PERSPECTIVES OF THE SCOTTISH CITY

PERSPECTIVES OF THE SCOTTISH CITY

Edited by

GEORGE GORDON

ABERDEEN UNIVERSITY PRESS

First published 1985
Aberdeen University Press
A member of the Pergamon Group
© The Contributors 1985

The publisher acknowledges subsidy from the Scottish
Arts Council towards the publication of this volume.

British Library Cataloguing in Publication Data

Perspectives of the Scottish City
  1. Sociology, Urban—Scotland—History
  2. Scotland—Social conditions
  I. Gordon, George, *1939-*
  941.1′009′732   HN398.S3
  ISBN 0 08 030371 4

PRINTED IN GREAT BRITAIN
THE UNIVERSITY PRESS
ABERDEEN

PREFACE

Cities are possibly the most striking man-made phenomena of the modern world. They are not merely assemblages of buildings and streets but integral components of the economic, functional, social, administrative and cultural organisation of society. The scale of cities means that urban problems are substantial matters of concern which require various policy initiatives. The images of cities are often conflicting or antipodal: power and poverty; east and west end; vitality and corruption; knowledge and neglect; development and decay. This volume of·multi-disciplinary essays seeks to investigate some of these perspectives in the context of the Scottish City during the last one hundred and fifty years.

Between 1901 and 1951 the four Scottish Cities accounted for between 38 and 41 per cent of the population of the nation. Subsequently, continued suburbanisation, the development of the New Towns and the emergence of a trend labelled counter-urbanisation, reduced their share to barely 31 per cent in the 1981 Census. That statistic is somewhat misleading because a growing number of commuters reside beyond city boundaries. Additionally, the cities remain the dominant administrative and commercial centres in Scotland, the foci of regional and national transport networks and the principal sources of diffusion of information, ideas and innovations. As an example, one can cite the dominant role of the cities in newspaper publication, broadcasting, television and publishing, the vital means of disseminating information and shaping attitudes. Six of the eight Scottish universities are located in the cities. The importance of market accessibility has encouraged a wide array of commercial and cultural activities to locate in cities. The congregation of such functions compounded the images of opportunity and excitement which have become associated with the 'bright lights' syndrome of city-ward migration. Yet, cities have recurrently been associated with spatial and social injustice and with the poverty and ill-health of large numbers of deprived citizens.

This volume seeks to examine several aspects of form, economy and society in the four cities in the Victorian, Edwardian and modern periods. The treatment is selective rather than comprehensive. Several themes have been surveyed in a companion volume, *Scottish Urban History*. Others have been discussed in other publications. Several topics warrant further investigation but, for want of space and my perception of balance, that must await another occasion.

In writing this book the authors received help and support from many individuals. Detailed acknowledgements are listed at the end of chapters but thanks are due to all who supplied information, stimulated ideas, read drafts, typed manuscripts, drew maps and printed photographs. The authors are indebted to the printers for the careful setting of the book and to Colin MacLean and Marjorie Leith of Aberdeen University Press for their enthusiastic support and for the benefit of their publishing skills. Finally, I owe an enormous personal debt to my wife and daughters for their patience and their loving support.

GEORGE GORDON

CONTENTS

CONTRIBUTORS

John Butt BA (London), PhD (Glasgow)
Professor of Economic History in the University of Strathclyde. He has published widely in the general area of Modern British Economic and Social History and contributed a number of items relating to Scottish urban history especially in the field of housing. His recent books include *A History of the SCWS* (Jointly with J A Kinloch) and *Industrial Archaeology in the British Isles* (with Ian Donnachie).

Brian Dicks BSc, PhD (Wales), FSA (Scot)
Lecturer in Geography, King Alfred's College, Winchester. Formerly Senior Lecturer in Geography, University of Strathclyde. He is co-editor with George Gordon of *Scottish Urban History* and has contributed to *The Stirling Region* and *Quality of Life and Human Welfare*. His articles on historical and contemporary geographical themes have appeared in *The National Library of Wales Journal, Area, Town Planning Review, The Geographical Magazine, Landscape Research,* and *Tidjschrift voor Economische en Sociale Geographie.*

W Hamish Fraser MA (Aberdeen) D Phil (Sussex)
Senior Lecturer in History, University of Strathclyde. Author of *Trade Unions and Society: The Struggle for Acceptance 1850–1880, The Coming of the Mass Market* and co-author of *Workers and Employers.* He has contributed to a number of essay collections and to learned journals.

George Gordon MA, PhD (Edinburgh)
Dean of the Faculty of Arts and Social Studies and Senior Lecturer in Geography in the University of Strathclyde. He is co-editor of books on *Scottish Urban History* and *Quality of Life and Human Welfare,* editor of *Regional Cities of the UK 1890–1980* and contributed to *A Geography of Scotland, An Historical Geography of Scotland, The Stirling Region* and to various academic journals.

William L Miller MA (Edinburgh), PhD (Newcastle)
Senior Lecturer in Politics, University of Strathclyde. Author of *Electoral Dynamics in Britain since 1918, The End of British Politics? Scots and English Political Behaviour in the Seventies,* and *The Survey Method in the Social and Political Sciences: Achievements, Failures, Prospects.* Contributor to various books and journals including *Political Studies, British Journal of Political Science, West European Politics, Parliamentary Affairs* and *Political Quarterly.*

Andrew Noble MA (Aberdeen), D Phil (Sussex)
Senior Lecturer in English Studies, University of Strathclyde. Edited *Edwin Muir: Uncollected Scottish Criticism* and *Robert Louis Stevenson* (Vison Critical Studies). Contributed 'Some Versions of Scottish Pastoral' to *Order in Space and Society.*

Michael Pacione MA, PhD (Dundee)
Senior Lecturer in Geography, University of Strathclyde. Previously lecturer in Geography, Queens University, Belfast. Author of *Rural Geography.* Editor of *Urban Problems and Planning in the Developed World, Problems and Planning in the Third World Cities, Progress in Rural Geography,* and *Progress in Urban Geography.* Co-editor of *Quality of Life and Human Welfare.* Contributor to several books, and author of articles published in an international range of academic journals.

Richard G Rodger MA, PhD (Edinburgh)
Lecturer in Economic and Social History, Leicester University. In 1982–83 Visiting Professor and Fulbright Scholar, University of Kansas, Lawrence. Contributor to several books including *The Pursuit of Urban History, The Structure of Nineteenth Century Cities, The Growth and Transformation of the City.* Other publications include *Bibliography of European Economic and Social History* and various articles on social and urban topics in *Business History Review, Victorian Studies, Journal of Historical Geography and Urban History Yearbook.*

Frank Arneil Walker B Arch, PhD (Strathclyde), RIBA, ARIAS, FSA (Scot)
Senior Lecturer in Architecture, University of Strathclyde. Formerly in private practice. Co-author of *Order in Space and Society.* Articles published in several journals including *Architectural Design, Architectural Association Quarterly, RIBA Journal, Country Life.*

1

THE CHANGING CITY

George Gordon

INTRODUCTION

The term Scottish City is used with some caution. It will be argued that a distinctive species does exist but it must also be recognised that the Scottish City has been variously affected by experiences, developments, innovations and forces from furth of Scotland. Furthermore, in detail every city has a substantial measure of uniqueness and individuality arising from a specific resolution of the common ingredients of site, situation, function, morphology, development, management and population. Ward[1] refers to the passionate pride of place of Glaswegians and similar territorial affection for their native city is found amongst the residents of Aberdeen, Dundee and Edinburgh. Another source of divergence is the fact that the city is a dynamic phenomenon which since Georgian times has changed substantially in various dimensions such as build, extent, functional character, management and social ecology.

The basis of the thesis that the cities of Scotland have sufficient in common to justify the use of the term Scottish City primarily stems from the distinctiveness of the institutional framework. Lea[2] argued that the influence of religious, educational and legal systems gave 'a distinctive character to many aspects of Scottish culture and social life'. In relation to the city the distinctive legal system of Scotland has been particularly important in determining the character of property law and necessitating separate government legislation on Scottish affairs. Thus the basic contextual framework of the city in Scotland is different in detail from that of comparable settlements in England and Wales. A more complex and tenuous force has been that of Scottish culture. For example, Walker outlines the emergence of one particularly Scottish architectural style which succeeded an era when imported ideas were dominant (*see* Chapter 5).

The tenement is probably the most widely perceived visual manifestation of the Scottish City and it is a built-form which combines the strands of law and culture. Worsdall[3] has outlined the development of the law of the tenement in Scotland which was administered by Burgh and Dean of Guild Courts.[4] By the seventeenth century towering tenement lands had become a characteristic feature of Edinburgh. Subsequently, more standardised four and five storey versions dominated pre-1914 provision of working-class housing in the Scottish cities. By their numerical magnitude and powerful visual image, the Victorian tenements virtually became the stereotype of the townscape of the Scottish City. In that form the Scottish City markedly diverged from contemporaneous developments in England and Wales, although there were some similarities to parts of inner London and central

Newcastle. Those English examples were normally constructed in brick and to a different design from the stone-built Scottish tenement. The tradition of high-rise buildings was not uniquely Scottish, being found in many European cities, e.g. Paris or Vienna, but it did distinguish the Scottish City from cities in other parts of Britain where, in the nineteenth century, the terraced building dominated the supply of working-class housing. The tenement inevitably entailed shared responsibilities and communal interests whereas the terrace conveyed separated territorial rights with fewer common interests. Most tenements were rented from landlords and progressively the owners' interests were handled by a specialist group, factors. The latter acted as agents for the owners particularly in relation to the administration of the properties and the commissioning of repairs. Many writers[5] have described the spirit of community which developed in tenement districts. Physical propinquity and human friendship clearly contributed to that spirit and the unavoidable presence of shared property interests may have been another contributory factor. However, much of the literature on the spirit of community in the tenement areas relates to the period after the cessation of tenement building and before the implementation in the 1950s of widespread urban redevelopment. By then migration to the cities had declined markedly and many tenement districts experienced a phase of demographic stability between the comparatively restless phases of Victorian construction and recent destruction. The demolition of numerous tenements might appear to undermine part of the criteria for the definition of the Scottish City. However, it must be emphasised that the tenement was merely a powerful image rather than the sole, or even necessarily a primary, basis of distinctiveness.

The volume is not intended as a sustained philosophical discourse on the thesis of the Scottish City but rather a detailed empirical examination, through a multi-disciplinary approach, of various aspects of the evolving and changing character of the Scottish cities and of the life and work of their citizens in Victorian, Edwardian and modern times. Through that mechanism the volume seeks to articulate the complex and changing features, images and components of the Scottish City.

THE BURGEONING CITY

The cities experienced substantial population growth in the nineteenth century and early decades of the twentieth century, although there were important variations in the detailed patterns of increase. Statistical comparison is complicated by the fact that there were also a number of large extensions in the administrative areas of the cities. Data exist both for the actual incorporated area at a point in time and for computations using subsequent boundaries as the spatial bases. The possible variation is shown by the fact that Carstairs[6] calculated the population of Aberdeen in 1911 to be approximately 164,000 whereas Rhind,[7] using the area of the modern Aberdeen District Council, computed a figure of 184,028. A further complication resulted from the annexation of substantial settlements in the late nineteenth and early twentieth centuries such as the burghs of Partick, Govan and Pollokshaws by Glasgow or Leith by Edinburgh. This process tended to exaggerate the apparent rate of population growth in the cities if the actual incorporate area was used and graphs of population should be interpreted with caution. Notwithstanding these caveats the cities did experience rapid urbanisation and in a more sporadic and lagged pattern, urban extension. In 1801 the four cities accounted for 11 per cent of the population of Scotland. By 1901 the proportion had increased to 35 per cent.[8] The maximum share, 40 per cent, occurred in 1951 but by 1981 the cities, as defined by the four District authorities, only accommodated 31 per cent of the total population. All of the cities suffered a loss of population between 1971–81, the decline being most marked in the case of Glasgow (1971—982,203; 1981—763,162).[9] By the middle of the twentieth century the dominant processes were decentralisation and suburbanisation rather than urbanisation, industrialisation and city expansion although the situation was complicated by the restrictions upon boundary extensions by the cities between 1940 and the reorganisation of local government in 1974.

Doherty[10] has noted that, in the nineteenth century, the 'trends towards urban concentration were a direct result of a combination of legislative (boundary extensions) and demographic (natural increase and migration) changes'. They were 'an integral part of the whole process of economic growth and expansion associated with the transition of Scotland during the course of the nineteenth century from an essentially agricultural society to a predominantly industrial[11] society'.[12] Doherty continued, 'Urbanization in the nineteenth century was more than a demographic manifestation of economic and social processes: it entailed the production of a built environment (factories, roads, houses, ports, etc.) on an unprecedented scale, the creation of a physical infrastructure which facilitated the expansion of industrial capitalism.'[13]

During the nineteenth century Edinburgh lost the primate place in the urban hierarchy to Glasgow. Nonetheless the capital experienced a fivefold growth of population between 1801 and 1911. The rate of increase was slightly greater in the early part of the period (1801–51) although the larger absolute increment occurred during the later phase (1851–1911). Over a wide spectrum of industry the Georgian and early Victorian periods were characterised by industrial growth in Edinburgh, with the founding of new elements such as the silk mills beside the Union Canal and the expansion of traditional industries, e.g. brewing, milling, glass-making, paper-making, printing and publishing. However, Edinburgh experienced a slower rate of industrial growth than Glasgow, the most notable difference being in the sector of textile manufacturing (see Chapter 2, Appendix 1). By contrast, the tertiary sector assumed greater importance in the development of the capital with expansion in banking, insurance, law, medicine, education and commerce. Later in the century further manufacturing specialisms were developed including whisky distilling and blending, engineering and rubber-making but Edinburgh primarily performed the roles of national administrative, cultural and legal centre and regional city for the Lothians, with manufacturing occupying a secondary rank and, for the most part, related to local resources or industrial traditions. The population of Edinburgh peaked in 1961 when, according to Rhind,[14] it had increased by 69,000 since 1911. Subsequently the total declined by approximately 48,000 according to the data from the 1981 Census.

The population of the Parliamentary Burgh of Glasgow rose from 193,030 in 1831 to 784,496 in 1911,[15] although the latter statistic becomes 976,418[16] when the spatial base of the modern Glasgow District is utilised. The highest rates of increase occurred between 1831 and 1881 but, as in Edinburgh, the largest absolute increment happened in the second half of the nineteenth century. Glasgow epitomised the model of the burgeoning industrial city. Successive phases of industrial prominence occurred in textiles, engineering and shipbuilding.[17] Dramatic demographic change was fed initially by migration, particularly from the Highlands[18] and from Ireland,[19] and subsequently primarily by natural increase. The urban area mushroomed and there was a rapid development of distinct morphological[20] and functional[21] areas (Figure 1) within the city. By comparison, in Edinburgh the restricted flowering of the industrial sector restrained the scale of migration although there was an influx of Irish immigrants in the second quarter of the nineteenth century. Within the capital the urban area increased and there was greater articulation of the urban structure with the emergence of various social shadings of status areas[22] and of commercial and industrial districts[23] but the rate of evolution was generally slower than that in Glasgow.

From 1921 to 1961 Glasgow housed more than one million inhabitants, with the maximum being recorded in 1951. Subsequently redevelopment (*see* Chapter 10), overspill, the development of the New Towns and the sustained process of suburbanisation has reduced the total to that of the late Victorian period. The decline of heavy industry (Figure 2) has been partially compensated by the attraction of light industries, particularly from the middle of the 1930s, to industrial estates and by the growth of the tertiary sector. In fact, the growth of the office sector (Figure 3) predates the present century but the proportionate importance has increased with the more recent structural shift in employment. Glasgow reaped the dual commercial benefits of external prominence in trade and shipping and a strengthening role as a regional city serving an extensive hinterland in West Central Scotland. As in the other cities recent additions to the administrative functions include the headquarters of the Regional Council. Later in this volume Butt (Chapter 8) presents a detailed analysis and discussion of changes in the employment structure of the cities in the twentieth century while Rodger (Chapter 2) examines the changes between 1841 and 1911.

For almost two centuries Aberdeen and Dundee have contested for the rank of third largest city in Scotland. By the middle of the nineteenth century Dundee had edged into a lead of some 7,000 but by 1881 the gap had stretched to 35,000. However by 1911 the two settlements were almost equal in population size. The two totals remained in step until 1961 when

Figure 1 Broomielaw—Jamaica Street, Glasgow c.1914, the interface between the retailing area and the port facilities. *Source:* Strathclyde Regional Archives.

Figure 2   Govan 1930. *Source:* Strathclyde Regional Archives.

Figure 3 St Vincent Place, Glasgow c.1890. *Source:* Strathclyde Regional Archives.

the population of Aberdeen exceeded the figure for Dundee by some 15,000 and that position has continued in the 1981 Census.[24] Despite the similarity in demographic trends for a substantial period, the two cities differ on crucial dimensions. Dundee, in the phase of rapid demographic increase from 1831 to 1881, conformed even more closely to the image of the industrial city than Glasgow. For example, in the late Victorian period Dundee had a remarkably high percentage of the female labour force engaged in manufacturing activity (*see* Chapters 2 and 8). Moreover, the overwhelming dependence upon the jute industry meant that Dundee's Victorian prosperity was almost exclusively based upon one industrial activity[25] whereas the economic base of Glasgow was more widely secured in a number of sectors of manufacturing and in commerce and trade. In 1851 Dundee (19 per cent) ranked second in Britain to Liverpool (22 per cent) and ahead of Glasgow (18 per cent) in the proportion of Irish-born in the population. The Irish migration to Dundee in the 1840s and 1850s, attracted in large measure by the opportunities in the textile industry, particularly the emerging jute industry, included a substantial stream of unmarried females and widows who tended to lodge with other Irish mill families. In her analysis of this migration Collins[26] found that 55 per cent of the mid-nineteenth-century female textile workforce in Dundee consisted of Irish girls living in lodgings.

The decline and ultimately the virtual collapse of the jute industry in recent decades transformed the economic structure of the city, despite the successful development of industrial estates after World War II (*see* Chapter 8). Progressively Dundee has assumed the role of regional centre for Tayside with consequential effects upon the land use pattern of the city in terms of changing demands for space and access (*see* Chapter 9).

If Dundee was the classic Scottish example of a mono-industrial city in the late nineteenth century, Aberdeen was perceived by Saunders[27] as a true regional capital. Moreover, the rural–urban migration to Aberdeen in the nineteenth century overwhelmingly tapped the Highlands and northeast Scotland, with Aberdeen being the only Scottish city which failed to attract a substantial number of Irish immigrants.

Aberdeen was not only a regional city but progressively it formed a major portion of the region as the city's share of the regional population increased from one-sixth in 1801, to one-third by 1901 and almost half by 1971.[28] Until the middle of the nineteenth century demographic and economic growth was fuelled by a varied economic base including a buoyant textile industry. As the latter declined in the second half of the century other enterprises, most notably sea trawling, emerged to support and enhance the function of regional centre for the North East. That role, in turn, was strengthened by the phase of railway extension in the second half of the century which reinforced the nodal position of Aberdeen in the regional transport network and its terminal situation in the national pattern. The population of Aberdeen trebled between 1801 and 1851 and increased by a further 250 per cent between 1851 and 1911, with the largest absolute increment occurring in the period 1881 to 1911. During the latter phase demographic growth was primarily the result of natural increase. Indeed in the decade 1901–11 the city actually suffered a net loss by migration of nearly 10,000 people which was more than compensated for by a natural increase of 20,332.[29] As in the case of Dundee, Aberdeen suffered a decrease in population between 1911 and 1921, due to war losses and continuing, and indeed increased, net outward migration which exceeded natural increase by almost 5,000. Thereafter the population increased steadily to reach a maximum in 1971 before declining by more than 8,000 to 203,612[30] in 1981. The recent downturn in the total echoed the trend in the other Scottish cities despite the oil-led industrial success in and around Aberdeen. (Figure 4) There has been considerable suburban growth in the penumbra of the city in recent decades which principally explains the reduction in the population of Aberdeen. Additionally the general downward trend in the birth-rate in Scotland since the late 1960s has also been a contributory factor of varying regional significance, in the changing demography of the cities.

Flinn[31] noted 'that in the period 1861 to 1930 the cities did not by any means always draw heavily on the rest of the country for their growth'. Indeed, as has been shown above, there were occasions when the dominant migratory stream was outward from the city, e.g. Glasgow in the 1870s. Flinn added that 'it was not often, even in the nineteenth century, that the cities grew at rates in excess of their own natural increase rate'.[32] That, however, does not imply an absence of migration. In fact inter-regional flows, of varying scale and orientation, have been an important part of the Victorian, Edwardian and modern demographic history of Scotland.

In several instances migrants introduced a different dimension into the recipient city, in terms of language, religion, ethnicity or culture. In the nineteenth century Glasgow received substantial influxes of Gaelic-speaking Highlanders and both Protestant and Catholic Irish. Contemporaneously the first Jewish synagogue was consecrated in a building on the west side of the High Street. Daiches[33] estimated that the Jewish community in Glasgow numbered about 1,000 by the late Victorian period and nearly 20,000 by the middle of the twentieth century. By the latter period another international stream of migrants had started to arrive in Glasgow, the Indian and Pakistani community which by 1971 was estimated to total approximately 12,000.[34] Subsequently a further flow developed which resulted in the establishment of Chinese communities in Glasgow and Edinburgh. With the exception of the Irish migration, none of the flows constituted a sizeable proportion of the contemporary population of the city but each, at particular periods, has introduced distinctive functional institutions such as Gaelic-speaking Protestant congregations, Catholic churches and schools, synagogues and mosques. Moreover the immigrants tended to cluster in certain parts of the city, forming distinctive sub-groups within the urban population. In time, the segregated pattern of residence often declined as members were assimilated into urban society and become socially, spatially, and to some extent culturally, mobile but the process is complex and there have been substantial inter-group variations in the extent and patterns of geographical residential relocation. There are of course dangers in exaggerating the significance of distinctive but comparatively minor migratory flows. For example almost 8 per cent of the residents of Edinburgh in 1971 had been born in England. In the same year the Asian immigrants in Glasgow accounted for less than 2 per cent of the population of that city.

Areal development

During the nineteenth century the area of Glasgow increased from 715 to 5,134 hectares. In 1846, 1891 and 1912 there were major extensions to the bounds of the city, involving agricultural land and established urban communities. Thus the boundary extension of 1891 included the Police Burghs of Crosshill, Govanhill, Maryhill, Hillhead and Pollokshields with a combined population of over 50,000. That figure was surpassed in the 1912 extension when more than a quarter of a million people were added to Glasgow by the incorporation of the Police Burghs of Partick, Govan and Pollokshaws, the industrial districts of Shettleston and Tollcross and the suburbs of Cathcart and Newlands.[35] In essence the extensions appeared to result from two different pressures. First, there was a continuing need for additional space to accommodate the residential, industrial, and latterly recreational, demands of the burgeoning city. However, the incorporation of established settlements can only partly be explained in relation to those pressures. In some cases, at least, the separate burghs, districts or suburbs probably could have remained independent albeit as inliers within the enlarging city. It should be remembered that Manchester and Salford retained separate administrative identities, as did Newcastle and Gateshead. Indeed until 1920 Edinburgh and Leith were separate administrative units. Thus Glasgow's annexation of substantial settled districts may also indicate a desire to extend the influence and control of the central city within the emerging conurbation. Nowadays that strategy might be advanced on the grounds of efficient management of central government services and planning co-ordination. Whilst there is no evidence of a coherent plan by the City Council to create a metropolis, there is sufficient inferential material about the optimistic hopes of late Victorian Glasgow industrialists and businessmen to advance the suggestion that the incorporation of other settlements was viewed by councillors and leading citizens as part of the aggrandisement of the city and its region. Moreover, Fraser (Chapter 6) outlines the rapid development of an array of local government services in the late Victorian era, at least some of which benefited from the economies of scale offered by enlarged administrative units. Some of the early flowers of municipal socialism were transitory but others, such as the extensive Glasgow Corporation tramway network,[36] were forerunners of later ideas about regional transportation networks in West Central Scotland.

The two boundary extensions of 1926 and 1938 doubled the area under the municipal control of Glasgow. Most of the new territory was undeveloped farmland which, in the 1950s, provided the sites for massive developments of public sector housing at Drumchapel, Easterhouse and

Castlemilk. The prescience of the City Council in acquiring a major source of future building land was amply repaid in the 1950s. Glasgow's public sector programme was implemented within its own administrative boundaries whereas several large English cities, e.g. London and Manchester, had to build on sites beyond their administrative limits.

By 1939 Glasgow was surrounded by a ring of settlements which included the royal burghs of Paisley and Rutherglen and the growing suburbs of Bearsden, Bishopbriggs, Clarkston, Giffnock and Newton Mearns. The previous precedent of annexation did not occur and, with the exception of Rutherglen which became part of Glasgow District in the 1974 local government re-organisation, these areas remained outside the administrative bounds of the city. Whilst several factors may have contributed to that outcome, the principal reason was the opposition of the middle-class suburbs and the royal burghs to possible incorporation within the city. Indeed in the marriage in 1974 Rutherglen could certainly be cast as a reluctant partner.

In the 1940s Glasgow determined to resolve its housing problems within the administrative area of the city. The city objected to some recommendations of the Clyde Valley Plan, particularly the idea that a substantial section of the people relocated in the planned redevelopment of the densely-inhabited central tenement districts would inevitably have to be accommodated in New Towns at East Kilbride and Cumbernauld (*see* Chapter 10). The city engineer, Bruce, supported by the majority of the Council, believed that conurbation planning and decentralisation to new towns were incompatible strategies, and it was not until almost a decade later that Glasgow finally accepted the practical benefits of dispersal for a redevelopment policy aimed at a radical reduction in the population density of the inner city.

Apart from points of detail, the areal development of the other Scottish cities differed from that of Glasgow in one important dimension, namely the fact that they were not at the centre of a conurbation or surrounded by an extensive pattern of urban and industrial settlements.

In the process of expansion Edinburgh incorporated Leith, Portobello, several villages and suburbs in addition to extensive tracts of undeveloped farmland and open space. For example, the seven boundary extensions Acts between 1856 and 1901 added over 2,400 hectares to the city,[37] trebling the area under municipal control. Extensive areas of open space were annexed including Braid Hills, Blackford Hill, Corstorphine Hill, Craiglockhart Hills and part of the Pentland Hills. With the implementation of a Green Belt policy after 1945 the remaining undeveloped farmland and open space served as a barrier between the capital city and the settlements in the Esk Valley and in the adjoining parts of West Lothian. However, a south-western sector involving Currie and Balerno was omitted from the Green Belt and, consequently that zone became the focus of suburban growth in recent decades.

In Dundee and Aberdeen areal development in the twentieth century facilitated the construction of private and public housing and the building of industrial estates. Between 1831 and 1946 the boundaries of Dundee were altered on nine occasions.[38] Landward expansion occurred in the present century although an earlier component of that trend, the incorporation of Lochee in 1859, had emphasised the northwesterly industrial axis which had developed along the Scouring Burn. The annexation of Broughty Ferry in 1913 involved the largest settlement in the immediate environs of the city. Jones[39] noted that, in the nineteenth century, building in Dundee tended to lag behind boundary extensions. One consequence was an ample supply of open spaces with views across the Tay such as Baxter Park, The Law, Dudhope Park, Balgay Park, Victoria Park and Lochee Park. Local government re-organisation in the 1970s resulted in the creation of Dundee District with authority over an enlarged area, including a substantial landward zone of undeveloped farmland. Yet, just a few years earlier, Jones speculated that 'now Dundee faces opposition to further expansion to the north from the county of Angus and to the west . . . from Perthshire. Expansion to the south of the Tay, made increasingly possible by the opening of the Tay Road Bridge, may well meet the combined opposition of the small burghs on the south shore of the estuary and of the county of Fife.'[40] The latter did materialise but the opposition of Angus and Perthshire was spiked by administrative reform. Like the other cities Dundee had overcome opposition to extension on a number of occasions, most notable being the annexation of Lochee and Broughty Ferry.[41]

The various boundary extensions of Aberdeen primarily added to the potential building land although on occasion small settlements were included. For example the 1891 Act annexed Old Aberdeen, the industrial suburb of Woodside and, beyond the Dee, the suburb of Torry.[42] Cumulatively, between 1801 and 1950 the boundary extensions almost doubled the area of the city. One particularly substantial increase in 1934 added some 1,700 hectares. After 1914 the city acquired a ring of surrounding estates, including Tullos, Kincorth, Hazlehead, Sheddocksley, Kepplehills, Middlefield, Powis, Hilton and Rosehill[43] which became the sites of inter-war and post-war residential developments. Generally, the possible sources of opposition to the expansion of the Granite City were restricted to individual landowners, farming interests and the County Council. Local government reform in 1974 reduced the powers of the landward lobby but the various parties had rarely presented a united opposition, possibly because urban growth offered the prospect of increased land values for property owners in the affected portion of the urban fringe.

Social and functional topography

Chapters 4, 9 and 10 deal with particular aspects of the topic. Dicks outlines the character and development of fashionable residential districts in Victorian Glasgow, Gordon discusses the conservation of areas of architectural and historic merit, whilst Pacione considers the processes of renewal, redevelopment and rehabilitation in the modern city.

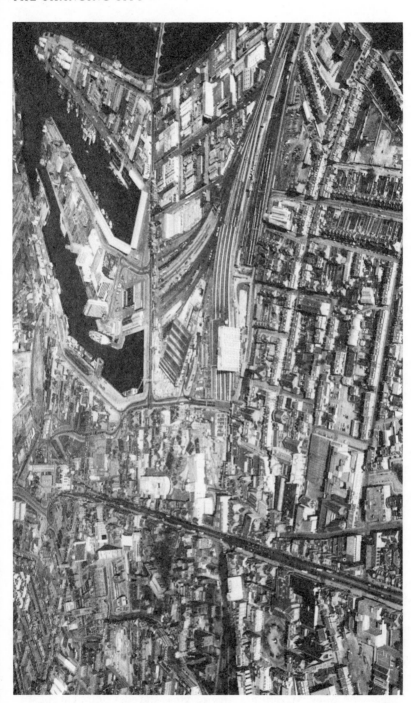

Figure 4 Aerial view of Aberdeen. *Source:* Aerofilms Limited.

In the Victorian era the social topography of the city was sharply drawn with the elegance of the high-status districts, in terms of building[44] and the life-style of the inhabitants, seemingly polarised from the poverty and wretchedness of the worst slums.[45] A detailed analysis of the changing pattern of status areas in Edinburgh between 1855 and 1962[46] illustrated the multi-factorial character of the processes and the spatial complexity of the patterns. 'By 1914 the dominant high-status poles were located centrally in terraced mansion districts to the north and west of the original Georgian New Town. The principal middle-status zone ocurred in the southern suburbs although there were clusters of middle-status flats in certain streets within, or adjacent to, the central high-status districts. The Old Town constituted the central portion of an arcuate zone of working-class housing which linked Gorgie to central Leith . . . suburban growth had extended Stevenson's notion of two distinct cities based upon the Old Town and New Town districts into at least three, and possibly four, components. The finely-shaded middle-class suburbs were a distinctive new component. Additionally, the emergence of a spatially discrete pattern of residential districts for the lower middle class and respectable working class . . . possibly added a fourth dimension to the spatial structure.'[47] Apart from the construction of new areas, central redevelopment occurred in the wake of the Improvement Acts and functional change resulted from the expansion of the office and retail sectors and from institutional invasion of central residential districts.[48] Thus the operative processes included suburban growth, localised infill, renewal and redevelopment, functional change and morphological adaptation and alteration and the social evolution of residential districts. Frequently the latter process meant social decline, although with considerable variations in rate of change, as housing filtered down the economic and social pyramid[49] but some neighbourhoods achieved an increase in social status with the passage of time. Moreover, certain districts such as the New Town areas in Edinburgh retained comparative stability in social rank for lengthy periods. These processes continued throughout the twentieth century although the relative importance of each component varied periodically. Major additional variables were the emergence of a substantial public housing sector[50] and, after 1950, the redevelopment, renewal and rehabilitation of many working-class housing areas (see Chapter 10).

Whilst the Scottish cities differed in detail, in every case the development of the social topography produced a notable West End of middle- and high-status residences, the spatial association of pre-1914 low-status housing districts and industrial zones and, in the inter-war and post-war periods, extensive peripheral public housing estates. In Glasgow the latter constituted the overwhelming majority of modern housing in the outer zone with most of the middle-class suburban development located beyond the bounds of the city. By contrast, in the other cities the peripheral ring included a segregated inter-digitation of areas of private and public housing.

Walker (Chapter 5) outlines the origins and development of one distinctive architectural style. Even when a style or building type was implanted from elsewhere the use of materials and the strictures of Scottish building regulations normally added a characteristically regional or national imprint. Similarities in morphology derived from diverse sources, including common practices such as the use of the feu-charter as an instrument of planning[51] or the adoption by local authorities of Scottish Office plans and guidance about the location and design of public sector housing.[52] Doherty[53] argued that most work on the built environment appeared to have concentrated upon housing construction. Various writers[54] examined the relationships between supply, demand and investment in housing in the Victorian and Edwardian eras, invariably identifying cyclical patterns of activity with successive booms and slumps. The cycles affected the rate of development and rate of change of other types of land use. For example, Whitehand[55] found that investment in institutional uses in the urban fringe tended to increase during a slump in house-building activity because land prices, a crucial factor for institutional uses, were depressed and competition for sites reduced. In contrast commercial uses corresponded more closely to housing cycles although the increased role of the public sector and of national government in regional and national matters complicated the correlation. For example, despite the recent economic recession substantial sections of redundant dockland in Glasgow have been redeveloped for use by offices, industry, an exhibition centre, transport, recreation and housing. Whilst some of these changes originated in strictly economic decisions, many resulted from governmental, local and national, initiatives and incentives.

Detailed studies[56] of renewal and redevelopment of the centre of Glasgow for the period 1840 to 1970 revealed complex temporal, sectoral and spatial variations. In general terms the highest rates of redevelopment affected the principal retailing streets, Argyle Street and Sauchiehall Street, and were substantially lower in the office areas.[57] However, in the office sector marked differences in rates of redevelopment appeared to correlate with period of origin, with Edwardian blocks showing the lowest rates of change[58] (see Chapter 9).

In the nineteenth century a hierarchy of service areas developed within the city serving local and sub-regional needs. The hierarchy continued to develop with subsequent urban growth but other factors also affected the structure and pattern of service centres including the redevelopment of inner city districts, planning policies and changes in retailing, intra-city transportation, consumer fashions and tastes and the precise array of services offered in the whole system and, especially at particular levels in the hierarchy. In Glasgow, for example, redevelopment was primarily responsible for the removal of the substantial shopping centres at St George's Cross and Gorbals whilst massive peripheral growth necessitated the construction of new centres at Drumchapel, Castlemilk and Pollok. In every city the development of supermarkets or superstores and of health centres illustrated organisational changes which had consequences in terms of the spatial distribution of outlets of particular activities. One characteristic result of such trends was an increase in the size of the area served and a corresponding rise in the average distance which consumers travelled.

Early in the Victorian period there was some decentralisation of industrial locations as firms sought larger, more accessible or less restricted sites. Major changes in resources or transport accelerated the trend, as did the development of industrial estates. The pattern also altered because of the closures of firms. Thus the modern distribution[59] reflects the interplay of various factors and trends which can only be fully understood by reference to detailed formative, evolutionary and adaptive processes.

The development of parks, playing fields and other formal and informal recreational spaces varied temporally, perhaps in relation to fluctuations in building cycles and changes in fashions and tastes. Generalisation is complicated by the policy implications of factors such as ownership of the space, public or private, or by points of detail related to a particular site such as the restrictions on change of use which were frequently attached to bequests of land for public parks.

Urbanism and urban conditions

'Cities which were expected to be places of civilisation were increasingly (in the nineteenth century) found to be full of the most loathsome problems. . . . From the 1820s the question of mass poverty was central to the argument about cities: in particular the industrial towns' vulnerability to the trade cycle produced widespread distress of a kind hard to ignore.'[60]

Rodger (Chapter 2) relates labour data for the Scottish cities 1841–1914 to a range of indicators of poverty and social distress such as overcrowding, death rates and anthropometric statistics. The analysis illustrates the conditions in cities and illuminates the different structural relationships in each of the Scottish cities.

Noble (Chapter 3) discusses the marked neglect of the themes of urbanisation, industrialisation and urbanism in nineteenth-century Scottish fiction. Romanticism may partly be interpreted as an implicit reaction to the hardship and unpalatable facets of urbanisation and urbanism. However, there were critics of industrialisation such as Carlyle and, from the mid nineteenth century onward, numerous commentators and recorders of urban conditions, and their writings have provided an important source of archival images for students of the city. Almost from the birth of the art, photography contributed to the archival material with views of places and of urban life. The massive collection of photographs by George Washington Wilson[61] included many city scenes whilst the work of Thomas Annan[62] provided a remarkable visual record of slums in mid-Victorian Glasgow. Novels, reports, paintings, drawings, photographs, biographies and diaries, minutes of societies and councils offer valuable insights into city life and conditions which extend and add further dimensions to the data of major sources such as Census enumerators' books, rate-books, Board of Trade figures and Medical Officers' Reports.

Society reacted to pressing urban problems[63] by instigating a wide array of reforms related to various aspects of living and working conditions such as housing,[64] health,[65] sanitation and sewage systems[66] and education.[67] Statutory changes were also made to the organisation of local government (*see* Chapters 6 and 7). The latter progressively developed an expanded managerial and functional role and in Chapter 6 Fraser discusses some facets of that situation. Adams noted that the 'transition from oligarchic incompetence (of the eighteenth-century burghs) to bureaucratic omnipotence was only achieved after numerous commissions and inquiries into every aspect of urban life'.[68] Whilst the rate of reform was often slow and the product of lengthy deliberation, the cumulative effect was substantial. New interests and groups emerged, became organised and sought influence in civic, social, economic and national matters (*see* Chapter 7). Political parties, Trades Councils and Trades Unions were important examples of these trends. Nonetheless the important role of other non-political societies and organisations in improving the conditions or way of life of city dwellers should not be forgotten. For example, various philanthropic bodies, as initiators of schemes of improved housing in the mid-Victorian period, contributed by example to the establishment of the standards embodied in later regulations.[69] Evidence presented to the various commissions and inquiries often referred to the dangers to morals of overcrowding, poor housing, squalor, alcoholism and other perceived defects of urban life. Many movements and organisations addressed themselves to moral development including the Boy's Brigade, the Salvation Army, temperance societies and the Band of Hope. The Boy's Brigade originated in Glasgow and Miller recounts how in the inter-war period temperance groups achieved representation on some city councils. Whilst other movements started outside Scotland, they are linked by a desire to counter the perceived degeneration of morals and social standards which in substantial measure were blamed upon urbanisation, industrialisation and urbanism.

'Glasgow's International Exhibition of 1888 was a great source of of civic pride to the respectable but, like so many other things in the city that gave satisfaction to its genteel middle-class citizens, it was liable to provoke satirical mirth in other quarters. The theatres and music halls of Victorian Glasgow attracted and reflected an altogether more rambunctious element in the population than the occupants of genteel terraces by Great Western Road or in Pollokshields.'[70] That tradition of popular comedy survived in Scottish cities for several decades and in the 1960s the earthy humour of Lex McLean regularly filled the Pavilion in Glasgow and the Palladium in Edinburgh. In addition to theatre and music halls,[71] the principal sources of working-class entertainment in the late Victorian cities were professional football and public houses. Daiches[72] suggested that the development of football was partly in response to the problems of drinking and drunkenness which, in 1873, was the cause of more than 150,000 arrests in Glasgow. Football quickly acquired popularity and the major clubs erected stadia to accommodate tens of thousands of spectators. The success of the sport did not result in a reduction in drunkenness or criminal offences but it added a new dimension to urban life as the fortunes of the 'team' came to dominate the match day ritual for many working-class families.

When the cinema first appeared in the Edwardian era the premises consisted of converted shops but subsequently halls and theatres were adapted and new specialised buildings were constructed. The demand for entertainment was illustrated by the rapid spread of cinemas, with, by 1917, one hundred being in operation in Glasgow.[73] In fact, the potential market for cinemas was very large, for whilst football and public houses were primarily bastions of masculinity, the cinema catered for both sexes and almost every age-group.

It is difficult to quantify the contribution which entertainment or moral fortitude made to the quality of life of the working-class residents of the cities. The creation of several commissions to investigate living and working conditions testified to the societal perception of the fundamental importance of factors such as housing standards, rents, wages, nutrition and health. The Glasgow Rent Strike provided further proof of the importance of these basic parameters of well-being. However, entertainment not only offered the prospect of release from the hardships of every day life but it was more directly within the decision-making control of the individual than factors such as wage-levels or housing standards. Consequently, these less tangible facets of quality of life may have offered an important veneer of pleasure, happiness, excitement or contentment for many city-dwellers.

THE MODERN CITY

Handlin[74] observed that 'the modern city edges imperceptibly out of its setting. There are no clear boundaries . . . it is hard to tell where city begins and country ends.' Knox provided a description of the forces of centralisation and decentralisation which shaped the pattern of urban life of the modern city.

> On the one hand the concentration of economic and political power in giant corporations and in larger and larger public authorities has made for a centralization of administrative and bureaucratic activity in the central business districts of cities. On the other hand, the new locational freedom of many shops and business enterprises has prompted a decentralization of jobs, and the vast increase in the number of white-collar workers, together with the consequent rise in average incomes and the more widespread availability of automobiles, has decentralized the residential structure of the city, creating enormous tracts of low-density suburban development.[75]

Nonetheless the product of the processes has been a state of evolutionary change rather than revolutionary transformation, albeit with accelerative thrusts and structural shifts deriving from particular events and innovations. Thus, the legislation[76] enabling the creation of the public housing sector simultaneously resulted in an alteration in the organisation of the housing market and in the rate, location and quality of provision of working-class housing.[77] Similarly, whilst the origins of urban planning predated the burgeoning city,[78] the highly influential reports, plans and Acts of the 1940s allocated planners a primary role in the shaping of the broad structure and detailed form of the modern city and city region (see Chapters 9 and 10). Adams assessing the benefits of modern planning controls concluded that:

> Fortunes have been made or lost when a change of land use has first been pinpointed on a development plan; individuals have found that rights of property are not sacrosanct; when objectors have been successful they have sometimes seen victory signed away by the Secretary of State; an urban ring road on a development map can create a swathe of planning blight. On the other hand, planning has saved us from the ugly uncontrolled urban sprawl, ribbon development and haphazard land use which scar the United States, West Germany and other countries.[79]

Indeed planning has contributed to the improvements in the quality of life of urban dwellers particularly in terms of basic dimensions such as housing and amenity. Unfortunately not all policies prove unqualified successes. Comprehensive re-development encountered serious programming faults, in addition to the disadvantages of social upheaval and the dislocation of communities. Similarly some new forms of housing, such as multi-storey blocks, and some new techniques of building, created an apparently unexpected series of technical and social problems which certainly did not indicate the achievement of the intended improvement in the quality of life and state of well-being of many of the residents of these properties. With reference to multi-storey blocks the problems of vandalism and the difficulties of particular groups of residents are well-documented[80] and adjustments have been made both in house-building policy and in the allocative procedures. Greater care in selection of tenants, improved standards of security and investment in environmental enhancement projects should ensure that much of this expensive modern stock can remain in effective use, although the success of management strategies will be determined by factors such as location and consumer preferences. Recently, local authorities adopted a more sensitive approach to demand for public sector housing, developing responses directed towards particular sections of the community. One consequence of the strategy was the effective abandonment of the concept of general stock which, in any case, had never matched consumer perception. The latter readily identified major spatial variations in location, quality and desirability within the public sector stock.[81]

To varying degrees there was also development of private sector housing in the Scottish cities in the post-1945 period. In the case of Glasgow the primacy, in scale and policy, of the public sector, resulted in the virtual exclusion of new private sector developments. The latter were attracted to established extra-mural locations and to small villages in the metropolitan fringe. Similar tendencies occurred in the other cities but in each case a substantial proportion of new buildings was situated within the administrative territory of the respective city.

The processes of suburbanisation, redevelopment and renewal altered the morphology and social geography of the cities. Demographic changes related to decline in average family size and increased rates of household formation, and reformation as a consequence of divorce or separation, affected the character of demand for housing. Additionally, changes in economic circumstances and social aspirations influenced consumer preferences. A study of residential movement in Glasgow[82] in 1974 illustrated the spatial outcome of these factors and forces. Marked differences were found between the patterns for the public and private sectors, although in both cases the Clyde acted as a barrier to residential mobility. In the public sector inner city redevelopment explained the radial movement to peripheral estates whilst short-distance moves predominantly reflected tenants seeking enhancement of quality, location and type of house.[83] Despite the pervasive effects of change, Pacione found evidence of the continued importance of the neighbourhood community in a detailed survey of part of the West End in Glasgow,[84] an area which featured prominently in short-distance private sector residential moves in the study by Forbes and Robertson.[85]

Employment patterns also changed as Butt (Chapter 8) recounts in an analysis which highlights differences and similarities in intercity profiles and trends. For Glasgow and, to a lesser extent, Edinburgh the process of decentralisation of employment introduced a complication as some employment opportunities were relocated beyond the civic boundaries.

Spatial variations remain in the quality of life within cities in terms of parameters such as housing, health and employment and there has been a substantial amount of research into the spatial and structural dimensions of the topic. Twine and Williams[86] found distinct patterns of social segregation in public sector housing in Aberdeen. Estates built in the 1930s under slum clearance and overcrowding legislation had significantly high concentrations of unskilled and semi-skilled manual households. In addition to the well-established role of allocative policies Twine and Williams highlighted the effect of rental policies in Aberdeen which, in the 1930s, effectively divided the public sector housing stock into higher rented non-rebated properties and lower rented rebated properties. As a consequence poorer families found themselves restricted to cheaper, rebated but less desirable properties.[87] Additionally, overcrowding and a concentration of social problems meant that certain public sector estates in each city acquired an adverse reputation which resulted in stigmatisation and the spiral of difficult-to-let housing and increased focalisation of multiply-deprived households.[88] Areas of deprivation occurred in each city but particularly high levels persisted in Glasgow. Concentrations of multiply-deprived households are found in most high-density inter-war public sector estates but similar levels of deprivation also occur in some parts of peripheral post-war public sector estates and in some tenemental private rented housing.[89] An array of housing, environmental, community and client-based policies have been implemented within the past two decades aimed at reducing the level of deprivation and resolving some associated problems such as vacant housing and environmental blight. Refurbishment of properties, the experiments in homesteading, and environmental improvement schemes were primarily directed towards physical dimensions of the multi-faceted topic whilst educational priority areas, community development projects and area-based social work teams have endeavoured to tackle social problems at the local scale. Authorities also embarked upon a re-organisation of their delivery services to improve levels of efficiency and effectiveness and special funding was made available through avenues such as the Urban Aid programme. Whilst much has been achieved through these various measures the rate of progress has been hindered and the policy jeopardised by the present high levels of unemployment (*see* Chapter 8), particularly because of the above average rates which are found in deprived areas.

Howe described a striking correspondence between areas of Glasgow with higher Standarised Mortality Ratios (SMRs) for ischaemic heart disease and lung-bronchus cancer and the less affluent wards of the city.[90] He concluded that the evidence supported 'the view that mortality experience is related to occupational class . . . (which) relates, in turn, to such features as nutrition levels, utilisation of health and hospital services, occupational hazards, poverty or affluence, overcrowding or otherwise, levels of occupation and also to stress in its various forms. Intra-urban inequalities in health undoubtedly involve a constellation of interacting factors, of which occupational class would seem to offer a significant indicator.'[91] Knox and Pacione[92] analysed the distribution of general practitioners in Edinburgh and Glasgow in the mid 1970s. In Glasgow there was still a localisation of surgeries in older central areas of the city whereas some peripheral estates had few local surgeries. Since levels of personal mobility in these peripheral estates were characteristically low the mismatch between the distribution of services and patients was exacerbated. A similar pattern was found for Edinburgh with the worst-served areas corresponding to deprived public-sector estates. Health Boards are now reacting to the misalignment of resources and seeking to enhance service provision in deprived areas but it will probably be some time before any redistribution has a significant impact upon the geography of intra-urban variations in morbidity and mortality.

The seeds of future trends, patterns and problems of the city are already sown but the rate and nature of development is not predetermined and, therefore, precisely predicted. Future changes in economic, political or social circumstance would have a profound influence upon the cities. If they remained unaltered it is likely that the cities will continue to decline in total population, although in the case of Glasgow at a slower rate than in the 1971–81 period. The problems of deprivation, unemployment and high vacancy rates in particular public sector estates will remain although the scale and spatial distribution might alter. Continued economic recession would dampen the rate of absolute improvement of living standards but improvement in average conditions would occur, although correspondingly increased levels of satisfaction might not be achieved, for the latter are subject to temporal redefinition. Rather than paint gloomy pictures or enunciate optimistic prognostications of the future it is suggested that examination of the past indicates that future changes will have varied spatial, economic and social dimensions which can be influenced by inheritance, contextual factors and future decisions about land, buildings, resources, communities and individual problems and needs.

REFERENCES

1   R Ward *Some City Glasgow* (Glasgow 1982)
2   K J Lea (ed) *A Geography of Scotland* (Newton Abbot 1977), p 8
3   F Worsdall *The Tenement, A Way of Life* (Edinburgh 1979), pp 14–15
4   R G Rodger 'The Evolution of Scottish Town Planning' in G Gordon and B Dicks (eds) *Scottish Urban History* (Aberdeen 1983), pp 71–91
5   M Weir *Shoes were for Sunday* (London 1970); C Hanley *Dancing in the Streets* (London 1958); J House *The Heart of Glasgow* (London 1972)
6   A M Carstairs 'The Nature and Diversification of Employment in Dundee in the Twentieth Century' in S Jones (ed) *Dundee and District*. British Association Handbook (Dundee 1968), p 319
7   D Rhind (ed) *A Census Users' Handbook* (London 1983), pp 363–4
8   Lea *op. cit.* p 58
9   Rhind *op. cit.* p 364
10 J Doherty 'Urbanization, Capital Accumulation and Class Struggle in Scotland, 1750–1914' in G Whittington and I D Whyte (eds) *An Historical Geography of Scotland* (London 1983), p 243
11 G Gordon 'Industrial Development, *c.*1750–1980' in Whittington and Whyte (eds) *op. cit.* pp 165–90
12 Doherty *op. cit.* p 243
13 *Ibid.* p 254
14 Rhind *op. cit.* p 364
15 J Cunnison and J B S Gilfillan *The Third Statistical Account of Scotland Vol. V. The City of Glasgow* (Glasgow 1958), p 54
16 Rhind *op. cit.* p 364
17 Gordon *op. cit.*; A Gibb *Glasgow—The Making of a City* (London 1983)
18 C Withers *Gaelic in Scotland 1698–1981: the geographical history of a language* (Edinburgh 1983), ch 9
19 M Flinn (ed) *Scottish Population History* (Cambridge 1977), pp 455–9
20 Gibb *op. cit.*
21 J W Whitehand 'Long-Term Changes in the Form of the City Centre: The Case of Redevelopment', *Geogr. Annaler* 1978, 60B, pp 79–86; G Gordon 'Victorian Edinburgh' *Scotia* VI 1982, pp 60–8
22 G Gordon 'The Status Areas of early to mid-Victorian Edinburgh', *Trans. Inst. Brit. Geogr.* 1979 (new series 4), pp 168–91
23 Gordon *op. cit.* note 21
24 Rhind *op. cit.* pp 363–4
25 B P Lenman and E E Gauldie 'The Industrial History of the Dundee Region from the Eighteenth to the Early Twentieth Century' in Jones *op. cit.* pp 162–73
26 B Collins 'Aspects of the Irish Immigration into two Scottish Towns (Dundee and Paisley) during the mid-nineteenth century.' MPhil thesis, University of Edinburgh 1978
27 L J Saunders *The Making of the Scottish Democracy* (Edinburgh 1950), p 130

28   R Jones 'The Growth and Development of Aberdeen' in C M Clapperton (ed)
      North East Scotland Geographical Essays (Aberdeen 1972) p 37
29   W D Chapman and C F Riley *Granite City: A Plan for Aberdeen* (London
      1952), p 15
30   Rhind *op. cit.* p 363
31   Flinn *op. cit.* p 311
32   *Ibid.*
33   D. Daiches *Glasgow* (London 1977) p 139
34   G W Kearsley and S R. Srivastava 'The Spatial Evolution of Glagow's Asian
      Community', *Scot. Geog. Mag.* 1974, 90, p 110
35   G Gordon 'Urban Scotland' in Lea *op. cit.* p 211
36   J R Hume 'Transport and Towns in Victorian Scotland' in Gordon and Dicks
      (eds) *op. cit.* pp 197–232
37   Gordon *op. cit.* note 21, p 65
38   S Jones 'Historical Geography of Dundee' in S Jones (ed) *op. cit.* p 273
39   *Ibid.* p 275
40   *Ibid.*
41   *Ibid.*
42   R Jones *op. cit.* p 37
43   Chapman and Riley *op. cit.* p 6
44   T A Markus (ed.) *Order in Space and Society* (Edinburgh 1982); A J Youngson
      The Making of Classical Edinburgh (Edinburgh 1966)
45   Gordon *op. cit.* note 21, p 65
46   G Gordon 'The Status Areas of Edinburgh: a historical analysis.' Ph.D Thesis
      (1971) University of Edinburgh
47   Gordon and Dicks *op. cit.* pp 15–16
48   G Gordon 'The Status Areas of Edinburgh in 1914' in Gordon and Dicks (eds)
      op. cit.
49   J G Robb 'Suburb and Slum in Gorbals: Social and Residential Change
      1800–1900' in Gordon and Dicks (eds) *op. cit.* pp 130–67
50   J Butt 'Working Class Housing in the Scottish Cities 1900–1950' in Gordon and
      Dicks (eds) *op. cit.* pp 233–68
51   G Gordon 'The Historico-Geographic Explanation of Urban Morphology: A
      Discussion of Some Scottish Evidence,' *Scot. Geog. Mag.* 1981, 97, pp 16–26
52   *Ibid.*
53   Doherty *op. cit.* p 255
54   A K Cairncross *Home and Foreign Investment* 1870–1913 (Cambridge 1953); J
      W Whitehand 'Building cycles and the spatial pattern of urban growth', *Trans.
      Inst. Brit. Geogr.* 1972, 56, pp 39–56
55   Whitehand *op. cit.* note 54
56   Whitehand *op. cit.* note 21
57   *Ibid.* pp 87–8
58   D Sim *Change in the City Centre* (Aldershot 1982)
59   R V Welch 'Manufacturing change on Greater Clydeside in the 1950s and
      1960s', *Scot. Geog. Mag.* 1974, 90, pp 168–78; C Carter 'Some Changes in the
      Post War Industrial Geography of the Clydeside Conurbation', *Scot. Geog.
      Mag.* 1974, 90, pp 14–26
60   I H Adams 'The Urban Scene, 1760–1980' in C M Clapperton (ed)
      Scotland—A New Study (Newton Abbot 1983), p 159
61   R Taylor *George Washington Wilson* (Aberdeen 1981)
62   T Annan *Photographs of Old Closes and Streets of Glasgow 1868–1877* (New
      York 1977)

63   I H Adams *The Making of Urban Scotland* (London 1978), pp 127–54
64   Butt *op. cit.* note 50
65   Adams *op. cit.* pp 137–43; E O A Checkland and M M Lamb (eds) *Health Care as Social History* (Aberdeen 1982)
66   Adams *op. cit.* pp 133–6
67   H M Knox *Two Hundred and Fifty Years of Scottish Education, 1696–1945* (Edinburgh 1953)
68   Adams *op. cit.* p 127
69   G Gordon 'Working Class Housing in Edinburgh 1837–1974' in *Festschrift K. A. Sinnhuber,* vol II (Vienna 1979), pp 75–6
70   Daiches *op. cit.* p 180
71   *Ibid.* pp 89–90, 180–9, 207–9
72   *Ibid.* p 212
73   *Ibid.*
74   O Handlin 'The Modern City as a Field of Historical Study' in O Handlin and J Burchard (eds) *The Historian and the City* (Cambridge, Mass 1966), p 1
75   P Knox *Urban Social Geography* (London 1982), p 16
76   Butt *op. cit.*
77   *Ibid.*; Gordon *op. cit.* note 69
78   Rodger *op. cit.* note 4
79   Adams, *op. cit.* note 63, p 242
80   Scottish Development Department 'The Social Effects of Living off the Ground', Housing Development Group Occasional Paper 1, 1975; M Pacione 'Housing Policies in Glasgow since 1880', *Geog. Rev.* 1979, 69, pp 409–10
81   Pacione *op. cit.* note 80
82   J Forbes and I Robertson 'Patterns of Residential Movement in Greater Glasgow', *Scot. Geog. Mag.* 1981, 97, pp 86–97
83   *Ibid.* p 90
84   M Pacione 'Neighbourhood Communities in the Modern City: Some Evidence from Glasgow' *Scot. Geog. Mag.* 1983, 99, pp 169–81
85   Forbes and Robertson *op. cit.* p 91
86   F Twine and N J Williams 'Social segregation in public sector housing: a case study', *Trans. Inst. Brit. Geogr.* 1983, N.S.8, pp 253–66
87   *Ibid.* p 265
88   M Pacione and G Gordon (eds) *Quality of Life and Human Welfare* (Norwich 1984)
89   Scottish Office 'A Study of Multiply Deprived Households in Scotland', *Central Research Unit* (Edinburgh 1980)
90   G M Howe 'London and Glasgow: A Spatial Analysis of Mortality Experience in Contrasting Metropolitan Centres', *Scot. Geog. Mag.* 1982, 98, p 126
91   *Ibid.* pp 126–7
92   P Knox and M Pacione 'Locational behaviour, place preferences and the inverse care law in the distribution of primary medical care', *Geoforum* 1980, 11, pp 43–55

2

EMPLOYMENT, WAGES AND POVERTY IN THE SCOTTISH CITIES 1841–1914

Richard Rodger

I

At the dawn of the Victorian age Scotland had already achieved a place among the elite in the industrial league table.[1] In the slipstream of the English economy Scottish cotton textiles and the iron industry projected Scottish industry to international eminence, based not only on an amalgam of accumulated advantages—developed banking structure, educational attainment, agricultural and intellectual enlightenment, social mobility—but also on real economic leverage, lower unit costs of production. This leverage was in fact two-fold: firstly, labour costs conspicuously lower than in her major competitor, England; secondly, locational advantages, geological in the coal and iron industries, geographical in the cotton industry, both of which conveyed a sufficient edge to secure a Scottish foothold in the industrialisation of western Europe. Technological solutions to the metallurgical problems of coke smelting in the iron industry and to the mechanisation of cotton textile production, pioneered in the main in England and only adopted haltingly in eighteenth-century Scotland, experienced a rapidity of diffusion in the nineteenth century which contributed to a technical leadership with possibilities for self-sustaining growth and expansion in late Victorian Scottish industry. Underlying the transmission of an initial forward impulse to the Scottish economy was a favourable, partly fortuitous, factor endowment. Cotton textiles, coal and iron working proceeded on the basis of standardised, mechanised and thus unskilled or semi-skilled labour fused with low priced raw materials—cheap cotton imports, suitable, accessible and abundant coal and iron deposits.

Factor endowments, both raw material and labour, proved not inexhaustible. Urban immigration and natural increase slowed while emigration accelerated; ore and coal seams encountered geological difficulties and diminishing returns; cotton imports were subject to interruptions and fluctuations, and output to increasing foreign competition. The balance of responsibility for continued industrial expansion passed increasingly after the 1870s to the specialised and highly skilled heavy engineering and shipbuilding sectors. But while this blood transfusion to the Scottish industrial economy sustained the aggregate performance in the intervening years before World War I, it simultaneously generated immense problems of adjustment for those workers previously at the spearhead of the economy.

This picture is, of course, the 'authorised version', the textbook treatment of Scottish industrialisation. And yet it is really a Clydeside/Clydesdale version. Lip-service is paid to minor aberrations, pockets of industrial non-conformity—Dundee jute, Kirkcaldy linoleum, Dunfermline linens. To music hall comedians and general public alike the archetypal Scot is a Glaswegian. The assumed homogeneity could not be further from reality and the variance between the four principal cities of Scotland, viewed through their employment structure which is central to this chapter, offers some light on the economic and social diversity in Victorian Scotland. Nonetheless, some common denominators such as the causes of poverty and attitudes to it are briefly examined because of their general relevance to each of the Scottish cities.

II

Scottish middle-class attitudes to unemployment reflected for much of the Victorian age prevailing responses to poverty and urban discipline in general.[2] Intemperance, idleness and moral degeneracy were interpreted as character defects, remediable only through denial of relief and the recognition that no institutional long-stop existed to cushion the impact of unemployment. Personal revelation and individual resurrection in the biblical sense of rediscovery and rebirth were central pillars in attitudes towards the disadvantaged in Victorian society. Understandably, middle-class concern surrounded falling church attendances, evident even in the 1850s, and with this instrument of moral rearmament structurally weakened at an early stage philanthropic gestures offered limited short term palliatives to the unemployed and poor, whilst simultaneously appeasing middle-class consciences. Whether motivated out of evangelical ardour, concern for safety on the streets, or the containment of disease and moral contamination, cleansing the moral environment was complementary to cleansing the physical environment of burghs, and Scottish pamphleteers missed few opportunities to exhort constant vigilance in the campaign for improved urban behaviour. Entirely consistent with such fears and aspirations, middle-class attitudes to unemployment, as reflected in editorial columns, letters to newspapers, societies, official enquiries and committee reports, stressed non-intervention from officialdom on the grounds that fundamental character reform was the only enduring solution. Any other approach not only failed to offer a long-term solution, but made it more remote by rewarding indiscipline and idleness.

In a Scottish urban context it has been noted that this Victorian self-help stance on unemployment, and poverty in general, underwent some revision in the 1890s.[3] As the Tory chairman of a Glasgow Parish Council stated in 1901, 'Hitherto the administrators of the Poor Law have had to accept final results, and act without regard to causes; but the relief of this class (unemployed) cannot be satisfactorily undertaken without breaking that ancient policy. Now the time would seem to have come when power should be transferred on Parish Councils to take causes of pauperism into account.'[4] Almost certainly the philosophical debate and startling sociological research of Mearns, Mayhew, Booth, Rowntree and others had some role in this regard, arguing as they did that 27–43 per cent of primary poverty was directly attributable to sickness, old age, widowhood, and family size, that is, irrespective of the will to work.[5] More recently Rose has confirmed the upper estimates of contemporaries as more accurate.[6] Nowhere better illustrated the triangle of employment–poverty–morality than both the rag trade, which depressed Sherwell sufficiently to conclude in 1897 that 'morals fluctuate with trade',[7] and port employment, where Drage's study of dockers showed that between October 1891 and March 1892 employment exhibited severe volatility, the numbers ranging in London in each month from 1,350 to 4,000.[8] English parallels did not go unremarked in Scotland.[9] The social conditions of neighbourhoods in London St Giles and Seven Dials, other provincial cities and Scottish burghs were compared, especially with reference to the unsafe nature of the streets, and related to the intensification of problems associated with irregular employment in Scotland from about 1860 to 1900.[10]

That the role of the Christian church in the reformation of character was central to the remedial efforts to deal with poverty in Scottish burghs remained unshakeable. 'It is essentially the function of the Christian church to organise such agencies and to bring to bear such influences as shall move the poor to live decent and clean lives in the decent and clean houses provided for them', argued the Presbytery of Glasgow in their Report on the Housing of the Poor in 1891.[11] The acceptance of their responsibility and that of the town council was explicit: 'The work of the Corporation and the work of the Church must go hand in hand.'[12] If this moral rearmament did no more than reassert the central tenets of Victorian social policy, one important departure gave the key to the direction opinion, and ultimately policy, was moving. The report noted that, 'sheer poverty has much to answer for',[13] a conclusion based upon employment patterns. One witness, Glasier, when asked, 'You are of opinion (sic) that poverty is the chief, if not the only cause of the crowded and insanitary dwellings of the poor?', replied emphatically, 'Exactly', and referred particularly to labourers, foundry workers, warehouse porters, cobblers and, significantly, 'old and debilitated workmen, widows with little children and women and girls without male support' as the sources of poverty.[14] More specifically and in relation to immigrants, it was 'the fact that the bulk of them are not craftsmen' and that 'they get very uncertain work' that consigned them, their families and succeeding generations to poverty. In general, it was both the employment structure and remuneration levels which created poverty, and Glasier concurred with his questioner 'that there are many families whose position is not due in any measure to drunkenness or sloth, or any other form of personal misbehaviour.'[15] In 1890 Glasier identified in Glasgow 4,500 dock labourers, 3,144 tailors, 4,850 carters and 5,293 iron workers, themselves totalling nearly 18,000 workers but representative of a much larger pool of 50,000 adult men 'who do not average more than 20s. a week'. This accounted for 27 per cent of the occupied adult male workforce and took no account of thousands of vagrants, of the irregularly employed, or of customarily low-paid female workers. What Glasier demonstrated conclusively was that with wages of £1 per week, or £52 over the year, 27 per cent of Glasgow workers were expected to feed, clothe and house their families on less than it cost the City Poor House (£55.9s.2d.) or the Prison (£62.13s.3½d.) per year for an equivalent number of inmates in their care. Telling, informed and quantified, such bald inconsistencies did much to loosen the mortar of the character deficiency argument though its adherents still managed to reassert the theme to enquiries in 1902–3, 1911 and 1911–17.

If economic theory, social investigations and philosophical debate were from the 1880s undermining the unanimity of character deficiency as an explanation of poverty, a faltering industrial performance and declining military capability accelerated the process. Within the space of fifteen to twenty years of Glasier's remarks, workmen's compensation for accidents, old age pensions, sickness and unemployment insurance, welfare entitlements ranging from school meals to milk and medical inspections, further restrictions on the length of the working day judged prejudicial to health, minimum wages in sweated trades, and early closing and general restraints on shop hours reflected a tacit acceptance of the fundamental causes of poverty—inadequate income.

Such diversity of legislative initiatives implicitly recognised that inadequate income stemmed from several sources—irregular work, casual and seasonal, low-paid sweated work, often female, and domestic circumstances, such as large family size, widowhood, interrupted earnings due to disablement or disease. However hesitantly, the distributional implications of industrialisation were in receipt of some attention, though these industrial casualties were in no way considered in a socialist, Marxist or paternalist framework, but more in keeping with entrenched liberal views of assisting individuals to get back on their financial feet.[16]

III

The number of low and irregularly paid workers, and equally important their susceptibility to trade fluctuations, was crucial to the depth and extent of poverty in the Scottish cities. Put another way, the stability of employment prospects, the dependability of work allowed predictability and continuity of consumption patterns at above minimum levels. Table 1 shows that the occupational composition of the four Scottish cities was dissimilar in some essentials.[17]

Logically, in an urban setting, agriculture and fishing maintained only a minimal presence. If anything its importance declined after mid-century as the sophistication of the Scottish urban economy eroded agricultural opportunities within urban boundaries. Exceptional to this pattern was Aberdeen. The third quarter of the nineteenth century saw a sustained expansion in east coast herring fishing, with Aberdeen gaining an important role as a fishing station.[18] Thereafter, with occasional interruptions, the availability of transport and credit facilities assisted Aberdeen to attain a position of paramountcy in the expansion of the herring fishery. Curing,

Table 1

Occupational Structure in Scottish Cities 1841-1911[a]

		Total occupied population (100%)		% Employment by sector, sex									
				Professional		Domestic		Commercial		Agriculture and Fishing		Industrial	
		M	F	M	F	M	F	M	F	M	F	M	F
1911	Glasgow	253210	111603	10.03	7.51	0.73	19.67	19.59	3.24	0.40	0.11	69.25	69.47
	Edinburgh	93631	55128	15.54	9.65	2.50	39.82	15.94	2.43	1.79	3.14	64.23	44.96
	Dundee	47374	36836	8.23	3.58	0.89	8.54	14.56	0.93	1.13	0.07	75.19	86.88
	Aberdeen	45467	22860	10.16	9.26	1.10	23.75	19.27	2.61	11.16	6.02	58.31	58.36
1901	Glasgow	250441	111472	4.56	5.30	0.74	21.61	23.84	7.65	0.37	0.16	70.50	65.28
	Edinburgh	93595	53658	11.08	8.00	1.89	42.53	22.75	6.79	1.29	0.28	62.61	42.40
	Dundee	46504	37567	4.02	2.90	0.77	8.00	18.59	2.15	0.82	0.07	75.80	86.87
	Aberdeen	43381	21836	6.09	6.99	0.98	25.63	23.75	6.10	4.13	0.23	65.05	61.04
1891	Glasgow	184270	86555	5.18	4.55	2.03	21.26	21.70	4.42	0.47	0.20	70.63	69.57
	Edinburgh	77849	44623	15.64	10.70	2.61	45.87	18.80	3.80	1.51	0.28	61.45	39.35
	Dundee	43782	36659	4.93	3.53	0.92	10.04	15.53	0.91	1.20	0.12	77.43	85.40
	Aberdeen	34409	18743	9.15	9.50	0.83	31.45	21.33	3.12	4.07	0.18	64.63	55.75
1881	Glasgow	155518	78464	5.18	4.63	1.13	20.66	19.71	2.31	0.69	0.21	73.29	72.19
	Edinburgh	66659	38326	14.86	10.76	3.93	49.32	16.43	2.67	1.56	0.64	63.23	36.62
	Dundee	37533	31617	4.20	2.64	1.21	8.38	14.54	0.53	0.91	0.09	79.14	88.36
	Aberdeen	28975	16507	8.91	9.93	2.09	32.39	17.24	1.99	3.52	1.08	68.25	54.61
1871	Glasgow	140044	75268	4.77	1.62	2.05	21.35	19.42	5.13	0.95	0.17	72.80	71.74
	Edinburgh	54437	31822	12.71	4.17	3.73	55.22	16.44	5.32	3.18	0.97	63.93	34.31
	Dundee	30170	27667	3.87	1.05	1.68	10.28	14.10	0.86	1.80	0.20	78.54	87.62
	Aberdeen	21665	13295	9.86	2.67	1.97	34.11	18.92	2.81	5.52	1.05	63.74	59.36
1851[b]	Glasgow	104475	62901	4.89	0.65	0.95	25.45	14.55	2.31	2.08	0.38	77.53	71.21
	Dundee	23452	15934	3.61	0.73	0.43	14.98	11.28	1.12	1.92	0.30	82.76	82.87
	Aberdeen	19145	12301	13.99	2.98	1.15	32.41	14.72	2.70	6.76	1.05	63.47	60.86
1841	Glasgow (+ suburbs)	81308	41744	4.53	0.57	2.03	31.60	15.09	2.87	4.43	0.37	73.92	64.59
	Edinburgh (+ suburbs)	36685	20941	13.34	1.93	6.53	70.36	14.10	2.71	2.77	1.39	63.26	23.61
	Dundee	16636	8149	4.98	0.88	1.95	27.30	13.70	2.79	2.80	0.38	76.57	68.65
	Aberdeen	16006	8841	6.46	2.24	4.05	40.37	14.57	2.44	6.21	0.97	68.71	53.98

Notes: (a) Dependents included in 1861 Census
     (b) Edinburgh and Leith data combined in 1851 and therefore omitted
        from Table 1
Sources: *See* note 17

gutting and packing offered sizeable if seasonal employment for women, as reflected in the 1911 figures.

Commercial employment—merchants, dealers, bankers, accountants, valuers, clerks, insurance agents, salesmen, railway, road and other employees in distribution—displayed rather different characteristics. Firstly, consistent with a developing economy and the rise of a tertiary sector, there was a long run tendency for male employment to expand in these areas from about one in seven male workers to one in five between 1841 and 1901, though this expansion was weakest in Dundee. Secondly, the level of employment in commercial and distributive activities was in two sets of pairs throughout 1841-1911, with Glasgow and Aberdeen both similar and above Dundee and Edinburgh, which were themselves similar. Even within this broad pattern of commercial employment there were significant differences with implications for the pattern of consumption. In Edinburgh, financial prowess meant that the contribution to commercial employment from middle-class and petit-bourgeois elements was roughly equivalent to that from the transport sector with its heavier reliance on manual and unskilled workers. By contrast, in Glasgow, Aberdeen and Dundee transport workers were twice as numerous as white-collar workers in the banking, insurance and merchanting classifications. Thirdly, female commercial employment exhibited considerable instability between censuses, albeit at a low level. Although the census dates were not cyclical turning points themselves, sizeable intra-cyclical variations in commercial travelling, messengering, selling, and even telegraphy and telephones existed. Women employees in commerce and distribution were, therefore, prone to short-term shifts in employment prospects.

Interestingly, the four Scottish cities do not seem to have participated in a 'white-blouse' revolution, a secular expansion in female commercial employment opportunities in telephone exchanges, office work and related employment after 1870.[19] Nor does scrutiny of the professional tier of employment, despite rising rapidly in 1881, suggest a marked proliferation of women's work opportunities. In fact, the increase in female professional employment in 1881 is attributable to the inclusion of students in the workforce. Women students were numerically equivalent to the remainder of female professional workers—principally schoolteachers, governesses, nurses, musicians and artists—and if the percentages for professional female employment are halved in the three university towns to take account of the inclusion of students, the expansion is understandably more gradual.[20] Even so, female professional work was, in the last third of the nineteenth century, expanding, most noticeably in Edinburgh and Aberdeen and if hardly of 'revolutionary' proportions, the number of women students was at least a portent of future involvement.

Male professional employment in Aberdeen and Edinburgh was until 1911 decisively more important than in Glasgow and Dundee. Until 1911 some 12–15 per cent of employment in Edinburgh was in the professions, the order of importance, for example in 1881 showing the entrenched position of legal, medical, cultural and administrative occupations. Indeed, only in the representation of the armed forces did Edinburgh fall below the national average and overall the percentage of professional workers was 215 per cent that of the UK.[21] In the most numerous branches of professional work the Edinburgh proportion was 450–500 per cent above the national average and the self-sustaining nature of this employment structure can be seen by the fact that Edinburgh students were equivalent to 2.3 per cent of the workforce.[22] Comparative figures are given in Table 2 for the other Scottish cities.

These illustrate the emphatically more stable employment base in Edinburgh with one worker in eight in professional work. Representatives of the professional middle classes in Dundee and Glasgow were not only far fewer than in Aberdeen and Edinburgh but were also below the national average.

Table 2

Stability of Employment: Professional Occupations 1881

Percentage of occupied population

	Glasgow	Edinburgh	Dundee	Aberdeen	UK
Law	0.42	2.51	0.39	1.26	0.56
Medicine, dentistry	0.48	2.09	0.48	1.17	0.40
Arts, entertainment, music	0.80	1.66	0.63	0.82	0.60
Civil service	0.59	1.61	0.50	0.51	0.60
Army, navy	0.21	1.43	0.33	1.26	1.60
Teaching	0.45	0.97	0.47	0.74	0.61
Church	0.36	0.95	0.40	0.57	0.56
Police, municipal officers	0.86	0.90	0.61	0.59	0.65
Science, engineering	0.20	0.36	0.08	0.16	0.22
Total professional	4.37	12.47	3.60	7.10	5.79

Sources: Census of England and Wales 1881, *PP 1883 LXXX*; Census of Scotland, *PP 1883 LXXXI*; C. Booth, 'Occupations of the People of the UK, 1801–81', *Journal of the Royal Statistical Society* 49 1886, p 414

Even so, in Glasgow and Dundee some areas of professional work were better represented than in national terms—medicine and entertainment, for example, and significantly employment of police, prison and municipal officials, that is the agents of environmental and social control.

Salaried employment was synonymous with security of employment. Security of employment meant stability of income, predictability of domestic expenditure. The salary 'bargain', in contrast to the wage bargain, implied not only higher income and different terms of engagement—regular hours, notice of termination, payment in lieu of notice, pension entitlements in certain professions, an element of discretion regarding deductions for unpunctuality, and censure rather than sacking over other minor misdemeanours—but also greater security of employment. In fact a degree of regulated entry ensured insulation against the machinations of the labour market. Educational standards, articles, ordination, and medical assistantships served to regulate the professional labour supply as effectively, if not more so than the apprenticeship system for skilled manual workers. This cyclical insulation was enhanced by secular growth. The maturing industrial economy attached increasing importance to the service sector, and the professions participated in this trend. Booth calculated a rise from 3.6 per cent to 5.6 per cent between 1841 and 1881 and this upward drift with occasional interruptions and different intensity was replicated in the Scottish cities, the percentage rising from 6.9 per cent in 1841 to 7.7 per cent in 1881 and 11.02 per cent in 1911.[23] The importance of this salaried component in each city cannot be underestimated. In late Victorian Edinburgh one in seven male workers was in the professional grouping and if some such as municipal officials and entertainers lacked the status or income flow of lawyers and clerics there were other non-professional salaried occupations, as for example previously noted in the commercial sector, who compensated for them. As early as 1865 the Edinburgh Medical Officer, Henry Littlejohn, observed this peculiar occupational structure. In his famous medical report on health in Edinburgh he noted, 'Edinburgh has no pretensions to be a manufacturing city . . . the establishment of a University and of the highest courts of judicature appears to have diverted the attention of the inhabitants from mercantile pursuits.'[24] Littlejohn also noted the attraction of Edinburgh to the gentry. Leisure and amusements, soirées and concert parties, artistic and other cultural pursuits derived substantial patronage from such a heavily represented class, and as Lee noted, 'There can be no doubt that it was the metropolitan role of Edinburgh which gave the Lothian economy its structural similarity to the South East of England and that mixture of professions, commerce, personal services and consumer goods industries such as printing and publishing.'[25] Dundee, at the other end of the spectrum, offered professional employment to no more than one male worker in twenty during the Victorian era and the stabilising, counter-cyclical consumption patterns were correspondingly weak.

The importance of this hard core of professional occupations was not confined to the middle class themselves. The size and stability affected the strength of demand locally for a broad range of goods and services. The aggregate effect of a higher marginal propensity to save amongst the middle classes was more than offset by the regularity and scale of expenditure, and this injection of purchasing power sustained ancillary occupations to varying degrees in the four Scottish cities. Retailing, housing maintenance and clothing were amongst those branches of employment in which middle-class patronage cushioned variations in the volume of overall business. Just as professional employment was important in Edinburgh for its stabilising qualities, so the reduced presence of the professional element was of major significance to the employment structure of Dundee and Glasgow, denying a counterweight to the volatility of manufacturing employment.

Closely associated with the purchasing power of the middle class was the demand for domestic service (Table 1). This was pre-eminently a female sphere of work; employment for male servants, mostly coachmen, grooms and gardeners, though most resilient in Edinburgh, diminishing from 3.3 per cent of the occupied workforce of the four cities in 1841 to a nadir of 1.0 per cent in 1901. Widely divergent patterns of female employment existed in the four cities. In Edinburgh, the concentration of middle-class demand patterns generated unprecedented opportunities for women, 70 per cent of the female workforce in 1841 being in domestic service, four out of five of whom were indoor servants in private houses. Although this ratio of indoor servants remained much the same over the mid-Victorian censuses, by 1871 female domestic service in Edinburgh had declined to a still formidable 55 per cent of employed women.[26]Thereafer there was a 10 per cent reduction 1871–81, and three successive 7 per cent decennial reductions to 1911, so that on the eve of war 40 per cent of female employees in Edinburgh were in domestic service. The pattern was not replicated elsewhere. In Aberdeen domestic service accounted for 30–40 per cent of female employment between 1841 and 1891 and slipped to about 25 per cent in the twentieth century. The decline to 25 per cent was registered as early as the 1840s in Glasgow; thereafter it hovered around 20 per cent during the years 1871 to 1911. In Dundee, in sharp contrast to Edinburgh and Aberdeen, though echoing Glasgow at a lower level, domestic service was halved in the 1840s and following a more gradual fall in mid-century contributed a fairly steady 8–10 per cent of women's employment in the years 1871 to 1911. In each burgh, however, indoor service remained the dominant occupation; in 1911 it still accounted for seven out of ten servants.

Table 3

Female Employment in Scottish Cities by Marital Status, 1911

Age groups	Glasgow		Edinburgh		Dundee		Aberdeen	
	A	B	A	B	A	B	A	B
15–19	10.2	—	17.5	—	54.6	—	6.1	—
20–24	7.5	69.0	7.3	72.0	41.1	71.4	3.3	81.8
25–44	5.3	54.1	5.0	56.7	25.2	74.6	2.9	52.7
45–64	5.6	30.0	5.2	31.4	18.8	48.2	3.2	27.2
65–69	3.8	16.9	3.5	18.0	8.1	27.3	3.7	18.4
70 +	2.8	6.5	1.8	6.8	3.9	10.1	1.1	5.3
All ages	5.5	26.5	5.1	26.4	23.4	39.0	3.0	22.6

A—% married and working   B—% widowed and working

Source: PP 1912–13 CXIX, Table XXIII B, pp 35, 76, 112, 152

Several features are worth stressing in relation to female employment generally. Firstly, there is some reason to believe that there was pressure on the household economics of the Scottish urban middle class. The proportion of female domestic indoor servants fell between 1881 and 1911—from 85 per cent to 70 per cent in Edinburgh, from 86 per cent to 76 per cent in Aberdeen, 77 per cent to 69 per cent in Dundee, though the proportion remained static, 74 per cent, in Glasgow. Thus in Edinburgh and Aberdeen, until the twentieth century, there was a greater reliance on indoor servants; conversely, the emphasis on occasional female work as chars and washer-women was more pronounced in Glasgow and Dundee. Secondly, the age structure of domestic servants divided roughly equally into thirds, in the age groups 15–19, 20–24, and 25–44. Widows in domestic work outnumbered married women by a ratio of approximately 2:1 in each of the Scottish burghs in 1911. Thirdly, with the exception of Dundee which is discussed later, marriage was virtually synonymous with withdrawal from the labour force.

In earlier Victorian years the frequency of pregnancy and childbirth did much to impose this pattern; latterly rising real wages of the husband, if employed, enhanced emphasis on family life and the emulation of middle-class child-rearing attitudes, and diminished prospects for re-entry into a domestic sector which had stabilised or was even contracting slightly maintained married women's employment at very low levels. From age twenty the proportion of working married women changed very little, a reflection of the social acceptability in certain occupations and of the number of childless marriages. Finally, faced with the prospect of poverty, widows vigorously sought and obtained employment. Married women in employment exceeded widows by a ratio of at least 3.5:1 in each of the cities, but certain occupational areas were firmly associated with widows. These are shown in Table 4 where the ratio exceeds 1.0.

Table 4

Ratio of Widowed to Married Women in Principal Industries, 1911

	Glasgow	Edinburgh	Dundee	Aberdeen
Sick nurses	2.4	2.5	3.5	5.9
Domestic indoor servants				
—not hotels	1.8	2.1	2.3	1.7
—hotels		0.7		
Caretakers		2.1		3.1
Charwomen, cleaners	2.1	2.4	2.3	4.3
Laundry workers	1.1	1.1	1.6	1.9
Flax, linen manufacture			0.4	1.2
Jute manufacture			0.4	
Cotton manufacture	0.8			
Dressmakers	1.1	1.4	1.7	1.7
Shirtmakers, seamstresses	1.2	2.0		4.0
Provision dealers				1.5
Fish curers				1.1
Fishmongers, poulterers				1.3
Grocers			2.1	3.7
Greengrocers, fruiterers	1.0	1.3		
Eating house keepers				2.1
Lodging house keepers	4.1	3.9		4.8
Hawkers, street sellers	0.7	0.7	0.6	0.7
Canvas, sailcloth, sacking			0.3	
Carpeting, rugmaking			0.7	
Bakers, confectioners	1.3	1.0	1.1	
Teachers		1.9		
India rubber, gutta percha		0.5		
Printing, bookbinding		0.8		
Paper manufacture		0.5		
Milksellers	1.1	1.4		
Shopkeepers	0.8	1.0		
Cooks (not domestic)	1.6			
Ironmongers, hardware	1.4			
Jam, preserves	0.7			

Source: *PP 1912–13 CXIX*, Table XXIIIA, pp 35, 76, 112, 152

For example, even though in Glasgow there were four times more married than widowed working women in 1911, there were 2.4 times more widowed than married sick nurses. Thus as nurses, and teachers, shopkeepers, lodging and eating housekeepers, caretakers, chars, and laundry workers, in shirt-making and as seamstresses widows could obtain an income, however insufficient to support themselves and their families. If it did have to be supplemented by charitable societies' and distress committees' payments, it did keep them out of the workhouse. By contrast, manufacturing industry and food processing attracted more married women, and reflected their work experience as single women and as newly-weds before they had a family, and is borne out by the drop of employed married women between the 15–19 and 20–24 age groups (Table 3).

IV

For most Scottish women at the opening of the twentieth century, however, industrial work was the most common sector of employment, even in Edinburgh (Table 1). Throughout the period 1841–1911 a steady 65 per cent to 72 per cent of employed Glaswegian women pursued industrial work, and in Aberdeen, too, the female industrial workforce remained consistently in the 55–60 per cent range during the Victorian and Edwardian period. In Edinburgh, with the lowest proportion of women industrial workers in 1841, approximately one in four, a mid-century expansion continued with a 10.7 per cent decennial increase in each census between 1871 and 1901, and a further 6 per cent increase during 1901–11. Thus over the half century female industrial employment in the capital expanded by an average 1 per cent per annum, so that on the eve of war 45 per cent were in this sector—printing, bookbinding, food processing and clothing accounting for the majority. For Dundee, the 1840s were 'a prosperous period' for the textile industry.[27] Female employment already reflected this emphasis—69 per cent of working women were textiles hands in 1841 and this jumped to 83 per cent in 1851. The outbreak of the Crimean War in 1854 'marked an unprecedented acceleration in the expansion of Dundee's already prosperous economy'[28] and from 1871 until 1911 a virtually static 85 per cent of Dundee women obtained work in textile manufacturing, despite the adversity created by foreign competition from the 1880s. No wonder Collins concluded that it was 'an almost wholly working class town'.[29]

Although the composition of male industrial employment exhibited marked differences both between the four cities and in the balance of its constituent elements, the absolute size of the industrial workforce remained remarkably constant throughout the period 1841 to 1911. Industrial employment as a percentage of the occupied workforce wavered by only one or two points either side of 77 per cent in Dundee, 72 per cent in Glasgow, 64 per cent in Aberdeen and 63 per cent in Edinburgh over the Victorian and Edwardian years (Table 1). Divergent industrial emphasis, partially reflected longstanding locational advantages in each city and the comparative advantage in costs of production in the selected specialisms of each city—centralised government, judiciary and administration in Edinburgh, accumulated textile expertise in Dundee, the cotton-iron-engineering complex of Glasgow, and fishing, quarrying and regional economic servicing in Aberdeen. Tables 5(a)–(d) show these and other branches of industrial employment for each city, and their changes over the period 1841–1911.

Certain general characteristics of industrial employment in the Scottish cities stand out. First, and most conspicuous, is the early dominance of textiles and clothing in 1841. Even in Edinburgh, though far more pronounced in the other three cities, this was the largest employer. By 1911, however, the general wastage of the textile sector singled out Dundee as exceptional in the retention of this area of industrial employment.[30] A

Table 5

(a)   Composition of Industrial Employment: Glasgow 1841–1911[a]

	1841 %	1851 %	1871 %	1881 %	1891 %	1901 %	1911 %
Printing and Publishing	1.12	1.38	1.90	2.21	2.58	2.37	2.82
Engineering, Toolmaking and Metalworking	7.17	8.67	14.08	12.81	14.17	14.84	16.86
Shipbuilding	0.35	0.14	1.33	0.68	0.72	0.84	1.80
Coachbuilding	0.40	0.13	0.48	0.46	0.62	0.63	0.72
Building	5.84	5.64	7.42	6.30	5.47	6.71	4.83
Furniture and Woodworking	1.06	1.41	1.17	1.79	1.77	2.03	3.18
Chemicals	1.22	1.00	1.17	0.64	0.60	0.79[b]	1.89[b]
Food, Drink and Tobacco	5.24	6.41	5.63	7.65	7.85	9.75	12.41
Textiles and Clothing	37.56	41.86	31.97	25.42	20.75	17.16	16.86
Other manufacturing[c]	2.90	3.36	3.32	3.21	3.37	3.45	3.34
General labouring	8.40	2.90	4.41	3.92	4.31	3.72	2.23

(b)   Composition of Industrial Employment: Edinburgh 1841–1911[a]

	1841 %	1871 %	1881 %	1891 %	1901 %	1911 %
Printing and Publishing	3.88	4.89	5.16	5.02	5.14	6.69
Engineering, Toolmaking and Metalworking	6.07	6.85	5.86	5.88	6.51	6.16
Shipbuilding	0.17	0.05	0.06	0.10	0.09	0.08
Coachbuilding	0.92	0.80	0.64	0.66	0.46	0.56
Building	5.73	9.64	9.28	6.92	8.98	6.24
Furniture and Woodworking	2.73	2.37	2.38	1.69	1.74	2.22
Chemicals	0.24	0.27	0.46	0.62	1.50[b]	3.22[b]
Food, Drink and Tobacco	8.31	7.36	8.54	9.34	10.40	11.57
Textiles and Clothing	13.04	14.64	11.17	11.49	10.00	11.00
Other manufacturing[c]	3.02	4.06	4.34	4.25	3.73	3.10
General labouring	3.69	2.32	1.90	2.63	1.67	1.69

(c)   *Composition of Industrial Employment: Dundee 1841-1911*[a]

	1841 %	1851 %	1871 %	1881 %	1891 %	1901 %	1911 %
Printing and Publishing	0.56	0.55	0.58	0.73	0.71	1.02	1.56
Engineering, Toolmaking and Metalworking	5.59	4.38	5.63	6.11	6.10	6.54	5.62
Shipbuilding	1.14	0.91	1.08	1.24	2.24	1.64	1.89
Coachbuilding	0.21	0.15	0.20	0.23	0.35	0.20	0.25
Building	6.05	4.04	5.64	4.38	3.48	5.56	3.46
Furniture and Woodworking	0.77	0.90	0.63	0.78	0.84	0.94	1.86
Chemicals	0.19	0.21	0.16	0.12	0.23	0.17[b]	0.62[b]
Food, Drink and Tobacco	5.27	4.62	4.38	5.53	6.27	6.93	7.59
Textiles and Clothing	50.54	61.36	61.81	54.42	52.28	51.73	53.52
Other manufacturing[c]	1.29	0.97	1.54	1.22	1.82	0.85	0.91
General labouring	3.84	3.60	3.15	3.24	2.27	1.65	1.32

(d)   *Composition of Industrial Employment: Aberdeen 1841-1911*[a]

	1841 %	1851 %	1871 %	1881 %	1891 %	1901 %	1911 %
Printing and Publishing	0.91	1.03	1.42	1.62	1.89	2.04	2.51
Engineering, Toolmaking and Metalworking	6.32	5.04	5.89	5.76	6.02	6.50	5.78
Shipbuilding	1.24	1.14	1.37	1.01	1.24	1.19	2.54
Coachbuilding	0.34	0.19	0.56	0.57	0.72	0.76	0.78
Building	5.99	5.06	7.81	7.90	6.74	7.80	4.72
Furniture and Woodworking	0.87	0.95	1.03	1.29	1.19	1.52	2.92
Chemicals	0.37	0.22	0.70	0.52	0.52	1.81[b]	1.65[b]
Food, Drink and Tobacco	4.66	6.89	7.07	8.61	7.65	11.00	10.13
Textiles and Clothing	34.68	35.08	25.45	17.38	17.43	15.56	16.16
Other manufacturing[c]	3.18	4.69	7.23	6.16	5.81	3.13	3.12
General labouring	6.87	4.32	4.13	4.91	4.75	3.30	1.81

Notes: (a) Data for 1861 includes dependents and for purposes of comparison is excluded
   (b) includes rubber
   (c) glass, paper, pottery, oil, cane, gum, grease
Sources: *See* note 17

second general characteristic, to be expected, was the developing specialisation of the industrial base, of which mechanical engineering and metalworking in Glasgow, and printing and publishing in Edinburgh are the most obvious examples. A third feature was the effect of rising real incomes on the food, drink and tobacco industries, where the proportions employed in each burgh in 1871 were much the same as in 1841, but by 1911 had doubled.[31] Fourth, the cyclical effect of building was apparent in for example the upswing of the early 1870s, sustained into 1880-1 in Edinburgh and Aberdeen and a further example of their eclectic employment bases with stabilising and countercyclical properties.[32] The cyclical decline, post 1905, which brought a virtual cessation to housebuilding and was so serious as to warrant a special report in the 1911 census, was represented by the lowest ever recorded percentage of building workers in each burgh in 1911.[33] Woodworking offered countercyclical employment by way of compensation to some. Fifth, the 'other manufacturing' base was largest in Aberdeen and Edinburgh where diversity represented an insurance premium against trade cycle downturns. By the same token the upswing also had a reduced dynamic. Finally, the general labouring category supplemented this pattern, the pool of unskilled labour being deepest in Glasgow, and, surprisingly, Aberdeen. The implications of this casual employment of which general labouring is only a part are examined later.

Attention to changes in employment structure over time within each of the burghs should not obscure the comparative importance of a particular branch of industry at any one time. Appendix 1(a)–(g) allows a static analysis whereby for each census date, 1861 excepted, the proportionate contribution of a particular industry to the occupied workforce of a burgh is presented, and can be contrasted with the proportionate contribution in another city. While this has been done for industrial employment, a more detailed analysis of 53 occupational headings, male and female, in 1911 is presented in Appendix II and permits a static, end of period view of the relative importance of various types of employment for each city. These 'location quotients' indicate the degree to which in comparison to its proportionate contribution to Scottish employment as a whole, any one occupational grouping was represented in each of the cities. A ratio of 1.00 indicates that a particular occupation was as important proportionately to the city as it was to the country as a whole. For example, in category 12, banking (males), the ratio for Edinburgh was 2.00; there were proportionately twice as many male employees in the banking sector of the capital as there were in Scotland as a whole. In Dundee, the ratio was 0.50; banking employed proportionately half as many males in 1911 as nationally. In Glasgow, the ratio was 1.58; male banking employment in Glasgow was three times more significant for the composition of the workforce than it was for Dundee, was one and a half times more important than for Scotland as a whole, but made only threequarters the contribution to employment as it did in Edinburgh. Thus, the higher the ratio the more important that area of work for the city; the lower the ratio the less the significance for the composition of city employment.

In Glasgow, (Table 5(a)), traditional industries with high skill components—printing, woodworking, coachbuilding for example, enjoyed slight growth of employment at low levels. It was this trend of regular and gently expanding employment which most differentiated the aristocracy of labour for it was on this that the distinctive cultural, educational and recreational activities depended. Though intercensal variations reflected the instability of the industry, there was no long term upward or downward trend in building, and much the same applied to the 'other manufacturing' category. The chemical industry, until 1911, meant declining labour opportunities. By contrast the surge of engineering and the metal trades from the 1860s, which has been extensively covered elsewhere,[34] and food and drink industries in the 1870s compensated for the continuous decline of textiles, lower in each census after 1851.

'Edinburgh', Helen Kerr commented in 1912, 'is not an industrial centre.'[35] After finding it 'startling to discover that Edinburgh's principal occupation is that of service', Kerr observed that, excepting the service sector, 'the principal occupations would be found in printing and publishing, for which Edinburgh has always had a very high reputation, rubber works, distilling and brewing, together with the building industry and its allied trades'.[36] Presumably Kerr did not consult the censuses. Textiles and clothing and food, drink and tobacco remained the most important industries, accounting for one-fifth of all employment together, though the rankings changed with textiles and clothing conceding primacy by the turn of the century (Table 5(b)). Fragmented into small workshops and retailing concerns, Kerr could be forgiven for thinking the areas she identified as the most important, though rubber attained prominence only in the last Victorian decade, and engineering and metalworking retained its position throughout the years 1841 to 1911, employing about one worker in sixteen. As a reflection of the class composition of the capital, previously noted, the importance of the consumer industries—furniture, printing, publishing and coachbuilding—was in the main greater than in the other Scottish cities, and this applied to the building industry, too, where in each census, 1841 to 1911, the proportion of the labour force in this sector was higher than in any of the other cities.[37] The same was true of the percentage employed in food, drink and tobacco. In mid-century Edinburgh this sustained about 8 out of every 100 in the workforce, compared to 5 or 6 per 100 in the other cities, though the differential was eroded somewhat over the course of the Victorian period, and eventually overhauled in twentieth-century Aberdeen and Glasgow. Greater stability of demand not just for food and drink, but other essentials too, shelter and clothing, meant improved opportunities for regular manual work in the lee of Edinburgh's professional middle-class expenditure patterns. Reinforcing this regularity were two other influences. Firstly, the demand preference for high quality and thus hand-made, skilled craftsmanship. As Bremner described this in the case of jewellery, 'All the work done is of a superior kind.'[38] Consequently the labour aristocracy was heavily represented in Edinburgh, with associated implications for greater continuity of employment, higher average earnings and the growth of small savings.[39] Secondly, the size of philanthropic efforts in Edinburgh—some 150 charities disbursing £250,000 annually in the 1900s[40]—was itself a measure of comfortable life styles in the capital, and indicated middle-class efforts to improve the comfort of others. Even this weekly buffer of approximately £7,000, like all transfer payments, gave some support to consumption levels and with marginal propensities to consume virtually 1.0 the re-circulation of this cash injection had wider employment implications for shopkeepers, landlords and small businesses in general.

Of the other Scottish cities, the employment, income and poverty structure of Aberdeen most closely approximated that of Edinburgh. Where national administration, bank and company headquarters, and supreme judicial functions were discharged in Edinburgh, local and regional responsibilities for the northeast and eastern highlands were executed from Aberdeen.[41] Coupled with an industrial base of important proportions until textile contraction, linens and woollens, in the 1850s reduced this element to half its former significance by 1881, Aberdeen enjoyed a balanced economy (Table 5(a)). This complementarity distinguished Aberdonian employment from that of Edinburgh, but conveyed a similar advantage—reasonable stability. Consumption patterns reflected this. Additionally, three other features supported the occupational balance. Firstly, the 'other manufacturing' category was more pronounced than in any other Scottish city. This diversification, associated with small workshop production, offered a degree of insurance against recession and bankruptcy in any one branch of employment. Secondly, it offered a larger pool of potential industrial developers, the 'springs of technical progress'.[42] Thirdly, Aberdeen enjoyed some industrial expansion to compensate for contraction. To offset the mid-century textile peak, food and drink, and chemicals were areas of industrial expansion after 1870, though the increase of female professional employment also from that decade was hardly likely to be accessible to unemployed linen workers. Skilled male employment by contrast was fairly steady after 1851, though there was an employment surge in coachbuilding in the 1880s, chemicals and food processing in the 1890s, and shipbuilding, woodworking and fishing related industries in the 1900s gave an impetus to skilled and unskilled alike. Employment prospects were further diversified with the presence of an important quarrying industry.[43] Amongst unskilled labourers in quarries and skilled workers in masons' and granitecutters' yards, an increasing percentage of the occupied Aberdonian male workforce found their employment, rising from 0.44 per cent in 1841 to 3.77 per cent in 1881 and to 5.23 per cent in 1911. The granite industry in fact contributed a countercyclical force, for a substantial volume of its output found its way to London, with its sustained building levels in the 1880s, and to a wide range of civic buildings which also tended to ignore the normal trade cycle timing.[44]

In the sharpest possible contrast to this balance and diversity it was clear by 1900 that the economic base in Dundee 'was dangerously lopsided'.[45] Dundee Social Union, the Town Council and the Chamber of Commerce recognised that the burgh's fortunes were hostage to the production and market penetration of new Calcutta jute mills and random influences such as tariff barriers and wars, for example in America and Argentina.[46] Well established as a jute centre by 1841, peak expansion took place during 1861–68, in association with the American Civil War demand for bagging. The conclusion of this conflict and the Franco-Prussian War, a trade cycle downturn in 1873, and a Scottish banking and credit crisis in the late 1870s meant an abrupt reduction in jute employment. But the absence of alternatives meant that the percentage associated, however intermittently, with jute and linen employment in Dundee remained almost unchanged until World War I (Table 5(d)). In the 1900s, the sale of two shipping fleets, the migration of another to the Tyne, the decline of the whaling industry and the liquidation of Gourlay's shipbuilding yard in 1908 served to narrow further this industrial base and more than compensated for the nascent developments in electrical engineering, biscuit making, stationery and post-card manufacture.[47] Hence the absence of virile 'other manufacturing' was critical, narrowing the skill and work experience base and limiting the development options. This eclectic 'other manufacturing' grouping actually fell by 50 per cent in the 1890s. Heavy reliance on unskilled female labour meant few industries were attracted to Dundee, and the generally low and interrupted wage levels and scarcity of middle-class occupations depressed the consumer industries to levels well below those of the other Scottish cities.[48] Textile wages were 20 per cent below those in Glasgow in the 1870s,[49] and in 1905 the Dundee Social Union reported that only 8 per cent of male textile workers received wages of more than £1 per week, and mostly they were mechanics and overseers, not operatives.[50] No women earned £1 a week in the jute industry. Flax and jute spinners' wages, hovering around 6–7 shillings per week in the 1850s reached a peak in the 1870s at about 12–14 shillings and then fell back to 7–10 shillings per week, 1880–1900, depending on the grade and stage of production. In 1905 the Social Union report recorded 12 shillings per week ·for women rovers, reelers, winders and weavers, with shift mistresses earning the highest wage of 14 shillings. Spinners (10s.4d.), twisters (10 shillings) calenders, tylers and bundlers (9 shillings) were all paid at lower levels. At such rates it was more than most workers could expect to have sufficient for food and shelter, and demand for other manufactured goods and services was unresponsive to even quite large price changes.[51]

Throughout the period 1841–1911 more than 50 per cent of employment was in jute and linen textiles, and clothing, itself not noted for high wages or regular work.[52] One study reported Dundonians poorly nourished in comparison to Lancashire textile workers.[53] Almost certainly, steadier employment between 1853 and 1872 brought improving and more regular wages. But the pattern of interrupted time and lengthy unemployment thereafter were more significant determinants of health and poverty than a declining cost of living index.[54] In any event, the retailing habits and the pressure on rents caused by casual workers' need for proximity to the place of work pushed the cost of living in Dundee beyond that of any other Scottish city, indeed beyond the cost of living in London.[55] Even without low wage levels the cost of living index itself throttled the volume of demand in the consumption industries of Dundee. The final quarter of the nineteenth century, therefore, witnessed intensified pressure on living standards, and the mortality rates in Dundee, which were substantially above those in the other cities, reflected this.[56] Low and irregular pay killed Dundonians by reducing affordable nutritional and accommodation standards to such minimal levels as to expose large numbers of workers, and weaken their resistance, to environmental diseases.

V

In what respects then did this employment and wage structure influence poverty and prosperity in the four Scottish cities? At the commencement of industrialisation labour costs were substantially lower than in English boroughs. In the 1870s the differential, which had already narrowed somewhat, was at least 3–4 shillings per week, some 10–15 per cent lower in a wide range of Scottish industries.[57] R H Campbell's measured judgement of the relative Scotland-UK wage levels in 1886 was of 'an unequivocal interpretation of Scotland as a low wage economy'.[58] As can be seen in Table 6, high wages were possible in certain sectors of the Scottish economy, though rarely were these more than a few points above the national average and even then in some industries such as silk, employed very few Scots. In fact even though the gap had narrowed further by 1912, the unweighted mean wage in the Scottish economy was 94.8 per cent of the UK wage (Table 6). This position continued beyond World War I and had parallels in the salary structure too, as A D Campbell concluded, 'Income per head has been lower in Scotland fluctuating between 87 and 96 per cent of the United Kingdom average.'[59] This lower figure was more in keeping with an extensive regional survey of wages undertaken by the Board of Trade in 1905.[60]

Table 6

Scottish Wages as a % of English Wages, 1886

Employment	%	Employment	%
Cotton	77.8	Gasworks	89.0
Woollen	88.6	Waterworks	92.5
Worsted	67.9	Iron and steel shipbuilding	92.1
Hemp	93.8	Brass and metalworking	92.7
Hosiery	97.1	Pig iron (blast furnaces)	101.4
Jute	100.0	Engineering	100.0
Carpets	100.0		
Linen	104.0	Building	93.9
Silk	111.1	Sawmilling	92.5
		Cooperage	94.7
Mining: coal, iron ore	101.9	Coachbuilding	98.1
slate	84.9	Breweries	86.7
Quarrying: granite	104.1	Distilleries	100.0
stone	108.5	Brickmaking	100.0
		Printing (large works)	86.8
Police	94.4		
Roads	94.1	Unweighted Mean:	94.8

Source: Calculated from R H Campbell, *The Rise and Fall of Scottish Industry, 1707–1939* (Edinburgh 1980), p 190

Lower wages in the four Scottish cities would have been of no great import had prices been correspondingly lower. In fact, as the Board of Trade noted in 1912, they were not.[61] Scottish urban price levels were consistently above those of English boroughs, and would have been much higher had not Scottish fuel prices been below those in the English cost of living basket of goods. Irrespective of earnings, especially prone though they were in Glasgow and Dundee to interruptions, wage rates in the four cities were appreciably lower (Table 6) and costs of living higher than in English boroughs (Table 7).

Table 7

Retail Price Indices in Scottish and English Cities, 1912
(Central London = 100)

	Retail prices (incl. rent)	Retail prices (excl. rent)
Dundee	97	104
Edinburgh and Leith	96	103
Aberdeen	93	101
Glasgow	93	99
Liverpool and Bootle	89	95
Manchester and Salford	88	94
Birmingham	87	93
Sheffield	87	94
Leeds	87	94
Nottingham	86	94

Source: Board of Trade, *Report of Enquiry into Working Class Rents and Retail Prices with the Rates of Wages in Certain Occupations in Industrial Towns of the United Kingdom in 1912*, Cd 6955, 1913, pp xxxvi–xxxvii

For an identical basket of food Dundonians paid 10.2 per cent more, and Glaswegians 5.7 per cent more than Mancunians, a differential which had already narrowed by 1912. Taking rent into account also, which with food represented 80 per cent of working-class weekly expenditure, and again compared to Manchester (though the same applied to Leeds, Sheffield or Nottingham) Glasgow residents paid a further 5.3 per cent, in Aberdeen the cost of living was 7.4 per cent above the English boroughs, and in Edinburgh and Dundee these inflexible elements of weekly expenditure required respectively 9.6 per cent and 10.6 per cent more than in the English cities and were on a par, or even above, the cost of living in London.[62]

But whereas the poverty implications of the adverse living costs are self evident, the impact of the structure of industrial production was less obvious, but no less adverse. Labour productivity in Scotland remained below the national average. Across the 97 branches of employment recorded in Table 8, the unweighted mean of Scottish labour output registered only 96.6 per cent of UK labour productivity. With wages at 94.8 per cent of the UK level and labour productivity at 96.6 per cent Scottish employers in aggregate rationally preferred labour intensive to capital intensive production where that choice was technically available to them.[63] The leverage of low labour costs so significant in the early phase of Scottish industrialisation found an echo therefore until World War I, and while this

Table 8

Scottish Industrial Productivity, 1907

	Net output per head Scotland as a % of UK		Net output per head Scotland as a % of UK
Coal & ironstone miners	108.6	Rope, twine, net	82.7
Coke works at collieries	134.4	Flock, rag	90.4
Oil shale mines	180.0	Bleaching, dyeing, finishing,	
Shale oil works	100.0	printing	79.2
Limestone quarries and kilns	96.5		
Slate quarries	63.9	Clothing, handkerchief,	
Quarries other than iron,		millinery	85.5
slate, limestone	88.0	Boot and shoe	88.7
		Hat, bonnet and cap	86.6
		Umbrella and walking stick	93.8
Iron and steel (smelting,		Fancy fur	113.4
rolling, foundry)	92.2	Laundry, cleaning, dyeing	
Wrought iron and steel tube	100.0	(private)	107.2
Wire trades	94.0		
Anchor, chain, nail, screw,		Grain and milling	91.6
rivet	119.3	Bread and biscuit	104.8
Galvanized sheet	95.4	Cocoa, confectionery, fruit	
Engineering trades	100.0	pies	98.8
Shipbuilding and marine		Bacon curing	97.3
engineering	99.0	Preserved meat	48.2
Cycle and motor trade	62.4	Butter, cheese, margarine	99.2
Cutlery trade	61.6	Fish curing	90.0
Tool and implement	96.6		
Blacksmithing	100.0	Ice trade	101.4
Lock and safe	75.6	Sugar and glucose	103.4
Small arms trade	72.1	Brewing and malting	82.2
Heating, lighting, ventilation,		Spirit distilling	103.5
sanitary	116.5	Spirit compounding	89.3
Railway, carriage and wagon	105.7	Bottling	132.3
Railways (construction, repair,		Aerated waters	89.6
maintenance)	95.6		
		Seed crushing	91.6
Copper and brass (smelting,		Oil and tallow	111.1
rolling)	76.6	Fertiliser, glue, sheep-dip,	
Finished brass	110.0	disinfectant	103.2
Lead, tin, zinc, other	128.6	Soap and candle	99.4
Plate and jewellery	78.7	Paint, colour and varnish	91.9
		Paper trade	92.8
Cotton	n.a.	Printing and bookbinding	
Woollen and worsted	102.9	(private)	84.1
Jute, hemp, linen	100.0	Printing, newspapers	107.4
Silk	109.1	Typefounding	102.0
Lace	71.4	Manufactured stationery	82.7
Hosiery	98.4	Cardboard box	84.6
Coconut fibre	152.9	Ink, gum and sealing wax	76.1

Table 8 (*Contd.*)

Fellmongery	116.9	Building and contracting	95.2
Leather (tanning and		HM Naval establishments	
dressing)	119.7	(Building)	98.6
Saddlery	105.9		
Travelling bag and fancy		Scientific instruments	108.3
leather	79.2	Musical instruments	85.7
Canvas goods	107.4	Billiard table and sports	72.2
Timber	104.9	Gas (companies)	106.6
Wooden crates, etc.	105.5	Gas (public)	95.5
Carriage, cart and wagon	89.0	Waterworks (public)	103.1
Brush	122.7	Electricity (companies)	40.0
Coopering	93.4	Electricity (public)	97.2
		Local authorities	98.6
Brick and fireclay	106.4	Tramways	102.9
China and earthenware	98.5	GPO telegraph, telephone	115.6
Asbestos and boiler		National Telephone Company	76.7
coverings	100.7		
Glass, stone, roofing felts	91.5	Unweighted Mean	96.6

Sources: R H Campbell, *The Rise and Fall of Scottish Industry, 1707–1939* (Edinburgh 1980), pp 195–6; Census of Production, 1907, *PP 1909 CII; 1912–13 CIX*

sustained Scotland's position in the pre-war industrial league table, lack of capital deepening and industrial diversification meant relegation to the second division in the inter-war years, and problems of structural adjustment even now.[64]

If the long-term production structure favoured labour intensive methods short-run adjustments to manufacturing output were in the main translated into adjustments in labour inputs. The reservoir of labour was the mechanism by which employers reduced total costs in recession, that is, by cutting variable costs. By increasing shifts, hours and piece rates in the upswing, in other words by avoiding additions to fixed costs through capital expenditure in a boom which might prove temporary and long term increments to capacity unnecessary, employers again varied labour inputs. With raw material or semi-manufactured prices exogenously determined and final prices increasingly pressurised by foreign competition, employers chose to impose the burden of adjustment to variations in their order books upon the volume of employment available to the workforce. The trade cycle was no more than an employment cycle by another name.

This is not to argue that technical development and capital expenditure were stagnant. Clearly the engineering expansion post-1870 in west central Scotland belied this, though the long-run stability of engineering in the other cities is equally striking. More, it stresses that both the nature of industrial products and the lower labour costs in Scotland conspired to reassert labour intensive production methods. Ultimately this meant that variations in business conditions would be felt more acutely in cities where an unskilled labour force was more conspicuous or where that workforce was subject to substantial variation in the demand for the product of its labours.

For many Scottish city dwellers, then, even though wage rates were below and the cost of living above national levels, the cause and course of poverty was determined by another consideration—irregular employment. Several authors have shown that technical change and the expansion of a mass consumer market revived many part-time opportunities for the self-employed.[65] The sewing machine rekindled dress-making, tailoring and the clothing trades in the last third of the nineteenth century. Jam, lemonade and confectionery consumption generated new areas of occasional employment for women; and brewing achieved the same for men. And the advent of advertising created opportunities for handbilling, bill posters, sandwich-board men, newspaper vendors and postal workers for whom a revolution in Victorian information technology spawned opportunities for casual work. All of this added to already well-established, numerically significant, irregular employment in portering, messengering, carting, street-selling and general labouring for men, and sporadic employment as chars, washer-women and paper bag, box-makers and other factory and workshop employment for women. Treble has done much to illuminate these developments in a Glasgow setting[66] and his data for Glasgow unskilled male and female workers irregularly employed are presented in Table 9 with directly comparable classifications for Edinburgh, Dundee and Aberdeen.

Amongst male workers in Scottish cities one in four (25.49 per cent) were in employment subject to interrupted time. Some were engaged in seasonal trades—dock workers with mid-winter doldrums (even more pronounced in the sailing ship era), building workers' slack time in winter, contrasting with peak employment for gas workers, and the most noted and seasonally varied branch of employment, the garment trade. Seasonality meant erratic wages for all but the artisan elite, a short cut to deprivation and poverty. In Glasgow, Treble's calculations show that between 1891 and 1911 20–23 per cent of male and 26–29 per cent of female employment was in occupations closely associated with seasonal variations.[67]

In comparison to the 26.1 per cent of female employment susceptible to seasonal employment in Glasgow in 1911, the percentages based on identical occupations in Edinburgh and in Aberdeen were 20.3 per cent and 18.6 per cent (Table 10). For Dundee seasonality in these trades was 7.8 per cent, though in fact virtually the entire textile sector in Dundee could be said to be seasonal.

Many workers were, however, subject to the same characteristic, irregular income, but from a less visible direction. Trade cycle variations generated sizeable changes in the demand for labour in a society still heavily reliant on animate energy sources—portering, navvying, messengering, carting. Elasticity of demand for such occupations, engaged on an hourly or half-daily basis, presented considerable scope for accommodating changes in output, with none of the risk borne by the entrepreneur. The adjustment was through labour costs only. With a large reservoir of unskilled labour

Table 9

Male Occupations Susceptible to Irregular Employment: Scottish Cities 1911

Census category	Occupation	% of total occupied male work force			
		G	E	D	A
2	Civil service messenger, letter carrier	0.54	0.87	0.48	0.72
42	Inn, hotel servant	0.10	0.34	0.06	0.11
363	Others in hotel, eating house service	0.36	0.66	0.34	0.20
362	Barmen	0.46	0.43	0.51	0.48
68	Railway porters, servants	0.61	0.64	0.45	0.43
76	Coachman, grooms, cabmen	0.55	1.13	0.38	0.44
74	Railway labourers (not contractors)	0.91	1.06	0.45	0.53
78	Carters, carriers, vanmen	4.35	3.24	3.65	4.23
93	Warehousemen	0.39	0.39	0.14	0.26
91	Dock, wharf labourers	1.57	0.29	1.20	2.26
95	Messengers, porters, watchmen	2.90	2.72	2.27	3.78
115, 123, 130	Coalheavers, coal porters, labourers	0.30	0.31	0.03	0.01
147	Labourers in engineering	1.10	0.19	0.18	0.22
181	Ship painters, shipyard labourers	0.94	0.03	1.18	1.18
203	Builders' labourers	0.14	0.29	0.11	0.06
205	Carpenters'/joiners' labourers	0.04	0.04	0.03	0.03
207	Bricklayers' labourers	0.25	0.12	0.06	0.01
209	Masons' labourers	0.44	0.70	0.68	0.35
212	Plasterers' labourers	0.10	0.37	0.10	0.11
218	Navvies, railway contractors' labourers	0.10	0.04	0.04	0.08
221	Paviours, road labourers	0.27	0.32	0.25	0.36
213	Painters, plumbers, decorators	1.52	2.28	1.20	1.35
317	Tailors	1.63	2.06	1.14	1.53
325	Boot and shoe factory hands	1.01	0.99	0.86	1.01
364	Gas works	1.01	0.63	0.53	0.62
368	Scavengers	0.24	0.30	0.22	0.30
390	Coster mongers, hawkers, street sellers	0.35	0.40	0.33	0.45
371	Bill posting	0.11	0.02	0.04	0.03
392	Newsboys	0.10	0.05	0.01	0.04
346	Sweetmakers, jams & preserves	0.18	0.10	0.28	0.11
334	Milksellers, dairymen	0.34	0.46	0.34	0.22
350	Aerated water, ginger beer	0.11	0.12	0.12	0.09
175	Iron goods workers (undefined)	0.41	0.04	0.05	0.05
237	Other wood workers	0.14	0.05	0.08	0.18
306	Factory hands (textiles undefined)	0.62	0.02	0.06	0.05
396	Factory labour (undefined)	0.09	0.04	0.13	0.04
393	General labourers	2.88	2.50	2.06	2.52
		27.16	24.24	20.04	24.44

Sources: *PP 1912–13 CXIX*; J H Treble, 'The Market for Unskilled Male Labour in Glasgow 1891–1914' in I MacDougall (ed), *Essays in Scottish Labour History* (Edinburgh 1979), Appendix, col. 6. [Note Treble uses the figure for female not male 'Undefined Factory Hands (textile)'. This has been amended.]

G = Glasgow; E = Edinburgh; D = Dundee; A = Aberdeen

Table 10

Female Occupations Susceptible to Irregular Employment: Scottish Cities 1911

Census category	Occupation	% of total occupied female work force			
		G	E	D	A
52	Charwomen	3.17	3.29	1.03	2.57
53, 54	Laundry, wash house and baths	1.58	3.17	1.04	2.17
317	Tailoresses	4.36	2.41	0.87	1.47
321	Shirtmakers, seamstresses	4.66	0.65	0.32	0.96
315	Milliners	1.15	1.45	0.74	1.65
319	Dressmakers	5.75	7.27	2.47	7.41
320	Stay and corset makers	0.18	0.03	—	0.03
325, 327	Shoe, boot, patten and clogmakers	0.46	0.30	0.09	0.12
330	Umbrella, parasol, stick makers	0.27	0.04	—	0.01
241	Earthenware, china, pottery, porcelain	0.48	0.10	—	—
269	Brush, broom, hairbrush	0.25	0.01	—	0.01
275	Paper bag, box making	1.17	0.74	0.10	1.36
350	Ginger beer, mineral water	0.17	0.10	—	0.13
346	Jam, preserve and sweetmaking	1.65	0.22	0.97	0.28
390	Hawker, pedlar, streetseller	0.76	0.49	0.17	0.38
		26.06	20.27	7.80	18.55

Sources: *PP 1912–13 CXIX*; J H Treble, 'The Seasonal Demand for Adult Labour in Glasgow, 1890–1914', *Social History* 3 1978, p 60, Appendix 1, col. 6

supplemented by what Samuel called 'comers and goers',[68] vagrants and migrants, output variations were achieved by laying off, or in the upswing, engaging labour. Stockpiling, cocooning plant, scrapping and updating policies, whatever the technical disposition of management, could not be easier than hiring and firing unskilled labour. Such elasticity in both demand and supply schedules for labour meant frequently interrupted incomes, albeit often for short periods only. Not surprisingly, therefore, in Glasgow 27 per cent, in Edinburgh and Aberdeen 24 per cent, and in Dundee, 20 per cent of male workers were prone to such influences (Table 9).

There were opportunities for dovetailing seasonal work; family income sources might be phased complementarily, cyclical downswing in one sector could be offset by buoyancy in another, and so on, and for some this counteracted the effect of interrupted income. With diligent household economy, income could be spread through spells of short time and short run unemployment, and lay-offs did offer a respite to arduous toil for unskilled workers. And only some of the 27 per cent in Glasgow, 24 per cent in Edinburgh and Aberdeen, 20 per cent in Dundee were affected by interrupted work at any one time, though all might well experience it at some stage of an employment year. Although the percentage of city workers potentially exposed to irregular work did not vary very greatly between the four cities, the actual experience of interrupted time could and did differ appreciably, and in this respect the industrial balance and the scale of professional work substantially determined the extent, frequency and duration of irregular work. The more stable the employment and expenditure base of the city, the less the actual experience of interrupted time of those exposed to the possibility.

This susceptibility was indeed the crucial influence on living standards. It was the average weekly income taken over the duration of an employment year which dictated consumption patterns.[69] Wage rates, and earnings when in employment were lesser considerations than the average affordable levels of expenditure throughout the year. In this respect Scottish rental leases were particularly decisive.[70] Commonly the long-let, a one year rental from Whitsunday was contracted up to four months before the commencement of the lease.[71] In the context of variable employment prospects the standard of accommodation affordable over the duration of one year's lease had to take account of interrupted earnings. English short lets allowed a tenant *in extremis* to move to cheaper accommodation. In Scotland, a very large segment of the working population, 25.5 per cent in the cities, was prone to interrupted income yet committed for up to 16 months to a rental component of their weekly expenditure from which it was difficult to escape, and even then only with financial penalties. Not surprisingly the letting and ejectment system produced unusually hostile landlord–tenant relations before World War I and rent strikes during it.[72] In this uncertain climate of household accounting many tenants understandably chose a level of accommodation at such minimal levels that they felt reasonably confident that whatever the nature of seasonal and casual employment in the ensuing twelve month period they should be able to maintain rental payments. It was a delicate balancing act. For 20,000 Glaswegians per annum evicted for non-payment of rent it was clearly beyond them.[73] Many achieved some equilibrium in the phasing of domestic income and expenditure, though, as seen from Table 11 to do so meant settling for a standard of accommodation—typically a one- or two-roomed tenement flat with minimal and shared amenities—at a level prejudicial to health and life expectancy, and thus, in the vicious circle of poverty, to employment prospects and regularity of income.

In Edinburgh and Aberdeen one-third, and in Glasgow and Dundee, one-half of the population lived in a one- or two-roomed house, and at an overcrowded density of more than two per room.[74] Even then such accommodation was palatial for many tenants. So problematical was the management of household income and expenditure that the customary yearly letting system which accounted for 80 per cent of working-class housing and for approximately 60–90 per cent of all houses rented at between £5 to £10 per annum, gave encouragement to short letting to take account of irregular employment and variable income.[75] '(L)andlords were forced to introduce greater flexibility in the long let property, but as a consolation secured a speedier process of summary eviction which could be used against the

Table 11

Poverty in Scottish Cities, 1911: Housing, Overcrowding and Mortality

	Mean death rate per 1000 1896–1905	% of total houses having					% of population in houses having					% of population living more than		
		1 room	2 rooms	3 rooms	4 rooms	5 rooms	1 room	2 rooms	3 rooms	4 rooms	5 rooms	2 per room*	3 per room†	4 per room
G	20.4	20.0	46.3	18.9	6.6	8.2	13.8	48.7	21.2	7.2	9.1	55.7	27.9	10.7
E	18.2	9.5	31.4	21.9	14.4	22.8	5.8	30.9	22.8	15.1	25.4	32.6	12.7	4.1
D	20.0	16.9	53.0	17.3	5.2	7.6	9.9	53.2	21.5	6.4	9.0	48.2	20.0	6.1
A	17.8	9.8	36.8	27.9	11.3	14.2	4.8	33.8	32.0	13.0	16.4	37.8	12.3	2.2

* overcrowded housing: English standard
† overcrowded housing: Scottish standard
G = Glasgow; E = Edinburgh; D = Dundee; A = Aberdeen

Sources: Scottish Land Enquiry Committee, Report, *Scottish Land* (London 1914), pp 350–1, *PP 1912–13 CXIX*; Board of Trade, *Report of Enquiry into Working Class Rents, Housing, and Retail Prices, etc.*, Cd 3864, 1908, pp 511, 516, 521, 535

monthly tenants.'[76] Eviction from these short lease properties was common. In fact there was 'one application for ejectment for every 1.2 short let houses' in Glasgow in 1905–6,[77] and the number of eviction proceedings rose dramatically from a low point of 2,780 in 1875 to 6,376 in 1880, 8,760 in 1885, 10,350 in 1889 and 20,887 in 1908,[78] though 'the respectable yearly tenant of a house above £10 annual rental was not often taken to court'.[79] Such overcrowded living conditions and landlord-tenant tensions suggest that Daunton's image of improving home life was far from general, especially in the Scottish cities.

The distinction between the unskilled and others in housing was evident elsewhere. Mortality and morbidity reflected similar patterns.[80] For example the mean death rate of the Old Town, was 52.8 per cent above that of the southern suburbs of Edinburgh between 1875 and 1900.[81] But

Table 12

Height and Weight of Schoolchildren, by House Size, Glasgow 1904

	Boys		Girls	
	Height (in)	Weight (lb)	Height (in)	Weight (lb)
1-roomed houses	46.6	52.6	46.3	51.5
2-roomed houses	48.1	56.1	47.8	54.8
3-roomed houses	50.0	60.6	49.6	59.4
4-roomed houses	51.3	64.3	51.6	65.5

Number of children 72,857)

Source: Scotch Education Department, *Report as to the Physical Condition of Children Attending the Public Schools of the School Board for Glasgow,* (HMSO, 1907) Table VIIIa,b.

Table 13

Physical Differences in Edinburgh Children 1904: A Comparison of Broughton and North Canongate Schools according to Fathers' Occupation

Occupation	N (children)	Mean difference (inches)	S.D.	Coefficient of variation
Printers	43	1.88	2.29	1.22
Bookbinders	15	1.96	2.20	1.12
Masons	27	2.15	2.72	1.27
Joiners	22	2.33	1.73	0.74
Painters	64	2.40	2.60	1.08
Engineers	17	0.93	3.12	3.35
Metal trades	25	2.06	2.44	1.18
Shoemakers	32	1.76	2.48	1.41
Misc. skilled	30	1.74	2.19	1.26
Semi- and unskilled	40	3.29	2.80	0.85

Source: R Q Gray, *The Labour Aristocracy in Victorian Edinburgh* (Oxford 1976), p 85, Table 4.10

perhaps the most striking instance of class difference was in the anthropometric data collected by the Dundee Social Union, the Edinburgh Charity Organisation Society and, in the largest survey of its kind ever undertaken, by the School Board of Glasgow.[82] An emphatic empirical link was forged between income and health, or as the official report put it, 'The numbers examined are so large, and the results are so uniform that only one conclusion is possible, viz.:— that the poorest child suffers most in nutrition and in growth.'[83]

In Table 12 and Figure 1 this connection is presented according to room

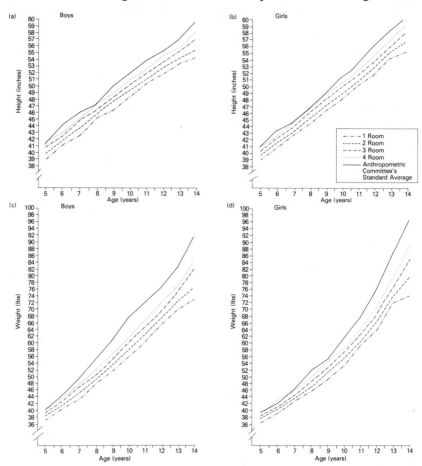

Figure 1   Glasgow Children compared to the National Average, 1904; height and weight according to house size

Source: Scotch Education Department, *Report as to the Physical Condition of Children Attending the Public Schools Board for Glasgow* (HMSO, 1907) table VIIIA–B

size, a reflection of employment and affordable income, and in Table 13 it is presented according to skill and residential location. Broughton School in Edinburgh was 'attended by children of small shopkeepers, of skilled artisans, and of clerks'.[84] The mean heights of these children of the lower middle and prosperous upper working classes, compared to children of equivalent occupations in the North Canongate School, 'the old, central working class area . . . serving the poorest parts of the city . . . (where) the skilled trades are underrepresented compared to the industrial population of the city generally at the 1901 census',[85] showed that the children were between one and three inches taller than the children of north Canongate. Despite genetic and migratory influences, Gray concluded, 'The children of the semi- and unskilled sample have the largest mean difference from all Broughton School' and that 'engineers and the semi-and unskilled workers are thus both sharply distinguished from a central group comprising most of the skilled workers.'[86]

VI

The structure of employment and wages in Scottish cities diverged appreciably in the Victorian period. Though superficial similarities between Edinburgh and Aberdeen, as one pairing, and Glasgow and Dundee are apparent at the aggregate level of analysis, closer scrutiny reveals significant structural differences in employment within each pairing. As a low wage economy with pockets of intensely irregular income, effective demand levels were subdued for the Scottish people as a whole and for the working class in particular, as the adverse cost of living and wage rate data demonstrate. More significantly for the long term, low wages encouraged continued labour intensive production methods in late Victorian Scottish cities which, with lower productivity than the UK, constrained the growth and diversification of the Scottish economy. This narrow employment base was particularly important in Dundee and Glasgow and the prevailing Victorian ethos of self-help in relation to poverty meant solutions were cosmetic. The Scottish Poor Law provided a basic minimum; philanthropic endeavours produced a multi-faceted social support system. Without a Booth or Rowntree for Glasgow, without empirical work on the west of Scotland labour market, English surveys of poverty could be pigeon-holed as inappropriate by a newly created, though largely impotent, Scottish Office whose officials, drawn from the middle-class milieu of the Edinburgh bourgeoisie, could point to intemperance and improvidence as long-standing character deficiencies. In the context of the capital's counter-cyclical employment experience, insulated through its tertiary sector from the late Victorian squeeze on credit and profits visible in west central Scotland, any analysis of housing or wider social problems which identified inadequate incomes of the working class was heretical . An embryonic Scottish Office was therefore unlikely to recommend a fundamental shift of policy to its Whitehall superiors.[87] No wonder then, that the Edinburgh–Glasgow axis was, and remains, one of suspicion and antagonism.

Appendix I

The Structure of Industrial Employment in the Scottish Cities

Percentage of workforce in	*Glasgow*	*Edinburgh*	*Dundee*	*Aberdeen*
(a) *1841*				
Printing and Publishing	1.12	3.88	0.56	0.91
Engineering, Toolmaking and				
Metalworking	7.17	6.07	5.59	6.32
Shipbuilding	0.35	0.17	1.14	1.24
Coachbuilding	0.40	0.92	0.21	0.34
Building	5.84	5.73	6.05	5.99
Furniture and Woodworking	1.06	2.73	0.77	0.87
Chemicals	1.22	0.24	0.19	0.37
Food, Drink and Tobacco	5.24	8.31	5.27	4.66
Textiles and Clothing	37.56	13.04	50.54	34.68
Other manufacturing[a]	2.90	3.02	1.29	3.18
General labouring	8.40	3.69	3.84	6.87
(b) *1851*[b]				
Printing and Publishing	1.38		0.55	1.03
Engineering, Toolmaking and				
Metalworking	8.67		4.38	5.04
Shipbuilding	0.14		0.91	1.14
Coachbuilding	0.13		0.15	0.19
Building	5.64		4.04	5.06
Furniture and Woodworking	1.41		0.90	0.95
Chemicals	1.00		0.21	0.22
Food, Drink and Tobacco	6.41		4.62	6.89
Textiles and Clothing	27.60		53.82	21.19
Other manufacturing[a]	3.36		0.97	4.69
General labouring	2.90		3.60	4.32
(c) *1871*				
Printing and Publishing	1.90	4.89	0.58	1.42
Engineering, Toolmaking and				
Metalworking	14.08	6.85	5.63	4.23
Shipbuilding	1.33	0.05	1.08	1.37
Coachbuilding	0.48	0.80	0.20	0.56
Building	7.42	9.64	5.64	7.81
Furniture and Woodworking	1.17	2.37	0.63	1.03
Chemicals	1.17	0.27	0.16	1.70
Food, Drink and Tobacco	5.63	7.36	4.38	7.07
Textiles and Clothing	31.97	14.64	61.81	23.65
Other manufacturing[a]	3.32	4.06	1.54	7.23
General manufacturing	4.41	2.32	3.15	4.13
(d) *1881*				
Printing and Publishing	2.21	5.16	0.73	1.62
Engineering, Toolmaking and				
Metalworking	12.81	5.86	6.11	5.76
Shipbuilding	0.68	0.06	1.24	1.01
Coachbuilding	0.46	0.64	0.23	0.57
Building	6.30	9.28	4.38	7.90

Furniture and Woodworking	1.79	2.38	0.78	1.29
Chemicals	0.64	0.46	0.12	0.52
Food, Drink and Tobacco	7.65	8.54	5.53	8.61
Textiles and Clothing	25.42	11.17	54.42	17.38
Other manufacturing[a]	3.21	4.34	1.22	6.16
General labouring	3.92	1.90	3.24	4.91
(e) *1891*				
Printing and Publishing	2.58	5.02	0.71	1.89
Engineering, Toolmaking and				
Metalworking	14.17	5.88	6.10	6.02
Shipbuilding	0.72	0.10	2.24	1.30
Coachbuilding	0.62	0.66	0.35	0.72
Building	5.47	6.92	3.48	6.74
Furniture and Woodworking	1.77	1.69	0.84	1.19
Chemicals	0.60	0.62	0.23	0.52
Food, Drink and Tobacco	7.85	9.34	6.27	7.65
Textiles and Clothing	20.75	11.49	52.28	17.43
Other manufacturing[a]	3.37	4.25	1.82	5.81
General labouring	4.31	2.63	2.27	4.75
(f) *1901*				
Printing and Publishing	2.37	5.14	1.02	2.04
Engineering, Toolmaking and				
Metalworking	14.84	6.51	6.54	6.50
Shipbuilding	0.84	0.09	1.64	1.19
Coachbuilding	0.63	0.46	0.20	0.76
Building	6.71	8.98	5.56	7.80
Furniture and Woodworking	2.03	1.74	0.94	1.52
Chemicals[c]	0.79	1.50	0.17	1.81
Food, Drink and Tobacco	9.75	10.40	6.93	11.00
Textiles and Clothing	17.16	10.00	51.73	15.56
Other manufacturing[a]	3.45	3.73	0.85	3.13
General labouring	3.72	1.67	1.65	3.30
(g) *1911*				
Printing and Publishing	2.82	6.69	1.56	2.51
Engineering, Toolmaking and				
Metalworking	16.86	6.16	5.62	5.78
Shipbuilding	1.80	0.08	1.89	2.54
Coachbuilding	0.72	0.56	0.25	0.78
Building	4.83	6.24	3.46	4.72
Furniture and Woodworking	3.18	2.22	1.86	2.92
Chemicals[c]	1.89	3.22	0.62	1.65
Food, Drink and Tobacco	12.41	11.57	7.59	10.13
Textiles and Clothing	16.86	11.00	53.52	16.16
Other manufacturing[a]	3.34	3.10	0.91	3.12
General labouring	2.23	1.69	1.32	1.81

Notes: (a) glass, pottery, earthenware, paper, gum, grease, cane
      (b) Edinburgh and Leith are only available as a combined urban population, and for the sake of comparability with other censuses, have been omitted
      (c) includes rubber

Sources: See note 17

Appendix II

Employment in Scottish Cities, 1911: Location Quotients*

Census Category	Occupation	Location Quotients: Males				Location Quotients: Females			
		G	E	D	A	G	E	D	A
1	Civil Service	0.97	2.61	0.80	1.26	0.82	0.96	0.26	0.58
2	Local Government Service	1.64	1.21	1.22	1.28	0.90	0.78	0.45	1.18
3	Naval and Military Services	0.45	1.49	0.65	0.53	—	—	—	—
4	Clerical Profession and Service	0.72	1.46	0.78	0.80	0.61	1.44	0.72	1.83
5	Legal Profession and Service	0.79	3.84	0.65	1.65	0.85	2.41	0.44	1.61
6	Medical Profession and Service	1.11	2.56	0.94	1.31	1.17	1.66	0.30	1.25
7	Teaching Profession and Service (not under Local Authority)	1.06	3.69	2.13	2.94	0.83	1.45	0.62	1.30
8	Other Professions and their Services	1.43	2.24	1.11	1.49	1.43	1.61	0.88	1.45
9	Domestic and Institution Service	0.33	1.12	0.40	0.49	0.73	1.40	0.32	0.88
10	Hotel, Eating house Service	1.57	1.85	1.25	1.05	1.29	1.54	0.47	1.07
11	Commerce	2.04	2.10	1.03	1.40	1.69	1.23	0.53	1.42
12	Banking and Insurance	1.07	2.25	0.96	1.56	1.58	2.00	0.50	1.17
13	Railway Service	1.30	1.33	0.77	0.79	1.55	1.09	0.18	0.73
14	Road Transport Service	1.51	1.84	0.99	1.15	1.33	1.50	0.33	0.83
15	Railway, Road, Canal, Harbour Construction	0.76	0.59	0.45	0.55	—	—	—	—
16	Coach, Motor Cycle Building	1.30	1.08	0.56	1.47	1.29	1.29	0.29	1.29
17	Shipping and Docks	1.52	0.38	1.26	2.06	2.00	0.75	0.38	1.25
18	Shipbuilding	0.61	0.28	0.79	0.89	0.50	0.00	0.00	0.60
19	Agriculture	0.03	0.13	0.09	0.16	0.20	0.70	0.01	0.30
20	Fishing	0.04	0.15	0.06	4.00	0.00	0.00	0.00	5.27
21	Coal Industry	0.20	0.21	0.13	0.15	0.20	0.31	0.08	0.14
22	Shale Industry	—	—	—	—	—	—	—	—
23	Other Mining Industries	0.13	0.13	0.00	0.00	—	—	—	—
24	Quarrying	0.24	0.23	0.42	6.00	1.50	0.00	0.50	8.50
25	Iron Manufacture	1.76	0.43	0.70	0.56	1.67	0.38	0.22	0.33
26	Metal Manufacture other than iron	2.21	1.83	1.21	0.90	1.86	1.36	0.68	1.23
27	Precious Metals, Jewels, Musical and Scientific Instruments Manufacture and Sale	1.58	3.59	0.76	1.31	2.03	1.83	0.14	1.90
28	House, &c., Building and Decorating	1.13	1.61	1.02	1.16	1.68	2.05	0.45	1.27
29	Wood and Furniture Industries	1.74	1.41	1.44	1.83	2.31	1.01	3.53	1.08

30	Brick, Cement, Pottery, Glass Industries	1.42	1.46	0.18	0.32	1.91	0.59	0.16	0.22
31	Chemical and Rubber Industries	1.60	2.35	0.70	1.65	1.12	3.02	0.17	0.44
32	Leather and Leather Goods Manufacture	1.85	1.83	0.98	0.76	2.00	1.88	1.31	0.50
33	Paper and Stationery Manufacture	1.05	1.42	0.49	1.51	1.58	1.24	0.27	2.67
34	Printing, Publishing and Allied Industries	1.73	4.92	1.53	1.61	1.95	3.38	0.47	1.58
35	Cotton Industry	2.39	0.06	0.06	0.09	2.62	0.19	0.19	0.21
36	Wool Industry	0.18	0.25	0.02	1.69	0.17	0.08	0.01	1.33
37	Silk Industry	0.67	0.67	0.00	0.00	0.64	0.21	0.00	0.00
38	Linen Industry	0.06	0.06	1.77	1.69	0.03	0.01	0.70	1.89
39	Hemp, Jute, Rope, Mat Industries	0.12	0.07	22.84	0.57	0.05	0.00	11.91	0.50
40	Thread, Hosiery, and Other Textile Industries	1.16	0.27	0.67	0.30	0.89	0.21	0.12	0.33
41	Bleaching, Dyeing, and Allied Industries	0.72	0.11	2.07	0.18	0.65	0.35	0.41	0.20
42	Dealing in Drapery and Textiles	1.91	1.30	1.01	1.48	1.50	1.26	0.80	1.37
43	Hat Making and Selling	2.33	2.50	1.00	1.33	1.31	1.30	0.62	1.35
44	Tailoring, Dressmaking	1.37	1.83	0.94	1.32	1.31	1.23	0.40	1.08
45	Bootmaking	1.20	1.10	1.01	1.21	1.36	0.94	0.42	0.83
46	Other Dress Industries	1.81	1.44	1.26	1.30	2.96	0.39	0.22	1.14
47	Preparation and Sale of Provisions	1.30	1.46	1.24	1.48	1.51	1.06	0.71	1.17
48	Tobacco Manufacture and Sale	2.60	2.00	1.20	1.40	2.53	1.60	0.66	0.49
49	Brewing, Distilling	1.25	3.94	0.71	0.50	2.14	0.59	0.77	0.36
50	Gas, Water, Electricity Supply (not under Local Authority)	0.45	0.25	0.09	0.18	—	—	—	—
51	Drainage and Sanitary Service (not under Local Authority)	0.20	0.20	0.00	0.00	—	—	—	—
52	General Shopkeeping and Dealing	1.25	1.12	1.17	1.29	1.09	0.96	0.52	1.03
53	Other and Undefined Industries	1.26	1.21	0.96	1.44	1.73	1.18	0.49	1.66

G = Glasgow; E = Edinburgh; D = Dundee; A = Aberdeen

* For method of calculation see G S Jones, *Outcast London*, Appendix 2, Table 5

Source: PP 1913 LXXX

ACKNOWLEDGEMENTS

The author wishes to thank R Siddiqi and the Stack Service Librarians, University of Leicester.

REFERENCES

1   For accounts of the industrial revolution in Scotland see for example R H Campbell *Scotland Since 1707* (Oxford 1965), and *The Rise and Fall of Scottish Industry 1707–1939* (Edinburgh 1980); A Slaven *The Development of the West of Scotland 1750–1960* (London 1975); S G E Lythe and J Butt *An Economic History of Scotland, 1100–1939* (Glasgow 1975); B Lenman *An Economic History of Modern Scotland 1660–1976* (London 1977); C H Lee 'Modern Economic Growth and Structural Change in Scotland: the Service Sector Reconsidered' *Scottish Economic and Social History* 3 1983, pp 115–35 provides a critique of these and other approaches to Scottish economic growth.

2   A Paterson 'The Poor Law in Nineteenth Century Scotland' in D Fraser (ed) *The New Poor Law in the Nineteenth Century* (London 1976), pp 171–93; O Checkland *Philanthropy in Scotland: Social Welfare and the Voluntary Principle* (Edinburgh 1980), pp 30–64, 90–191; A S Wohl *The Eternal Slum: Housing and Social Policy in Victorian London* (London 1977); W Logan, *The Moral Statistics of Glasgow* (Glasgow 1844)

3   J H Treble *Urban Poverty in Britain 1830–1914* (London, 1979), p 52, and 'Unemployment and Unemployment Policies in Glasgow 1890–1905', in P Thane (ed) *The Origins of British Social Policy* (London 1978), pp 147–72; I Levitt, 'The Scottish Poor Law and Unemployment, 1890–1929' in T C Smout, (ed), *The Search for Wealth and Stability: Essays in Economic and Social History presented to M W Flinn* (London 1979), pp 263–8

4   I Levitt *op. cit.* pp 266–7

5   J R Hay *The Origins of the Liberal Welfare Reforms, 1906–14* (London 1975) and references cited

6   M E Rose *The Relief of Poverty 1834–1914* (London 1972), pp 15–16

7   A Sherwell *Life in West London* (London 1897), p 146

8   G Drage *The Unemployed* (London 1894), pp 130–1

9   O Checkland *op. cit.* p 338

10 Presbytery of Glasgow *Report of Commission on the Housing of the Poor in Relation to their Social Condition* (Glasgow 1891), p 10, and Evidence of J Morrison p 54

11 *Ibid.* p 22

12 *Ibid.* See also S Mechie *The Church and Scottish Social Development 1780–1870* (London 1960)

13 Presbytery of Glasgow Report *op. cit.*

14 *Ibid.* Evidence of Glasier, pp 178–9

15 *Ibid.* p 179

16 For an interesting view of housing provision on this aspect see J Melling, 'Employers Industrial Housing and the Evolution of Company Welfare Policies in Britain's Heavy Industry: West Scotland 1870–1920', *International Review of Social History* 26 1981, pp 255–301

17 The occupational classifications used throughout this chapter are essentially those of W A Armstrong 'The Use of Information about Occupation' in E A

Wrigley (ed), *Nineteenth Century Society: Essays in the Use of Quantitative Methods for the Study of Social Data* (Cambridge 1972), pp 191–310. Adaptations in a Scottish context are explained in R Q Gray *The Labour Aristocracy in Victorian Edinburgh* (Oxford 1976), Appendix II. In the interests of brevity a full explanation of Scottish occupational classification in the Scottish cities is not given here but is available from the author. Though relegated to a footnote, two methodological points should be made. Firstly, classification of the 1841 Census is acknowledged to be weak. Secondly, the classification of female employment, particularly in relation to textile and domestic work, is problematical. Orders of magnitude and trends are more appropriate in this census than precise percentage measures of occupational activity. Occupational data have been extracted from the following censuses of Great Britain, and Scotland: *PP 1844 XXVII; PP 1852–53 LXXXVIII Pt. II; PP 1862 L; PP 1873 LXXII; PP 1883 LXXXI; PP 1893–94 CVIII; PP 1904 CVIII; PP 1912–13 CXIX; PP 1913 LXXX*

18 M Gray 'Organisation and Growth in the East Coast Herring Fishing 1800–1885' in P L Payne (ed) *Studies in Scottish Business History* (London 1967), pp 206–13, and *The Fishing Industries of Scotland 1790–1914: a Study on Regional Adaptation* (Aberdeen 1978), pp 166–80

19 P Branca *Women in Europe since 1750* (London 1978), pp 51–65 explains the concept. *See also* D Garrison 'The Tender Technicians: the Feminization of Public Librarianship, 1876–1905', *Journal of Social History* 6 1972, pp 131–59

20 *PP 1893–94, XXI* Table LVI

21 C Booth 'Occupations of the People of the UK, 1801–1881', *Journal of the Royal Statistical Society* 49 1886, p 414. Booth quotes the total professional occupied population as 5.6 per cent, rather than 5.79 per cent obtained using census data, *PP 1883 LXXX*

22 *PP 1893–94, XXI* Table LVI reveals the different involvement of the city population in education in 1891. In Aberdeen 22.62 per cent of males, 17.85 per cent females were in education; in Dundee 19.94 per cent males, 16.03 per cent females; in Edinburgh 21.01 per cent males, 16.42 per cent females; in Glasgow 16.83 per cent of males, and 15.98 per cent of females were in education.

23 C Booth *op. cit.*; *PP 1844 XXVII; PP 1883 LXXXI; PP 1912–13 CXIX*

24 H D Littlejohn *Report on the Sanitary Condition of the City of Edinburgh, with Relative Appendices, etc.* (Edinburgh 1865), p 45

25 C H Lee *op. cit.* p 22; J. Heiton *The Castes of Edinburgh* (2nd edn Edinburgh 1860), p 37. *See also* T C Smout *A History of the Scottish People 1560–1830* (London 1969), pp 366–79; G Gordon 'The Status Areas of Edinburgh in 1914' in G Gordon and B Dicks (eds) *Scottish Urban History* (Aberdeen 1983) pp 168–96; R Q Gray *op. cit.* p 20

26 T McBride *The Domestic Revolution* (London 1976) argues that the apogee of domestic service was in 1891. Scottish data would confirm the rather earlier high water mark of 1871 suggested by F K Prochaska 'Female Philanthropy and Domestic Service in Victorian England', *Bulletin of the Institute of Historical Research* 54 1981, pp. 79–85, and M Ebery and B Preston, *Domestic Service in Late Victorian and Edwardian England 1871–1914* (Reading 1976). *See* E Higgs 'Domestic Servants and Households in Victorian England', *Social History* 8 1983, pp 201–10 for a wider discussion of these issues and the basis of census classification of domestic servants.

27 B Lenman, C Lythe and E Gauldie *Dundee and its Textile Industry 1851–1914* (Dundee 1969), p 23

28 *Ibid.*
29 B E A Collins 'Aspects of Irish Immigration into Two Scottish Towns (Dundee
    and Paisley) during the Mid-Nineteenth Century'. Unpublished M Phil thesis
    Edinburgh University 1978, p 184
30 A J Robertson 'The Decline of the Scottish Cotton Industry, 1860–1914',
    Business History 12 1970, pp 116–28; B Lenman *et al. op. cit.* pp 23–42
31 W H Fraser *The Coming of the Mass Market 1850–1914* (London 1981)
32 R G Rodger 'Scottish Urban Housebuilding, 1870–1914'. Unpublished PhD
    thesis, Edinburgh University 1975, table 3.4, fig. 3.1
33 *Ibid.* and table 5. The percentage employment in Edinburgh building trades in
    1841 was in fact below that of 1911
34 A Slaven *op. cit.*; R H Campbell *op. cit.*; T J Byres 'Entrepreneurship in the
    Scottish Heavy Industries, 1870–1900' in P L Payne (ed) *op. cit.* pp 250–96
35 H L Kerr 'Edinburgh' in H Bosanquet (ed), *Social Conditions in Provincial
    Towns* (London 1912), p 55
36 *Ibid.* pp 54–5
37 R Q Gray *op. cit.* p 24; I Levitt and T C Smout *The State of the Scottish
    Working Class in 1843* (Edinburgh 1979), p 9 note the Edinburgh–Glasgow
    income and wealth differential at the start of the Victorian period.
38 D Bremner *The Industries of Scotland* (Edinburgh 1869), p 131
39 R Q Gray *op. cit.* pp 26–7, 28–42, and 'Thrift and Working Class Mobility in
    Victorian Edinburgh' in A A MacLaren (ed), *Social Class in Scotland: Past and
    Present* (Edinburgh, 1976), pp 128–42 and 'Styles of Life, the "Labour
    Aristocracy" and Class Relations in Later Nineteenth Century Edinburgh',
    International Review of Social History 18 1973, pp 428–52
40 H L Kerr *op. cit.* pp 56–8; S Blackden 'The Poor Law and Health: A Survey of
    Parochial Medical Aid in Glasgow, 1845–1900' in T C Smout (ed) *op. cit.* p 262
    notes that until the 1870s Edinburgh enjoyed three times as much medical treat-
    ment per 1000 population as Glasgow.
41 R C Michie 'Trade and Transport in the Economic Development of North East
    Scotland in the Nineteenth Century', *Scottish Economic and Social History* 3
    1983, pp 66–94; M Gray *The Fishing Industries, op. cit.* pp 78, 179; A A
    MacLaren 'Class Formation and Class Fractions: the Aberdeen Bourgeoisie,
    1830–1850' in G Gordon and B Dicks (eds) *op. cit.* pp 112–29, and, *Religion
    and Social Class: the Disruption Years in Aberdeen* (London 1974), pp 1–25
42 R S Sayers 'The Springs of Technical Progress in Britain 1914–39', *Economic
    Journal* 60 1950, pp 275–91
43 W Diack *Rise and Progress of the Granite Industry in Aberdeen* (Aberdeen
    1950), p 77; T Donnelly 'The Development of the Aberdeen Granite Industry
    1750–1939. Unpublished PhD thesis, Aberdeen University 1975
44 M J Daunton 'The Building Cycle and the Urban Fringe in Victorian Cities: a
    comment' and J W R Whitehand 'The Building Cycle and the Urban Fringe in
    Victorian Cities: a reply', both in *Journal of Historical Geography* 4 1978, pp
    175–91; and R G Rodger 'The Building Cycle and the Urban Fringe in
    Victorian Cities: another comment', *Journal of Historical Geography* 5 1979,
    pp 72–8
45 B Lenman *et al. op. cit.* p 37
46 *Ibid.* pp 23–40; D R Wallace *The Romance of Jute: a Short History of the
    Calcutta Jute Mill Industry, 1855–1927* (London 1927)
47 S G E Lythe *Gourlays of Dundee: the Rise and Fall of a Scottish Shipbuilding
    Firm* (Dundee 1964) and 'The Dundee Whale Fishery', *Scottish Journal of
    Political Economy* 11, 1964, pp 158–69; R C Michie 'North-East Scotland and

the Northern Whale Fishing, 1752–1893', *Northern Scotland* 3 1979, pp 62–85; B Lenman *et al. op. cit.* 38

48   J C Gilbert *A History of Investment Trusts in Dundee 1873–1938* (London 1939) and W G Kerr, *Scottish Capital on the American Credit Frontier* (Austin Texas 1976), pp 169–89 show that the Dundee middle class were present in certain areas.

49   B Lenman *et al. op. cit.* p 70; Corporation of the City of Glasgow, *Glasgow Municipal Commission on the Housing of the Poor, Minutes of Evidence,* Irwin, p 523

50   Dundee Social Union *Report on Housing and Industrial Conditions and Medical Inspection of School Children* (Dundee 1905)

51   J H Treble *Urban Poverty op. cit.* p 149 states that 'weaving households in Dundee were devoting eighty per cent of their meagre incomes during 1834 to acquire the limited range of foodstuffs which comprised their inadequate diet'.

52   J A Schmiechen *Sweated Industries and Sweated Labor: the London Clothing Trades, 1860–1914* (London 1984) investigates the general problems associated with employment in sweated industries.

53   J Lennox 'Working Class Life in Dundee 1895–1903'. Unpublished PhD thesis Dundee University, quoted in B Lenman *et al. op. cit.* p 66

54   B R Mitchell and P Deane *Abstract of British Historical Statistics* (Cambridge 1972) gives data on cost of living in Britain generally

55   *See* Table 7

56   B Lenman *et al. op. cit.* pp 77–99. Dundee Dean of Guild Court responsibilities for environmental and building control were confined in the mid-nineteenth century to the central city areas. The expansion of tenement building to house the population influx associated with textile expansion was thus unsupervised and considerable structural and sanitary problems ensued. This administrative control in Dundee was far weaker than in the other cities

57   R G Rodger 'The "Invisible Hand": Market Forces, Housing and the Urban Form in Victorian Cities' in D Fraser and A Sutcliffe (eds) *The Pursuit of Urban History* (London 1983), pp 194–7; A L Bowley 'The Statistics of Wages in the United Kingdom in the Last Hundred Years', *Journal of the Royal Statistical Society* 62 1899, pp 708–15; 63 1900, pp 297–315; 64 1901, pp 102–12; 68 1905, pp 563–614; E H Hunt *Regional Wage Variations in Britain 1850–1914* (Oxford 1973); *PP 1887, LXXXIX,* Returns of Wages Published between 1830 and 1886; *PP 1893–94, LXXIII* (ii), Wages of the Manual Labour Classes; Industrial Remuneration Conference *Report* (London 1885) pp 142, 515

58   R H Campbell (1980) *op. cit.* p 80

59   A D Campbell 'Changes in Scottish Incomes 1924–49' *Economic Journal* 65 1955, pp 225–40

60   Board of Trade *Report of Enquiry into Working Class Rents, Housing and Retail Prices, etc.* 1908, Cd 3864, xl

61   Board of Trade *Report of Enquiry into Working Class Rents and Retail Prices with the Rates of Wages in Certain Occupations in Industrial Towns of the United Kingdom in 1912* 1913, Cd 6955, p xxxvi, concluded, 'The index numbers for the Scottish towns . . . are considerably higher on the whole than those for English and Welsh towns'

62   Calculated from Table 7

63   R H Campbell 'Introductory Essay' in Campbell (ed) *Scottish Industrial History: A Miscellany* (Edinburgh 1978), p xxxix

64   H W Singer and C E V Leser 'Industrial Productivity in England and Scotland',
     Journal of the Royal Statistical Society 111 1948, p 309; N K Buxton 'Economic
     Growth in Scotland Between the Wars: the Role of Production Structure and
     Rationalization', *Economic History Review* 33 1980, pp 538–55; A D Campbell
     op. cit.; T Dickson 'From Client to Supplicant: Capital and Labour in
     Scotland, 1870–1945' in *Scottish Capitalism: Class, State and Nation from
     before the Union to the Present* (London 1980), p 284
65   B S Rowntree and B Lasker *Unemployment: a Social Study* (London 1911); D
     Bythell *The Sweated Trades: Outwork in Nineteenth Century Britain* (London
     1978); J A Schmiechen 'State Reform and the Local Economy', *Economic
     History Review* 28 1975, pp 418–22; J H Treble *op. cit.* pp 67–70; J A
     Schmiechen *Sweated Industries op. cit.* p 185 states that 'sweating was the
     result of growth not stagnation'.
66   J H Treble 'The Market for Unskilled Male Labour in Glasgow, 1891–1914' in
     I MacDougall (ed), *Essays in Scottish Labour History: a Tribute to W H
     Marwick* (Edinburgh 1979), pp 115–42.
67   J H Treble 'The Seasonal Demand for Adult Labour in Glasgow, 1890–1914',
     Social History 3 1978, pp 43–60
68   R Samuel 'Comers and Goers' in H J Dyos and M Wolff (eds) *The Victorian
     City: Images and Realities,* vol. I (London 1977 edn), pp 123–60
69   R G Rodger 'The "Invisible Hand" . . . ' *op. cit.*
70   R G Rodger 'The Law and Urban Change: Some Nineteenth Century Scottish
     Evidence', *Urban History Yearbook* 1979, pp 85–6; *see also PP 1907 XXXVII,*
     and *PP 1908 XLII,* Report of the Departmental Committee on House-Letting
     in Scotland, vols I and II for characteristics of tenancies in Scotland
71   D Englander *Landlord and Tenant in Urban Britain, 1838–1914* (Oxford 1983),
     pp. 167–70 and M J Daunton *House and Home in the Victorian City: Working
     Class Housing 1850–1914* (London 1983), pp 132–9 give accounts of the house-
     letting system in Scotland
72   J Melling *Rent Strikes: People's Struggle for Housing in West Scotland
     1890–1916* (Edinburgh 1983); S Damer 'State, Class and Housing: Glasgow
     1885–1919' in J Melling (ed) *Housing, Social Policy and the State* (London
     1980); D Englander 'Landlord and Tenant in Urban Scotland—the Back-
     ground to the Clyde Rent Strikes', *Journal of Scottish Labour History Society,*
     15 1981, pp 4–16
73   M J Daunton *op. cit.* p 136
74   Scottish Land Enquiry Committee Report *Scottish Land* (London 1914), pp
     350–1
75   Report of the Departmental Committee on House-Letting in Scotland, *PP 1907
     XXXVI,* p 3
76   N J Morgan and M J Daunton 'Landlords in Glasgow: a Study of 1900'
     Business History 25 1983, p 279
77   *Ibid.* and M J Daunton *op. cit.* p 137
78   Presbytery of Glasgow Report *op. cit.* p 96
79   N J Morgan and M J Daunton *op. cit.* p 279 and M J Daunton *op. cit.* pp 137–8
80   C Pennington 'Tuberculosis' in O Checkland and M Lamb (eds) *Health Care as
     Social History* (Aberdeen 1982), pp 90, 96–7
81   H MacDonald 'Public Health Legislation and Problems in Victorian
     Edinburgh, with Special Reference to the Work of Dr Littlejohn as Medical
     Officer of Health'. Unpublished PhD thesis, Edinburgh University 1972, vol 2,
     graph A

82 Dundee Social Union *Report on Housing and Industrial Conditions and Medical Inspection of School Children* (Dundee 1905); City of Edinburgh Charity Organisation Society *Report on the Physical Condition of Fourteen Hundred Schoolchildren in the City together with Some Account of their Homes and Surroundings* (London, 1906); Scotch Education Department, *Report as to the Physical Condition of Children Attending the Public Schools of the School Board for Glasgow* (HMSO 1907), Cd 3637
83 SED *Report op. cit.* p v
84 R Q Gray *op. cit.* p 85
85 *Ibid.* pp 83–4
86 *Ibid.* p 86
87 D Milne *The Scottish Office* (London 1957), pp 15–17; K Burgess 'Workshop of the World: Client Capitalism at its Zenith, 1830–1870' in T Dickson (ed) *op. cit.* pp 230–4

3

URBANE SILENCE:
SCOTTISH WRITING AND THE NINETEENTH-
CENTURY CITY

Andrew Noble

Like all theorists he was not good at drawing practical conclusions from his
theory.   Nadezhda Mandelstam

Rich and poor

A life of self-indulgence is for us,
  A life of self-denial is for them;
For us the streets, broad-built and populous,
  For them unhealthy corners, garrets dim,
    And cellars where the water-rats may swim!
For us green paths, refreshed by fragrant rain;
  For them dark alleys where the dust lies grim!
Not doomed by us to this appointed pain—
  God made us—rich and poor—of what do these complain?

Mrs Norton

A fact so obvious as perhaps not to have been given the attention it merits is
that Scottish nineteenth-century fiction—unlike the English, European and,
even, the American novel—scarcely deals with the chronic problem of the
age, the new industrial city. Yet Scotland was by no means the society least
shaped by the often brutal energy of industrialisation. The purpose of the
following essay is to make some suggestions as to the cause and consequences of this strange, sorry state of affairs when a society with a self-
avowed appetite for facts was incapable of contributing to the great realist
tradition of the nineteenth-century novel.

Scotland's movement to such peripheral fictional impotence was almost
as abrupt as it was odd. In the eighteenth century the extraordinary
intellectual phenomenon of the Scottish Enlightenment had placed the
country at the cosmopolitan centre of change in Western society. Even
odder is the fact that the innovative nature of Scottish thought with its truly
radical achievements in epistemology, history, economics and sociology
would seem to portend a state of mind precisely attuned to the creation of a
realistic fiction. It has been argued, of course, that Sir Walter Scott's house
of fiction, built on the foundations of the Scottish Enlightenment, presents
us with precisely such a welcome outcome. I shall be arguing that this
rambling, mock-gothic structure presents us with no such vital transition
nor livable achievement. If, however, Scott's achievement is that of
innovative realism (as opposed to pioneering historicism) it can be

immediately remarked that the fictional hiatus that follows him becomes even harder to comprehend. Was his genius so enormous that for a century it exhausted the formal and linguistic possibilities of self and social representation in Scottish fiction?

Following Duncan Forbes's seminal article, 'The Rationalism of Sir Walter Scott', the pattern of relating Scott to the Englightenment has, obviously and sensibly, been to see his fiction in the context of the earlier non-fictional prose.[1] Joseph Brodsky has remarked, however, that 'poetry always precedes prose'. While he conceives of this in the Russian tradition (for example the organic evolution from Pushkin and Dostoevsky) it is a hypothesis which might be fruitfully tested with regard to the relationship between Scottish poetry in mid eighteenth century and the subsequent Scottish prose of the latter part of that century and the nineteenth century. The credibility and utility of this experiment is enhanced by the fact that the poet I assume to be particularly exemplary, James Thomson, author of *The Seasons,* reflects with extra-ordinary accuracy the intellectual, economic and social values of the thought of the Scottish Enlightenment. His poetry, unlike that of our age, is not at odds with the public aspirations of its society. Thus in terms of both language and values he can be reasonably postulated as not only Scott's predecessor but of much subsequent, often 'anglicised', Scottish writing. For good or ill he is one of our genuine ancestors.

If he is in some ways their precursor, Thomson is also manifestly dissimilar to the later English Romantics. This is most obvious in direct relation to Wordsworth. Under the impact of enclosing agrarian capitalism Wordsworth's poetry deals with the dissolution of rural society and its people. The uprooted figures in his landscape are alone and often distraught. Wordsworth conceived of city life as leading to another sort of human disintegration. Writing before this vortex of social change, Thomson's world is understandably far more mellow and promising. Although there are undercurrents of anxiety in him, his most characteristic tone is that of belief in social progress. It is, however, a tone which to varying degrees reflects more aspiration than achieved fact. There is an unreal, enamelled glaze over the surface of the 'Britannia' of which he is so proud. Something suspect, too, in the harmony between property and labour which he asserts has been realised:

> . . . thy Valleys float
> With golden Waves; and on thy Mountains Flocks
> Bleat, numberless, while roving round their Sides.
> Bellow the blackening Herds in lusty Droves
> Beneath, thy Meadows slow, and rise unequall'd,
> Against the Mower's Sythe. On every Hand,
> Thy Villas shine. Thy Country teems with Wealth;
> And Property assures it to the Swain,
> Pleas'd, and unweary'd, in his guarded Toil.[2]

'The swain/pleas'd, and unweary'd in his guarded Toil' is a central figure

in *The Castle of Indolence*. This, to say the least, is a paradoxical creation.
It is a poem by a Scotsman written in Spenserian stanzas with an equally
contrived archaic vocabulary in praise of British social and political
progress extending itself into the realms of a righteous imperial destiny.
Hence the activity of the hero, 'The Knight of Arts and Industry':

> Then towns he quicken'd by mechanic arts,
> And bade the fervent city glow with toil;
> Bade social Commerce raise renowned marts,
> Join land to land, and marry soil to soil,
> Unite the poles, and without bloody spoil
> Bring home of either Ind the gorgeous stores;
> Or, should despotic rage the world embroil,
> Bade tyrants tremble on remotest shores.
> While o'er th' encircling deep Britannia's thunder roars.[3]

Imperial prosperity without guilty blood on its hands certainly belongs
more to the world of romance than reality. Thus Thomson's deliberate
choice of his medium. Aided by abandoning the tough specificity of his own
Scottish language, his 'mythic' poetry veers towards propaganda as it
insinuates that the desires of the establishment, of the propertied classes and
their economic and social theoreticians, are the reality of eighteenth-century
Britain.

Myth is exploited in terms of content as well as for its linguistic and
formal atmosphere. While the poem contains some standard, pious aspirations, it is theologically much more unconventional, even heretical, in the
true object of its praise. A post-Newtonian god of energy has replaced a god
of love:

> What is th'adored Supreme Perfection? say!
> What, but eternal never-resting Soul,
> Almighty Power, and all-directing Day,
> By whom each atom stirs, the planets roll;
> Who fills, surrounds, informs and agitates the whole.[4]

Energy, activity, the work ethic, this is the new divinity and redemptive
force. Characteristic of the Enlightenment's secularisation of Christianity
for its humanist purposes, Thomson reinterprets the primary myth of the
Fall. There was an Eden of agricultural bounty but this was lost in the
course of history so that men emerged from 'Barbarism' apathetic and
listless. Into this state of entropy Thomson injects human energy and
practicality. If we had eaten of the tree of knowledge this was actually to
our benefit because it unleashed human inventiveness: 'Vain is the tree of
knowledge without fruit.' Thomson was, of course, well aware that this
contravened one of the primary meanings of the Fall; that henceforth
labour was to be for man a harsh curse. As much as exhorting 'these new
created men', the entrepreneurs, Thomson directs his activities to pointing
out the blessings of labour to the agrarian working class:

Better the toiling swain; oh, happier far!
Perhaps the happiest of the sons of men!
Who vigorous plies the plough, the team, the car;
Who houghs the field, or ditches in the glen,
Delves in his garden or secures his pen.
The tooth of Avarice poisons not his peace;
He tosses not in Sloth's abhorred den;
From Vanity he has a full release;
And, rich in Nature's wealth, he thinks not of increase.

Good Lord! how keen are his sensations all!
His bread is sweeter than the glutton's cates:
The wines of France upon the palate pall,
Compared with what his simple soul elates,—
The native cup, whose flavour thirst creates.
At one deep draught of sleep he takes the night:
And for that heartfelt joy which nothing mates,
Of the pure nuptial-bed the chaste delight,
The losel is to him a miserable wight.

Ah! what avail the largest gifts of Heaven,
When drooping health and spirits go amiss?
How tasteless then whatever can be given!
Health is the vital principle of bliss;
And exercise, of health. In proof of this,
Behold the wretch, who slugs his life away,
Soon swallow'd in disease's sad abyss;
While he whom toil has braced, or mainly play,
Has light as air each limb, each thought as clear as day.[5]

As Roy Porter has recently pointed out, life for all ranks in the eighteenth-century was rawly exposed and painful.[6] For the agricultural worker domestic conditions were poor and the nature of his work often extremely burdensome. This stereotype of a placid peasantry, whose appetites, fiscal and sexual, were regulated by the pleasurable nature of his therapeutic labour, was nearer the reverse of the truth than the truth. The power of this stereotype was such, however, that someone who felt as passionately as Burns about the way he had been socially humiliated and physically brutalised by his life as a small farmer wrote 'The Cottar's Saturday Night'; a poem which is in quite obvious line of descent from Thomson's work. Burns, of course, in that poem was pandering to the predilections of his genteel audience. By Burns' time the middle and upper classes wished not only not to be exposed to the grim facts of rural destitution—they were to be even less keen to bear witness to the industrial slum—but to believe that rural life was inherently not only domestically placid but politically stable. Increasingly in the shadow of the French Revolution the notion of a contented, loyal peasantry as a moral counterweight to their dissident urban brethren became evident. The population density of the expanding cities made them ever more likely centres for insurrectionary mobs. At the level of mythical association, the city had been from time immemorial the haunt of fratricidal Cain. The bourgeois mind has at its disposal some enormously powerful archetypes with which to manipulate desires and fears and thereby maintain its irresponsibility and control.

Shadows of such anxieties flit all through Thomson's work but he is more concerned with aspiration. He ignores the difficult problem of how a static peasantry is to relate to a dynamic urban economy and population but takes for granted that rising prosperity created by released energy will change the face of both the British countryside and town. As Raymond Williams has remarked: Thomson's is an 'idealization of a productive order that is scattering and guarding plenty'.[7] Energy, fiscal rectitude, all lead to harmony and civilisation. Confident that they had left behind them the fanatical repressions of a superstitious past, the thinkers of the Enlightenment felt it within their power to build a world prosperous, rational and good. The secular city was the inevitable goal of their ambition and invention: 'Then towns he quicken'd by mechanic arts,/And bade the fervent city glow with toil.' In *The Seasons* we can perceive a more detailed image of the results of the entrepreneurial impregnation:

> Hence every form of cultivated life
> In order set, protected and inspired
> Into perfection wrought. Uniting all,
> Society grew numerous, high, polite,
> And happy. Nurse of art, the city reared
> In beauteous pride her tower-encircled head;
> And stretching street on street, by thousands drew,
> From twining woody haunts, or the tough yew
> To bows strong-straining, her aspiring sons.
>   Then Commerce brought into the public walk;
> The busy merchant; the big warehouse built;
> Raised the strong crane; choked up the loaded street
> With foreign plenty; and thy stream, O Thames,
> Large, gentle, deep, majestic king of floods!
> Chose for his grand Resort.[8]

Like peasant labour, the pronounced demographic change involved in urban growth, in reality a painful business, is allegedly a harmonious, self-regulating activity. The new city is for Thomson, like Voltaire, 'the perfector of rational civilization'. Voltaire, too, envisaged a state arising better than Eden. Rural Adam and Eve were rough creatures with matted hair and broken fingernails. 'They lacked industry and pleasure: Is this virtue? No, pure ignorance.'[9] Loss of innocence is for Voltaire a positive advantage since it leads not only to productive knowledge but this causes the aristocrat in his amoral search for pleasure to pump prime the economy. He hires labour to meet his gross material demands and, for the common good, causes those socially beneath him to attempt to emulate his luxurious life. It is not a cynical but a logical reversal of Christianity's command that the rich should be charitable towards the poor given that moral problems are in practical terms wholly solvable.

Scottish thinkers in the eighteenth century also saw increased productivity and consequent prosperity as the key to the creation of a new civilisation whose principal manifestation would be the city. David Hume believed that increased agrarian wealth provided the foundation for the new, desirable urban order. His city was to grow organically from its quickening rural roots.

If prosperity was rooted in the land, the human medium of its transfer into urban terms was to be what Hume termed the new 'middling class'. Unlike Voltaire, Hume could not countenance the good life emerging from the amoral, cynical activities of the aristocrat. Luxury and its emulation had to be innocent. 'Vicious luxury' worked only in terms of being an antidote to other poisons in the body politic. 'Virtue,' he wrote, 'like wholesome food, is better than poisons, however corrected.' Hume's prescription for social success is founded on an increase in the numbers and virtues of the middle class. He saw the economic inertia and political animosity of Scotland's past as caused by the gulf between aristocrat and peasant. The middle class were to bridge this gulf. The very nature of their middle situation was inherently suited to such benevolence.

Those who are placed among the lower ranks of men, have little opportunity of exerting any other virtue besides those of patience, resignation, industry and integrity. Those who are advanced into the higher stations, have full employment for their generosity, humanity, affability and charity. When a man lies between the two extremes, he can exert the former virtues towards his superiors and the latter towards his inferiors. Every moral quality which the human soul is susceptible of, may have its turn, and be called up to action; and a man may, after this manner, be much more certain of his progress in virtue, than where his good qualities lie dormant, and without employment.[10]

Like Thomson, indeed like almost every other Scottish eighteenth-century thinker, Hume constantly reiterates the psychological and economic value of activity. The men of the Scottish Enlightenment were haunted as much by the poverty inducing stasis caused by past Scottish economic inadequacies and malpractices as they were by the bloody fratricide caused by religious fanaticism or alleged Highland barbarism. Regression to such torpor haunted them: thus the constant invocations of industry and inventiveness. Like Thomson, Hume feared—even loathed—indolence. At best, it was a necessary but transitory respite from action. Action primarily expressed itself in trade and in the mechanical arts. These gave birth to progress in the liberal arts. An economically dynamic society will, Hume believed, inevitably achieve derivative, parallel improvements in the refined arts. This quantitative and hence qualitative rise in social life would find natural expression in more civil and civilising cities.

The more these refined arts advance, the more sociable men become: nor is it possible, that, when enriched with science, and possessed of a fund of conversation, they should be contented to remain in solitude, or live with their fellow-citizens in that distant manner, which is peculiar to ignorant and barbarous nations. They flock into cities; love to receive and communicate knowledge; to show their wit or their breeding; their taste in conversation or living, in clothes or furniture. Curiosity allures the wise; vanity the foolish; and pleasure both. Particular clubs and societies are everywhere formed: both sexes meet in an easy and sociable manner; and the tempers of men, as well as their behaviour, refine apace. So that, beside the improvements which they receive from knowledge and the liberal arts, it is impossible but they must feel an increase of humanity, from the very habit of conversing together, and contributing to each other's pleasure and entertainment. Thus *industry, knowlege*, and *humanity*, are linked together, by an indissoluble chain, and are found, from experience as well as reason, to be peculiar to the more polished, and, what are commonly denominated, the more luxurious ages.[11]

Hume's vision is that of the main stream of the Scottish Enlightenment. There were, of course, dissenting voices, most notably that of Adam Ferguson. In part Hume's vision was part act of faith in the 'middling class' and part calculated gamble. Further he believed that any activity was better than the prior swamp of social and economic despond. Also much of the evidence that his own age presented him with seemed solid proof of the veracity of the social experiment. As Jacques Ellul has remarked:

The optimistic atmosphere of the eighteenth century . . . created a climate favourable to the rise of technical applications. The fear of evil diminished. There was an improvement in manners; a softening of the conditions of war; an increasing sense of man's responsibility for his fellows; a certain delight in life, which was greatly increased by the improvement of living conditions in nearly all classes except the artisan; the building of fine houses in great numbers. All these helped persuade Europeans that progress could only be achieved by the exploitation of scientific discoveries.[12]

Scotland's two major cities, Edinburgh and Glasgow, in different respects, seem to confirm this improvement. In Edinburgh the city is transformed as a dramatic, innovative combination of wealth and architectural skill builds the New Town. Wealth also allows the growth of debating societies, clubs and literary groups. With real foresight the civic authorities decide to refashion Edinburgh University on the best available continental models and hire the best possible professors. In an age of near total Oxbridge inertia, Edinburgh becomes a centre of international renown; a position it was to hold throughout the eighteenth century.[13]

These were by no means superficial achievements but, in Hume's own words, 'no advantages in this world are pure and unmixed'. If the New Town in terms of building space, amenities and, not least, sanitation was a vast improvement it was also a manifest division in Edinburgh society. The old life of the high tenements was gone. Wealth had taken itself elsewhere and the inhabitants of such areas as the Canongate were left to look after themselves as they might. A more rigid sense of class, with the fear and anger such division entailed, came into operation.

Further, if Edinburgh were a capital city, it was the capital of an entity which lay in an uneasy state between nation and province. Even before the

Union the shadow of London had lain over Edinburgh's destiny. Almost inevitably it was Andrew Fletcher of Saltoun who saw the threat with greatest clarity:

> For this vast city [London] is like the head of a rickety child, which by drawing to itself the nourishment that should be distributed in due proportions to the rest of the languishing body, becomes so overcharged, that frenzy and death unavoidably ensue. And if the number of people and their riches would be far greater in twelve cities than now in one, which I think no man will dispute; and that these cities were such as are situated in convenient distances from each other, the relief they would bring to every part of these kingdoms would be unspeakable.[14]

With regard to law, Fletcher believed that injustice prevailed in direct proportion to the physical centre of justice. Executive power was similarly harmed by the concept of one, dominant centre.

> For all the same offices that belong to a great kingdom must be in each of them; with this difference, that the offices of such a kingdom being always burdened with more business than any one man can rightly execute, most things are abandoned to the rapacity of servants; and the extravagant profits of all great officers plunge them into all manner of luxury, and debauch them from doing good: whereas the offices of these lesser governments extending only over a moderate number of people, will be duly executed, and many men have occasions put into their hands of doing good to their fellow citizens. So many different seats of government will highly tend to the improvement of all arts and sciences; and afford great variety of entertainment to all foreigners and others of a curious and inquisitive genius, as the ancient cities of Greece did. I perceive now, said Sir Edward, the tendency of all this discourse. On my conscience he has contrived the whole scheme to no other end than to set his own country on an equal foot with England and the rest of the world. To tell you the truth, said I, the insuperable difficulty I found of making my country happy by any other way, led me insensibly to the discovery of these things, which, if I mistake not, have no other tendency than to render, not only my own country, but all mankind as happy as the imperfections of human nature will admit. For I considered that in a state of separation from England, my country would be perpetually involved in bloody and destructive wars. And if we should be united to that kingdom in any other manner, we must of necessity fall under the miserable and languishing condition of all places that depend upon a remote seat of government. And pray where lies the prejudice, if the three kingdoms were united on so equal a foot, as for ever to take away all suspicion and jealousy of separation? that virtue and industry might be universally encouraged, and every part contribute cheerfully and in due proportion to the security and defence of this union, which will preserve us so effectually from those two great calamities, war and corruption of manners. This is the only just and rational kind of union. All other coalitions are but the unjust subjection of one people to another.[15]

Eighteenth-century Edinburgh, in fact, presents contradictory patterns of growth and decay. The university, particularly the medical school, flourished. The law maintained its national integrity. The church was not to divide till the next century. Real political power had, however, departed. Perhaps most ominously, the culture became divided between the genteel and increasingly anglicised middle class and the common people. T S Eliot was rightly to remark that in cultural terms eighteenth-century Edinburgh was like Boston a province of London values.[16] That is to say its literary values were not only those of the rather sterile eighteenth-century aesthetics but were derivative. Creative literature and imitation are irreconcilable. As we shall see, despite the enormous circulation and wealth of the great Scottish reviews their true accents were those of the sentimental cosmopolitan bourgeoisie and not of their own nation. They were also transient phenomena. They and Scottish writers in general could not resist the magnetic attraction of London. What Smollett called the 'dropsical head' either infected or sucked off Scottish creative life.

If the fate of the Edinburgh common people was that they were left behind to decay in their crumbling tenements, the people of Glasgow were to be even less fortunate victims of innovation. Glasgow was to be one of the first of the new industrial cities, with all the attendant horrors of that state. The Humean equation of wealth with improved civic amenity did not prevail in these new cities. Profit came from property speculation. A superficial rational order, that lowest common denominator of architectural design, the grid system, produced both unregulated growth and a high density of population. Rent returns depended on this density. The buildings were so packed in the poorest areas that much life was lived in underground, basement space. Such density, combined with inadequate sanitation and polluted water, made disease rife.[17]

Smith and his successors had considered that the operation of the division of labour would have an integrating effect on society. In theory, the notion that since no man could be any longer wholly independent in his labour it would lead to a healthy kind of social interdependence was perfectly reasonable. The reality of money and power was not at all like this. In the new water and then steam driven factories the nature of the work removed the craft element. This not ony diminished a sense of worth in the worker but the time and energy he had to spend ministering these crude machines was ruinous to his health. Economic fluctuation also led to varying degrees of unemployment. The condition of the new urban industrial man was that of exhaustion and malnutrition. Hence the appearance on a massive scale of laudanum and alcohol as pain killers for this terrifyingly unnatural life.

It was *this* Scotland, a land in agrarian and proto-industrial travail divided by fascination with and fear of French inspired revolution, which was contemporary with Sir Walter Scott. At one level of that strangely divided personality, he was as able as any Scotsman of his age to articulate its problems. In 1829 he wrote:

> The state of high civilization to which we have arrived is scarcely a national blessing, since, while the *few* are improved to the highest point, the *many* are in proportion brutalized and degraded, at the same time the very highest and lowest state in which the human race can exist in point of intellect.[18]

This was precisely the condition which the optimistic faith of the Enlightenment was supposed not to lead. Their 'conjectural history' by no means envisaged the disappearance of class but had believed that the conditions of all classes would relatively improve: 'As society advanced, the difference of ranks advances with it.' In direct refutation of Smith's doctrine of the division of labour Scott clearly saw that the new steam technology would cause a dangerous demographic shift from rural water sources to congested, fraught urban enclaves:

> The actual Radicals in Scotland are only to be found in the large manufacturing towns where a certain number always entertain those sentiments which are always more or less widely extended amongst the giddy multitude according to the pressure of the times, the price of provisions the plenty or want of work and so forth. The situation and habits of the Scottish manufacturers, considered as part of the community, have been powerfully affected, and much for the worse, by the general introduction of steam for driving engines. Since I remember Scotland manufactures were usually situated within the vicinity of waterfalls for convenience of driving machinery—this drove the undertaker into remote and solitary places where they erected their cotton mills while their workmen formed a little village round them, . . . In hard times a man was obliged to maintain his work-people till work came round, and was usually assisted on such occasions by the country gentlemen. In short, the employer possessed the natural influence over the employed which go so far to strengthen the bonds of society. But where the engines are driven by steam there is and can be nothing of this—the buildings are erected nearly as possible if not in the actual precincts of Glasgow or Paisley—when a manufacturer wishes to do a particular job he gets some two hundred weavers from lanes, streets and garrets without the slightest attention to character or circumstances or to anything but they have ten fingers and can work a shuttle. These men are employed for perhaps a fortnight and are then turned off, the employer knowing no more than if they were so many old pirns and shuttles.[19]

The movement from country to congested town, then, is accompanied by a deep degeneration in relations between masters and men due to the implementation under the influence of steam of harsh, utilitarian arithmetic. However flawed they may have been, Scott saw a genuine loss in the older paternal forms of responsibility.

The nineteenth-century novel is suffused with nostalgia for a lost green world. The literary intelligence is perhaps too prone to exaggerating relative differences into the absolute polarities of myth: the good country as opposed to the evil town. This, however, is not Scott's error. Like most enlightened Scotsmen he felt the fratricidal violence of Scottish history as being too recent to allow this particular fantasy. The distinction between town and country was in his mind of a different nature. Thus he wrote in *Chronicles of the Canongate*:

> A nobler contrast can hardly exist than that of the huge city, dark with the smoke of ages, and groaning with the various sounds of active industry or idle revel, and the lofty craggy hill, silent and solitary as the grave; one exhibiting the full tide of existence, pressing and precipitating itself forward with the force of an inundation; the other resembling some timeworn anchorite, whose life passes as silent and unobserved as the slender rill which escapes unheard, and scarce seen, from the fountain of his patron saint. The city resembles the busy temple, where

the modern Comus and Mammon hold their court, and thousands sacrifice ease, independence, and virtue itself at their shrine; the misty and lonely mountain seems as a throne to the majestic but terrible Genius of feudal times, when the same divinites dispensed coronets and domains to those who had heads to devize, and arms to execute, bold enterprises.[20]

Thus, although there has been a significant shift from silence to brutalising noise, cupidity and ambition are seen as the ruling deities in both feudal and capitalist society. Hume and Smith had placed emulation as a key, healthy cause of progress. The force that Scott detects at the heart of any form of society seems an altogether darker, more dangerous, entity.

When we move, however, from either Scott's incidental or personal writing to the main body of his fiction we find a quite different balance between feudalism and capitalism. It has been frequently remarked that Scott's fictional historical perspective permits him to show the benign causality of social development. It is also usually assumed that this causality results from an objective neutral assessment of the facts. The novelist is seen not only as historian but embryo social scientist. Hence Duncan Forbes:

> He practised what the Scottish philosophers preached: he avoided the 'mist of metaphysics' and lived, by the light of commonsense, a life of action and observation in society—the great laboratory of the Philosophers—the sort of life recommended by Adam Ferguson: full of bustle.[21]

One can agree with Forbes that Scott was not merely the 'King of the Romantics', an intensely popular Gothic fabulator—though this was the essence of his enormous commercial success—and that his novels do express the fundamental progressive theme of the historicism of the Scottish Enlightenment. As Forbes states:

> He accepted the leading principle of conjectural history: the law of the necessary progress of society through successive stages, and used it, as has been seen, as a weapon. For instance, against codification he argued that one cannot expect law to be simple in an advanced state of society. Napoleon's conduct in war as tending 'to retrograde towards the brutal violence of primitive hostility', and the Continental System 'consisted of the nation, as in the days of primitive barbarism, to remain satisfied with its own productions, however inadequate to the real or artificial wants to which its progress in society had gradually given rise'.[22]

It is dangerous, however, for an artist to so accept theory, far less use it as a weapon. Art is the reverse of ideology. Forbes and the numerous critics who have followed his lead in relating Scott to Enlightenment historicism represent, at best, a profound naïveté regarding the relationship of fiction to the history of ideas. Facts not theories are the sacred, primary sustenance of fiction. What contemporary life presented Scott with were some very harsh facts which revealed that the melioristic progress initiated by *laissez faire* economics had, at the least, some very severe side effects. We can almost reverse Forbes's analogy. Rather than Scott's fiction being a sort of laboratory where the hypotheses of the Enlightenment were tested by their empirical results, especially the conditions becoming manifest in urban Scotland, Scott manipulated the form and content of his fiction to evade confronting these disturbing facts. A key symptom of this is evident in the astonishing difference between Scott's private political writings and the repressed world of his public fiction. Though he does not pursue the logic of his argument, Tom Crawford has remarked on the disruption of his art by his politics:

> Scott's difficulties as an artist were due not so much to any defect in the life of the Scottish people—this was an age of industrial expansion and social ferment—as to his Toryism, his pathological fear of radical weavers and contemporary mobs, combined with a refusal to put art first, and a disastrous compromise with the market.[23]

Despite Graham MacMaster's recent interesting attempt in *Scott and Society*, no one has yet adequately explained how this mixture of aesthetic bad faith combined with Scott's fear and anger with what he regarded as a disintegrating society was transmuted into 'progressive', unbiased, generous fiction.[24] Should we really trust the tale rather than the teller in this instance?

Scott is generally credited with introducing a new historical dimension into the English novel; character and action are shown as evolving out of the past. The actual nature of the causality is less often discussed. Nor is it often noted that if Scott added something to the world of the eighteenth-century novel, he simultaneously took something away. As Edwin Muir has written:

> The eighteenth century English novel was a criticism of society, manners and life. It set out to amuse but it had a serious intention; its criticism however wittily expressed was sincere and being sincere it made for more civilized manners and a more sensitive understanding of human life. Scott marks a definite degeneration of that tradition: after him certain qualities are lost to the novel which are not recovered for a long time. The novel becomes the idlest of all forms of literary art and by a natural consequence the most popular. Instead of providing an intelligent criticism of life, it is content to enunciate moral platitudes and it does this all the more confidently because such platitudes are certain to be agreeable to the reader. It skims over every aspect of experience that could be obnoxious to the most tender or prudish feelings and in fact renounces both freedom and responsibility. Scott, it seems to me, was largely instrumental in bringing the novel to that point; with his enormous prestige he helped to establish the mediocre and the trivial.[25]

Coleridge, an irascible Hamlet to Scott's Polonius, writing at the time of their publication similarly felt that these novels were really valued for their anodyne power. In an age of pervasive anxiety they disseminated a sense of false security. When, in fact, one looks at their language, underlying aesthetic and historical theories and their manipulation of fictional form one can see how, by instinct and calculation, Scott manufactured novels precisely suited to the aspirations and anxiety of his international bourgeois audience.

Largely on account of provinciality, the cult of gentility and senti-mentality had bitten deeper in middle-class Scotland than elsewhere. James Hogg has accused Scott of bowdlerisation of traditional Scottish poetic sources. The consequences for his fiction were worse. The salty virility of the Scottish language was either watered down or repressed in favour of anglicised diction. 'Tender and prudish feelings' dominated taste. Sentimental fantasy indulged in rural scenes which had never existed. The disconcerting, politically threatening urban world was simply not engaged with. As well as an emasculated diction, an aesthetic theory was also necessary for keeping reality at a safe distance. That theory is not hard to discern in Scott. Revealingly, he came upon the writing of Sir Uvedale Price at the beginning of his career as a novelist. As he wrote to Lady Abercorn:

> I have been studying Price with all my eyes and [am] not without hopes of converting an old gravel-pit into a bower and an exhausted quarry into a bathing-house. So you see my dear Madam how deeply I am bit with the madness of the picturesque and if your Ladyship hears that I have caught a rheumatic fever in the gravel-pit or have been drowned in the quarry I trust you will give me credit for dying a martyr to taste.[26]

Though it was to become such a personal financial disaster, Abbotsford for Scott initially became both an antiquarian symbol for a departed Scot-land and a scene where improving landscaping could be carried out. At a *private* level he hoped to have the best of ancient and modern worlds. The 'madness of the picturesque', however, not only engaged his personal extravagance, that obsessive need for money and afforested land, but, with even sadder results, wrought harm in his fiction. The following passage from Scott's journals shows exactly the damaging nature of Price's picturesque theory not with regard to landscaping but the rendition of Scottish common life:

> I saw the poor childs funeral from a distance—Ah that distance. What a magician for conjuring up scenes of joy and sorrow, smoothing all asperities reconciling all incongruities veiling all absurdness softening every coarseness doubling every effect by the influence of imagination.[27]

Here, ironically in the name of imagination, is that very surrender of freedom and responsibility that Muir perceived. Price's blatant theory was that unappealing subjects could be treated in direct proportion to the *distance* maintained from them. While it is one thing to convert a gravel pit into a pleasing bower, it is another to transmute socially uncomfortable human beings into a pleasing picture. Political fear engenders a false aesthetic. Hence the picture Scott goes on to compose:

> A Scottish wedding should be seen at a distance the gay bound of the dancers just distinguished amid the elderly groupe of the spectators—the glass held high & the distant cheers as it swallowed should be only a sketch not a finished Dutch picture when it becomes brutal & boorish. Scottish psalmody too should (be) heard from a distance—The grunt and the snuffle and the whine and the scream should all be

blended in that deep and distant sound which rising and falling like the Eolian harp may have some title to be called the praise of our makers,—Even so the distant funeral the few mourners on horseback with their plaids wrapped around them. The father heading the procession as they entered the river and pointing out the ford by which his darling was to be carried on the last long road—not (one) of the subordinate figures in discord with the general tone of the incident—the presence of the mourners seeming just accessories and no more to the general purpose of the procession this affecting—to be in the midst of bustle is incongruous and unpleasant from the contradictions which it involves.[28]

Safely distanced by this picturesque aesthetic distasteful forms and sound can then be sentimentally indulged. This, too, it should be remembered is a rural group. The bustle of 'the incongruous and unpleasant' was far more present in the stagnant life of the Canongate or among the radical, unemployed weavers in the West. The techniques of Dutch pictorial realism were the last means to be employed in a composition of these troubling forms of life.

If spatial distance was one way of dealing with this problem, there was also for Scott a temporal solution. Scott was preoccupied with violence in a variety of contradictory ways. At one level he fantasised a militant role for himself. As Phillipson suggests this may stem from his crippled and hence insecure masculinity.[29] It may also stem from a national sense of martial deprivation which he shared with many middle-class Scots.[30] At another level he was obsessed not with participating in violence but with violence breaking out in popular insurrection. He also shared this with Scots of his class.

At a *fictional* level Scott resolved this problem by adhering firmly to enlightenment historicism. This, it will be recalled, entailed that society advanced by definite stages marked by different economic modes and that these successive stages entailed not only a quantitative improvement in material life but in the quality of civilisation. As Scott was well aware, Scottish history provided a remarkably proximate and apparently clear cut transition from one stage to another. As Duncan Forbes has remarked:

Scott's stories do not hinge on the psychological conflict, but on the contrast between different 'degrees of civilization' and 'states of society', especially between Highland and Lowland, barbarism and civilization, as in *Waverley, Rob Roy, The Fair Maid of Perth, Anne of Geierstein, The Two Drovers*. The contrast between Highland and Lowland, so sharply exhibited in eighteenth-century Scotland, the existence of a 'barbarous society', a sociological museum at Edinburgh's back door, and the eruption of the Highlands in 1745, must have been a most potent factor in the outburst of sociological speculation after 1750, speculation which centred round the idea of progress of society from rudeness to refinement. Adam Ferguson, hailed by some as the founder of sociology, was a Highlander who settled down near Edinburgh. Scott was fascinated by a character like Rob Roy, 'blending the wild virtues, the subtle policy and unrestrained licence of an American Indian . . . flourishing in Scotland during the Augustan age . . .'. He was especially interested in the transition period from barbarism to civilization,' the most picturesque period of history'.[31]

It is indisputable that militarism is an essential aspect of Highland feudalism, presumably what Scott meant by 'the majestic but terrible Genius of feudal times'. It should be immediately remarked, however, that during the '45 those with the 'unrestrained licence' of American Indians had displayed in their campaign remarkable order and chivalry towards the civilian population. The sole genocidal brutality of that campaign, as Scott well knew, was inflicted after Culloden by the civilised Hanoverian army. Thus in this particular, crucial instance the whole theory of progress as an antidote to violent behaviour did not hold good.

In enlightened Edinburgh there was a mixture of ancestral fear combined with contemporary condescension to the Highlander. It was assumed that the distinction between Highland and Lowland was a movement from barbarism to civilisation. Scott unthinkingly inherited this attitude. It combined with his fear of the fact that society might 'retrograde towards the brutal violence of primitive hostility'. In direct proportion to his fear of violence breaking out in his own society, Scott's fiction displays an increasing need to stress the terror of *regressive* violence. In *Waverley* the insurrectionary Highland anti-hero is finally, safely framed in a pleasingly nostalgic portrait. By the time of *Redgauntlet* the book pulses with a Gothic, diabolic clamour of Jacobite danger so that its menacing language is ludicrously contradicted by its plot when a Hanoverian *deus ex machina* steps in to resolve the near hysterical political terrors.

What lies behind such artistic confusion? Obsessed with the possibility of violent insurrection—an attitude based on a profoundly unreal analysis of the actual nature of Scottish society—Scott retreated from facing the elements tending toward violence in his own society to projecting violence backwards into the past and the Highlands. Thus instead of the complex analysis of the disturbing present as a product of history as we find in Scott's contemporary, Stendhal, we are given a kind of simplistic anthropology. The archetypal pattern of the Scott novel is of an immature hero who crosses a geographical boundary, the Highland line, to be brought face to face with real and not fantasy violence. Suitably chastened he happily retreats into marriage, inheritance and the allegedly safe creature comforts of the social secure man of the new world. Fearing Jacobinism, Scott seized on Jacobitism as a safe surrogate enemy. The Highlander became a kind of ritual scapegoat. It was not, however, this kind of ancestral violence that really troubled Scott but the violence of harsh industrial and agricultural change. This historical bad faith accounts for the aesthetic confusion and vacuity of his fiction. It is nowhere more apparent than in *Rob Roy*. The following passage is a masterpiece of insinuation and evasion of social reality, as those odd Gaels come South not only to wonder but reside. Goethe, incidentally, was astonished at the physique of the men in the Highland regiments he saw. The 'poison dwarves' of later Scottish military history were an urban mutant.

The dusky mountains of the Western Highlands often sent forth wilder tribes to frequent the marts of St. Mungo's favourite city. Hordes of wild, shaggy, dwarfish cattle and ponies, conducted by Highlanders as wild, as shaggy, and sometimes as dwarfish, as the animals they had in charge, often traversed the streets of Glasgow. Strangers gazed with surprise on the antique and fantastic dress, and listened to the unknown and dissonant sounds of their language, while the mountaineers, armed, even while engaged in this peaceful occupation, with musket and pistol, sword, dagger, and target, stared with astonishment on the articles of luxury of which they knew not the use, and with an avidity which seemed somewhat alarming on the articles which they knew and valued. It is always with unwillingness that the Highlander quits his deserts, and at this early period it was like tearing a pine from its rock, to plant him elsewhere. Yet even then the mountain glens were over-peopled, although thinned occasionally by famine or by the sword, and many of their inhabitants strayed down to Glasgow—there formed settlements—there sought and found employment, although different, indeed, from that of their native hills. This supply of hardy and useful population was of consequence to the prosperity of the place, furnished the means of carrying on the few manufactures which the town already boasted, and laid the foundation of its future prosperity.

The exterior of the city corresponded with these promising circumstances. The principal street was broad and important, decorated with public buildings, of an architecture rather striking than correct in point of taste, and running between rows of tall houses, built of stone, the fronts of which were occasionally richly ornamented with mason-work—a circumstances which gave the street an imposing air of dignity and grandeur, of which most English towns are in some measure deprived by the slight, unsubstantial, and perishable quality and appearance of the bricks with which they are constructed.[32]

At this point it is almost as if Glasgow vanished from the literary imagination of educated Scotland for almost a century. When it does make a brief appearance as in *Peter's Letters to his Kinsfolk* it is only to evade the harsh reality of its grinding slum poverty, factories and its ostentatious wealth which Lockhart, a West of Scotland man and Scott's son-in-law, knew only too well.[33] Different in degree though not in principle to other industrialising cultures, the Scottish imagination retreated into the safe pseudo-pastoral; into a world of pietistic peasants of no radical aspiration or revolutionary protest and potential whatsoever.

Even at the height of the Scottish Enlightenment there had been grave doubts about urban life. It has been suggested that Adam Smith himself believed that the urban capitalist as a type was 'a rather unpatriotic nomad'. As Schorske has remarked of Smith:

Other vices of a subtler sort accompany the urban virtues: 'unnaturalness and dependence.' Smith maintained that 'to cultivate the ground was the natural destination of man.' Both by interest and by sentiment, man tended to return to the land. Labor and capital gravitated naturally to the relatively risk-free countryside. But above all, the psychic satisfactions of the planter surpassed those of the urban merchant or manufacturer. Here Adam Smith showed himself an English preromantic: 'The beauty of the country, the pleasures of country life, the tranquility of mind which it promises and, wherever the injustice of human law does not disturb it, the independency which it really afford, have charms that more or less attract everybody.'[34]

This anti-urban bias was by no means an exclusively Scottish phenomenon. English and American writing are replete with similar examples of aesthetic and political bias. No culture, however, achieved such a repression of representation of urban life by promulgating such mythical rural alternatives. Myth is employed here in Roland Barthes' definition. So much of nineteenth-century Scottish pastoral writing, especially that of *Blackwood's Magazine*, fits precisely Barthes' description of the evasion of history by recourse to alleged eternal, mythical verities.

> Everything here . . . aims to suppress the determining weight of History: we are held back at the surface of an identity, prevented precisely by sentimentality from penetrating into this ulterior zone of human behaviour where historical alienation introduces some 'differences' which we shall here quite simply call 'injustices'.[35]

Of course, economic injustice and utilitarian methodology were almost as prevalent in the capitalist agricultural economy of nineteenth century Scotland as in the cities.[36] In the deeply influential *Noctes Ambrosianae* of *Blackwood's*, however, James Hogg is turned into court-jester to give false witness against life in both urban and rural Scotland. Though it was increasingly disguised by sentimentality, Calvinistic dualism did not give up its grip on the Scottish mind. If the literary rustics of nineteenth-century Scotland are not quite angels it is certainly devils who populate the teeming slums and wynds of Glasgow and Edinburgh. In the following two passages one can not only note the corrupt crudity of the polarity between urban and rural Scotland but remark that these passages are merely the tip of a literary iceberg. Bourgeois Scottish writing is replete with them. Such a false polarity was not to release its grip among Scottish writers till the beginning of the twentieth century. Here is John Wilson, 'Christopher North', on Edinburgh:

> Things hae really come to a queer pass when towns' bodies, leevin in shops and cellars, and garrets and common stairs, and lanes and streets that, wi' a' their fine gas lamp-posts, are pestilential wi' filth and foulzie; and infested wi' lean, mangy dowgs, ruggin out stinking banes frae the sewers; and wi' auld wives, like broken-backed witches, that are little mair than bundles o' movin rags, clautin among the bakiefu's o' ashes; and wi' squads o' routin or spewin bullies o' chiels, staggerin hame frae tripe-soopers, to the disturbance o' the flaes in their yellow-tinged-lookin blankets; and wi' anes, and twas, and threes, o' what's far waur than a' these, great lang-legged, tawdry, and tawpy limmers, standin at closes, wi' mouths red wi' paint, and stinkin o' gin like the bungs o' speerit-casks, when the speerit has been years in the wudd; while far and wide over the city (I'm speakin o' the Auld Town) you hear a hellish howl o' thieves and prostitutes carousin on red herrings and distillery-whuskey, deep down in dungeons aneath the verra stanes o' the street; and faint far-aff echoes o' fechts wi' watchmen, and cries o' 'murder, murder—fire, fire' drowned in the fiercer hubbub o' curses.[37]

This was very much the house style in treatment of urban themes. *Noctes* has several companion pieces dealing with Glasgow in almost indistinguishable terms. It is concerned neither with charity or justice. In the nineteenth century genuinely realistic prose was essentially reformative in its nature. These people are not only irretrievably fallen but, it is insinuated, solely to blame for their promiscuity and alcoholism. They are creatures of licence who have placed themselves beyond the pale. In this passage from Wilson's close associate, Lockhart, Scottish rural man is presented in terms of almost precisely reversed image. Licence is replaced by restraint; thrift and obedience is of the essence of the Scottish soul. This has nothing to do with a realistic presentation of Scottish rural life but is a manifestation of the repressed, political anxiety of the propertied class. There is more devious fantasy in this than in Thomson's earlier poetry:

> These Elders were a most interesting set of persons, and I believe I could have studied their solemn physiognomies as long as I had done those of the young rural beauties at the burn side. I regarded them as the *élite* of this pious peasantry, men selected to discharge these functions on account of the exemplary propriety and purity of their long lives spent among the same people, over whom they were now raised to some priest-like measure of authority. Some among them were very old men, with fine hoary ringlets floating half-way down their backs—arrayed in suits of black, the venerably antique outlines of which shewed manifestly how long they had been needed, and how carefully they had been preserved for these rare occasions of solemnity—the only occasions, I imagine, on which they are worn. The heads of these were very comfortably covered with the old flat blue bonnet, which throws a deep and dark shadow over the half of the countenance. Others, who had not yet attained to such venerable years, had adopted the more recent fashion of hats, and one could see more easily beneath their scantier margins the keen and piercing eyes with which these surveyed every person as he passed—scrutinizing with a dragon-like glance the quantum of his contribution to the heap of guarded copper before them. As for passing their capacious plates without putting in something, that is a thing of which the meanest Scottish peasant, that supports himself by the labour of his hands, would never dream for a moment.[38]

These are not eccentric, wilfully chosen examples of Scottish writing of the period. They can be endlessly duplicated from a variety of sources both Whig and Tory. What they represent is a wholly artificial and politically corrupt treatment of town versus country. Literature rather than correcting the ideological fantasy life of the time did, in fact, endorse it. It was stuff of this kind which fuelled Thomas Chalmers' absurd campaign to divide Scotland up into 2,000 parishes in which allegedly old fashioned communal values would reassert themselves. It was also such a polarity which directly led to the Kailyard novel of the latter part of the nineteenth century and the notion that Scotland was an ahistorical collection of discrete if somewhat indiscreet small towns.

If the Edinburgh poor were to be objects of both denial and denunciation, the capital as a whole could not be so written off. In the wake of the Union, deeply anxious about the continuity of Scottish identity, the Scottish literati set about manufacturing a series of national symbols: hence, for example, we have the tartanisation of the nation. Lockhart's *Peter's Letters to his Kinsfolk* is essentially an exercise in such 'mythologising' of Scottish personalities and phenomena. Not only genteel Edinburgh society but the

city itself is of central importance in this activity. This is a brief excerpt
from Lockhart's verbose 'picture' of the capital.

> . . . But here, as every-where, moonlight is the best. Wherever I spend the
> evening, I must always walk home by the long line of Prince's-Street; and along all
> that spacious line, the midnight shadows of the Castle-rock for ever spread
> themselves forth, and wrap the ground on which I tread in their broad repose and
> blackness. It is not possible to imagine a more majestic accompaniment for the
> deep pause of that hour. The uniform splendour of the habitations on the left
> opening every now and then broken glimpses up into the very heart of the modern
> city—the magnificent terrace itself, with its stable breadth of surface—the few
> dying lamps that here and there glimmer faintly—and no sound, but the heavy
> tread of some far-off watchman of the night—this alone might be enough, and it is
> more than almost any other city could afford. But turn to the right, and see what a
> glorious contrast is there. The eternal rock sleeping in the stillness of nature—its
> cliffs of granite—its tufts of verdure—all alike steeped in the same unvarying hue
> of mystery—its towers and pinnacles rising like a grove of quiet poplars on its
> crest—the whole colourless as if the sun had never shone there, as silent as if no
> voice of man had ever disturbed the echoes of the solemn scene.[39]

As Scott's use of the picturesque, this debased romantic coinage is
deliberately employed to hide more than reveal. While there is some pride in
the New Town, the real impulse is to turn Edinburgh into a thing more
elemental than the product of human ingenuity and labour. The city is also
symbol of Scotland's enduring greatness: 'The Capitol itself is but a pigmy
to this giant.' To create such a sense of Scotland having an eternal city
Lockhart runs not only the gamut of artistic tricks of the light but makes no
attempt to present a detailed social picture of the life of all the streets as the
essential factor in that city's evaluation. The following report of another
politically symbolic event which took place three years after the publication
of Lockhart's book places the interpretation of symbolic Edinburgh in a
somewhat different context.

> I had grown disgusted with the fulsome 'loyalty' of all classes in Edinburgh
> towards this approaching 'George Fourth Visit'; whom though called and
> reckoned a 'King', I, in my private radicalism of mind, could consider only as
> a—what shall I call him?—and loyalty was not the feeling I had toward any part of
> the phenomenon. At length, reading one day, in a public Placard from the Magis-
> trates (of which there had been several), That on His Majesty's Advent it was
> expected that everybody would be carefully well-dressed, 'black coat and white
> duck trousers,' if at all convenient,—I grumbled to myself, 'Scandalous flunkeys,
> I, if I were changing my dress at all, should incline rather to be in white coat and
> black trousers!'—but resolved rather to quit the City altogether, and be absent
> and silent in such efflorescence and flunkeyisms. Which I was, for a week or more
> (in Annandale and at Kirkchrist with the Churches in Galloway,—ride to Lochin-
> brack Well, by Kenmure Lake, etc., how vivid still!)—and found all comfortbly
> rolled away at my return to Edinburgh.[40]

Unmistakably these are Carlyle's iconoclastic accents. Certainly it was an
occasion for satire. The House of Hanover responsible for the destruction

of the clans at Culloden had its pink tartan swathed representative welcomed in 1822 to a lowland tartan bedecked city. It is hard to imagine any nation with a more fabricated, illusory tradition than this. What Carlyle's account also reveals is the characteristic romantic desire for escape from the city to the country. At the end of the same year as he avoided seeing the king, Carlyle wrote to David Hope:

> In Edinr all things are just about as they were. Two thousand dull heads set a-working in the university; twenty times as many hard hands in the various workshops of the place, manufacturing shawls and instruments and furnishings and all the apparatus of luxury; politicians wrangling; the 'mob of gentlemen' talking insipidities and giving dinners, or gone forth to slaughter hares and woodcocks; all minding the solid prose of life, and seeking to invest it with what little decoration they can find in literature, ale, champagne, devotion, whiskey, love, etc., etc., quite in the usual way. For me, I keep as much apart from all their operations as I can; it is not above once a fortnight that I enter their old black harlot of a city, and then my stay in it is as brief as an angel's visit. I never think without shuddering of the life that is led there; the very atmosphere-compounded of coal-smoke and more gases and odours than ever chemist or perfumer dreamed of—were itself enough to make me loathe the whole concern. My paradise must lie many miles from any paved streetsome green nook, it should be, in a far valley of the Highlands, by the clear and quiet waters, with smooth lawns around me, mountains in the distance, and the free sky overhead. Put a bright white cottage down in such a place, give me books and food and raiment and conveniences, with liberty to break the heads of all that come within a furlong of me (except some few select persons, to be hereafter specified) and then—should I be pleased? I know not—but if you hear of any such establishment, I beg you will give me notice.[41]

In part this letter merely reiterates that romantically inspired impulse to rural escape: 'the bright white cottage' is the stuff that clichés are made of. Romanticism, however, is not mere escapism. In its great practioners it was a form of incisive realism created to counteract the profound social crisis initiated by industrialism towards the end of the late eighteenth century. Carlyle is exceptional among nineteenth-century Scottish writers in assuming the burden of this stringent romantic social critique. Whether we find any of his solutions acceptable or not, his virtue, as his English compatriots clearly understood, was that he was constantly engaged in not only documenting the horror of the industrial city but was involved with the political problem that lies unresolved at the heart of modern life: the nature of authority and responsibility in mass industrial culture.

Carlyle's early dislike of genteel Edinburgh—'the "mob of gentlemen" talking insipidities and giving dinners'—was to lead to his move to London. Obsessed with giving meaningful depth back to life, Carlyle from the outset of his career was opposed to what he considered to be the shallow, evasive humanism of the Scottish Enlightenment and, in particular, to the capitalist system of *laissez faire* economics he believed lay at its centre. Inevitably this led to aesthetic quarrels with the Edinburgh literati. Thus although his initial work was published in Jeffrey's *Edinburgh Review* it was from the outset an uneasy alliance in that Carlyle was deeply hostile to the very propertied and entrepreneurial class whose political views the magazine not only supported but formed.[42] Edinburgh was a literary centre which could neither support nor hold him. London he found more vital and responsive. Fletcher of Saltoun's fear had come true. Despite its enormous commercial success and prestige, Edinburgh by the early nineteenth century had collapsed as a vital literary and cultural centre. Had Carlyle remained, Scottish gentility would have repressed his documentation of the plight of the urban, industrial poor which is perhaps his most important strength.

Though he went south, industrial Scotland was still the object of Carlyle's attention. What he stressed was the very fact that so much other Scottish writing was designed to obscure: not only the terrible squalor of the deprived but that such criminal neglect by the ruling class could well have insurrectionary consequences. By manipulation of history and by false rural stereotypes most Scottish writing disguised this deep rooted fear and sought with varying degrees of success to indoctrinate the populace with torpor. Scotland became an ahistorical culture. What Carlyle was trying to do, hence part of his stridency, was to waken Scotland from its sinister sleep. Hence his account of his *Chartism*:

> The melancholy fact remains, that this thing known as Chartism does exist; has existed; and, either 'put down' into secret treason, with rusty pistols, vitriol-bottle and match box, or openly brandishing pike and torch (one knows not in which case *more* fatal looking), is like to exist till quite other methods have been tried with it. What means the bitter discontent of the Working Classes? Whence comes it, whither goes it? Above all, at what price, on what terms, will it probably consent to depart from us and die into the rest? These are questions.[43]

Carlyle is a kind of psychoanalyst not so much of personal but of the political repressions of the prosperous. Horrifying phenomena swam up from the nether social depths:

> 'Glasgow Thuggery', 'Glasgow Thugs;' it is a witty nickname: the practice of 'Number 60' entering his dark room, to contract for and settle the price of blood with operative assasins, in a Christian city, once distinguished by its rigorous Christianism, is doubtless a fact worthy of all horror: but what will horror do for it.[44]

The political assassination of the 1837 Glasgow Cotton Spinners strike runs like a thematic bloody thread through *Chartism*. It is both an ominous violence and a herald of the greater violence which Carlyle obsessively thought imminent. This is no pastoral Scotland nor incipient Kailyard:

> It is in Glasgow among the class operatives that 'Number 60' in his dark room, pays down the price of blood. Be it with reason or unreason, too surely in verity find the time all out of joint; this world is for them no home, but a dingy prison-house, of reckless unthrift, rebellion, rancour, indignation against themselves and against all men. Is it a green flowery world, with azure everlasting sky stretched over it, the work and government of a God; or a murky simmering Tophet, of copperas-fumes, cotton-fuzz, gin-riot, wrath and toil, created by a Demon,

governed by a Demon? The sun of their wretchedness merited and unmerited welters, huge, dark and baleful, like a Dantean Hell, visible there in the statistics of Gin. . . . [45]

Ironically, Carlyle's eccentric rhetoric is by far the most accurate mode of urban realism in Scottish writing in the first half of the nineteenth century. Thomas Chalmers apart, it is to the more sensible clerical and medical reports which we must have recourse to find how grim things were for the urban poor. The nineteenth-century novel is either silent or evasive.

1857 saw the publication of a remarkable little book, *Shadow's Midnight Scenes and Social Photographs* where the realistic technology of the camera undermined the corrupt literary analogies derived from painting on which sentimental Scottish writing depended.[46] The squalor, destitution, alcoholism and prostitution of the Glasgow slums seem near incredible. We have, of course, by this time the remarkable Annan photographs to corroborate Shadow's evidence.

Shadow was the pseudonym for Alexander Brown, a letterpress printer. His is a quite remarkable book in terms of its detail and compassion. The 'photographs' he takes are of a heart of darkness in slum Glasgow which needed only nocturnal exploration to reveal. He reveals that in terms of drink and prostitution the only thing Wilson had exaggerated was his mendacious prose style. The life of the poor seems largely to be led in basements: a seamy underground of poverty and filth. Hence his description of a blind widow and her sons:

They live in a cellar, within a yard or two of a dung-heap, sending forth its noxious smells, and fever-causing exhalations. By the uncertain light of a small glimmering fire, we can recognise at a glance the wretchedness of the abode. It reminds us more of a charnel house than a dwelling place for the living. Amid this desolation sits the afflicted widow in her faded tattered weeds. Poor woman! she has seen 'better days'—worse she cannot. Around the hearth are squatted her dirty ragged boys, each tearing from the other a filthy bone picked up in the street. On our expressing surprise at a thing so horrible, she says, 'Ou aye, sir, they're glad o' ony thing, puir things, but they maun gang to bed.' Upon this the youngest of the four—a poor fleshless child of four years old, pale and emaciated—rises, rubs his little eyes, scratches his hands, and shakes himself terribly as if suffering from some cutaneous disease. The scene is sadly pitiful. In a corner of the room is their bed of dirty matted straw. Fortunately, a wreck of a bedstead keeps them from the damp floor. We visited this place again at mid-day, and found that this 'home' was dark as the grave! God pity us, we exclaimed,—can such things be in a Christian land![47]

Running through Brown's writing is the irony of such destitution in a Christian country. He was also incipiently aware of a contradiction between Scotland's historical self-image and the reality of its contemporary industrial condition. Having dealt with the sad plight of Blythswood Square's prostitutes his attention turned to the city's statuary:

Little or nothing else calls for notice, we amuse ourselves by noticing the long tortuous windings of the two rows of street lamps, in unbroken links of nearly two miles. However much we admire Sir Walter Scott as a poet and novelist, on observing these little luminaries, we feel disposed to depreciate his faith in science, and his gift of prophecy, remembering the old story of how he ridiculed the idea of lighting a city with gas. But poor Sir Walter has, in the flesh long since passed away; and as we approach the foot of Miller Street, we are enabled to see, partly by the aid of these sad lamps, the dark and lofty column raised to his memory, peering up into the heavens,—a striking contrast to monuments of less note, though not of less men—for there also the illustrious Watt sits, as he was wont, in a reflecting mood, blessing the world with the fruits of his rare genius. That the novelist should occupy a higher position, even in stone and lime, than the discoverer of the steam engine is, in the nature of our tastes and industrial pursuits, somewhat anomalous, seeing that the sons of Sanct Mungo are now a more practical than an imaginative people—that they are more indebted to the one for their magnificent steamers and princely wealth than they are to the other for any particular refinement they possess in the cultivation of letters.[48]

There is a dour, anti-aesthetic material practicality to this which has been endemic in Scotland since Knox. Like many Scots, Brown sees literature as not functional. One of its essential functions, however, is intelligent dissent to social injustice. In that sense Scott and the Scottish historical novel he gave birth to are culpable. The 'Highland' novels of James Grant and William Black pandered to militaristic and erotic bourgeois fantasy. Along with pastoral fantasy, what Scottish nineteenth century fiction engendered was the concept of a country peculiarly rooted in its past.

It was such an image that drew one of the greatest of nineteenth century novelists to visit Scotland. Nathaniel Hawthorne who in the mid 1850's was American consul in Liverpool visited Scotland in both 1856 and 1857. He had long admired Scott and Abbotsford was a magnet for him. The actual impact of that house had a strange effect on him. Enthusiasm for Scott turned first to apprehension and then dismay. As he wrote of Abbotsford: 'One learns from it, too, that Scott could not have been a really wise man, nor an earnest one, nor one that grasped the truth of life;—he did but play, and the play grew very sad towards its close.'[49] Shocked by the clutter of historical memorabilia and even more by the expression on the death mask—'a perturbed slumber, perhaps nothing short of nightmare'—he saw the house as a historical extravaganza like Strawberry Hill. 'In a certain way,' Hawthorne wrote, 'I understand his romances the better for having seen his house; and his house the better, for having read his romances. They throw light on one another .'[50]

What this relation of writer, dwelling and historical romances suggested to Hawthorne, historical novelist of genius himself, was the actual discontinuity of Scottish history and fiction. Unlike his own revelation of the tragic intensity of American history, like Scotland's in its fanatical, bloody religiosity, Hawthorne felt that Scott had turned Scottish history into devious fantasy. This experience was undoubtedly central to Hawthorne's inability to accept the historical Scotland of nineteenth century tourism. Thus he consistently saw Scotland in dualistic terms of sentimentality conflicting with realism. This was particularly true of his experience of urban Scotland.

Here, while I smoked a cigar, the sun was setting, and gilded the Old Town with its parting rays, making it absolutely the most picturesque scene that I ever beheld. The mass of tall ancient houses, heaped densely together, looked like a Gothic dream; for there seemed to be towers, and all sorts of stately architecture, and spires ascended out of the mass; and above all was the Castle with a crown of gold on its topmost turret. It wanted less than a quarter of nine when the last gleam faded from the window of the old town and left the mass of the buildings dim and indistinguishable; to reappear on the morrow in squalor, lifting their meanness skyward, the home of layer upon layer of unfortunate humanity. The change symbolized the difference between the poet's imagination of life in the past—or in a state which he looks at through a coloured and illuminated medium—and the sad reality.[51]

Such a 'coloured and illuminated medium' is the essential aesthetic of nineteenth-century fiction. It involved a deliberate distortion of vision and, indeed, of another sense as well. As Hawthorne wrote:

As we leaned over this parapet, my nose was conscious of the bad smell of Edinburgh, although the streets, whence it must have come, were hundreds of feet below. I have had some experience of this ugly fragrance in the poor streets of Liverpool; but I think I never smelt it before crossing the Atlantic. It is the odor of the old system of life; the scent of the pine-forests is still too recent with us for it to be known in America.[52]

While the stink of Edinburgh reminded him of Liverpool, he found Glasgow's slums even more appalling.

I think the poorer classes of Glasgow excel even those of Liverpool in the bad eminence of filth, uncombed and unwashed children, disorderly deportment, evil smell and all that makes city-poverty disgusting.[53]

What struck Hawthorne equally forcibly was the degree to which prosperous and impoverished Glasgow lived cheek by jowl.

. . . my wife and I walked out, and saw something of the newer portion of Glasgow; and really I am inclined to think it the stateliest city I ever beheld. The Exchange, the other public buildings and the shops, especially in Buchanan-street, are very magnificent; the latter, especially excelling those of London. . . . Later in the forenoon, we again walked out, and went along Argyle-street, and through the Trongate and the Saltmarket. The two latter were formerly the principal business streets, and, with the High-street, the abode of the rich merchants and other great people of the town. The High street, and still more the Saltmarket, now swarm with the lower orders, to a degree which I never witnessed elsewhere; so that it is difficult to make one's way among the sallow and unclean crowd, and not at all pleasant to breathe in the noisomeness of the atmosphere. The children seem to go unwashed from birth, and perhaps they go on gathering a thicker and thicker coating of dirt till their dying days. Some of the gray houses appear to have been stately and handsome in their day, and have their high gable-ends notched at the edges.[54]

The reality not the fantasy of Scottish history is that the urban poor are condemned to live out their lives among the squalid near ruins of the architectural past. Edinburgh provided Hawthorne with as telling an example as Glasgow of people using not only the rags but the houses abandoned by their social superiors:

> We left the palace, and toiled up through the dirty canongate, looking vainly for a fly, and employing our time as well as we could in looking at the squalid mob of Edinburgh, and peeping down the horrible vistas of the closes, which were swarming with dirty human life as some mouldy and half-decayed substance might swarm with insects;—vistas down alleys where sin, sorrow and poverty, drunkenness, all manner of sombre and sordid earthy circumstances had imbued the stone, brick and wood of the inhabitants, for hundreds of years. And such a multitude of children, too;—that was a most striking feature.[55]

The stink of such slum areas was for Hawthorne a manifest sign of a purposeless rotting away of human life. A 'redundant' population living without hope amidst such squalor and deprivation struck Hawthorne as not simply a social or political but a spiritual problem. We rightly associate the rise of science, with its associated law of intractable causality, with the loss of faith among nineteenth-century writers and intellectuals. This industrial, urban experience, with the inhabitants of the lower depths apparently irredeemably condemned to moral and physical destitution, also shook the foundations of faith. Such horror transcended social and political justice and called in question the existence of a loving God. The vast Liverpool asylums of orphaned and abandoned children—especially those pre-natally maimed by venereal disease—confronted Hawthorne with a test of faith even harsher than that posed by the determinist, Calvinist god of his American ancestors.

It is not in Scottish prose fiction but in poetry that such anxieties are given voice. Ironically the poet is called James Thomson. His *City of Dreadful Night* is the inverse of the energetic, optimistic prognostications of *The Castle of Indolence*. In that century the Scottish novel did not break out of the restraints Scott had placed on it. In R L Stevenson we see a gallant but failed attempt. As Edwin Muir has remarked:

> So one of the earliest ideas which must have been implanted in Stevenson's mind by universal suggestion was that story-telling was an idle occupation, and could be tolerated only as long as it remained so. He had before him, moreover, the example of his great countryman Scott, and he was probably too young, and too securely enclosed in national literary prejudice, to see that Scott's immense powers too were made idle by the general expectation of his countrymen that they should be idle.[56]

Much of Stevenson's talent was misused in adolescent adventure. In dealing with Scottish history he fitted it to Scott's deceitful paradigm of the evolution of commercial civilisation out of Highland barbarism.[57] He was, however, fascinated by the city. In part he dealt with this by either playing the bohemian or by writing about the detective who is the natural hero of this strange new urban world. More serious is *Dr Jeckyll and Mr Hyde*. Often analysed in Freudian terms the horror behind it seems more like a

Gothic variant of Carlyle's political nightmare that homicidal violence would erupt from deprivation. Hence that peculiarly sinister image of the house whose middle-class front faces into a working class street and whose back fronts a middle-class street. It is characteristic of the failure of Scottish literary nerve which lasted till the beginning of the twentieth century that Stevenson's masterpiece of social realism, *The Amateur Emigrant*, is a travel book dealing with the Atlantic and transcontinental train journey to California.[58] Even that, however, his father and friends suppressed. From Scott to Stevenson Scottish fiction almost entirely represents—compared to other national traditions—a sorry failure of nerve.

REFERENCES

1 Duncan Forbes 'The Rationalism of Sir Walter Scott', *The Cambridge Journal* VII, no. 1 October 1953, pp 20–35

2 'Summer', *The Seasons* (ed James Sambook) (Oxford 1981), p 126

3 *The Castle of Indolence* (Intro Blunden, ed Hardie) (London 1956), p 34

4 *Ibid.* p 43

5 *Ibid.* pp 44–6

6 *English Society in the Eighteenth Century* (London 1982)

7 *The Country and the City* (London 1975), pp 174–5

8 'Autumn', *The Seasons,* p 148

9 Quoted by Carl E Schorske 'The Idea of the City in European Thought: Voltaire to Spengler' in *The Historian and the City* (ed Handlin and Burchard) (New York 1966), p 97

10 'Of the Middle Station of Life' in *Essays Moral, Political and Literary* (Oxford 1963), p 580

11 'On Refinement in the Arts', p 278

12 *The Technological Society* (New York 1964), p 47

13 Lawrence Stone 'Social Control and Intellectual Excellence: Oxbridge and Edinburgh 1560–1983' in *Universities, Society and the Future* (ed Phillipson) (Edinburgh 1983), pp 3–30

14 *An Account of a Conversation Concerning the Right Regulation of Governments for the Common Good of Mankind, Selected Writings and Political Speeches* (ed David Daiches) (Edinburgh 1979), p 135

15 *Ibid.* pp 136–7

16 T S Eliot 'Was There a Scottish Literature?', *The Athenaeum* 1 August 1919, pp 680–1

17 Lewis Mumford's chapter 'Palaeotechnic Paradise: Coketown' in *The City in History* (London 1979), pp 508–48 remains the classic account of just how desperate conditions were

18 *Letters* (ed H J C Grierson), vol. XI (London 1932), p 128

19 *The Correspondence of George IV* (ed A Aspinall) (Cambridge 1938), p 539

20 *Castle Dangerous and Chronicles of the Canongate* (ed Andrew Lang) (Waverley Novels/Border Edition) XXIV (London 1899), pp 428–9

21 'The Rationalism of Sir Walter Scott', p 23

22 *Ibid.* pp 27–8

23 *Walter Scott,* Scottish Writers Series (Edinburgh 1982), p 18

24 *Scott and Society* (London 1981)

25   'Scott and Tradition', *Edwin Muir-Uncollected Scottish Criticism* (ed Andrew
     Noble) (London 1982), pp 209–10.
26   *Letters 1811–1814*, p 240
27   *Scott on Himself* (ed David Hewitt) (Edinburgh 1981), p 225
28   *Ibid.*
29   'Scott as Storyteller: An Essay in Psychobiography', *Scott Bicentenary Essays*
     (ed Alan Bell) (Edinburgh 1973), pp 87–99
30   See my 'Scott, Stevenson and the Scottish Historical Novel', *Robert Louis
     Stevenson* (ed Andrew Noble) (London 1983), pp 134–87
31   'The Rationalism of Sir Walter Scott', pp 31–2
32   *Rob Roy* (ed Andrew Lang) (Border Edition) IV (London 1906), pp 260–1
33   *Peter's Letters to his Kinsfolk* (ed William Ruddick) (Edinburgh 1977)
34   'The Idea of the City in European Thought', p 99
35   Roland Barthes 'The Great Family of Man', *Mythologies* (London 1983), p 101
36   See *Farm Servants and Labour in Lowland Scotland* (ed T M Devine) to be
     published by John Donald summer 1984
37   *Noctes Ambrosianae* (Edinburgh 1860), vol. I, pp 174–5
38   *Peter's Letters to his Kinsfolk*, p 183
39   *Ibid.* pp 61–2. *See also* pp 2–5
40   *Reminiscences* (London 1972), p 222
41   *The Collected Letters of Thomas and Jane Welsh Carlyle* (ed Sanders and
     Fielding), vol. 2, 1822–23 (Durham NC 1970), pp 245–6
42   Peter F Morgan, *Literary Critics and Reviewers in Early 19th-Century Britain*
     (London 1983)
43   *Selected Writings* (ed Alan Shelston) (London 1971), p 152
44   *Ibid.*
45   *Ibid.* pp 175–6
46   *Glasgow 1858: Shadow's Midnight Scenes and Social Photographs* (Glasgow
     1976)
47   *Ibid.* pp 20–1
48   *Ibid.* pp 56–7
49   *The English Notebooks of Nathaniel Hawthorne* (ed Randall Stewart) (New
     York 1962), p 344
50   *Ibid.*
51   *Ibid.* pp 535–6
52   *Ibid.* p 337
53   *Ibid.* p 329
54   *Ibid.* p 512
55   *Ibid.* p 535
56   'Robert Louis Stevenson' in *Edwin Muir-Uncollected Scottish Criticism,* p 229
57   'Scott, Stevenson and the Scottish Historical Novel', *op. cit.* pp 134–187
58   A new, illustrated edition of Stevenson's American travels, *From the Clyde to
     California,* edited and introduced by Andrew Noble, is to be published in 1985
     by Aberdeen University Press.

4

CHOICE AND CONSTRAINT: FURTHER PERSPECTIVES ON SOCIO-RESIDENTIAL SEGREGATION IN NINETEENTH-CENTURY GLASGOW WITH PARTICULAR REFERENCE TO ITS WEST END

Brian Dicks

The broad theme of this essay acknowledges a study by Pooley which focuses attention on some of the processes responsible for residential change and social differentiation in mid-Victorian Liverpool. In it he forwards a conceptual framework which views segregation, a major and ubiquitous feature of nineteenth-century industrialising cities, as the outcome of 'the interaction of those elements of choice and constraint which affected various aspects of residential location'.[1] In effect he isolates what Dyos and Reeder collectively referred to as 'centrifugal' and 'centripetal' forces, the former drawing 'the rich into airy suburbs' and the latter confining the 'poor in airless slums'.[2] Already apparent in London and in many of Britain's provincial cities during the early decades of the century, such socio-residential patterns were firmly established towards its end.

Contemporaries were fascinated, excited and often alarmed by the rapidity of nineteenth-century urban growth and also by what was one of its main concomitants, class segregation or class struggle which manifested itself most clearly at the extremes of society. Slums, in particular, attracted startling, sometimes sensational, accounts of their conditions and as the nineteenth century progressed the term 'suburbia' became increasingly associated with the flight from the worst parts of the city to areas of superior amenities including 'the pure breath of heaven.'[3] There is considerable evidence, official and otherwise, of the macro-dichotomies in London life and, as Best notes, 'the novels of Dickens were accepted by his contemporaries as extraordinarily faithful, in one mode or another, to the middle and lower class realities they represented'.[4] Ultimately, London's extreme residential polarity was subsumed under the descriptions East End and West End, the inhabitants of the former apparently 'knowing little of western districts other than from hearsay and report'. As John Richardson continues, 'there was little communication of sympathy between the respective classes by which the two ends of London were occupied. They differed in external appearance, clothes, pursuits and pleasures.'[5]

Britain's other large nineteenth-century cities also exhibited increasing socio-residential segregation and the progressive separation, for the more affluent classes at least, of workplace from residence. This has been fully demonstrated for mid-Victorian Liverpool which, like Leeds, Sheffield, Cardiff, Nottingham and Manchester, inspired graphic eye-witness accounts of their contemporary social patterns and problems. Speaking of Manchester in 1839, Canon Parkinson commented that 'there is no town in the world where distance between the rich and poor is so great or the barrier between them so difficult to be crossed. The separation between the different classes and the consequent ignorance of each other's habits and conditions are far more complete in this place than in any other country.'[6]

Highly significant as these macro-residential patterns were in the nineteenth-century city it would be misguided to accept too readily that extremes were the only spatial features of contemporary urban-social geography. Empirical studies have indicated that, in addition to affluent suburb and immigrant slum, the Victorian city was also characterised by a more subtle intermixing of groups and classes albeit, in many urban districts, marking a transitional phase in the formation of segregated areas on a broader canvas. This has been argued by Ward[7] in his work on Leeds, while areas of Victorian Liverpool,[8] when viewed at the local level, reflected significant variations in social standing. Such patterns are particularly relevant in the Scottish context where close residential association between diverse social elements was a traditional aspect of urban structure. Gordon's study of mid-Victorian Edinburgh,[9] emphasising the transitional nature of its social geography, illustrates how elements of the pre-nine-teenth-century urban pattern were retained within a re-organised economy and society. Similarly, Robb's work on Glasgow's Gorbals–Hutchesontown[10] area indicates the persistence of local sub-areas, some of which continued to harbour middle-class properties, despite, as the century progressed, its increasing working-class proportions. Gorbals, however, presents a complex case of an old centre that witnessed an important phase of middle-class speculative development which subsequently suffered from the malaise of in-migration and the penetration of other incompatible activities. It marks, therefore, a transitional period during which the competition of more attractive residential locations forced its 'genteel residents to seek the more guaranteed exclusiveness of Glasgow's growing West End.'[11]

THE SHOCK CITY

If Manchester, on account of its rapid growth and resultant slum problems, was regarded as England's first 'shock city', this perjorative title north of the Border fell unchallenged to Glasgow. Without exception, Scotland's expanding manufacturing towns and seats of commercial industry had nurtured an intimidating growth of social malaise, but Sir Archibald Alison had Glasgow firmly in mind when he commented that 'one side of the picture exhibits the elements of prosperity in unprecedented vigour amongst us, the other points not less clearly to a still more alarming augmentation of misery, pauperism and crime'.[12] Scotland's Victorian city *par excellence,* Glasgow had dramatically outpaced London with respect to both cities increasing shares in the respective population totals of England and Scotland. The city's expansion from its position as an old regional centre was assured with the development of substantial entrepot activities, the economic results of the Act of Union. With remarkable adaptability it responded to the collapse of old opportunities and the rise of new challenges. The tobacco trade provided the first impetus for growth but it was cotton textiles that, towards the end of the eighteenth century, created the manufacturing base for the subsequent burgeoning of the city.[13] The 1830s saw important developments in coal, iron, chemicals and engineering, activities which sustained Glasgow's growth when cotton faltered in 1847. The cumulative effects of such commercial-industrial cycles were demonstrated in the city's rapid population increase in which immigration, chiefly from rural Scotland and Ireland, played a leading role. By 1851 the city totalled some 375,000 inhabitants, a figure which made it one of Britain's largest provincial centres, demographically surpassed only by Manchester, Liverpool and Dublin.[14] From mid-century onwards its population rose from 443,000 in 1861 to 568,000 in 1871 and to 673,000 in 1881. During the century's last quarter it emerged as the 'Second City of the Empire' while in the Scottish context its 1891 population accounted for 20 per cent of the country's total, Glaswegians outnumbering the aggregate populations of Scotland's seven next largest settlements.

Hand in hand with economic vitality went social squalor and the emergence of Glasgow's notorious slums which, as the century progressed, threatened the material interests of the bourgeoise. It is not the purpose of this essay to discuss Victorian attitudes to slum formation and the plight of the lower classes. Suffice it to say that it varied from one of 'sentimental philanthropy', as Saunders[15] calls it, to one of disdain and total neglect, at least in the early decades of the century when, prior to national legislation, urban government was firmly in the hands of the town oligarchies. The philosophy and spirit of *laissez-faire* was seen as moulding social as well as economic life and to many industrial capitalists the underpriviledged classes were the victims of their own circumstances.[16] Even with the Reform Acts and the instigation of elected councils such attitudes were slow to change and there seems little doubt that for many, middle-class segregation was accompanied by a psychological abandonment of the lower classes, a prejudice that served to strengthen the barriers, real and perceived, between the social orders. Thus, for all its seeming whimsy, an extract from *A Lament of Glasgow Green*[17] which ran:

> The rich maun ha'e their West End Park,
> Wi pure and caller air
> But tho' the poor should choke in smoke
> The great folk dinna care.

. . . was basically an indictment not so much of physical segregation but of indifference on the part of the middle classes. If initial unconcern was indeed the middle-class norm, then it has to be interpreted as the desire, calculated or otherwise, for self preservation during an age when 'the threat of the slum' fully entered the 'consciousness of the suburb'.[18]

THE BEGINNINGS OF SEGREGATION

Although strongly articulated in Victorian times, the tendencies towards residential segregation on class lines were apparent in Glasgow from as early as the middle and later years of the eighteenth century. Essentially a commercial city, economic progress brought with it a substantial increase in the merchant class and it was the self-assured Tobacco Lords—the 'strutting grandees' as Worsdall[19] calls them—who were initially responsible for radical changes in thought and fashion. As Adams[20] affirms, the era of Georgian town planning, albeit piecemeal in conception and a pale equivalent of Edinburgh's New Town, was instituted by these commercial barons who spearheaded the move westwards from the old city centred around Glasgow Cross. By nineteenth-century standards the distances involved were minimal though the act of separating residence from business broke with tradition and instituted a movement that increased in scale and momentum as the city increased in size.

A mansion house and an estate was undoubtedly the seal of social success for both merchants and professional people, and in Glasgow, as elsewhere, the new demand was for *rus in urbe*[21] within easy distance of the business centre. The concept was essentially urban with the country confined to a garden and, if possible (though this became increasingly difficult) a view. In an age of ostentation, the elegant and fashionable Shawfield Mansion[22] (long demolished) was, without doubt, one of the most imposing dwellings in Glasgow's 'Tobaccoland' and one of the earliest examples of a Palladian urban villa in Britain. Built in 1717 on the north side of Trongate at the junction of what became Glassford Street, it was purchased in 1760 by John Glassford who owned large and extensive business enterprises on both sides of the Atlantic. The mansion was complete with three and a half acres of garden ornamentally laid out and abundantly provided with fruit trees. In 1792 the residence and grounds passed to William Horn, a builder who demolished the house and laid through its grounds a new street originally called Great Glassford Street. Large mansions were also erected in Virginia Street (opened in 1753) where traces of their earlier grandeur can still be seen. Provost Andrew Buchanan's house was situated between Ingram Street (1772) and Wilson Street, the initial extension to the town taking the form of new access ways leading to large residences.[23] Other early streets of the Georgian suburb were Jamaica (1760), Miller (1762), Queen (1765), Buchanan (1765), Howard (1769), Maxwell (1772) and Dunlop (1772), the majority perpetuating the names of city notables or overseas lands where many had made their fortunes. To the north elegant residences were also built around George Square on the lands of Ramshorn and Meadowflats.

A few merchants flaunted their wealth and prestige in estates and country mansions acquired some distance from the city centre in areas that a hundred years later were engulfed by the middle-class villas, terraces and institutional buildings that collectively came to characterise Glasgow's West End. The sites chosen, all contiguous to the sylvan valley of the Kelvin, were essentially rural, separated from the city, yet close enough to it to allow access without undue inconvenience if urgent business arose.[24] Robert Bogle Junior, successor to a great commercial dynasty made Gilmorehill his country retreat and in 1782 Patrick Colquhoun, another respected second generation Glasgow merchant and Lord Provost, bought 12 acres of land on the banks of the Kelvin and commissioned Robert Adam to design his mansion. Kelvingrove House was long regarded as one of the most beautiful country houses in southern Scotland.[25] Both these residences, however, post-dated Kelvinside House and North Woodlands House which were built in 1756 within ornamental and landscaped grounds. Yet the ability and, indeed, the desire to acquire such residences, thus securing what Devine[26] hints at as 'nouveaux riches' titles, rested with a small minority. Many merchants and professional people regarded sites as far west as the Kelvin as too isolated from Glasgow's city centre. In 1802 James McNayr's house on Woodland's Hill was nicknamed 'McNayr's Folly' by his contemporaries who saw it as an out of the way place from which to pursue business in the city.[27]

Yet the impact of these country estates was substantial. They were the scenes of splendid occasions where famous and influential people were received in elegant drawing rooms filled with the finest works of art that money could buy. Their prominent situation in an area of farms, cottages and rural industry prompted John Mayne[28] to poetically write in 1795:

> Now sirs, its wonderful to trace,
> How commerce has improved this place,
> Changing bare house room's narrow space
> And want of money,
> To seeds of elegance and grace
> And milk and honey.

In terms of the area's subsequent nineteenth-century speculative development these country estates formed an important stage in a process marked by the rapid sale and transference of land titles. The West End was seen to provide great potential for residential speculation, especially at a time when middle-class desires were firmly fixed westwards. Though the factors in its popularity are complex there seems little doubt that part, at least, of its attractiveness lay in the bid by the middle class to follow in the steps of earlier established social 'sets.'[29]

SUCCESSION AND SEGREGATION

To return to the city, however, the pattern and extent of Glasgow's Georgian suburbs is revealed on James Barry's map of 1782 and the character of this townscape has been described by a number of authors.[30] Here it might be said that this initial residential segregation, limited to the most affluent class, appears to have been mainly a reflection of substantial changes in fashion and taste associated with the Georgian era in general. As the nineteenth century arrived and advanced residential relocation became a more positive response to major changes in the city centre where land, reacting to pressures of changing economic organisation became increasingly specialised. Contemporary observers of the Victorian urban scene identified two interrelated processes stemming from what was a new regime in land values: succession and segregation.[31] With the increasing demand for space for non-residential purposes there emerged a more articulately specialised commercial core and the formation of a series of urban zones or districts which Engels informatively describes for Manchester in 1842. 'At its heart', he wrote, 'is a rather extended commercial district . . . consisting almost wholly of offices and ware-houses. Nearby the whole district is abandoned by dwellers and is lonely and deserted at night.' Surrounding it were 'unmixed working people's quarters stretching like a girdle averaging a mile and a half in breadth', and beyond lived 'the upper and middle bourgeoisie, the middle bourgeoisie in regularly laid out streets in the vicinity of the working quarters . . . the upper bourgeoisie in villas with gardens . . . in free, wholesome country air, in fine comfortable homes'.[32]

It cannot be claimed that Glasgow also typified what appears in Manchester to have been a mid-Victorian illustration of classic concentric zonal theory. There was, however, a rapid invasion of commerce into the city's Georgian extensions, a process that caused a bow-wave effect as the middle class sought residences to the west, in advance of the encroaching business tide with its inflationary impact on land and property values. The constraint exerted by early commercial colonisation of residential areas requires further investigation though it was apparent in George Square, short-lived as a middle-class suburb, and in the area beyond the West Port, whose streets were originally built for access to town houses. The business fervour of early nineteenth-century Glasgow is detailed in banking returns and in the often lengthy letters regularly sent by agents to head offices. Robert Moncrieff, Agent in Glasgow for the Royal Bank, wrote in 1802 that 'the building going on in and around Glasgow this summer is no less than £200,000—yet the population is growing more rapidly and the accommodation is scarce'.[33] By accommodation he seems to be referring to business as well as residential properties for much of his correspondence takes the form of practical advice to his bank which was searching for premises in which to expand.

Banks and other financial institutions were one of the major forms of business encroachment. In 1840, Andrew Buchanan's mansion in Virginia Street was demolished to make way for the Union Bank and no less than four other independent banks were to colonise this thoroughfare.[34] Buchanan Street suffered a similar fate. Developed in the last three decades of the eighteenth century as a street of self-contained residences, by the late 1820s the majority of these had been adapted for commercial purposes, shops and warehouses. As Worsdall notes,[35] the inauguration of the Argyle Arcade and the opening of the Royal Exchange and new offices of the Royal Bank in Exchange Square greatly boosted the street's commercial popularity. By the 1840s the nearby railway terminus at Queen Street had led to the conversion of adjacent dwellings to hotels and offices. The Bank of Scotland premises occupied the site of the demolished residences in George Square and was followed by the Merchant's House which had moved from cramped quarters in Hutcheson Street. Other banks and offices moved into St Vincent Place and commercial colonisation also reached Sauchiehall Street whose original farmland had been laid out with villas and terraces.

THE NEGATIVE ENVIRONMENT

Commercial encroachment, however, was but one factor in the growing pace of out-migration and segregation of the more affluent class. The deteriorating urban and social fabric of the old city has to be cited as a major contributory cause. The adjustment of the built environment, inherited from the pre-industrial era, to the requirements of the industrial age was fashioned by competition between working-class residential needs (greatly augmented by a massive influx of migrant labourers during the early decades of the nineteenth century) and the land use needs of industry, commerce and transport.[36] Together with the constraints imposed by the Scottish feuing system of land tenure (see below), scarcity contributed to the prevalence of high land values thereby encouraging the construction of high-density backland tenements and the creation of appalling living environments. Conditions in Glasgow's wynds, closes and vennels were graphically depicted by Symon:[37] 'I allude to the dense and motley community who inhabit the low districts of Glasgow, consisting chiefly of alleys leading out of High Street, the lands of Calton, but particularly in the closes and wynds which lie between Trongate and the Bridegate, the Saltmarket and Maxwell Street . . . I have seen degradation in some of the worst phases, both in England and abroad . . . but I did not believe until I visited Glasgow that so large an amount of filth, crime, misery and disease existed on one spot in any civilised country'. The wynds consisted of long, narrow lanes opening into courts surrounded by dwellings, mostly three-storeys high. These were sub-let 'to the lowest class of labourers or prostitutes or to lodging-house keepers (where) ten, twelve, and sometimes twenty persons of both sexes and of all ages sleep promiscuously on the floor in different degrees of nakedness. These places are, generally as regards to dirt, damp, and decay, such as no person of common humanity to animals would stable his horse in.'

Glasgow's nineteenth-century slum conditions are fully documented, not least as a result of the City Improvement Trust,[38] created in 1866 to tackle overcrowding and its attendant environmental issues. Contemporary with it was Thomas Annan's remarkable collection of photographs which portrayed startlingly the intolerable ghetto conditions. In addition, two important institutions, the Royal Infirmary and the University or Old College, occupied sites precariously close to some of the worst areas, and for academic and other reasons (which in the case of the University can only be attributed to a bid for self preservation) kept a watchful eye on the mounting social problem. Quoting from official papers, Kellett[39] describes why, by the 1840s, Principal and Professors were anxious to move: 'The area around the College had become appallingly decayed and overcrowded. The evening law classes had been abandoned because of the nightly pandemonium of screams and policemen's rattles, and the inexpediency of bringing young men through the parade of women of the town in front of the College entrance.' The adjacent area, in which the students lodged, included the notorious Vennel and Havannah slums, 'inhabited by rag dealers, thieves, prostitutes and receivers of stolen goods'. In an era long before the social sciences gained academic respectability, the University, though engulfed by an authentic sociological laboratory, ultimately succumbed to middle class trends and moved to new premises in the West End.

Opened in 1794, the Infirmary remained and was inevitably involved in the succession of epidemics that bred in the airless warrens, polluted streams and stagnant sewage. One of the most constant hazards of Victorian urban life was exposure to infectious diseases and mortality statistics at ward level demonstrate a simple relationship between high-density living and deaths from such virulent scourges as typhus and cholera.[40] Glasgow's drinking dens were also notorious breeding grounds and contemporary accounts suggest a link between alcoholism and infectious disease, the latter showing greater prevalence amongst Irish labourers. The cholera epidemic of 1832 is well documented and, together with others in 1848, 1849 and 1853–4, collectively led to over 10,500 deaths.[41] Children, destined to an environment of dirt, ignorance and malnutrition, were particularly susceptible to infection, falling victim to such diseases as scarlet fever, measles, diptheria, smallpox and pulmonary complaints. Glasgow's crude mortality rates rose from 1:41 in 1822 to 1:30 in 1828 to 1:24 in 1837. It hovered around this level for much of the remainder of the nineteenth century and on the death of Queen Victoria it still remained as high as 1:50.[42]

Although the virulence of disease demonstrated a direct relationship with overcrowding and squalor, cholera and typhus, in particular, were no respecters of class. In congested areas where only short distances, or even storeys, had separated the extremes of society, exposure to infection was an imperilment to all. Glasgow's 1832 cholera pestilence initially claimed its victims largely from the ranks of the poor but spread, in its second wave, to infect all classes and neighbourhoods.[43] Without doubt, aspirations for social advancement and the desire to locate in a residentially respectable area were significantly tempered by the threat of exposure to the 'filth diseases' and also to the gamut of 'nuisances' that plagued the University. Hence, it was commented that 'families who were formerly content to live in a flat of a house in the old town, have now handsome self-contained houses in new parts of the town'.[44] Pagan similarly noted that 'domiciles which last century formed the cosy retreats of city clergymen, physicians and merchants are now often tenanted by pickpocket and prostitute'.[45]

CHOICE AND CONSTRAINT

With the growing middle-class disaffection with the city centre in terms of intrusive land-users and environmental hazards, the attraction of alternate suburban locations, free of squalor, grime and congestion, might appear so obvious as to be undeserving of more than passing recognition. There is a grave danger, however, in erecting for the Victorian middle class an all pervading reason for residential relocation. As modern analogies indicate, the decision to move residence could not have been arrived at without first some considerable thought, nor for that matter was it a process that affected large groups simultaneously. In Gorbals—Hutchesontown, for example, many middle-class families operated an alternative strategy to segregation by coming to terms, at least for a time, with declining urban standards. Here the lowering of socio-economic aspirations were compensated by the ease of access to Glasgow's commercial core, proximity to the latter, rather than income constraints, being the main determinant of this persistent middle-class enclave.[46]

Viewing residential mobility in terms of a decision-making behavioural model, Brown and Moore[47] conveniently subdivide the process into the desire and determination to move, and the search for a new residence. The former, they argue, is a product of stress generated by disharmony between a household's needs, expectations and aspirations on the one hand, and its actual housing conditions and environmental setting on the other. From even a cursory study of the works of nineteenth-century novelists and other observers of the contemporary scene it is not a particularly difficult task to build up a picture of middle-class aspirations. The latter might be subsumed as the strive for respectability and the endeavours of those who had acquired such a status to preserve an exclusiveness which could best be achieved through socio-residential segregation in suburban settings.

No less than the situation today, the search for a new residence was a complex procedure and involved such processes as the specification of criteria for evaluating residences, the search for those which satisfied such criteria and the final choice of a new residence. Judging from nineteenth-century property advertisements dwelling amenities, environmental quality, the social composition of neighbourhoods and accessibility to various suburban facilities, were among the more frequently used criteria. According to Best's generalisations, 'a villa, detached for preference, in a private estate, became the rich mid-Victorian town dweller's ideal. . . . Semi-detached villas were the next best thing to wholly detached ones. . . . Between the less pretentious sort of semi-detached houses and the unabashed terrace, there was no significant difference in either social or economic terms. . . . Once below the carriage owning or carriage suggesting level . . . it became largely a matter of geographical chance and personal choice whether a semi-detached or a terraced house was taken. The dearer the land, the likelier a terraced house was to provide the quantity and kind of rooms required by the more stylish kind of respectability.'[48] Such an income-based model more neatly applies to English Victorian cities, although it is not entirely without relevance in explaining Scottish middle-class house preferences. Many of Glasgow's West End architects, however, not least Alexander Thomson, housed upper-middle-class clients in villas and terraces indiscriminately, but it was the latter form of residential building, splendid in style and scale, that predominated in the area. In all, no more than 160 villas were built in the West End, approximately half in Kelvinside, 50 on and around Partickhill and 25 in Dowanhill.[49]

Although individual preferences undoubtedly played an important role in the search procedure these cannot be divorced from wider decisions that on the one hand aided, but on the other limited, available choice. The idea that middle-class suburbanites, freed from the exigencies of poverty, had more freedom to live the lives they chose than those below them on the social scale lies far from reality. The concept of respectability itself greatly limited this apparent freedom and, as Thompson[50] has noted for Hampstead, the 'powerful urge for people of like condition to want to live in the same neighbourhood with their kind, to decline to be mixed up with their social inferiors' significantly reduced relocation choice. In more tangible terms the vagaries of the housing market,[51] reflecting sudden upward surges and downswings in land prices and building cycles, substantially controlled the scale and character of nineteenth-century suburbanisation frustrating middle-class objectives of finding the right property, at the right price and, importantly, at the right time. Hence, housing availability, social aspirations and the resulting need to locate in a 'respectable area' effectively reduced choice as much as poverty did for the lower classes. Market manipulation by land and property speculators was an important determinant of housing choice, a fact that has led many to argue that even among the most affluent, few residential location decisions were completely unconstrained.[52]

LANDOWNERSHIP AND SPECULATION

A large body of literature has discussed and assessed, from a number of standpoints, the role of the landowner and property speculator in shaping the character of Victorian cities, particularly the middle-class suburbs. Rodger[53] has stressed the landowner's ability to determine the supply and demand of building land through the partial and controlled release of sites for residential and other development. Such manipulations were most apparent in districts opened up, or likely to be opened up for transport improvements, for enhanced accessibility to central areas greatly inflated land price. Occasionally, through patronage and political leverage, the same landowners were able to influence projected transport routes and, accordingly, could determine precisely who the beneficiaries would be. Equally, however, many landowners were belligerent against transport developments which they saw as threats to the quietude and social exclusiveness of suburban areas. In Glasgow, no less than in other Victorian cities, varying shades of enthusiasm for the railways can be observed amongst landowners who also, for various reasons, welcomed or resisted the trams with as much vigour.[54]

The grip of the landowner on the suburbanisation process has been seen as a function of estate size, the contention being that the larger the land-holding, the greater the monopoly of control exercised on development and the greater the prospect that it would be comprehensively planned at the outset and to have its character maintained thereafter by the enforcement of covenants. Such estates were more likely to house middle-class residents, whereas working-class neighbourhoods were more likely to grow up in districts characterised by small and fragmented ownership.[55] The contrast between London's high-status West End, developed on large, prestigious estates, and the low-status East End, which colonised small landholdings, is usually held as evidence of this major role of landownership in the suburban process. Numerous provincial examples might also be cited, not least the powerful influence of the Dukes of Newcastle on Nottingham's Park Estate[56] and that of the Lords Calthorpe who turned Edgbaston[57] into an 'aristocratic' Victorian suburb whose renown extended far beyond the confines of Birmingham. Whereas it cannot be denied that the imposition of a master plan by large landowners accounted for the high social tone of many nineteenth-century suburbs it has also been argued that socio-residential patterns owed as much, if not more, to forces such as topography, general environmental conditions and the fashionable desire of the affluent to vacate the city centre. Cannadine[58] suggests that had London's landowning pattern been reversed the overall character of class segregation in the capital, if less coherent, would still have evolved. In fact, there are examples in London and many provincial cities of socially homogeneous middle class areas that were the collective result of unplanned, piecemeal embourgeoisement of small, but contiguous land-holdings. Hampstead was never singly owned or controlled, yet it provides, in the words of Thompson 'as near perfect a working model of single class residential zoning as one can expect to encounter over such a large area as 2,500 acres'.[59]

The middle-class suburbanisation of Glasgow's West End partly follows the Hampstead pattern though a more valid comparison might be made with Sheffield's western suburbs[60] where architectural as well as social consistency combined to produce a dramatic middle-class adjunct to its central area. The original pattern of Glasgow's estates, as Kellett[61] notes, was substantially determined during the Reformation. City and surroundings, however, had no exact equivalent of the landed aristocracy or gentry of the type common to many major cities south of the Border. The possible exception was the Maxwell family whose lands south of the Clyde were laid out from the mid nineteenth century in parkland and villas constituting the nucleus of the prosperous middle-class suburb of west Pollokshields. Its development in relation to the grounds and residence of Pollok House was similar in concept to that instituted at Edgbaston and Nottingham's Park Estate. Glasgow's West End, in marked contrast, totalled some 1,250 acres and, at the time of suburban encroachment was divided between 23 different freeholdings greatly varying in size (Figure 1). Some of the smallest, like Ashfield and Westbank, were scarcely over 3 acres, whereas

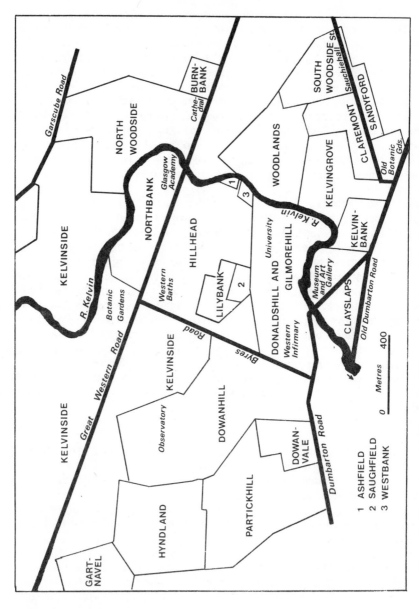

Figure 1   The pattern of Glasgow's West End estates and the sites of the area's principal institutions.

the largest, the combined property of Kelvinside and Gartnavel accounted for 516 acres. Its nearest rival in size was Dowanhill (around 100 acres) but the majority fell within the 10–30 acre range.[62]

As noted, eighteenth-century merchants, newly rich from overseas trade, had acquired lands and estates to the west of the city. These properties, or portions of them, passed quickly between a succession of owners and by the 1830s were mainly in the hands of speculative solicitors, builders and land agents. Acquisition and exchange continued for much of the century and towards its end it was reported that 'large syndicates (were) eagerly buying up land in districts opened up, or likely to be opened up, by the tramway system'.[63] Although realising the financial potential of their lands, restricted capital reserves prevented proprietors from emulating the grander speculative adventures of some of their English counterparts. The provisions of Scottish law, however, offered significant inducements to place land in the hands of entrepreneurs thus providing landowners both with an initial capital sale sum and a fixed annual payment, or feu.[64] The latter existed as a type of nominal land rent and though the terms of some feu contracts provided for its subsequent cancellation on payment of an agreed lump sum (usually 21 times the annual feu), more often than not it remained as an instalment in perpetuity. Such a system placed Scottish land values higher than those for England and Wales for building contractors were required to meet not only the current market price for land but the feu payment also. The value of the latter was legally set in the original sale document and it could not be reviewed again; consequently it tended to be stiff in relation to the initial value of the property and was invariably set high enough to take account of future inflation. These legal and financial constraints, as well as having repercussions on the type of residences built, also offer some explanation for the lagging nature of many building projects. Developers frequently operated on a hand to mouth basis, building (rarely no more than ten houses a year), selling and re-investing their profits in a speculative environment characterised by a succession of bankruptcies, sequestrations, trust foundations, reversions and sudden flight.[65] The pages of the *Glasgow Herald* are filled with reports of the financial troubles and disasters that commonly overtook Victorian speculators.

Not technically considered as part of the West End proper, but marking an important stage in middle-class westward colonisation, the development of the Blythswood Estate serves to illustrate the perils of early-nineteenth-century speculative building.[66] Its owners, the enlightened and strong-minded Campbells, were quick to realise the financial potential of their steep-sided drumlin land lying north of St Vincent Street, west of Renfield Street and within walking distance of George Square. A feuing plan was prepared to control development which was to follow a rigid grid-iron pattern similar to that of Garnet Hill, another drumlin site on Blythswood land north of Sauchiehall Street. The Glasgow Building Company purchased part of the northern flank of Blythswood Hill in 1800 and laid out what was to become Bath Street, named after baths built in 1804 by William

Harley, the estate's principal early speculator. Running into financial difficulties his affairs were taken over in 1814 by trustees who also went bankrupt. In 1816 many of the feus passed to the Garden family but they too were put in the hands of the trustees in 1826. Slowly, however, the hill was colonised as an elegant middle-class enclave centred on Blythswood Square, but even before it was fully built up its close proximity to the city centre led to the encroachment of non-residential buildings and functions, a process that was essentially a continuation of the previously noted CBD expansion. In this also, Blythswood provides an informative model of the suburbanisation process. Here the middle class again felt themselves under attack and once their *cordon supérieur* was breached they retreated to establish new bastions of exclusiveness farther out in Glasgow's West End.

In addition to the high price of land, the burden of the feu and the problems of non-residential encroachment, the difficulties faced by many speculators were often compounded by the clauses superiors included in the initial sale contracts. These were primarily a means of controlling the type and style of residential building and usually specified the maximum number of storeys and the minimum number of rooms to be provided in each house.[67] Some further stipulated the quality and type of building materials to be employed. By these means high-density working-class dwellings or commercial uses could be restricted or completely renegated in an effort to control and maintain high status development, thus enhancing the values of as yet undeveloped sites. Such measures were equally beneficial in attracting the right kind of buyer who sought some assurance that his residence would not be outflanked by speculative development of an inferior quality or the general area be penetrated by congested transport lines that would threaten its environmental exclusiveness.

The convictions of Mathew Montgomerie and partners about the status of their Kelvinside estate, shrewdly purchased in 1839, fully illustrates the way in which owners controlled and fashioned middle-class suburbs. 'From the first it was resolved . . . to make the suburb . . . the best residential district of the city'[68] and Montgomerie's implicit belief was that only the finest class of terraces and villas should be built along Great Western Road, fully opened in 1840 as 'the handsomest thoroughfare in Glasgow'. Montgomerie flatly refused to even consider the building of a road which would link the estate with Partick, maintaining that the latter was 'designed to be the workshop of Glasgow'. As Simpson notes,[69] feu charters granted for Kelvinside detailed not only the style and character of buildings but also specified every minor detail such as the width and quality of footpaths, the nature of shrubbery and the type of gas lamps. The owners had initially favoured the construction of villas, each costing not less than £2,000 and having no more than three storeys, though they could have a tower, an architectural feature freely developed. The estate, however, provides another example of the slow process of feuing, a fact explained as much by the constraints imposed by the owners on prospective builders as by its distance from the city centre. But access was important and when transport was improved, and important institutions gravitated to the area, the district became one where 'the spacious, opulent atmosphere of Western Glasgow (was) most apparent'.[70]

To conclude this section it can be noted that the feuars and builders were anything but free agents being subjected on the one hand to the dictates of superiors and on the other to the expectations of middle-class buyers. Hence it is important to view the quality Victorian suburb, in Glasgow and elsewhere, as the material manifestation of a complex of lofty ideals, desires and decisions that were inevitably tempered by the prosaic financial tenets that governed supply and demand. The solvents in this speculative game were those with the economic means and the social aspirations to vacate the central urban area and settle westwards. Importantly, however, these middle classes had still to be enticed and convinced of the excellence, indeed superiority, of a residential site both in terms of the accommodation it provided and its general environmental setting. Competition between respective housing speculators was keen, for the middle-class house hunter could afford to choose between several rival developments. To attract buyers emphasis was given, in addition to the architectural character and domestic amenities of residences, to such potential advantages as environmental quality, the proximity to institutions and leisure facilities, accessibility and the general social composition of neighbourhoods. In other words it paid those who catered for middle-class demand to satisfy requirements beyond the provision of affluent residences. Although such attractions can be regarded as the main suburban 'pull' factors which effectively summarise middle-class residential expectations, it is important to stress that individual households most certainly graded and valued them differently. Yet the detailed attention given to the development and promotion of these suburban assets produced in Glasgow's West End an extensive middle-class district which, despite its piecemeal and tardy growth, was characterised by a remarkable degree of physical uniformity and social cohesion, an ideal suburb, in fact, 'for nineteenth century grandees aspiring to health, gentility and seclusion'.[71]

ENVIRONMENTAL QUALITY

The exploitation of topographical advantages underlay the successful embourgeoisement of a number of classic Victorian suburbs and has prompted authors to argue the case for topographic determinism,[72] especially as many middle-class areas were situated west of urban-industrial concentrations where prevailing winds effectively carried 'noxious vapours' in the opposite direction. In this respect Glasgow's West End differed little from Headingley in Leeds, Edgbaston, Nottingham's Park Estate, Hampstead or Sheffield's western suburbs, all of which were characterised by higher altitudinal position in clean-air environments. Glasgow advertisements, either for feuing or house sales, continually stress the amenity value of 'open, airy and agreeable locations', conditions that also proved attractive to institutions (see below) which moved westwards from old sites in the city centre. When, for example, Gartnavel Royal Hospital (the lunatic asylum) moved from its old home in Parliamentary Road to a western site—described as 'a pleasant retreat for the insane'—the 'purity of the air' was seen as being beneficial to 'the bodily and mental health of the patients'.[73]

Another common component of advertisements was the emphasis placed on such elements as local scenery and attractive views, especially if they incorporated sylvan features. The West End's drumlin hills, rising to 200 feet, commanded extensive vistas southwards over the Howe of Clyde and, in places, over the wooded valley of the Kelvin. Already selected as the sites of earlier mansions, a hundred years later they were crowned by middle-class villas and terraces but, unlike Blythswood whose drumlin features were completely sacrificed to a rigid grid-iron street pattern, the building projects on many West End hills fully incorporated topographic detail into their designs. The results were some unique townscapes skilfully blending architecture with topography. As Muir wrote:[74] 'Over the wide valley where a river (the Kelvin) winds headlands and cliffs of stone rise on either hand. . . . Now trees appear screening terraces, and through them warm lights shine through open doors that mean the West End the world over.'

The initial residential developments of Partickhill and Dowanhill were contour-inspired, the latter being described as one of 'beautiful . . . villas that sit among trees'.[75] These were aimed at the wealthiest section of the bourgeoisie and were followed by impressive terraces of which Crown Terrace and Crown Circus, completed in 1860, offered expansive views over the Clyde and towards Gilmorehill, respectively. But the masterpiece in terms of hill-top composition was the Park Circus—Park Terrace complex (Figure 2) on Woodlands Hill, the brainchild of Charles Wilson. It provides an excellent illustration of how topography was used to enhance residential character and has been described as one of the finest examples of Victorian city planning. The hill-top was covered by two alignments of buildings— one inward-facing (Park Circus) and surrounding an ornamental garden and the other looking outwards (Park Terrace) over what was then the West End (Kelvingrove) Park and beyond it the Howe of Clyde. The Woodlands Hill development continued until about 1870 and its impact is recorded by *Senex* (alias Robert Reid), the popular reviewer and commentator of the local scene for the *Glasgow Herald*: 'Woodland's Hill and its environs . . . have become of great interest, the aspect of these formerly rural spots being now entirely changed and the locality at present forming the urban places of residence of our fashionable folk, whose elegant mansions are rearing up their heads on every side with magical rapidity.'[76]

The approaches to the Woodlands area were enhanced by developments on adjoining estates which also made full use of natural features to enhance environmental quality. South Woodside occupied the gentler slopes of Woodlands Hill and, as its name suggests, had been the fringe of a wooded area stretching from South Woodside, through Woodlands itself to North Woodlands. Sections of mature trees were preserved to form a central park serving Woodside Terrace, Woodside Place and Woodside Crescent (Figure 3). The adjacent Claremont estate followed South Woodside in its

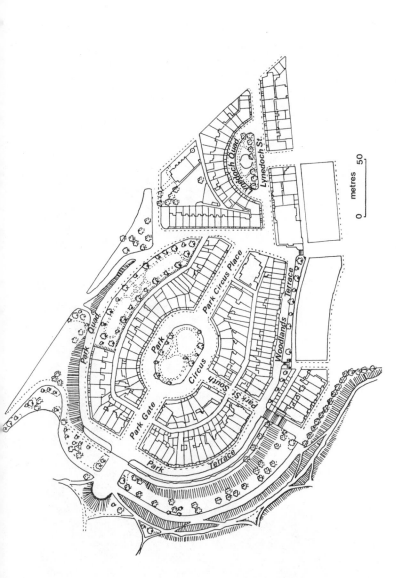

Figure 2   Charles Wilson's Park Circus development made full use of the topography of Woodlands Hill to produce a unique piece of nineteenth-century urban planning.

Figure 3 Woodlands Crescent in the 1840s centred around its private pleasure gardens.

development and included Royal Crescent, one of a series of fashionable terraces that were built along the western extension of Saughy Haugh Road 'which for its sylvan charms had long been the favourite promenade of the beauty and fashion of the city'. Many West End terraces, crescents, circuses and places were laid out in relation to gardens which attempted to either preserve or artificially create sylvan scenic outlooks within their midsts. It is reported that 'in places of trees (there are) plots of *pro indiviso* pleasure grounds with shrubs and gravel walks',[77] features that remain to regularly punctuate the West End townscape where 'gardens' is a particularly common descriptive suffix in local street names.

Yet, important as hilly and scenic situations were to middle-class segregation, such an environmental response has to be viewed in the context of a broader set of locational determinants. The West End's drumlin hills were no more appropriate for working-class housing than they were for industry and throughout the nineteenth century it was more rational to place both on low-lying land near lines of communication, leaving higher ground to the more affluent income groups. As large-scale industry sought sites beyond the crowded city, complexes of factories and tenements spread to such districts as Possil and Maryhill in the north-west and westward along both banks of the Clyde where shipbuilding and engineering brought concentrations of working-class housing to Partick, Whiteinch and Govan. Similarly, in Glasgow's East End there was a dense working-class build-up based on rapid industrialisation. Kellett[78] has cited the landowners who were more concerned with industrial than residential development, thereby welcoming the interest railway companies were showing in their lands. Houldsworth and Dixon, for example, were quick to realise the advantages improved communications would bring to their Clydeside lands at Anderston. In addition to the general areal pattern of segregation, therefore, there was also a significant zoning that was topographically determined, one aptly summarised by Muir who described Woodlands Hill as having 'the mansions of the wealthy who live in affluence on the silver clouds that hang over Govan'.[79]

THE INSTITUTIONS

Although the appeal of location and topography, as well as the laying out of wide tree-shrouded roads, were powerful forces in attracting middle-class tenants, the arrival of societies and institutions and the encouragement of churches and other amenities were factors that further served to popularise the West End and enhance its lofty social tone. Wilson's Free Church College (later Trinity) and the adjacent College Church added both architecturally and socially to the prestige of Woodlands Hill, while further west other institutions crowned the tops of drumlins or moved to locations that were environmentally attractive. This institutional colonisation both led and followed middle-class settlement and speculators lost few opportunities to emphasise the advantages they brought to the area. Two important societies, migrants from sites formerly closer to the city centre, arrived in the West End in 1841–2. The Glasgow Astronomical Institution[80] had been founded in 1760 and in 1810 a camera obscura and solar microscope, available to the interested public, occupied a site on Garnet Hill. But with the spread of industry to Maryhill, Possil and the canal locations of Port Dundas, the old observatory struggled with problems of a smoke-ladened atmosphere. This prompted its move to Dowanhill where, stated the *Glasgow Herald,* the 'plain, substantial edifice stands on an eminence commanding an extensive view'.[81]

In close proximity of the Observatory was the new site of the Botanic Gardens also anxious for a clean air environment and sylvan surroundings.[82] Its beginnings may be said to date from 1705 when a Physic Garden was established for teaching purposes in the grounds of the Old College in High Street. As an exclusive middle-class amenity, however, the gardens were founded on 15 May 1817, on the initiative of Thomas Hopkirk, an influential Glasgow merchant. Financed by shareholders and granted a Royal Charter in 1818, the site was at Sandyford at the west end of Saughy Haugh Road. As the city expanded westwards the attractiveness of its situation quickly deteriorated and by the 1830s atmospheric pollution was adversely affecting the growth of plants. In 1839 the Sandyford site, purchased for £1,000, was sold for £12,000 which more than financed the acquisition of a large 21-acre site in Kelvinside, Montgomerie and partners recognising the presence of a prestigious park-like garden as a major enticement for feuars and property developers. Although condemned by many for its exposure and heavy clay soils, the new site was good from the landscape point of view and importantly, the ground was 'completely rural (and) far removed from any public works which in any other quarter would have rendered the atmosphere too impure for healthy vegetation'.[83] The move, which included the transference of plants and the original range of greenhouses, was completed by April 1842.

The Botanic Gardens prepared the way for the first residential terraces to be erected on the Kelvinside Estate. In 1845 (although twenty years elapsed before its completion) work began on Windsor (later Kirklee) Terrace adjacent to the gardens to which it was given its own entrance. Another of Wilson's showpiece designs, it was a terrace whose ornate Florentine-Renaissance style put elegance before profit and fully illustrates the quality of residences the owners specified for their lands. Opposite, Kew Terrace (the first of the grand terraces on the south side of Great Western Road) and Grosvenor Terrace (built between 1855 and 1858 as a speculative venture of Thomas Philip) also gained substantially from their proximity to the gardens. When two of the latter's identical Venetian-Renaissance house units were offered for sale in 1858 the advertisement, albeit with some speculative licence, reads: 'This magnificent terrace . . . is the finest range of buildings in Great Britain, being designed after the most palatial style of architecture, placed in the most salubrious situation and commanding the whole range of the Royal Botanic Gardens, which it directly fronts and overlooks, with the umbrageous woods of Kelvinside beyond.'[84]

The presence of the gardens, the Observatory and the Gartnavel Asylum, all accessible from Great Western Road, led to a further succession of lavish and independently styled terraces along this thoroughfare's southern side—Belhaven, Great Western, Lancaster, Devonshire (Devonshire Gardens) and Marlborough (Devonshire Terrace). Competition between architects to design what could be regarded as the grandest collective edifice was rife, and for many the title goes to Alexander Thomson's Great Western Terrace (1867–9) in which attention to Scottish tradition allowed him to successfully conceal the separateness of the large included residences within a single monumental design set back from the road and reached at either end by flights of grand steps. Such terraces were complemented by those on the north side of Great Western Road, though here (but not until after 1869) villas were more characteristic, particularly along what was originally Kelvinside Gardens. The most grandiloquent palazzo was Carlston (now St Mungo's Academy Former Pupil's Centenary Club)[85] built in 1877 for James Marshall (an ironmaster) to the designs of James Boucher.

Another West End institution responsible for quickening the pace of residential development was the University whose towering mock-medieval edifice, the design of George Gilbert Scott, was the product of one of the largest building projects in Victorian Scotland. Work began on the Gilmorehill site in 1866 and four years later the University moved from its ancient quarters in the old town to an environment considered 'more in keeping with the middle-class backgrounds of its students'.[86] A firm offer by the Glasgow Railway Company in 1863 to purchase the High Street site gave the institution the necessary capital to purchase the 43 acres of Gilmorehill, together with the adjoining 5 acres of Donaldshill which in 1881 became the home of the Western Infirmary, the University's teaching hospital. Significantly, £81,000 was paid for the collective purchases, a massive price increase on the £8,500 for which the Bogle family had acquired the land in 1800. The main quadrangle of the University was laid out on the site of Gilmorehill House which had been demolished two years previously.

Although the area had been residentially developing prior to its move, the University provided great building impetus, especially on lands to the north and east—the Hillhead Estate and its small acolytes, Lilybank and Saughfield. Hillhead had started as a garden suburb but by mid-century villa construction was replaced by terraces and tenements along a rectilinear street pattern similar to that of Blythswood rather than the freer developments occurring on lands surrounding it. Most of the residences were of a high class, though some bordering the Kelvin and others encroaching towards the University northwards from Partick Cross along Byres Road were definitely down market. Feeling over this intrusion ran high, an anonymous commentator describing them as 'a string of very common houses which are anything but an ornament to the locality'.[87] Working-class housing in the heart of the West End, however, was extremely limited; rents restricted tenants to those in higher paid employment who were thus able to better themselves by moving out of the more congested areas of the city. Here it might be noted that it was not until the end of the century that tenement building was taken seriously in the West End, and even then (as now) residents disclaimed such a description of their properties. Hyndland, recently declared a conservation area, became the first all-tenement district, most of it built between 1898 and 1910. Its dwellings were of exceptionally high quality as an advertisement in the *Glasgow Herald* for 1908 indicates. It describes some of the smaller properties in York (now Novar) Drive as '. . . beautifully finished, high class new two and three room and kitchen houses (having) granite columns at entrances, large parlours, sculleries, light bathrooms, electric light fittings, ranges with tiled surrounds, polished mahogany mirrored mantelpieces (and) art tiled interiors'.[88] In this later, but socially conforming addition to the West End 'the ultimate in luxury', as Worsdall[89] comments, 'seems to have been achieved'.

RECREATIONAL AND ANCILLARY AMENITIES

Glasgow's West End suburbanites were both attracted by, and responsible for, the growth of recreational and other amenities—schools, retail establishments and a plethora of churches—that collectively helped to fashion what became a socially mature middle-class enclave. Parks and gardens played important roles in the area's private and public leisure activities. The tree-lined grounds that occupied the centres of most residential developments were strictly the domains of the 'key to the garden' residents whose houses overlooked them. Fenced and locked by gates, a situation that still prevails, they were the places for family promenades and picnics, for infant-minding and children's games. By mid-century, however, public parks had become the object of deliberate desire and in 1850 the residents and developers of Sandyford and the terraces along Saughy Haugh Road petitioned the City to provide a 'Queen's Park in the West' as an added amenity for the locality.[90] Agreement was eventually reached and in 1854 the 28-acre Kelvingrove Estate was purchased as the nucleus of the West End (Kelvingrove) Park which was later increased to 51 acres by the addition of portions of contiguous estates. Sir Joseph Paxton, designer of London's Crystal Palace and Glasgow's Queen's Park south of the Clyde, was invited to lay out the new pleasure ground along with Charles Wilson who successfully landscaped it with the unbuilt-on sections of Woodlands Hill.

Centrally situated to serve a number of West End neighbourhoods, the park was an immediate success and offered strong competition to the Botanic Gardens which, in addition to its scientific interest, was also, like its predecessor (Figure 4), promoted as a pleasure garden available to all who cared to pay the entrance fee. Initially the garden had been open only to vested members, their families and University students of botany. In a bid to meet heavy running costs admission was subsequently granted to annual subscribers, although the substantial fee—one guinea in 1842—largely limited its use to the middle class. Non-members were admitted on Saturdays on the payment of one shilling (a sum that also guaranteed

Figure 4 The Old Botanic Gardens advertised as a 'fashionable place to resort'.

exclusiveness) and, as an afterthought (perhaps a sop to the underprivi-leged), on certain days the gates were 'thrown open to the working classes on the payment of one penny each'.[91]

In addition to the ranges of glasshouses, trees, lawns and flower beds, the garden also acquired the Kibble Palace which hosted weekly concerts and 'musical promenades'. This huge glass-domed conservatory, 471 feet in circumference, had begun life attached to Coulport House on Loch Long, the home of John Kibble, a Paisley engineer. In 1871 it was presented to the City as an art gallery and concert hall but found its home in the gardens. When opened to the public on 20 June 1873, it was grandiloquently des-cribed as 'The Kibble Crystal Art Palace, newest and most magnificent hall for music or place for public speaking in Scotland, calculated to accom-modate upwards of 6,000 persons and containing outstanding picturesque mossery, rare plants, cases of the most celebrated specimens of ancient and modern statuary, and busts of persons eminent in science, literature and art'.[92]

Yet despite attempts to promote it as 'the fashionable place of resort,'[93] by 1887 the financial position of the gardens had grown so precarious that the directors believed it would only be a matter of years before it would have to close. It was the annexation of Kelvinside to the City and the transference of the gardens to the Parks Department (which also acquired its debts) that saved it. There can be little doubt that had the gardens been closed its land would have been feued to developers and this part of the West End would have lost much of its urban character.[94] Ironically, the rapid development of Kelvinside, itself partly the product of proximity to the gardens, was also responsible for the latter's decline for suburbanisation affected the site in much the same way as it had at Sandyford. Another factor appears to have been its staid character which was disparagingly described as 'pure West End, for Kelvinside encompasses it behind and before'.[95] In other words the gardens for some were 'far too respectable', one critic in 1887 being moved to suggest (no doubt to shock the Kelvinside establishment) that its image should become more worldly and 'be given over to the vulgar' as Glasgow's equivalent of Tivoli or Coney Island.[96]

Bath establishments were another of the West End's leisure features. The Western Baths in Cranworth Street was built to serve the Hillhead, Dowanhill and Kelvinside neighbourhoods while another in Arlington Street presumably catered for Woodlands Hill. Both housed large bath ponds and a complex of dressing-rooms, but of the two the Western Baths was the most prestigious having separate recreation rooms for smokers and non-smokers and a Turkish Bath which was its showpiece. Annual fees were high in order to preserve a middle-class membership.

The number of churches built in the West End during the course of the nineteenth century is legion. They catered for all denominations except Roman Catholics. Many had been forced to migrate westwards in pursuit of their membership. An important acquisition was St Mary's Scottish Episcopal Church in Great Western Road, which, significantly, became the episcopal cathedral for the entire city. Important schools were also built to serve the needs of the West End. In 1866 Glasgow Academy, a private school for boys moved to the old Holm Meadow site at Kelvinbridge. This was followed in 1878 by Park School for boys (later a girl's school) whose site in Lynedoch Street gleaned its pupils from the select Woodlands neighbourhood.

As the West End residentially matured shops gravitated to Byres Road, to sections of Great Western Road and to the area around Charing Cross—the important junction where city centre met the West End proper. By the 1860s may feuing advertisements were stressing some properties as being 'suitable for shops in this rapidly increasing district'.[97] Retail outlets tended to colonise the ground floors of less pretentious dwellings, the tenement design, in particular, enabling the efficient adaptation from residential to retail functions. Such a transformation was rarely possible in areas of high-class terraces and Great Western Road has only one example of shops that later colonised gardens that fronted terraces. Many West End residents were highly critical of this commercial intrusion fearing that it might become 'unrestrained adaptation which would threaten the residential ambience of quality streets'.[98] It is significant that commercial colonisation never extended into the heart of Kelvinside which still retains its purely residential character.

THE TRANSPORT FACTOR

Although the development of an effective suburban transport network has been seen as a necessary pre-condition for large-scale residential differentiation there is grave danger, especially in the case of Glasgow, of placing too much emphasis on the restrictive function of transport on middle-class suburban speculation. Certainly by the end of the nineteenth century cheap and efficient transport aided suburban sprawl, but the lack of it did not prevent earlier residential differentiation from occurring. As Gordon claims 'housing tastes and comparative evaluations of possible residential environments . . . were more decisive factors for the leaders of the middle class'.[99] A salient factor in this argument relates to the physical form of Victorian Glasgow which remained, largely on account of its working-class tenement structure, an extraordinarily compact, but densely populated city. Such descriptions of it as being 'a huge amorphousness'[100] are inaccurate.

That suburban life owed less to transport innovations is perhaps best illustrated by the slow development of local railways. Kelvinside, situated 2–3 miles from the city centre, was too close for rail services to be attractive and the rapidly expanding working-class areas such as Maryhill, Partick and, in the east, Bridgeton, were likewise within easy walking distance of the industries on which they depended.[101] As far as the West End is concerned it was not until 1896–97, within a few years of the electrification of the trams, that the area was served by stations of the Caledonian Railway Company's line which linked Rutherglen in the south east via Bridgeton and the city centre to Maryhill in the north west. Hence the contribution made by the railways to West End suburbanisation was modest and Kellett's conclusion on their impact on Victorian cities in general applies most forcibly to Glasgow in that 'it was the ground plan formed by property titles' which was the key to explaining 'the whole course of development of certain types of urban area and the emergence of characteristic residential and industrial zones'.[102]

Yet, obviously, the transport factor cannot be ignored and as the West End extended ever further from the city centre the landlords took a vested interest in accessibility in terms of roads and in bridges across the Kelvin. Initial improvements began in 1825 when a small ziz-zag stone bridge, replacing a ford, was erected over the river at Holm Meadow. In 1836, however, the Act of Parliament authorising the building of Great Western Road, necessitated a new Kelvin Bridge at this site which, at a cost of £40,000, many Glaswegians saw as an extravagance in that it 'was ridiculous to think that the city would ever extend beyond the Kelvin'.[103] In fact, Kelvin Bridge was continually widened and pressure on it was relieved in 1853 when the Eldon Street Bridge was constructed down-river to provide more direct access to Hillhead. Up-river Belmont Street Bridge (1867) and Queen Margaret Bridge (1871) connected lands laid out for feuing and development with Great Western Road, while in 1877 Partick Bridge greatly improved east–west access in the south. Here the junction between Dumbarton Road and Byars (Byres) Road was of great importance. The improvement of the latter, extending northeastwards from Partick Cross to Great Western Road had been viewed by Montgomerie and partners as being detrimental to their plans for Kelvinside. For the trustees of the Botanic Gardens, however, alternative access was enthusiastically received and a comment in the *Glasgow Herald* read: 'Another excellent road has been opened up via Partick from the Garden Gate to Dumbarton road; a drive outwards by one road and homewards by the other will undoubtedly become a favourite recreation.'[104]

Vehicular transport along the West End's roads was at first by private or hackney carriages and the mews lanes in many West End developments testify to the significance of the former.[105] Soon, however, speculators began to subsidise horse omnibuses which they saw as beneficial in attracting prospective buyers and property advertisements, in addition to stressing 'open, airy and agreeable situations', increasingly made reference to 'omnibus accommodation being complete'.[106] In 1847 Montgomerie and partners appointed James Walker, a city omnibus proprietor to run a service from Glasgow Cross to the Botanic Gardens. Contemporary prints (Figure 5) frequently depict the two- and three-horse vehicles that operated in the West End though, in keeping with the social standing of the area, they remained a privileged form of transport for fares were beyond the reach of the working class.[107] In 1849 Andrew Menzies acquired many of the small omnibus companies and it was his idea to lay tram lines, Glasgow securing the Act for its first routes in 1870. Although the trams and horses were privately owned the lines were leased from the city until 1894 when municipalisation and electrification followed.

The basic advantage of the tram as opposed to the omnibus was the

Figure 5 Royal Crescent, Sauchiehall Street, the terminus in the 1840s of a three-horse omnibus.

Figure 6 A turn of the century cartoon expresses Glasgow's socio-residential contrasts in terms of the clients of east- and west-bound trams.

greater load which could be pulled. Yet, the idea that they provided cheap transport for the working class lies far from the truth, the provision of the 1870 Act to operate cheap fares at certain times for 'artisans, mechanics and daily labourers' being largely ignored. Working on the economy of scale principle, that is, the longer the journey the lower the fare, the trams initially favoured the more affluent living in the outer suburbs and were instrumental in preserving the middle-class exclusiveness of the West End. The effect of electrification greatly stimulated house-building and it is significant that Hyndland's complex of red sandstone tenements was built close to one of the city's most respectable tram routes (Figure 6).

By the end of the century the West End's tram network was complemented by the Caledonian Railway's Glasgow District Subway.[108] The latter, consisting of a circular cable-worked underground railway was opened in January 1899. It served the western parts of the city on both sides of the Clyde and four of its stations were within or peripheral to the West End. Despite its uniqueness it was not initially popular, part of middle-class dissatisfaction stemming from its small unattractive stations which were usually hidden within down-market properties.[109] In marked contrast the Central Railway, which to appease criticism was built underground or in shallow cuttings, paid great attention to its stations, all being designed by eminent architects. The one at Botanic Gardens (demolished in 1970) was the work of James Miller and was built of red brick with half-timbered gables and a verandah in front. From its roof rose two tall towers capped with balconies and onion domes. As Worsdall comments the design 'was a splendid foil to the dignified terraces all around . . . the only light relief to be found in the solemn north-west of the city'.[110]

EXCLUSIVE 'SUBURB'

The factors discussed in the previous sections—environmental quality, the pull of the institutions, the growth of recreational and other amenities and the role of transport, albeit ambivalent, can be regarded as collectively responsible for the popularisation of the West End. Overriding them all, however, appears to have been what Thompson describes as 'the powerful urge for people of like condition to want to live in the same neighbourhood with their kind, to decline to be mixed up with their social inferiors'.[111] If this was indeed the strong tide making for segregation it was also the most powerful force in middle-class preservation. Measures to safeguard exclusiveness permeated all aspects of West End life and previous pages have noted the concern with which many residents viewed such threats as the encroachment of working-class housing, retail colonisation and the appearance of railways.

Yet equal displeasure was directed at the more petty 'nuisances' that socially trespassed into middle-class domains. In an age of socio-economic extremes the West End became a target for such undesirables as street vendors, loafers, beggars and itinerant musicians. Unlike London's Belgravia, Mayfair or parts of St Pancras and Marylebone,[112] the presence of street gates and road barriers to exclude intruders were less obvious in the West End, though many of its terraces, gardens, places and crescents were private preserves. Intruders there were, however, and their activities regularly reached criminal proportions. Housebreaking was a common hazard to West End residents and a letter to the *Glasgow Herald* in January 1863 and signed 'A Constant Reader', warned of 'a numerous gang of midnight robbers'. The writer continues: 'I keep a six-barrel revolver at all times fully charged, in my bed-room; and had I been awake in time to get in shot of them, I would have to a dead certainty, given them the full benefit.'[113] Extreme as this attitude appears, it tellingly reflects the middle-class revulsion for such violators and also hints (and other examples abound) of the cooperation that existed between West Enders to maintain the distinctive lifestyle they had fashioned.

As the product of many speculators who built in response to a variety of forces, it is remarkable how Glasgow's West End evolved from a series of unco-ordinated, piecemeal developments into an extensive area with an overall homogeneous tone. As Simpson writes: 'The district has a harmony which might be the work of a single authority or voluntary cooperation. It is difficult to tell where estates meet, and yet there seems to have been no cooperation between the developers to harmonise their plans.'[114] Certainly landowners' covenants, acting as safety nets, were important in ensuring residential standards but within these controls architects and builders were free to indulge in developments expressive of their personal and often innovative genres. The control was a process that has been termed 'growth by contagion', for the presence of a terrace or villa of a certain cost and quality encouraged speculators to build in keeping with existing developments.[115] Glasgow's West End, in fact, seems to confirm Olsen's view that 'given sufficient size and a favourable location, a Victorian suburban estate planned and managed itself'.[116]

In so far as the majority of its residents continued to look to the City for their employment the term 'suburb' technically applied to the West End, yet such an unqualified description belied its true character. In response to the number of important institutions within its bounds the West End came to develop some measure of functional coherence which complemented its social standing. Its recognition of being more than a suburb came in 1888 when Kelvingrove Park hosted the International Exhibition which, attracting 5.7 million visitors, was a resounding financial success. The £46,000 profit was used towards the erection of another prestigious West End building, a Museum and Art Gallery for the City.[117] Its opening in 1901 was combined with a second more ambitious International Exhibition whose attendance reached 11.5 million. The 'suburb' had certainly come of age.

POSTSCRIPT

This essay has attempted to evaluate the factors responsible for socio-residential segregation in nineteenth-century Glasgow which manifested itself most clearly at the extremes of urban society. It was responsible for the emergence of the city's West End as a prime example of a socially uniform middle-class district equal in status and character to similarly affluent enclaves in Britain's other large Victorian cities. Segregation was not entirely a nineteenth-century phenomenon and in Glasgow the pattern of westward migration, albeit limited in scale, had been set earlier, only to increasingly gather momentum as the nineteenth century progressed. The main theme of this study has viewed residential location in terms of a broad decision-making model where behavioural patterns were geared to existing choices and constraints that conditioned both individual and collective residential preferences. Pooley has regarded these as 'the sorting mechanisms operating in different strata of society' and, importantly, 'on different spatial and temporal scales'.[118] It cannot be claimed that the factors selected for discussion were the only ones involved in middle-class decision processes. Neither is it possible to isolate any as being more significant than the others for the interactions between them were complex. Important as income levels undoubtedly were to residential choice, the self-imposed constraints stemming from middle-class aspirations for social advancement and the resulting need to locate in socially respectable areas, has to be seen as a major determinant of segregation. Endowing the middle class with stereotype attitudes is dangerous and presumptuous, yet the many who conformed to behavioural norms served only to effectively reinforce the social distinctiveness of districts. Their residential advantages, real and perceived, were astutely promoted by speculators whose propaganda conditioned the middle class into accepting residential relocation as being the outcome of personal decision and unconstrained choice.

REFERENCES

1 C G Pooley 'Choice and constraint in the nineteenth century city', in J H Johnson and C G Pooley *The Structure of Nineteenth Century Cities* (London 1982), pp 199–235, p 213

2 H J Dyos and D A Reeder 'Slums and Suburbs' in H J Dyos and H Wolff *The Victorian City* (London 1973), p 360

3 A S A Briggs *Victorian Cities* (London 1980), pp 28–9

4 G Best *Mid-Victorian Britain, 1851–1875* (London 1971), p 316

5 J Richardson *Recollections of the Last Half Century* (London 1856) as quoted in A S A Briggs *Victorian Cities* (London 1980), p 314

6 Quoted by A S A Briggs *Victorian Cities* (London 1980), p 114

7 D Ward 'Environs and neighbours in the "Two Nations", residential differentiation in mid-nineteenth century Leeds', *Journal of Historical Geography* 6 (1980), pp 133–62

8 C G Pooley 'Migration, mobility and residential areas in nineteenth-century Liverpool'. Unpublished PhD thesis, University of Liverpool, 1978

9 G Gordon 'The status areas of early to mid-Victorian Edinburgh', *Transactions, Institute of British Geographers,* new series 4 (1979), pp 168–91

10   J G Robb 'Suburb and slum in Gorbals: social and residential change 1800–1900', in G Gordon and B Dicks (eds) *Scottish Urban History,* Aberdeen (1983), pp. 130–67

11   *See* J G Robb *ibid.*

12   A Alison (Sir) 'Social and moral conditions of the manufacturing districts in Scotland', *Blackwood's Magazine* 50 (1841), pp 659–73

13   J Doherty 'Urbanisation, capital accumulation, and class struggle in Scotland, 1750–1914', in G Whittington and I D Whyte *An Historical Geography of Scotland* (London 1983), p 252

14   *See* G Best (London 1971) *op. cit.* p 29

15   L J Saunders *Scottish Democracy* (London 1950), p 163

16   J Doherty *op. cit.* p 259

17   M L G MacLeod 'Glasgow's West End: a study of estate development 1830–1914'. Unpublished BSc thesis, Department of Geography, University of Strathclyde, 1979, pp 8–9

18   H J Dyos and D A Reeder (1973) *op. cit.* p 360

19   F Worsdall *The Tenement: A Way of Life* (London 1979), p 3

20   I H Adams *The Making of Urban Scotland* (London 1978), p 77

21   L Naimer *England in the Age of the American Revolution,* 2nd edn (London 1974), p 16; G Best *op. cit.* p 34

22   W W Barr *Glaswegiana* (Glasgow 1981), pp 7–10

23   A Gibb *Glasgow, The Making of a City* (London 1983), p 70–3

24   Anon *The Old Country Houses of the Old Glasgow Gentry* (Glasgow 1889)

25   F Worsdall *The City that Disappeared: Glasgow's Demolished Architecture,* (Glasgow 1981), p 27

26   T M Devine 'The merchant class of the larger Scottish towns in the later seventeenth and early eighteenth centuries' in Gordon and Dicks *op cit.* pp 104–7

27   *See* M M Brown 'Kelvingrove 1700–1971: The Role of Perception in the Development of an Urban Area'. Unpublished BA thesis, Department of Geography, University of Strathclyde, 1972, pp 4–15

28   Quoted in M M Brown *op. cit.* p 14

29   A Gibb (1983) *op. cit.* pp 95–104

30   *See* A Gibb *op. cit.* pp 69–78

31   P Knox *Urban Social Geography* (London 1982), p 11

32   F Engels *The Condition of the Working Class in England* (London 1844), (reprint London 1969), p 80

33   Royal Bank of· Scotland *The Royal Bank in Glasgow 1783–1983* (Glasgow 1983), p 13

34   W W Barr *op. cit.* p 37

35   F Worsdall *Victorian City, A Selection of Glasgow's Architecture* (Glasgow 1982), p 53

36   *See* J Doherty *op. cit.* pp 235–58

37   J C Symon 'The South of Scotland' in *Reports from Assistant Hand-Loom Weavers' Commissioners, Accounts and Papers* (1839), XLII, p 51

38   *See* C M Allan 'The genesis of British urban redevelopment with special reference to Glasgow', *Economic History Review* (2nd series), 18 (1965), pp 598–613

39   J R Kellett *The Impact of Railways on Victorian Cities* (London 1969), p 218

40   *See* W H Duncan *On the Physical Causes of the High Rate of Mortality in Liverpool* (Liverpool 1843)

41   G Watt 'On the origins and spread of malignant cholera in Glasgow and its

neighbourhood', *Glasgow Medical Journal* 5, no. 19 (1832), pp 298–308, no. 20 (1832), pp 384–94

42   A K Chalmers, *The Health of Glasgow 1818–1925* (Glasgow 1930), p 190

43   'Remarks on the proceedings of the Glasgow Board of Health', *Glasgow Medical Examiner,* nos. 10–11, January–February 1832

44   J Cleland *Statistical Facts Descriptive of the Former and Present State of Glasgow* (Glasgow 1837), p 24

45   J Pagan *Sketches of the History of Glasgow* (Glasgow 1847), p 105

46   J G Robb *op. cit.* p 164

47   L A Brown and E G Moore 'The intra-urban migration process: a perspective', *Geografiska Annaler,* 52 B (1970), pp 1–13

48   G Best (1982) *op. cit.* pp 35–7

49   M L G MacLeod (1979) *op. cit.* pp 14–15

50   F M L Thompson *Hampstead: Building a Borough, 1650–1964* (London 1974), p 241. *See also* F M L Thompson 'Hampstead, 1830–1914', in M A Simpson and T H Lloyd *Middle Class Housing in Britain* (London 1977), pp 86–113

51   A K Cairncross *Home and Foreign Investment, 1870–1913* (Cambridge 1953)

52   This is argued by C G Pooley (1982) *op. cit.*

53   R Rodger 'Rents and ground rents: housing and the land market in nineteenth-century Britain' in J H Johnson and C G Pooley (1982) *op. cit.* pp 39–75

54   J R Kellett (1969) *op. cit.* and D Cannadine 'Victorian cities: how different', *Social History* 11 (1977) p 466

55   D J Olsen *The Growth of Victorian London* (London 1976), p 154

56   K C Edwards 'The Park Estate, Nottingham' in M A Simpson and T H Lloyd (1977) *op. cit.* pp 153–69

57   D Cannadine *Lords and Landlords: The Aristocracy and the Towns 1774–1967* (Leicester 1980), pp 81–218

58   *Ibid.* p 401

59   F M L Thompson (1977) *op. cit.* p 87

60   J N Tarn 'Sheffield' in M A Simpson and T H Lloyd (1977) *op. cit.* pp 170–91. *See also* G Rowley 'Landownership in the spatial growth of towns: a Sheffield example', *East Midland Geographer* 6 (1975), pp 220–44

61   J R Kellett (1969) *op cit.* pp 208–10

62   M L G Macleod (1979) *op. cit.* p 17

63   Particulars and Plan of the Estate of Knightswood, 1885, *Scottish Records Office,* RHP. 3339

64   For an introduction to the Scottish legal background see, F Worsdall *op. cit.* (1979), pp 14–26

65   A Gomme and D Walker *Architecture in Glasgow* (London 1968), p 74

66   *See* A Gibb (1983) *op. cit.* p 99

67   R Rodger (London 1982) *op. cit.* p 54

68   J P Fleming *Kelvinside* (Glasgow 1894), pp 1, 8

69   M A Simpson 'The West End of Glagow, 1830–1914' in M A Simpson and T H Lloyd (1977) *op. cit.* p 50

70   A Gomme and D Walker (1968), *op. cit.* p 83

71   W W Barr (1981), *op. cit.* p 56

72   *See* D Cannadine (1980), *op. cit.* p 391 ff

73   *Glasgow Herald* 17 January 1863

74   J H Muir *Glasgow in 1901* (Glasgow and Edinburgh 1901), p 248

75   *Ibid.* p 28

76   *Glasgow Herald* 23 June 1856

77   J H Muir (1901) *op. cit.* p 115
78   J R Kellett (1969) *op. cit.* pp 211 ff
79   J H Muir (1901) *op. cit.* p 5
80   F Worsdall (1982) *op. cit.* pp. 94, 95
81   *Glasgow Herald* 16 April 1841
82   *Glasgow Herald* 8 March 1850. Supplement on progress of building in Glasgow
83   *Glasgow Herald* 14 April 1842. *See also* E W Curtis *Glasgow Botanic Gardens* (Glasgow 1979)
84   Quoted in F Worsdall (1982) *op. cit.* p 137
85   *Ibid.* p 107
86   A Gibb (1983) *op. cit.* p 121
87   *Glasgow Herald* 12 December 1870
88   *Glasgow Herald* 6 January 1908
89   F Worsdall (1983), *op. cit.* p 122
90   *See* M M Brown (1972) *op. cit.* pp 23–4; M L G Macleod (1979) *op. cit.* pp 20 ff
91   E W Curtis (1979) *op. cit.* p 3
92   *Glasgow Herald* 7 May 1873
93   *Ibid.*
94   E W Curtis (1979) *op. cit.* pp 3–4
95   J H Muir (1901) *op. cit.* p 116
96   *Quiz* 4 March 1887
97   *Glasgow Herald* 14 August 1863. Notice of feuing or selling the remaining portion of Burnbank estate
98   *Glasgow Herald* 7 August 1869
99   G Gordon and B Dicks (1983) *op. cit.* p 15
100 *See* J M Reid *Glasgow* (1957)
101 J R Kellett (1969) *op. cit.* p 354
102 *Ibid.* pp 125, 424, 521
103 M M Brown (1972) *op. cit.* pp 27–30
104 *Glasgow Herald* 16 April 1841
105 *See* J R Hume 'Transport and towns in Victorian Scotland' in G Gordon and B Dicks (1983) *op. cit.* pp 197–233
106 *Glasgow Herald* 13 January 1863. Advertisement for 27 Buckingham Terrace
107 I H Adams (1978) *op. cit.* p 122. *See* M A Simpson, 'Urban transport and the development of Glasgow's West End, 1830–1914', *Journal of Transport History*, new series 1(no. 3), 1973, pp 146–60
108 D L Thomson and D E Sinclair *The Glasgow Subway,* Scottish Tramway Museum Society (Glasgow 1964)
109 I H Adams (1978) *op. cit.* p 119
110 F Worsdall (1981) *op. cit.* p 142
111 F M L Thompson (1974) *op. cit.* p 241
112 G Best (1971) *op. cit.* pp 35–6
113 *Glasgow Herald* 12 January 1863
114 M A Simpson 'Middle-class housing and the growth of suburban communities in the West End of Glasgow, 1830–1914', BLitt thesis, University of Glasgow,1970, pp 381–2
115 S B Warner Jr *Streetcar Suburbs: The process of Growth in Boston, 1870–1900,* (Cambridge, Mass. 1962), p 124
116 D J Olsen *Growth of Victorian London* (1976), pp 247–8
117 *See* F Worsdall (1981) *op. cit.* pp 157–9
118 C G Pooley (1982) *op. cit.* p 225

5

NATIONAL ROMANTICISM AND THE
ARCHITECTURE OF THE CITY

Frank Walker

If we seek to investigate . . . we find the research all to (*sic*) cold and too methodical to accord with the tone of our feelings. . . . So it is with those who have harboured an early affection for the architecture of their native land . . . that deep and filial affection which many a youth untaught in art but gifted by nature with a perception for its beauties has entertained from his tenderest years towards the old castle of his neighbourhood or that irrestistable (*sic*) attraction which compels many . . . to visit the various castles and palaces of this country, not only under the balmy influences of summer, but along muddy roads and snowy path, and with glowing heart but shivering hand to sketch the humble cottage, the more pretentious mantion (*sic*) or the mutilated though venerable castle with feelings of the most indescribable delight.

It is this instinctive affection which is so difficult to reason upon. . . . [1]

With this heather-purple prose the young Charles Rennie Mackintosh began his 1891 paper on 'Scotch Baronial Architecture'. His words were deeply felt, his tone unashamedly nationalistic, but the members of the Glasgow Architectural Association whom Mackintosh addressed would not find his thesis exceptional; the claims made for the continuing relevance of the Scots Baronial idiom were not new. Since the middle of the nineteenth century the lineaments of the style had figured prominently in the literature of Scottish architecture while the robust and symbolic language of Baronial form permeated the urban fabric of Victorian Scotland. All this was, of course, no more than the most recent, although certainly the most extensive, manifestation of a long and almost uninterrupted lineage of revival. In the short term it stemmed from the country-house manner of William Burn and David Bryce developed during the second quarter of the nineteenth century. This in turn might be tracked back into the preceding century to that appropriately castellar manner adopted by Robert Adam, e.g. in his recasting of Oxenfoord, Midlothian, and Culzean, Ayrshire, and especially in his 'modernisation' at Cluny, Aberdeenshire. Even the great tower-house castles of the late sixteenth and seventeenth centuries, so often precedents for later architectural excursions, were themselves already 'an astonishing revival of old forms romantically presented'.[2] Moreover, as McWilliam tentatively suggests,[3] there may also be a case to be made for a Baronial *survival*: just as Street, Morris and Webb had discovered a Gothic survival in the deeply English countryside of the Cotswolds so Mackintosh was among those who sensed a persistent national vernacular in the crow-stepped gables, turnpike stairs and solidly austere three-dimensional quality which for centuries had characterised the humbler buildings of nearly every

Scots village and town. At any rate, the stylistic issue had been well rehearsed and Macleod is undoubtedly correct in pointing out that in this youthful paper delivered to the Glasgow Architectural Association in 1891 Mackintosh 'was not presenting a revolutionary document in any sense'.[4]

On 20 February 1891, *The Architect* carried a short paragraph reviewing Mackintosh's paper. The journal's anonymous correspondent was sufficiently discerning to make special reference to the 'very complete series of illustrations', many of which were by the speaker's own hand, and to observe of Mackintosh's introductory remarks that he 'prefaced the historical review of the style with a commendation of the claims it has on all architectural students as exhibiting the standard models of picturesque grouping' adding that 'to the Scot it should appeal with the added force of national association'.[5] These brief, even casual, remarks—the one directed to the issues of architectural form and composition, the other to questions of meaning and character—are peculiarly perceptive. In effect they specify the horns of the design dilemma on which the nineteenth-century architect had repeatedly found himself tossed.

The problem was that while most architects (as distinct from builders or engineers whose speculation or innovation proceeded at unbridled pace) recognised the doctrine that 'the presence of both good composition and appropriate character is essential in a successful building' they frequently found that 'the presence of the one is not automatically productive of the other'.[6] It was this dilemma of style which afforded national romanticism its opportunities. For, to the ramified architectural challenge of the nineteenth-century town-halls, sheriff courts, schools, office buildings, hotels, and, above all, urban housing, all of which had often to be devised for the most awkward and constrained city sites—the 'Scotch' Style could afford both formal and symbolical significance. Not only were its vocabulary of architectural elements and its compositional syntax less studied, less clearly codified, and thus more flexible than the more international styles of text-book orthodoxy but its evocation and message were also much more pervasively and immediately relevant to the political and cultural consciousness of nineteenth-century Scots society.

It might well be thought that this latter aspect of overt nationalism would be first and most strongly evident in the design of a *National* Monument. Such projects are, of course, exceptional and wholly untypical of urban building. Yet of all building types surely none is less beset by complex functional considerations in the resolution of its formal composition or more programmatic in character than the monument raised to the glory of country won in arms or letters. In the course of the nineteenth-century Scotland found the opportunity to erect several such piles—the National Monument on Calton Hill, Edinburgh (1822–9); the Scott Monument, Princes Street, Edinburgh (1840–6); and the Wallace Monument on the Abbey Craig near Stirling (1861–9) are perhaps the most notable—and

while their formal nature was perhaps almost as much sculptural as architectural and their settings could not in every case be regarded as fully urban,
the stylistic development that can be traced in their respective designs is
useful evidence of a gradual evolution in the wider public acceptance and
application of the Scottish Baronial idiom—at any rate as a vehicle of
national sentiment. To begin with, however, no doubt due to the strength of
Neoclassical architectural orthodoxy, but perhaps also because political
daring or desire was wanting, indigenous culture was spurned and national
ideals were to be imported from the other end of Europe: the National
Monument to be built above Scotland's capital city was to be quite explicitly
Greek!

When the proposal was first made in 1817 that a monument should be
raised as a memorial to those who had fallen in the Napoleonic Wars, letter
writers to *The Times* were quick to suggest the Parthenon as model.

> What then, can be more worthy of a nation—a building which was the boast of the
> country . . . from which we derive all our philosophy, all our morals, all our taste,
> all our love of liberty, all our eloquence, all our poetry; in short, all that is good.
> . . .[7]

So much for any *Scottish* sentiment. And, as funds accrued and the
possibility of building advanced, such abject deference to classicism
continued to be the order of the day. A correspondent to *The Scots
Magazine* in February 1820, outlined several more specific reasons why the
Committee on the National Monument should proceed with the 'Restoration of the Parthenon'.[8] Signing himself 'A Traveller', he claimed that the
scenic resemblances between Edinburgh and Athens virtually demanded the
erection of such a building on Calton Hill. Furthermore, aside from any
topographical parallel, as a paradigm of architectural excellence the
Parthenon was, he argued, undeniably pre-eminent and since detailed
measured information was available, the realisation of such a project was
not only desirable but feasible—provided, of course, 'a fit architect' could
be found. Nor was a suitable building material lacking: Edinburgh
freestone would prove just as good as Pentelic marble. Here at least, amid
all the eulogising of things Greek, was just a touch of local confidence! As
yet, such intimations were material rather than spiritual in character, none
more so than when the writer, betraying typical Scottish caution in financial
matters, warned that with a target sum of only £40,000 'it would be hopeless
to aim at distinction in any other known style of architecture'.[9]

In January 1822 a decision was finally taken when a sub committee of the
General Committee of subscribers 'unanimously resolved to restore the
Parthenon of Athens on the Calton Hill'.[10] Reasons given recounted the
natural advantages of the site, the availability of good building stone and
the existence of a pool of skilled masons schooled in the making of
Edinburgh's classical New Town. More grandly, restoration was justified
on the grounds that the Parthenon itself was already dilapidated and likely
to become more so during 'the first struggles of Grecian freedom'. Finally,

it was held that since it is only the '*habitual* study of the best models' (and here no distinction was made between facsimile and original) which raises standards in the arts,

> By doing this we give the greatest impulse to the *National Genius,* and are laying the surest foundation for our own future eminence in the arts of *original design.* (*sic*)[11]

Just over six months later, Sir Walter Scott, Lord Elgin, Henry Cockburn, Francis Jeffrey, and the rest of the General Committee invited the English architect C R Cockerell, then the leading archaeological and aesthetic authority on Greek architecture, to visit Edinburgh in order to determine the precise siting of the Monument on Calton Hill. Appointed as architect in the spring of 1823, Cockerell himself produced a brief memorandum once more justifying the choice of the Parthenon as model. For someone whose first-hand knowledge of classical architecture was in his day unsurpassed and who, therefore, might have been expected to base his case on a refined scholarship, his arguments are strangely perverse and romantic. Each country, he wrote, evolved its own architectural forms to suit climate, materials, etc. and not least to contrast with the outline of the landscape. Thus, for example, in flat countries 'an elevated or perpendicular architecture has been always adopted'—Egyptian pyramids, Assyrian ziggurats, Flemish cloth halls and Fenland cathedrals are all cited—while in mountainous countries such as Greece a horizontal low architecture was preferred in which the 'unbroken line, the order, the symetry (*sic*), contrasted admirably with the wild irregularity of the scene . . . .'[12] In effect, this is by no means an argument for the supremacy of the classical style but rather for the relativity of cultural forms. It is an essentially romantic thesis and as such similar to views expressed, for example, by Goethe, Coleridge, and, interestingly, the Scottish geologist Sir James Hall,[13] all of whom had found in the forests of northern Europe a metaphorical and even, most explicitly argued in the case of Hall, a directly structural link with medieval Gothic forms of pointed arch and tracery, and had thus derived exactly the opposite correlation between building and landscape to that of Cockerell. It is only by the somewhat specious adducing of the picturesque that Cockerell can, in fact, avoid the logical conclusion that Scottish architecture must have its roots in Scottish conditions. Such a conclusion could not be long delayed; but meanwhile the temporising sentiments of romantic classicism won the day.

   Cockerell, aided by his Scottish amanuensis, W H Playfair, went ahead, the somewhat embarrassing implications of his own *apologia* conveniently ignored. Other voices had, however, been raised in protest. An article in *The Quarterly Review*[14] was certainly not disposed to set aside the national critique. Besides questioning the relevance of a Greek temple to the functional role of war memorial ('Are the slender and graceful maidens of the Panathenaic procession to be considered as typical of the army list and the navy list . . . ?')[15] the writer pointed out that the Parthenon was necessarily and inescapably a Greek national monument 'and not a monument of Scotland',[16] the crags of Edinburgh could not seriously be likened to the Acropolis, and that

> To 'adapt' the Parthenon to this scene, we must begin by blotting out every memorial of Scottish antiquity, power, independence, or piety by which the 'Doric Temple' is surrounded.[17]

Instead of invoking an authentic pride in the Scottish identity, the National Monument would turn out to be 'a perpetual and painful solecism'.[18]

Whether or not time has vindicated this prophecy may be open to dispute. It would be difficult to gainsay the picturesque delight which the sight of the Monument's open peristyle perched high above the end of Princes Street adds to today's urban prospect. But to Playfair, writing to Cockerell in 1829 when the money had run out and only the columns of the west end had been constructed, disillusionment was complete: 'Our Parthenon is come to a dead halt, and is, I am afraid, likely to stand up a striking proof of the pride and poverty of us Scots.'[19] Even Robert Louis Stevenson, in his aptly titled *Picturesque Notes* written half a century later, cannot conceal feelings of national shame.

> It was meant to be a National Monument; and its present state is a very suitable monument to certain national characteristics.[20]

Parsimony is, of course, the obvious and legendary sin. But so too is that poverty of spirit, that cultural timidity which has made Scotland 'almost afraid to know itself'[21] since the Union. It was this affliction, masked for a time by 'enlightened' Neoclassical pride, that romanticism would attempt to cure.

It is, however, ironic that, just as the belief that Edinburgh might be turned into some kind of 'Modern Athens' was based on a delusion, so too, in one peculiarly Scottish particular, was the subversive power of the romantic imagination stimulated by a lie. During the 1760s, the very decade in which James Craig's plan had laid the basis for the capital's New Town classicism, what purported to be fragments of the lost poetry of the third-century Celtic bard Ossian were published. Despite Dr Johnson's prompt condemnation of Macpherson's forgeries, they had an immediate and astonishing impact throughout Europe and especially in Germany. There, Ossian had been enthusiastically ranked alongside Homer; 'The Scottish nation, previously regarded as near-barbarian, enthralled the literary world, who chose to regard it as the Greece of the North.'[22] Herder, for example, rhapsodising over the natural humanity of this epic verse,

> must go to the Scottish Highlands, to see the places described by the great Ossian himself and 'hear the living songs of a living people'. After all, 'the Greeks, too . . . were savage . . . and in the best period of their flowering far more of Nature remained in them then can be described by the narrow gaze of a scholiast or a classical scholar'.[23]

To Herder, Scotland was *not* Greece; it was the validity of the forces which shaped their respective cultures which mattered. But the more writers like Herder perceived that the qualities of Greek literature and art which they admired had not sprung Athene-like, fully formed , from some cultural godhead, but were the unique creation of a 'savage', freedom-loving people with its own quite specific roots in time and place, the more did international classicism wither into an etiolated and deracinated ideal. As the seeds of cultural relativism were sown, it was for each nation to find its own forms. And for Scotland there was irony here too. For it was from the pen of Sir Walter Scott, that prominent signatory to the resolutions of the committee promoting the Calton Hill Parthenon, that the vivid romance of Scotland's own historical heritage was now flowing. Moreover, although Scott's novels and poetry, with their sentimentalised view of Scotland's medieval past, might also be said to be built on a delusion, they had unquestionably wrought a sea change in the nation's consciousness. Just how deeply this change was running in the tide of public taste, and the extent to which it manifested architectural consequences, became clear a few years after his death.

Scott died on 21 September 1832. Two weeks later a public meeting, at which the largest ever representation of the Scottish nobility had assembled, was held in Edinburgh and the decision taken to raise a monument to the memory of the great man. Committees responsible for fund raising were set up in Edinburgh, Glasgow and London.

In February 1836, the Edinburgh Committee advertised in thirty two newspapers for the submission of designs, costing not more than £5000 'in which the combination of a Statue with Architecture is indispensable'.[24] No decision having been taken on a site, it was intimated that the Secretary had information on a number of locations being considered, though 'it will be open to Artists to suggest any other'. Similarly, although the Committee had earlier 'decided—though not unanimously—that this monument should be Gothic rather than Classical . . . ',[25] no specific guidance was given on the architectural style which competitors should adopt. In fact, of the fifty-four entries received, eleven were essentially sculptural in form rather than architectural; but fourteen entries, undaunted by the Cockerell–Playfair failure, were Grecian temples; there were five memorial pillars, an obelisk and a fountain; and the remaining twenty-two were, indeed, Gothic. Evidently, a taste for indigenous medievalism was superseding that for things Greek. In any event, it was pointed architecture which the Committee continued to favour, for the designs placed first, second and third were all Gothic memorial crosses.[26]

But still the Committee could not decide to build. New proposals were invited. Finally, in March 1838, the entry submitted under the pseudonym 'John Morvo', in fact a greatly revised version of that placed third in the original 1836 competition, was chosen. The fact that John Morvo had been a fifteenth-century mason involved in the rebuilding of Scott's 'fair Melrose' was not lost on the Committee whose minutes described an imposing structure . . . in beautiful proportions and in strict conformity with the purity of the taste and style of Melrose Abbey, from which the author states that it is in all its details derived.[27]

The author, George Meikle Kemp, an unknown joiner-draughtsman who had indeed studied Melrose Abbey closely, having made careful drawings of it earlier in a remarkably varied but far from successful career, was not at once able to begin building. Discussion on the choice of site dragged on. As Ruskin wrote later,

the proceeding of the committee, in requiring architects to furnish them with a design without knowing the situation, is about as reasonable as requiring them to determine two unknown quantities from one equation.[28]

There were those who, like Ruskin, favoured a distinctly natural setting. But the Editor of the *Edinburgh Courant* seemed to speak for most when he wrote that 'it is only in streets and elegant squares . . . that architectural ornaments or statues can be seen with advantage'.[29] Amongst such urban settings, Melville Crescent was canvassed as a possibility, as was Coates Crescent. Kemp himself seems to have given serious consideration to the eastern side of Charlotte Square on the axis of George Street. At length, just before Christmas 1838, the site was finally determined: it was to be in Princes Street gardens at the south end of St David's Street (Figure 1).

Somewhat paradoxically, then, where the mechanically precise elemental forms of the National Monument had been sited in a loose, or at any rate, picturesque relationship with hill and city, the crafted complexity of Kemp's pinnacle was to be located with all the exactitude of a Neoclassical *point-de-vue*. In this sense of urban setting, therefore, Youngson is wrong in his criticism that 'nothing could be more alien to classical Edinburgh than this monument'.[30] In addition, the Scott Monument effects a particularly subtle transition in the capital's townscape, mediating between the regularised patterns of 'classical Edinburgh' and the crocketed aggregative skyline of the Old Town. But, of course, in strictly architectural terms, it *is* clear that Kemp's work, in exchanging the precedent of Melrose Abbey for that of the Parthenon, has, so to say, pointed up the degree to which nationalist association had become a significant factor in the formation of stylistic character. Still, Youngson's praise appears grudging and faintly damning:

It is a gothic fantasy in a style of romantic nostalgia not unsuited for its purpose.[31]

Kemp's design has always been attacked for its departure from those classical standards of taste which surrounded it, standards which, of course, still prevailed in Rhind's interpretation at Glasgow. But it can be strongly defended for its constructional skill and its mastery of Gothic form—both of which had been achieved, according to William Burn, 'in such a manner as to satisfy any professional man'.[32] It is fitting, too, many have felt, that Scott, the chronicler of Scotland's medieval life and legend, should be commemorated by a Gothic spire conceived in the manner of Melrose rather

Figure 1 The Scott Monument, Edinburgh, under construction; photographed in 1844. Just in the background right is the incomplete peristyle of the earlier National Monument (by permission of National Galleries of Scotland, Edinburgh).

than by Grecian column or temple. Undoubtedly this was Kemp's intention, but he himself went further in his explanation adding the unusual gloss of empathy to the associational argument since it seemed to him that

> Enjoying a panoramic view of Edinburgh and the surrounding countryside from seventeen different galleries, at four easy stages from the ground, might create an excitement something like one of Scott's own romances.[33]

All this is but variation on the theme of nationalist sentiment that surfaced in architectural debate during the 1830s. No longer did it seem to make sense to seek public architectural respectability in the classical tradition alone. Nor indeed, as the attentions of historian, designer and theorist were directed down Puginian paths and turned increasingly to the hitherto 'hidden and unknown antiquities of surpassing interest'[34] that were to be found in that 'surrounding countryside', was it necessary to do so.

There was, of course, no Pugin writing in Scotland to articulate an explicit case for the infusion of a specifically Scottish nationalism in architectural design. Nevertheless, as the conscription of Melrose shows, the ecclesiasical sources drawn into Pugin's argument were acknowledged in Scotland too, though not at all with the same ecclesiological overtones. So, also, Pugin's recommendation to study the indigenous tradition of secular vernacular building found its echo in the Scottish context where the forms of post-Reformation tower houses were increasingly assimilated to the balance of character and composition predicated in the design of the early nineteenth-century country house. Often, indeed, in such problems, ecclesiastical and secular influences were confused one with the other, as well as with Tudor or Jacobean revivalism more genuinely English in derivation. Abbotsford, for example, Sir Walter Scott's country seat in Roxburghshire, has been regarded as 'the unsung prototype of Scots-Baronial architecture'[35] but the ascription may be doubted if not for the mixture of Tudor and Jacobean elements which his English architects William Atkinson and Edward Blore adduced to the new manorial manner (1816–23) then perhaps for Scott's own wish that the house should be an 'old English hall'. A somewhat less indiscriminate, or at any rate more national, eclecticism is evident at William Burn's Milton Lockhart (1829–36) set on a fine sweeping bend of the Clyde—'the prettiest place in Scotland',[36] as Scott described it—and in his transformation of Tyninghame, East Lothian (1829–30). Thereafter, during the thirties and forties, not only Burn but his rival William Henry Playfair and his partner-successor David Bryce built many such houses in which dynamic and asymmetrical compositions of plan and silhouette and 'a sharper historical aesthetic'[37] in the choice and execution of detail combined to produce an increasingly convincing if still rudely indeterminate Scottishness. To some extent these loosely massed Baronial piles were simply a direct consequence of new demands inherent in the Victorian country house commission: quite apart from the romantic attraction exerted on a class rich enough to maintain such a grand life-style by an architecture of nationalist allusion, a complex social hierarchy of master and servant, family and guests, male and female, inevitably provoked free and unprecedented planning solutions. But part of the reason for formal licence and experiment was occasioned by the absence of any significant literature dealing systematically with the historical architecture of Scotland. Certainly there was little upon which designers might rely as they had upon the pattern book precedents of Georgian building.

It is true that as early as 1693 John Slezer's *Theatrum Scotiae* . . . had made the outrageous claim that 'there is no country in Europe that can brag either of greater piles of buildings, or more regular architecture in its ancient churches and religious fabricks, than Scotland . . . '[38]. But, although Slezer's work remained of particular interest as the first important illustrated account of Scotland's buildings and, as the fifth edition of 1814 stressed, the last 'while it yet remained an independent kingdom',[39] the precision of its record and the accuracy of its draughtsmanship were suspect and unreliable. Somewhat better in these respects were the two volumes of Grose's *The Antiquities of Scotland* published between 1789 and 1791, although the author found in North Britain 'every sort of ancient monument usually found in the south'[40] and remarked only a few distinguishing peculiarities of Scottish architecture as, for example, in his note that

> At each end of the tower adjoining to the roof, is commonly a triangular gable, the sides diminishing by a number of steps called crow steps. . . . [41]

High gables and corbie steps as well as corbelling, conical roofs, battlemented eaves and bartizan turrets all figured in many of the illustrations in Robert Forsyth's five volumes of *The Beauties of Scotland* (1805–8)—a work compiled on a shire-by-shire basis closely modelled on the parish version of the 1790s' *Statistical Account of Scotland.* But Forsyth's engravings, drawn from various sources, were reproduced in such small size as to be valuable only as impressions. Numerous topographical publications recounting the tours of travellers up and down the country added incidental insight but, like Forsyth's work these were not concerned solely or even principally with buildings.

In 1833 two houses in the Baronial style were illustrated in J C Loudon's *Cottage, Farm and Villa Architecture.* . . . Each was of contemporary design but said to be 'a very good imitation in the old Scotch manner',[42] the antiquarian legitimacy of one—a projected villa by the Edinburgh architect David Cousin—supported by an appeal to several historical precedents, most of which, it was specifically stated, could be found in Forsyth. Loudon, decidely practical in his approach, had no real interest in recording the niceties of stylistic archaeology, but a simultaneous attempt to fill this gap in historical knowledge was even less successful when plans for a publication on *Scottish Cathedrals and Antiquities,* for which George Meikle Kemp was to have made a series of drawings, came to nothing. In fact, by 1840, when the foundation stone of the Scott Monument was laid, no accurate antiquarian study had yet pictured the corpus of Scottish architecture; still less had any analytical view or definition of a 'Scotch Style' been seriously attempted. By mid century, however, the picture had begun to change. Ironically enough, the achievement belonged to an Englishman. Financed by William Burn to the tune of £1,000 (a measure perhaps of the emigre country house architect's continuing interest in a Scottish national style), Robert William Billings (1813–74), architect, antiquarian and restorer, succeeded in producing *The Baronial and Ecclesiastical Antiquities of Scotland,* publishing its four volumes in Edinburgh between 1845 and 1852. Although the work did not construct a detailed developmental study of the style, nor yet a formal analysis—Billings' method was one of straightforward alphabetical presentation, each building being described architecturally and historically and illustrated by his own remarkable drawings—significantly it did maintain the claim for originality in Scotland's architecture, admitting what were believed to be 'its French affinities'[43] but arguing that these no more diminished the integrity of the Baronial style than did those Italian influences at work in the south render the historically parallel Elizabethan style any the less English. But it was not argument but image which made Billings' volumes so important. His beautifully sharp and vigorous delineations of the nation's architectural heritage surpassed all previous publications in number, size and detail. Consequently their impact was immediate and immense, reinforcing the somewhat isolated built achievements of the country house school by providing fertile source material, at once tolerably accurate and readily accessible. Now it became possible not only to adduce a more precise imagery to the creation of architectural character, something hitherto generally dependent only on a romantic and vaguely associational notion of what the buildings of Scotland's past actually looked like, but it was also feasible to exploit on a much broader scale than ever before a whole repertoire of clearly specified Baronial elements in attaining the compositional freedom and flexibility which the building demands of the nineteenth century town increasingly sought.

Of the former strategy, that is the deliberate declaration of nationalist character in architecture, the most celebrated example was undoubtedly the Wallace Monument begun in 1861 on the Abbey Craig, near Stirling. Designed by J T Rochead, who had been briefly articled to David Bryce, its dramatically stabbing Baronial tower (Figure 2) is the unsubtle culmination of decades of nationalist architectural aspiration. This is the Scotch Walhalla. At 'the centre of Scotland and . . . likewise the centre of the Scottish battle-ground for civil and religious liberty',[44] its tiered halls reliquaries of the nation's past, the monument rose two hundred and twenty feet in height from craggy base to crown. It was finally completed in 1869. Half a century earlier the idea of raising a memorial to the great hero of Scottish independence had first been put forward in Glasgow in 1818. But while Edinburgh was building its Parthenon on Calton Hill, Glasgow's plans to erect 'a lofty circular tower of unhewn whinstone' on 'a commanding eminence to the east of Glasgow Cathedral'[45] came to nothing.

Figure 2   The Wallace Monument, Stirling; photographed *c.*1890 (by permission of
National Monuments Record of Scotland).

Further initiatives in 1838 and 1846 seem to have fallen through 'in consequence of the proverbial jealousy which had so long existed between the Glasgow "folk" and the Edinburgh "people" . . . '[46] so that in the end Stirling was chosen not only for its associations with Wallace's role in Scottish history but also because of its central and 'neutral' location. Compromise site or not, on 24 June 1856, the anniversary of the battle of Bannockburn, no fewer than 20,000 people assembled in the King's Park to acclaim this final proposal to construct what was called, in the patriotic euphoria of the times, 'a National Monument to the Scottish Chief'.[47] Funds were now raised and in 1858 advertisements placed for an architectural competition. Over a hundred entries were received and duly displayed at Glasgow, Edinburgh and Stirling, Rochead's winning design being the choice not only of the adjudicating committee but of the general public who had been asked to record their preference in a manuscript volume which accompanied the exhibition of the competitors' drawings. Whatever the part played by aesthetic discernment in such popular approval, the stylistic symbolism of this third 'National Monument' of the century captured the public imagination more completely than any of its predecessors. Eschewing both classical Greek and ecclesiastical Gothic, the design was as Scottish as the plates of Billings could make it.

While the building of the Wallace Monument evidently confirmed the public's acceptance of the Scottish Baronial style as the most fitting architectural expression of national culture, it did not evoke universal critical approbation. The architect J J Stevenson, for example, wrote

> The enthusiasts for Scotch nationality have recently erected, as a monument to Wallace, a tower which alters, and some think destroys, the contour of a beautiful hill near Stirling. Corbelling has run mad in it, making marvellous protuberances where one does not expect them; corners are hacked out of it, and the pieces stuck on somewhere else. The design seems to aim at being wild.[48]

In a similar vein he castigated J Ingram's monument to Burns, erected at Kilmarnock in 1879—'something between a steeple and a castle'—and, tilting at both, he went on:

> Such productions are not true expressions of national feeling. National peculiarities and differences have of late become softened down and assimilated by more frequent intercommunication with England and the influence of common culture. We should therefore expect that the architecture of the two countries should become assimilated, as in fact has happened, except in this revival of Scotch 'Baronial' which has exaggerated the peculiarities of the old national style.[49]

These peculiarities had been summarily listed by Robert Kerr in *The Gentleman's House,* the first edition of which appeared in 1864 while

Rochead's monument was still under construction. No publication having dealt analytically with the 'the Scotch Baronial Style', Kerr's brief chapter was perhaps the most succinct literary description of the elements so profusely illustrated in Billings.

> small turrets on the angles of the building, sometimes carried up from the ground, and sometimes built out on corbelling; crowstepped gables; battlemented parapets; small windows generally; the introduction almost always of a main tower; and over the whole, in one form or another, a severe, heavy, crude, castellated character.[50]

Kerr and Stevenson, seduced by Johnson's 'noblest prospect', had both chosen, like many before and since, to take the high road to England: Kerr, an anglicized Aberdonian, to become the leading architectural polemicist of his day; Stevenson, a Glasgow architect, to found an office in the south which became 'the Scotsman's stepping-stone to London'.[51] Both were, therefore, emigres and so it is perhaps not surprising that they should have expressed rather reactionary views, depreciating their own tradition in deference to English culture. Such nationalism as they cared to admit was limited to an approval of 'the old Scotch style' for modern houses built in Scotland. Kerr commended the convenience of the planning models evolved by Burn and Bryce but nevertheless condemned 'the pepper-box corners, battlemented parapets, and corbiesteps of the dreary middle ages of the Northern Kingdom'.[52] Stevenson likewise maintained that 'the old Scotch style, when such extravagances are avoided, is well fitted for modern houses',[53] though he went further than Kerr in acknowledging that 'crow-steps, though an addition to the expense, did not affect the internal arrangements, and projected angle turrets, adopted for the sake of appearance, could be fitted up as water-closets or wardrobes'.[54]

Essentially, however, these theoretical discussions of the Baronial manner went little beyond the earlier practical achievements of the country house school. Certainly it is true that residential architecture, both rural and, increasingly, urban, continued to provide major scope for the Scottish Baronial style throughout the century. Country houses might have set the pattern, but from Charles Wilson's rather refined Scots villas in Dundee's west end (c.1851) to John Ednie's gnarled and quirky mansion at Whitting-hame Drive, Glasgow, (1910), suburban villas all across the country had proclaimed that a Scotsman's home too could be his castle. So much was this the case, indeed, that Mackintosh concluded his 1891 essay with the lament that 'It is a matter of regrets that we don't find any class of buildings but domestic in this style . . . '[55].

Yet this was by no means the whole truth, for throughout the second half of the Victorian era the Baronial was much more than the sentimentally romantic manner of monument and mansion. In a certain measure, indeed, it proved to be one of the 'essentially progressive styles'[56] averred by Loudon, another emigré Scot, as early as 1833, for

It must always be recollected that, in imitating any style we are not limited to copying particular forms; but are required to enter into the spirit of the subject or style to which they belong, and to form a new composition in that spirit, adapted to whatever use it maybe required for. When we hear, therefore, of Architects stating that there is no precedent for such and such things in the models which they take for imitation, we consider that it shows a want of comprehensive views, and indicates that man is a slave of his profession, rather than the master of it.[57]

The reasons for this comprehensive application, implied in Loudon's 'spirited' defence of Scotch Baronial (and also, incidentally, what he called the 'Old English Manor House' style) lay first in the style's ability to proclaim national affiliation: in the ramified range of semantic possibilities available to the historicist designer it afforded a readily recognisable architectural *character* rooted in indigenous culture. Secondly, the historical precedents themselves, so thoroughly pictured by Billings, were proof of the style's vigorous asymmetrical syntax which, as Loudon put it, 'admits of an unlimited extent of additions, spread out in any, or in every direction';[58] in short, Baronial *composition* was flexible and adaptable—it offered freedom not slavery. Throughout Europe similar creative combinations of meaning and grammar, drawn from revitalised national cultures, gave to the old concept of *l'architecture parlante* a new, romantic, subversive, and genuinely vernacular significance.

To some extent socially and politically generalised in the Wallace Monument, a new hard-edged urban manifestation of romantic nationalism replaced the soft-centred Scott-fostered Scottishness of the earlier decades of the century. The Baronial was no longer merely the predilection of a rural gentry, both aristocratic and *parvenu*, or of the suburban *nouveaux riches,* but had become a significant stylistic force readily adduced to a whole range of building types in the towns and cities of Victorian and Edwardian Scotland. Particular coincidences of form and function seemed to emerge and in this respect it is perhaps appropriate to look first at those areas of Scottish culture in which a distinct and very separate identity existed—the church, education and the law.

'Calvinism and the Shorter Catechism' have frequently been advanced as explanations for the dour Scottish character and particularly for having blighted the development of the country's visual arts. No doubt a relationship exists, though in the cold light of other climatic and economic factors the simple association of religious cause with cultural effect seems facile, while the inference that the Scottish character is somehow inferior or uncivilised by virtue of its austerity is the worst kind of cultural betrayal. Indeed, it was at just such rudely fundamental levels, in which the environmental and the spiritual coalesced, that Romanticism had revealed the relative, if raw, truths about culture. Unhappily, however, the church in Victorian Scotland effectively rejected this very proposition. Corrupted by the English Gothic Revival and the arguments of the ecclesiologists, in whose writings 'the invariable implication was that Scotland was a most barbarous and backward place'[59] because its reformed churches were customarily centrally planned with no chancel, it largely abandoned both liturgical and architectural inheritance for the alien forms of another tradition. That this should have happened in a time of such opportunity, when the General Assembly's 1828 enquiry into the adequacy of its accommodation had instituted a programme of church building and the Disruption of 1843 had turned this into an unparalleled boom, was a sad and debilitating irony. Instead of playing its part in a national revival of artistic consciousness, the church entered into an era of wholesale cultural apostasy.

There was, of course, no lack of direct religious precedent in medieval church building, but most architects, vying with one another for professional and, no doubt, commercial attention in the denominational 'free-for-all' of the second half of the nineteenth century, seemed to feel little obligation to find these in the Scottish tradition. On the contrary, English and Continental Gothic supplied the models for most commissions and, as Hay remarks bleakly,

> The fully developed mediocrity of the Gothic Revival, which by the time of the Disruption was holding undisputed sway over ecclesiastical and architectural minds alike, dragged its dreary course through the remainder of the century. . . .[60]

Meanwhile, however much Ruskin might rail against the pagan forms of classical architecture as 'base, unnatural, unfruitful, unenjoyable and impious',[61] the trabeated solidity of the Graeco-Roman temple also continued to find favour. In Glasgow, for example, John Honeyman, T L Watson and Hugh and David Barclay were still designing porticoed temple-churches in the 1880s; Alexander Skirving as late as the mid 1890s

Continuity with the traditions of *Scottish* ecclesiastical building remained a minority interest. Not surprisingly perhaps, David Bryce, master of the Scots Baronial country house, had occasionally tried to extend his national idiom to church building. At Carnwath (1865–69) his design was certainly indebted to the forms of the ruined collegiate church, while at St Mungo's, Lockerbie (1874–77) he created a 'rugged freestone church in late Scots Gothic with stumpy pinnacled buttresses and a massive defensive-type tower'.[62] But these were not the evidence of a convinced or convincing commitment and have to be regarded as aberrations in the context of Bryce's other religious commissions. Not until the last decades of the nineteenth century and the early years of the twentieth were the native forms so carefully recorded and illustrated by Billings seriously assimilated to contemporary church design. At the Barony, Glasgow (1886–90), J J Burnet responded practically, as Ruskin had delightedly done theoretically, to the west front of Dunblane Cathedral, adding crow-steps to the adjoining church halls for good Scots measure. Some magnificent crown steeples, recalling the late medieval skylines at King's College, Aberdeen, and St Giles, Edinburgh, which Billings had also pictured, were built; amongst such were those by J J Stevenson at St Leonard's-in-the-Fields, Perth (1885) and Belmont Street, Glasgow (1900) and, most spectacularly of all, that by Hippolyte Blanc at Coats' Memorial, Paisley (1894). In a series of commissions carried out across the country from Elgin to Ardrossan, Peter Macgregor Chalmers elaborated the theme of the Scottish Romanesque church, round-arched and apsidal like Dalmeny and Leuchars. But of a widespread church architecture comparable in its stylistic nationalism to the secular *oeuvre* already evolved by the country house designers there was little or nothing. A few crow-stepped gables might appear; the occasional round turret with conical roof; a gaunt square tower with corner bartizans perhaps, as much keep as kirk: and though all of these could, on close inspection, be found in Billings and, by the late 1890s, in MacGibbon and Ross's *Ecclesiastical Architecture* too, the historical distinction which these writers had rightly recognised between *The Baronial and Ecclesiastical Antiquities of Scotland* could not be overcome. Attempts to do so, such as P Allan-Fraser's 'late Presbyterian' mortuary chapel at Arbroath (1875), contrived as a complex imploded agglomeration of Kerr's Baronial elements, only proved ridiculous.

Thorough, hard-headed and severely moral, the distinct qualities of a Victorian Scottish education were closely tied to the ethos of the Scottish church. It was a relationship with a long and explicitly legal history. While 'the importance of education from the point of view of national welfare had been recognised as early as the Act of 1494',[63] the Reformers' enlightened desire for a school in every parish did not win an effective statutory validity until the 1696 Act which enjoined the heritors of the parish to 'provide a commodious house for a school',[64] if none already existed, and charged heritors and minister with the appointment of those who would teach there. For more than a hundred and fifty years ministers and presbyteries continued to exercise control over education: schoolmasters were obliged to sign the Confession of Faith and subscribe to the formulae of the Church of Scotland, and although these specific restrictions were relieved by the Act of 1861, it remained a legal requirement that no opinions contrary to the Bible or the Shorter Catechism should be taught.

This official Scottishness, so rigorously maintained in the administration and curriculum of Victorian education, seemed to find a rather more significantly national response in the forms of school building than its related religious equivalent did on those of church architecture. The parish school, 'side school' or 'parliamentary school'[65] was, of course, generally small and, being indeed frequently little more than 'a commodious house for a school' customarily called for only the most modest vernacular interpretation. On the other hand, the great foundation schools which were privately or corporately endowed during the nineteenth century found grander precedent. Collegiate Gothic was an obvious first choice and the formal schemata of late medieval secular architecture proved as readily amenable to the needs and aspirations of the large educational establishment as they had done for those of the large country house.

Such a college was effectively a large house—often a country house—made a grander and more 'commodious house for a school', catering for the educational, physical and moral well-being of a greatly extended family. Copying the contemporary architectural manners of the country house, Donaldson's School, Edinburgh (1842–54) by W H Playfair and Stewart's College, Edinburgh (1849–53) by David Rhind were carried out in the fashionable and adaptable idiom of an earlier era of stylistic transition: Tudor or Jacobean, romantic in conception and setting, 'overloaded with towers and turrets', but for the moment, with barely a hint of Scottishness.

The search for a picturesque effect soon took a French cast, steeply pitched roofs were peppered with 'towers and turrets', chimneys, finials and crocketted dormers to produce the skyline of the Loire chateaux, while plans were frequently organised more or less symmetrically around a single central tall turreted tower of French or Flemish provenance. David Bryce's Fettes College, Edinburgh (1862–70), 'possibly the most flamboyant French Gothic public building built in the British Isles'[66] was the most extravagant example, but in Glasgow Sir George Gilbert Scott's new university buildings on Gilmorehill (1866–70) also drew freely on Franco-Flemish models to develop a full-blown collegiate Gothic of comparable exuberance. Beneath the foreign formal complexities of Bryce's great school, however, it is possible to detect that Baronial vigour which animated so much of his architecture, while in Scott's style at Glasgow, as indeed in his slightly earlier 'trial run' at the Albert Institute, Dundee (1864–7), certain recognisably national features have been added:

> I adopted a style which I may call my own invention, having already initiated it in the Albert Institute at Dundee. It is simply a thirteenth or fourteenth century secular style with the addition of certain Scottish features peculiar in that country . . . [67]

Meanwhile in the work of Peddie & Kinnear at Morgan Academy, Dundee (1863–6) and Morrison's Academy, Crieff (1860), though the compositional structure is similar to the main front of Fettes, the French character has been much muted; in part, perhaps, as a simple result of a smaller budget; in part, perhaps, by deliberate design. Such stripped-down Frenchness seemed to expose a more rugged Scottish character in the architecture. 'Scotch only by modification'[68] it may be, but whether such modification was the historicist consequence of historical relationships pertaining between the architecture of France and Scotland, or whether, as seems more likely, the Baronial was a consciously adopted revival in parallel, from the 1860s a clearly national quality could be found in the design of a number of the country's large school buildings. It is evident, for example, in James Matthew's Aberdeen Grammar School (1861–3) and Robert Baldie's Bellahouston Academy (1876) in Glasgow.

Yet, despite a considerable building programme of urban 'public schools' stemming from the 1872 Act's creation of democratically elected School Boards and Scotch Education Department, the 'old Scotch style' failed to achieve more than sporadic success. A few designers developed along lines already established in the architecture of the large private schools—J Graham Fairley, for example, moved from a French manner at the girls' block of the High School, Dundee (1886) to the use of more Scottish elements at Linlithgow Academy (1900–1) and Bathgate, Torpichen Street (1904)—so that, by the turn of the century, crow-stepped gables, eaves dormers, and the occasional bartizan proved much less congenial to the stiff symmetry of plan which resulted from the rigid separation of the sexes[69] than did some prosaic application of classicism. Only Charles Rennie Mackintosh—appropriately enough at Scotland Street School, Glasgow (1904–6)—by combining the familiar schema of balanced staircases and classrooms with half-round towers, conical roofs, skews, and some highly abstracted decorative stone carving drawn from the motif of the thistle, succeeded in infusing school architecture with a Scottishness raised beyond the level of token allusion.

Perhaps rather surprisingly then, neither church nor school displayed that consistently Scottish quality in its architecture which an otherwise markedly national identity in these fields of culture might seem to suggest. Even in those cases—mostly educational buildings—where some such consonance was achieved, designers found little opportunity to exploit to the full that compositional freedom which had earlier been so effectively deployed in the formal dispositions of the country house. Stylistic congruity and flexible syntax were not, however, lacking in what might be termed the buildings of the law; perhaps more frequently and convincingly than any other building types the sheriff courthouses, police courts, county buildings and town halls of the nineteenth-century burghs took on an appearance as distinctively Scottish as the law they administered.

In 1860, the Sheriff Court Houses (Scotland) Act was introduced to improve and increase the accommodation available for the dispensation of civil and criminal justice throughout the country. Costs were to be met equally by the Treasury and from the assessment of local lands and heritages while the buildings themselves were to 'be erected and completed under the supervision of the Commissioners of Supply',[70] an originally nominated group of local dignatories whose authority to manage the affairs of the county was largely based on property, superiority or liferent and whose powers were not finally abolished until 1889. This shared patronage, which thus extended over a period of some thirty years, did much to explain not only the choice of architects favoured for the design of these new court houses, many of which were integrated with the provision of a variety of other local government offices and halls, but, indeed, the very nature of the architectural style adopted for such buildings. Those architects already engaged on Crown commissions, such as Thomas Brown, architect to the Prison Board of Scotland, or those whose Edinburgh practices put them close to the source of government funding, notably the firms of David Rhind, whose brother was a sheriff, and Peddie & Kinnear, found themselves well placed to benefit from this extensive programme of court house building. At the same time it was not entirely remarkable that the Commissioners of Supply, almost to a man landed gentry or aristocracy, should endorse that same Baronial manner already invested in the romantically conceived mansions of their own country estates, so that an apprenticeship served under David Bryce could prove an attractive and valuable asset. In any event, in the historicising mood of these mid-Victorian years, 'the old Scotch style' might seem eminently fitting for the Scots Law.

The court house work of Thomas Brown or more correctly, the practice of Brown and his partner James Maitland Wardrop, was not immediately national in character. That same flavouring of English and Continental sources seen in the evolution of the country house or the endowment school pertained. Linlithgow (1861–3), for example, was 'not quite symmetrical Tudor',[71] Alloa (1863) had Flemish overtones, while Forfar (1869–71) and Stranraer (1872–3) were still strongly Elizabethan, though not without a trace of Scottishness. On the other hand, at Falkirk (1866–8) and Stirling (1874–6) the feeling is more Scottish though not wholly so; Renaissance with, especially at Falkirk, an invigorating admixture of Baronial.

Peddie & Kinnear adopt a more robustly detailed medievalist Baronial at Greenock (1887) and Aberdeen (1868–74).[72] Both buildings bulk large in the local townscape not least because of their high bartizaned towers, placed centrally at Greenock but located on a corner in asymmetrical relationship with the much larger townhouse project at Aberdeen. Bryce at Fettes (1862) and Peddie & Kinnear themselves at Morgan Academy (1863) had already developed this powerful vertical element and, for the rest of the century, variants of the tower, spire-topped, with gablet or dormer sandwiched between conically roofed corbelled corner turrets, continued to make a significant impact at the centre of many towns throughout the country; for example, besides Aberdeen, such courts and town halls as Rutherglen (1861), Renfrew (1872), Lockerbie (1873, 1884), Dunfermline (1875), Hawick (1881), Bathgate (1899), et al. are all 'the continuation of a native type'.[73]

Possibly the most adept utilisation of both the vocabulary and the syntax of the Baronial style was that made by David Rhind. His sheriff courts at Dumfries (1863–6) and Selkirk (1870) (Figure 3), for example, are rich in all the architectural elements of the Scottish tradition—corbelled turrets, parapeted towers, machicolations, gabled eavesdormers, canted oriels, corbie-steps, rope mouldings. But it is the freedom with which these elements are asymmetrically grouped together which best illustrates Rhind's skill in adapting this national language to the contingencies of the brief and, particularly at Selkirk, those of the site. Here is vindication not merely of the associative power of the Baronial but, once again, as with the country house, of its flexibility and serviceability too.

Figure 3 Sheriff Court and County Buildings, Selkirk, under construction; photographed in 1870 (by permission of National Monuments Record of Scotland and Selkirk Antiquarian Society).

It becomes clear that the success of the Baronial Revival can not be explained by an appeal to romantic sentiment only. The evocation of the nation's past was certainly always important and frequently deemed, by architect and client alike, to be pertinent. The accessibility of the language, *in situ* or in Billings, was convenient. But every bit as attractive to the nineteenth-century designer trying to cope with an accelerating elaboration and diversification of building types was the way in which the elements of the style, collated but scarcely co-ordinated by Kerr, had not only avoided any kind of canonical atrophy in the past but continued to prove freely amenable to the novel aggregations demanded by the present. Paradoxically it was this characteristically British absence of codified formulae which, more than any other factor, fostered the 'old Scotch style', just as it did an Elizabethan or Old English Revival in the south. While it was largely for the former reasons that the tradition of country house and castle building was maintained through the century from the mansions of Burn and Bryce to the extravagant piles of Dunrobin in Sutherland (1844–50) and the royal residence at Balmoral, Aberdeenshire (1853–5) down to the twentieth-century domestic work of Lorimer at Ardkinglass, Argyll (1906–7), Rowallan, Ayrshire (1903–6) and Formakin, Renfrewshire (1903–13), each still 'saturated with the spirit of the old builders'[74], it was more for this last reason that, over the same period, all kinds of *urban* buildings also took to wearing full Scottish dress.

There was, therefore, something of a nationalist swagger in the architectural growth of the Scottish cities and towns. Besides the few churches, rather more schools and many court-houses already discussed, there were numerous town halls, public halls, police stations, corn exchanges, banks and, of course, suburban villas all carried out in Baronial style. There were several hospitals, notably Bryce's Royal Infirmary, Edinburgh (1870–9), and his smaller Lockhart Hospital in Lanark (1874) twin gabled 'with flanking wings ending in pairs of round towers with conical roofs like Edinburgh Royal . . . '.[75] In Aberdeen, James Souttar built a fairytale Salvation Army citadel (1893) on the axis of Union Street to enliven the city's seaward skyline and J Cumming Wyness a vast fortress of a post-office (1907) to protect the royal mail in Crown Street. In Glasgow, J T Rochead, later architect of the Wallace Monument, contrived a magnificent four-storeyed block of offices along the north side of the Trongate (1855), quite unkindly labelled a 'Baronial travesty'[76] by Gomme and Walker. Jagged turrets, gables and dormers, its saddleback tower on the corner of Candleriggs responding to the steeples of the Tron Kirk and the Tolbooth, it positively bursts with energy in a restless architectural reflection of the life that animates the street below (Figure 4). It seems as if the whole repertoire of Billings has been absorbed into Rochead's composition,[77] as well it might be since the Englishman had only recently published his seminal work and had himself taken a hand in the design of another large Baronial warehouse at 137 Ingram Street not far off on the northern edge of Glasgow's Merchant City. Similar, if less ebullient, commercial developments began to appear in all the Scottish cities. On Edinburgh's narrow Victoria Street,

Figure 4 Trongate, Glasgow, *c.*1890 (by permission of Mitchell Library, Glasgow).

India Buildings, 'a large and highly ornate block of offices'[78] was completed by David Cousin in 1868. A little to the north, across the Lawnmarket, on St Giles Street, David Bryce's buildings for the *Edinburgh Daily Review* (1872) and the *Edinburgh Evening Courant* (1873) enriched the Old Town skyline with yet more stepped gables and bartizans. Dundee could boast Scotland's major Baronial railway station—the West or Caledonian (1888–9) by T Barr of Perth—complete with the familiar courthouse or town hall tower asymmetrically placed on the facade but top-heavy, it seems, for want of an extra storey. And in cold Aberdeen there was even a bathing station (1896)—not granite, indeed, but 'Baronialism in brick'.[79]

But by far the biggest building task of the expanding nineteenth-century city was the provision of housing. And here, too, the ubiquitous Baronial played its part.

While earlier industrial and commercial expansion had brought some incidental residential amelioration in its wake and a number of isolated reports had, with limited success, drawn attention to deteriorating environmental conditions in the older quarters of the country's towns and cities, it was not until midcentury that a series of individual private ventures endeavoured to respond directly to the growing problem, and not until the 1860s that, through the various City Improvement Acts (Glasgow 1866, Edinburgh 1867, Dundee 1871),[80] the municipal authorities began to assume responsibility for slum clearance and the provision of better housing. The report of a committee of working men, set up in 1858 to investigate overcrowding in working-class dwellings in Edinburgh and make recommendations for its alleviation, not only gives some sense of the progressive fusion of social conscience and capitalist economics but hints at some of the cultural and stylistic issues which inevitably attended such calls for extensive residential redevelopment. Published in 1860, the report began by complaining that, despite the recent boom in commercial and public building in the city,

> For a number of years back the increase of population in Edinburgh has, from a variety of reasons, not been met with a corresponding increase in the number of houses.[81]

Curiously, the well-worn classical analogy which celebrated the Scottish capital, as the Athens of the North, adduced for wholly different reasons to those employed by the apologists for Cockerell's National Monument, now found fresh proletarian pertinence,

> for the greatest of all the Greek historians has recorded that even at Athens, in the time of Pericles, foreigners were struck with the contrast between the splendour of the public buildings and the mean dwellings of the common people.[82]

Moreover, 'animated with all the spirit and patriotism of Lord Cockburn or Sir Walter Scott',[83] the Committee went on to argue that the housing so desperately required should 'still bear a general relation to that of the city',[84] principally through the continuation of the traditional practice of building several-storeyed flats or tenements rather than the adoption of any alien English methods which favoured the erection of separate dwelling houses, but also by assimilating more of the correspondingly localised architectural *character* of the Old Town—a reference to 'pointed gables'[85] seems to conjure up the historic skyline of High Street and Canongate and with it the inference that such an architecture, genuinely romantic and genuinely national, might prove more culturally fertile than all the international 'wilderness of square-cut stone'[86] across the bridges to the north. And yet it must be stressed that, despite this deferential acknowledgement of Ruskin's contemporary critique of the classical New Town it is 'the necessaries of comfort' not 'the luxuries of ornament' which take priority: the report is 'a well-grounded appeal to the capitalists of Edinburgh' to provide more and better housing which will not only yield a reasonable financial return on investment but will

> promote the advancement of order and progress, give encouragement to industry, increase virtue and temperance, and improve the physical and moral condition of the working-classes.[87]

Meanwhile, as such theories proliferated, developments were already underway. Prompted entirely by commercial expediency, an Edinburgh company, anxious to improve the access to the city's new central railway termini by redeveloping the densely built-up slopes below High Street, had obtained a private Act of Parliament

> for making a Road or Street from the South End of Waverley Bridge Road, adjoining the General Railway Station at Princes Street, to the High Street in the City of Edinburgh.[88]

Not only did this Edinburgh Railway Station Access Act of 1853 allow the clearance of certain specified properties to permit the setting out of the new curving thoroughfare of Cockburn Street (Figure 5), but it also authorised the company to build new shops and flatted houses on either side of the street. Some years later, with the purchase of lands and properties carried out and the consequent demolition of between two and three hundred old houses complete, the development began to take shape. The architects, Peddie & Kinnear, conceived the entire scheme in their favourite Baronial idiom using all the elements of the style in creative combinations cleverly adapted to the swinging curves of the street plan and the awkward climbing contours of the slope. The choice of Baronial was no arbitrary design decision, however, for as section XXI of the Act instructed,

> . . . it is desirable to preserve as far as possible the architectural style and antique Character of the Buildings of that Part of the Old Town in the Line and Neighbourhood of the said street.[89]

But since James Peddie (father of Kinnear's partner John Dick Peddie?) was a director of the development company, his influence may well have

Figure 5　Cockburn Street development, Edinburgh; presentation design by Peddie & Kinnear, c. 1860 (by permission of National Monuments Record of Scotland).

been decisive in stipulating this concern for the *genius loci*. At any rate, Cockburn Street was the first area of urban redevelopment to be realised in full-blown Scots Baronial style.

The Edinburgh Railway Station Access Act provided a model for future municipal compulsory purchase powers directed towards the clearance of squalid and congested areas of outworn urban housing while the success of Baronial Cockburn Street (*c*.1860) in conserving the city's townscape probably helped lead to the incorporation of similar structures in the Edinburgh City Improvement Act of 1867. Design guidelines were made quite explicit:

> . . . elevations shall be of plain but marked *character* (my italics), in harmony with those fine specimens of national architecture in many of the neglected and overcrowded areas.[90]

In other words, although the promoters of the Improvement Act were motivated by a reforming zeal to rid the city of the insanitary living conditions which prevailed in these 'neglected and overcrowded areas' of the Old Town, they did not reject the historic architectural *character* of its streets. Extensive clearance began in June 1868 and several new streets were laid out on either side of High Street and Canongate—Market Street, Cranston Street, Jeffrey Street, Blackfriars Street, St Mary's Street, Chambers Street, Guthrie Street, Lady Lawson Street, Marshall Street, Howden Street.[91] Plots were feued to various private builders who were legally bound to conform to designs prepared by the Improvement Trust's architects, David Cousin and John Lessels, both of whom were already practised in 'the old Scotch style'. These designs ensured the visual coherence and historical credibility of Old Edinburgh, so much so, indeed, that it is as much due to the Baronial redevelopment of Victorian times as it is to the legacy of earlier centuries that the capital continues to exert its magical medievalist spell. Modelled perceptively on the Lawnmarket roof-scapes of Gladstone's Land and Mylne's Court, the steep crowstepped gables, tall eaves dormers and chimney stacks which characterise the high-rise elevations designed by Cousin and Lessels are, as *The Builder* observed at the time 'in keeping with the surroundings, and *group well*' (my italics).[92] Scottishness is here more than mere polemics, it is a formal matter too, justified by a deliberate policy of urban conservation. What is more, it is the easy vernacular syntax of these Baronial forms, their ability to 'group well',which makes it possible to realise this policy so successfully.

Edinburgh maintained its fascination with the Baronial all through the second half of the century. It did so even where there were no immediate contextual reasons to prompt its adoption. Nor was any social premium to be set on a style which adapted as readily to the working-class tenements of Fountainbridge—including some early examples on Grove Street (1864–5) in the idiosyncratic idiom of F T Pilkington—as it did to more elegant streets beyond the Meadows, where David Bryce's 'emphatically Baronial'[93] designs for the Warrender Estate Development (from 1869) and MacGibbon and Ross's Bruntsfield Crescent (1870) catered for a more up-market clientele and further south in Merchiston, 'the most imaginative of later Victorian suburbs',[94] Dunn and Findlay reached five grand storeys with turreted corner bays and crow-stepped dormers in their work for the Chisholm Trust (1894). In Dean Village, by the Water of Leith, A G Sydney Mitchell created a self-contained group of flatted working-class homes complete with caretaker's house, shop, club room, and clock tower, the whole composition arranged with deceptively casual subtlety around an inner courtyard. Carried off in fine seventeenth-century Scots style, Brown's Court (1883–4)—or Well Court, as it is now known—was the remarkable romantic conceit of J R Findlay, owner of *The Scotsman*! Equally romantic but infinitely more prominently sited were Ramsay Gardens (1892–4) perched high on Castle Hill, the combined design of Henbest Capper, Mitchell, and Patrick Geddes. Certainly English in detail and material, their aggregative composition of vertical elements—gabled blocks, window bays and chimney stacks—nonetheless not only fits picturesquely in the local scene but, as McWilliam reminds us,

> A century in which the Scottish tradition has been identified with a puritanical love of masonry has brought us near to forgetting that wood and plaster, the erratic outline of 'overhanging stories and lookern windows' were just as much part of it.[95]

The Baronial Revival tenement, evolved in Edinburgh in the late 1850s, became a familiar element in the streetscene of Victorian Scotland. In the course of the last quarter of the century few towns failed to acquire an example (Rothesay constructed a long range sweeping down Russell Street as late as 1910). In the country's largest city, however, despite the pioneering precedent of the Glasgow Improvements Act of 1866 and the even earlier employment of the Baronial style in some fine commercial buildings, Baronial housing was slow to appear. As in Edinburgh, the railways had led the way for in 1863, at Cowlairs, the Edinburgh and Glasgow Railway Company, using the Perth architect Andrew Heiton, had built a small residential development on the hill beside the locomotive works 'in the best Baronial manner'.[96] But this was an isolated example of the revival. Indeed, when the City Improvements Act trustees built a number of model lodging-houses and two rather severe gable-fronted tenements on the Drygate (1875) there were still several genuinely seventeenth-century houses, very similar in form, standing on Stockwell Street, Saltmarket and High Street. It was more than a decade after that before these prototypes were followed and the cleared east side of Saltmarket was built up with four-storey tenement housing designed again in a very restrained national idiom, its Scottishness almost apologetically announced by a few crow-stepped gables and the minimal accretion of strapwork. During the 1890s building activities were stepped up, however, and similar tenements were erected on the west side of Saltmarket continuing, in a now more elaborated Scots manner, around Glasgow Cross into London Road.[97]

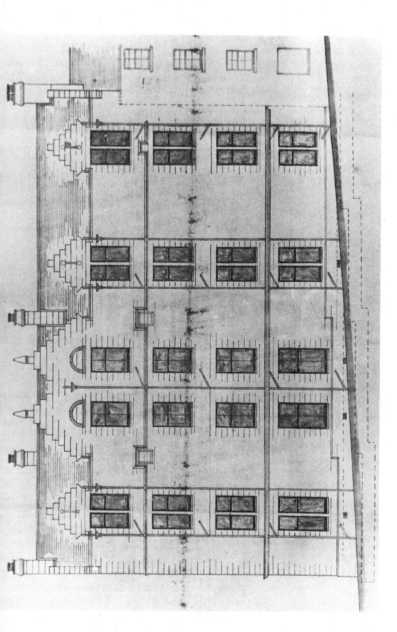

Figure 6 Workmen's dwellings, Morrin Square, Glasgow, 1894.

Though long delayed, such substantial stone blocks, generous in space standards, well lit, well ventilated, with proper sanitary provisions, were a vast improvement on the old backlands housing. Yet these very amenities put such property beyond the means of the poorer classes whose plight now deteriorated as they crowded into the older tenements that still remained in Calton and Bridgeton. Mounting criticism forced the City Improvements Trust to respond with a model development of workmen's dwellings at Morrin Square, Townhead (1894–8). Private concern, in the shape of the Glasgow Workmen's Dwellings Company, had already built nearby Cathedral Court (1892) and a few years later the same company, using the same architect, J J Burnet, provided additional low-cost accommodation at Greenhead Court, McKeith Street, Bridgeton (1897–8). All these developments were conceived in 'simple Scottish domestic style';[98] at Morrin Square the street facades were in red sandstone, though the inner courtyard elevations were of brick, while both Burnet's schemes were in harled brick throughout.

The combination of crow-stepped, eaves dormers and heavy chimney stacks with the plain white mass of soaring wall surfaces—especially evident at Burnet's Greenhead Court, Glasgow—brought the national revival closest to its roots. Glasgow could certainly boast a bolder Baronial. W J Boston's competition–winning design for the Improvement Trust's tenements on both sides of the High Street (1891–1903), for example, copes in a masterly aggregative way with the difficult demands of corner emphases, curving façades and rising contours—problems reminiscent of those first tackled by Peddie & Kinnear in Edinburgh's Cockburn Street half a century earlier. But Burnet's working-class Scotch, anticipating the domestic work of Charles Rennie Mackintosh and some of that by James Salmon, and, indeed, not dissimilar in character and composition, if not material, to Mackintosh's entry for the High Street competition (Figure 7) won by Boston, has an appropriately vernacular accent. That the Baronial and the vernacular should become one is, in some socio-cultural sense, paradoxical. But that the forms of cottage, mansion, castle and, doubtless, those of tenement, too, should alike evoke feelings to 'indescribable delight'[99] is less so since each belongs in the same landscape. Rough and severe in expression, these working-class tenements in Glasgow are undeniably Scottish. They are surely every bit as Scottish as the studied ashlar polish of an earlier Bryce- or Billings-derived Baronialism or the refined detail of a 'Scots Renaissance' predilection of which little has been said here.

By the turn of the century the historical landscape had finally been authoritatively presented by David MacGibbon and Thomas Ross in their five-volume Castellated and Domestic Architecture in Scotland (1887–92)—a work thoroughly studied by Mackintosh and as unscrupulously plundered by him in compiling the text of his 1891 paper to the Glasgow Architectural Association. By that time, too, the Baronial revival, no longer 'essentially an

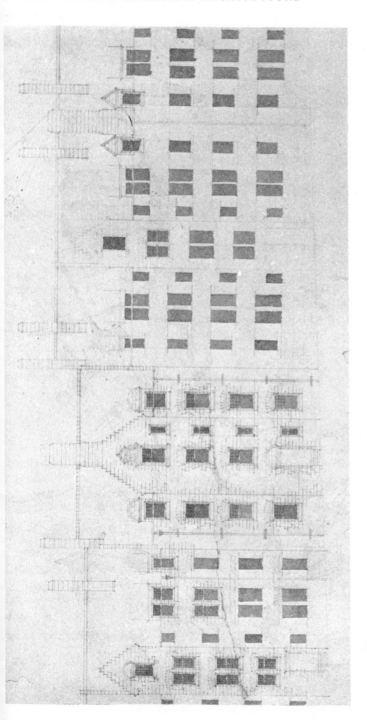

Figure 7 Workmen's dwellings, High Street, Glasgow; unpremiated competition design for City of Glasgow Improvement Trust, 1891, by C R Mackintosh (by permission of Hunterian Art Gallery, University of Glasgow, Mackintosh Collection).

upper-class style'[100] of castle or country house (though this remained largely the social *milieu* of Robert Lorimer's practice) had been democratised: first, by the immediate semantic import of its forms, its very nationalism; secondly, by that syntactical freedom, bound only by a tendency to verticality crowned by 'the most unexpected crustaceous projections',[101] which permitted its application to virtually every building type in the nineteenth-century city. Considered in these terms, the Scots Baronial may be seen to be far from the baneful and egregious influence a bad press has suggested. And yet, whatever the propensity of the Baronial tradition thereby to find an echo in what contemporary architectural theory now refers to as 'critical regionalism',[102] it remains a cultural tragedy that so few twentieth century Scots have been prepared to honour their own inheritance or create their future with that 'instinctive affection which', admittedly, 'is so difficult to reason upon'[103] but which Mackintosh had begun to draw and develop from the architecture of his native land.

ACKNOWLEDGEMENTS

The author is particularly indebted to David Walker, Senior Investigator at the Historic Buildings Branch of the Scottish Development Department, who generously took time to read and comment upon the text. Without this share in his unsurpassed knowledge of Scottish architecture the essay would have been much debilitated. For helpful information and discussion he is also grateful to Catherine Cruft, Pamela Reekie, Peter Robinson and Fiona Sinclair.

REFERENCES

1   C R Mackintosh 'Scotch Baronial Architecture', unpublished text (1891), Hunterian Museum Archive, F(c), Glasgow University
2   S Cruden *The Scottish Castle* (Edinburgh 1981), p 146
3   C McWilliam *Lothian,* The Buildings of Scotland series (Harmondsworth 1978), p 60
4   R MacLeod *Charles Rennie Mackintosh, Architect and Artist* (Glasgow and London 1983), p 27
5   *The Architect* 20 December 1891, p 113
6   C Rowe *The Mathematics of the Ideal Villa and Other Essays* (Cambridge, Mass. and London 1976), p 62
7   *The Times* 29 April 1817; see National Library of Scotland MS 638
8   *The Scots Magazine* February 1820; see NLS MS 638
9   *Ibid.*
10 Statement by subcommittee of the General Committee of Subscribers to the National Monument, 24 January 1822, NLS MS 638
11 *Ibid.*
12 'Memorandum by Cockerell on the principles of Greek architecture with reference to the adoption of the Parthenon as the model of the National Monument', 1823, NLS MS 639

13 *See* J Rykwert *On Adam's House in Paradise* (New York 1972), pp 82–7 for a discussion of Hall
14 *The Quarterly Review* , vol. XXVI (London 1822), pp 308–36
15 *Ibid.* p 329
16 *Ibid.* p 328
17 *Ibid.* p 330
18 *Ibid.*p 330
19 Letter from W H Playfair to C R Cockerell, 30 June 1829, NLS MS 638
20 R L Stevenson *Edinburgh, Picturesque Notes* (London 1889), p 123
21 W Shakespeare *Macbeth*, Act IV, Scene III, 164
22 D Daiches (ed) *The Penguin Companion to Literature,* vol. 1 (Harmondsworth 1971), p 406
23 I Berlin *Vico and Herder, Two Studies in the History of Ideas* (London 1980), p 172
24 *The Glasgow Herald* 5 February 1836
25 A M Wrinch 'George Kemp and the Scott Monument', *Country Life* 5 August 1971, pp 322–3
26 *See* N M McQ Holmes and L M Stubbs *The Scott Monument, a History and Architectural Guide* (Edinburgh 1979)
27 T Bonnar *Biographical Sketch of George Meikle Kemp* (Edinburgh 1892), p 85
28 J Ruskin 'Supplementary Chapter, being a contribution to a discussion in "The Architectural Review" as to the site of Scott's Monument', *The Poetry of Architecture* (London 1907), p 251
29 *Edinburgh Courant* 2 April 1838
30 A J Youngson *The Making of Classical Edinburgh* (Edinburgh 1975), p 279
31 *Ibid.* p 279
32 T Bonnar *op. cit.* p 110
33 G M Kemp, quoted in T Bonnar *op. cit.* p 108
34 A W N Pugin *Contrasts* (London 1841), p 17
35 J Macaulay *The Gothic Revival, 1745–1845* (Glasgow and London 1975), p 227
36 J Struthers 'Milton Lockhart', unpublished notes, Department of Architecture and Building Science, University of Strathclyde (Glasgow 1978), no. 41/78
37 V Fiddes and A Rowan 'David Bryce, 1803–1876', exhibition catalogue (Edinburgh 1976), p 60
38 J Slezer *Theatrum Scotiae containing the Prospects of their Majesties Castles and Palaces: together with those of the most considerable Towns and Colleges; the Ruins of many Ancient Abbeys, Churches, Monastries and Convents within the said Kingdom* (London 1693), fifth edition 1814
39 *Ibid.*
40 F Grose *The Antiquities of Scotland* (London 1797), p i
41 *Ibid.* p xviii
42 J C Loudon *Cottage, Farm and Villa Architecture and Furniture* (London 1833), p 879
43 R W Billings *The Baronial and Ecclesiastical Antiquities of Scotland* (Edinburgh 1852), p 6
44 Glasgow Scrapbook no. 21, Mitchell Library Glasgow, pp 8–9
45 'Proposal for erecting a Monument to the memory of Sir W Wallace of Elderslie', *Album Scoticarum Rerum* (Glasgow 1818), Mitchell Library Glasgow
46 *Some Records of the Origin and Progress of the National Wallace Monument Movement* (London 1880), private circulation, p 6

47 C Rogers *The National Wallace Monument, The Site and the Design* (Edinburgh 1860), p 3

48 J J Stevenson *House Architecture* (London 1880), p 377

49 *Ibid.* p 378

50 R Kerr *The Gentleman's House* (London 1864), p 376

51 A Gomme and D Walker *Architecture of Glasgow* (London 1968) p 280

52 R Kerr *op. cit.* p 450

53 J J Stevenson *op. cit.* p 378

54 *Ibid.* p 378

55 C R Mackintosh *op. cit.*

56 J C Loudon *op. cit.* p 890

57 *Ibid.* pp 879–80

58 *Ibid.* p 890

59 I Lindsay *The Scottish Parish Kirk* (Edinburgh 1960), p 142

60 G Hay *The Architecture of Scottish Post-Reformation Churches, 1560–1843* (Oxford 1957), p 142

61 J Ruskin *The Stones of Venice* (London 1907), vol. III p. 215 (ch. 2, p 35); first published 1853

62 V Fiddes and A Rowan *op. cit.* p 112

63 J L Wark (ed) *Encyclopedia of the Laws of Scotland* (Edinburgh 1928), pp 87–8)

64 Quoted in J L Wark *op. cit.* p 88

65 'Side Schools' were established by the Act of 1803 in those parishes where no school already existed; 'parliamentary schools' were introduced by the Act of 1838 as additional schools in divided parishes.

66 V Fiddes and A Rowan *op. cit.* p 58

67 G G Scott quoted in *The Curious Diversity, Glasgow University on Gilmorehill: the First Hundred Years* (Glasgow 1970), pp 11–12

68 R Kerr *op. cit.* p 377

69 *viz.* '. . . there will be separate entrances and playgrounds, and even separate staircases to enter the classrooms, so that the boys and girls may never associate except while under actual instruction in the eye of the teacher . . . ', article on Glasgow School Boards schools, *The Builder* 27 March 1875, p 274

70 *The Sheriff Court Houses (Scotland) Act, 1860*, 23° and 24° Victoriae c.79, section XI in G K Richards (ed), *The Statutes of the United Kingdom of Great Britain and Ireland* . . . (London 1860), pp 753–7

71 C McWilliam *op. cit.* p 305

72 The Commissioners of Supply responsible for the Aberdeen Court House clearly favoured a Scottish idiom since they held a limited competition inviting plans from Peddie & Kinnear, J Matthews—architect of Aberdeen Grammar School (1861–3), & W Smith—designer of Baronial Balmoral (1853–5)

73 C McWilliam *Scottish Townscape* (London 1975), p 145

74 Sir J Stirling Maxwell *Shrines & Homes of Scotland* (London 1937), p 206

75 V Fiddes and A Rowan *op. cit.* p 105

76 A Gomme and D Walker *op. cit.* p 296

77 Rochead was a subscriber to Billings' publication, as were several other exponents of the Scots Baronial revival, *viz.* J Matthews in Aberdeen, A Heiton in Perth, and D Rhind, D Cousins (*sic*), J Lessels, Kinnear, J Dick Peddie, and, of course, D Bryce, all in Edinburgh

78 *The Builder* 25 January 1868, p 57

79 F Wyness *Aberdeen, Century of Change* (Aberdeen 1971), p 158

80 Greenock (1877), Leith (1880), Aberdeen (1884), *see* I H Adams, *The Making of Urban Scotland* (London 1978), pp 159–60
81 'Report of a Committee of the Working Classes of Edinburgh on the Present Overcrowded and Uncomfortable State of Their Dwelling Houses' (Edinburgh 1860), p 1
82 *Ibid.* p 6
83 *Ibid.*p 6
84 *Ibid.* p 6
85 *Ibid.*p 7
86 J Ruskin *Lectures on Architecture and Painting* (London 1907), p 61; first published Edinburgh, November 1853
87 'Report of a Committee of the Working Classes of Edinburgh . . . ' *op. cit.* p 21
88 *A Collection of Local and Personal Acts . . . passed in the sixteenth and seventeenth year of the reign of her majesty Queen Victoria . . .* (London 1853), pp 577–86, sect. XXXV
89 *Ibid.* sect. XXI
90 Quoted in C McWilliam *op. cit.* p 196
91 *See* D King 'A Study of the Work of D Cousin (1809–1878)', unpublished dissertation, NMR (Edinburgh 1977), p 18
92 *The Builder* 7 August 1869, p 623
93 V Fiddes and A Rowan *op. cit.* p 101
94 C McKean *Edinburgh, an Illustrated Architectural Guide* (Edinburgh 1982), p 7
95 C McWilliam *op. cit.* p 198
96 F Worsdall *The Disappearing City* (Glasgow 1981), p 70
97 *See* M McNaught 'Glasgow: No Mean City (The Legal and Financial History of the Glasgow Tenement)', unpublished dissertation, Department of Architecture and Building Science, University of Strathclyde (Glasgow, 1972), for a history of the Glasgow Improvements Act
98 F Worsdall *The Tenement, A Way of Life* (Edinburgh 1979), p 110
99 C R Mackintosh *op. cit.* see above.
100 O Lancaster *Here, of all Places* (London 1959), p 96
101 N Pevsner *The Englishness of English Art* (Harmondsworth 1976), p 145
102 *See* K Frampton 'Modern architecture and critical regionalism', *Transactions* (RIBA) (London 1983), pp 15–25
103 C R Mackintosh *op. cit.* see above

6

LABOUR AND THE CHANGING CITY

Hamish Fraser

In a well-known essay Henry Pelling questioned how far the working class before 1914 supported social reform by means of state intervention.[1] He argued that there was, among the working class, a deeply entrenched suspicion of the state, as something that was inherently hostile to the working class. As a result, they were not likely to see social welfare measures emanating from the state as being to their ultimate advantage. As he also suggested, during the nineteenth and early twentieth centuries the state for most people did not mean Whitehall, but meant the local state, and this too was perceived by the working class as fundamentally hostile. The symbol of the local state was the police, which in a city like Glagow had, because of largely Highland recruitment, some of the characteristics of an alien, occupying force. The local state was the magistrate in the burgh courts handing out sentences to the drunk and disorderly, to the vagrant, to the dilatory ratepayer, and issuing warrants for the evictions of tenants. The local state was the sanitary officials raiding the ticketed houses between midnight and five in the morning in a hopeless effort to curb overcrowding, or reprimanding tenants for failing to keep clean the common stairs and closets. The local state was the work of the Improvement Trust, which by its slum-clearance policies drove the slum dwellers from their homes into the yet more crowded remaining houses. The local state was the new town hall, undoubtedly magnificent but on land gained at the cost of clearing the homes of the poor. The local state was the parochial board which treated the poor, in need or in sickness, with a parsimonious disregard for basic needs. The local state was the administrators of the Lord Provost's relief fund who treated applicants with what was intended to be a deterring harshness. The local state was the belt-happy teacher or the truancy officer of school boards that had made education compulsory but not free. None of these manifestations of urban authority was likely to endear it to the many of the working class.

Yet, at the beginning of the twentieth century the new Labour Party was firmly associated in the public mind with state intervention at all levels. It was particularly linked with greater power for the municipal authorities. Municipal enterprise had become municipal socialism, with councillors succumbing to pressure 'to provide everything the population required in its passage from the cradle to the grave'.[2] The aim of this essay is to examine some of the reactions of the working class in Scottish cities to the activities of local authorities and will seek to elucidate the changing attitude to the power of the municipality.

As with any work on the working class, one has the problem of identi-

fying what can be taken as its authentic voice or what fragment of the
working class any spokesman represents. Those most affected by either
deteriorating or 'improved' urban conditions were not necessarily the most
articulate. The organised working class, organised in its trade unions or
political parties, does not necessarily speak for the poorest. Yet, it is the
organised who leave much of the source material on which the historian has
to rely. For the unorganised and generally inarticulate one has to rely on an
interpretation of actions rather than of words.

In the actions of many of the poorest one can detect a very clear hostility
to any attempt by middle-class reformers to penetrate the dark recesses of
the city's vennels and rookeries. During the cholera epidemics doctors or
inspectors were, on occasions, the victims of assault, regarded as carriers of
the disease rather than as purveyors of much needed aid. When in the last
great outbreak of 1866 Glasgow's first medical officer of health issued 'a
kindly remonstrance' to a woman in a cholera-infested room he 'elicited
only angry abuse from her and friendly advice from a workman hard by to
hold our tongue and take ourselves off as quickly as possible'.[3] There was
no citizenry waiting to be cleaned. The baths and wash-houses, one of the
municipal glories of Glasgow in the late nineteenth century were not
particularly well patronised. After a decade of existence only 4000 washers
used the five wash-houses in 1895.[4] One does not need written confirmation
to imagine the attitude towards the sanitary authorities of those who
struggled for survival in some overcrowded, made-down house. Trapped in
poverty, often accentuated by a large family, and forced into the cheapest
of single rooms they would find themselves prosecuted for being so many.
One has a picture of a perpetual battle to beat the ticketed-house system.
John Butt has perceptively written of a 'communal obligation' to ensure
that blame was shared and that, whenever possible, a first offender was
brought to court so that he could, with luck, hope to get away with an
admonition or at most a 1s. fine.[5] There is no evidence that it deterred the
luckless inhabitants of such houses. Those whom social reform was
reputedly supposed to aid tended to see themselves as its victims.

The poor were right to see themselves as victims. They were seen as a
problem to be eradicated or manipulated, or as a group beyond the bounds
of civilisation that needed to be moralised. There was little sensitivity to
their feelings or their plight. Such attitudes were strengthened by the
assumption that their poverty was largely self-inflicted, through drink,
idleness or fecklessness, or was the product of an alien culture that
circumstances had injected into Scotland. The poorest were assumed to be
Irish immigrants who had brought with them habits that largely created the
urban social problems.

It proved extremely difficult to overcome the barrier of complete
indifference to matters of public health that existed in the Scottish cities.
Even Chadwick's conclusions that 'the mortality from fever is greater in
Glasgow, Edinburgh and Dundee than in the most crowded towns in
England' or the comment of the Health of Towns Committee that 'penury,
dirt, misery, drunkenness and crime culminate in Glasgow to a pitch

unparalleled in Great Britain'[6] did little to break through ignorance and indifference to how an ever growing section of the population lived. Only the terrors aroused by cholera were, briefly, enough to stimulate concerted action.

A few did care. Doctors operating in the slums were aware of the conditions. Dr W P Alison long and fruitlessly argued the case for the link between poverty and ill health. There were Christians who were concerned at the moral threat posed by bad living conditions. As Dr Callum Brown has shown, in his recent excellent thesis on religion in Glasgow,[7] evangelicals, well represented on the Town Council, played a vital role in trying to push forward social improvement. 'To give a man a comfortable dwelling and a clean face, is to start him on the path of intellectual and moral improvement' argued the evangelical *Glasgow Examiner*.[8] Moderate as it was in Scotland, Chartism too aroused fears and encouraged a new awareness of the working class:

> If the rich expect the gratitude and intention of the poor, they must first show that they feel and sympathise with them. . . . Employers now feel that it is in their interest that their workmen be sober, intelligent and happy, because they have invariably found that, when intelligent men are treated with integrity and justice, they have an interest in an employer's welfare, and, consequently, add to his continued prosperity and security.[9]

Yet at the end of the day it took thirty years of talk, debate and complaint to get round to tackling the fundamental problem of the water supply. The failure of the water companies to keep the pipes filled at night and to provide enough stop cocks for the fire engines, with the resultant threat to property from fire, was probably as important as public health concerns in eventually pushing through the Loch Katrine works in the 1850s.[10] From then on, however, there was, for two decades, a gathering momentum in public action. With no national legislation, since the 1848 Public Health Act did not cover Scotland, all initiatives had to come from the local authorities. Thanks largely to the enthusiasm and commitment of individual councillors like John Ure and John Blackie in Glasgow, powers were gathered into the hands of the Corporation to try to deal with some of the problems. Ure's committee in 1859 recommended additional powers to be obtained under the Police Acts to deal with overcrowding and insanitary housing, to prevent factory discharge into common drains, and to make ashes and night soil the property of the city.[11] Such powers were granted in the Glasgow Police Act of 1862 and it was under this legislation that the ticketing of housing with less than 2,000 cubic feet of space was brought in. Another recommendation was to acquire property by compulsory purchase for the sake of sanitary improvement. This was implemented by the Improvement Act of 1866, by which the City Improvement Trust could buy property, lay new streets and demolish the most insanitary buildings.

As with water, talk of municipalising gas had been around since the 1830s and a decade of battle with the gas companies in Glasgow ended in 1867 when the Corporation agreed to buy them out. High prices and a lack of competition had regularly brought complaints and there was active parliamentary encouragement to deal with the problem by means of municipalisation. It was a logical step since the Corporation was the largest consumer and it fitted with the current aim to open up the slums to inspection and control. Authority could more safely venture into a well-lit close.

The major typhus outbreak of 1869 resulted in the nation's first municipal fever hospital at Belvidere, with facilities for disinfecting the clothes of fever victims. The homeless poor were given an alternative to the private and notorious common lodging houses with the building of two 'model' lodging houses by the Improvement Trust in 1870. Another five followed in 1874, 1878 and 1879, by which time the city was providing a third of the total lodging accommodation. Later in the seventies another of Ure's recommendations of 1859 was taken up with the building of baths and wash-houses.[12]

Although the examples cited above are taken from Glasgow the pattern in the other Scottish cities is not dissimilar. Aberdeen had its municipal water works in 1866 and municipal gas in 1871 and a fever hospital in 1874. Dundee gas and water were first taken over in 1868 and 1869 and had its first public baths in 1871. Edinburgh had its City Improvement Act in 1868. By the early 1870s the local authorities had substantially increased their power to impinge on the lives of its citizens. In a relatively short period the Corporation of most cities had taken on new responsibilities to regulate and control and to provide services. In addition, parochial boards had taken the responsibility for poor relief from the Kirk and these boards too had increased their powers and responsibilities. Dangers of disease, of crime and of disorder led to the desire to control and check the patterns of life of the poor.

I

The response of the organised working class to these activities was remarkably muted. Demands for action to improve urban living conditions or the health of the working class did not feature prominently in the chartist programme, though it was not entirely absent. The Edinburgh chartist programme of 1839 called for 'sanitary police for dwellings, factories and workshops', and for the removal of 'taxes prejudicial to health'.[13] Chadwick showed some anxiety at the involvement of chartists in the health of towns movement.[14] In Glasgow, James Moir, a chartist activist and town councillor, interested himself in public health questions and was closely associated with John Ure in the 1859 committee which prodded the city fathers into action.[15] But, these would seem to be the exceptions rather than the rule.

By the 1860s in all Scottish cities trade unionists had in their trades councils a forum for expressing views on a range of local activities, yet here again references to conditions of life and to public health are few. The newly-formed Glasgow Council in 1858 found 'the efforts made by the municipal council to beautify and improve the city by the acquisition of public parks and a picture gallery . . . highly commendable', but, in an attitude that was to emerge again and again, they objected to plans to raise an additional rate for such purposes.[16] Rather they advocated a pet scheme of the veteran Owenite, Alexander Campbell, for a municipal bank with its own note issue. Throughout the 1860s the main solution of Glasgow unionists to the urban problem was state-aided emigration to remove the pressure of numbers on the city.[17]

By the end of the decade, however, there were signs of awareness among artisans of the implications of improvement. Edinburgh unionists, within months of the city's Improvement Act coming into force in 1868, were protesting at the demolition of working-class housing and the building of middle-class housing in its place, 'thereby inflicting a serious injury on the poorer portion of the community by crowding them into places that is (*sic*) already overcrowded'.[18] In 1870 the Trades Council tried to launch a wider public campaign of protest against overcrowded housing at exorbitant rents and called for the City Improvement Trust to erect the necessary houses.[19] The evidence of similar concern in Glasgow at this time is lacking, since the Trades Council was defunct in the late sixties. With its revival in 1870 there was discussion of sanitary conditions in the city and fairly mild resentment at the ticketed house system—'the expenditure for inspection (was) out of all proportion to the meagre results'.[20]

For the better off among the working class there were obvious gains to be made from city improvements. It is true that there was no dramatic fall in the death rate, but those with access to gas and water did gain from the new and better supplies. Municipalisation meant that water was now available to all who were plumbed into the system and the aim was to encourage as much consumption as possible by domestic consumers. Glasgow was very proud that it had the highest *per capita* consumption of water in the country, twice that of any English city.[21] The price of gas halved within a few years of municipalisation and by 1895 Glasgow had 156,980 consumers, Edinburgh 61,397, Dundee 32,629 and Aberdeen 24,475.[22] With the introduction of free cookers and the cheap hire of gas fires from 1885 consumption increased steadily.

In Scotland municipalisation of public utilities was not seen as a means of lowering rates. In most of the local acts by which municipalisation was carried out subsidy of the rates from profits was explicitly barred. This was in marked contrast to Joe Chamberlain's vision of Birmingham, where the profit-making gas works were intended to reduce the rates.[23] The emphasis in Scotland was always on cheapness of supply. To a large extent this can be accounted for by the different rating pattern in Scotland. Road and public water rates were paid by owners, but police rates (which covered watching, lighting, cleaning, baths, fire brigade), sanitary, parks, statute labour and domestic water rates were paid only by occupiers. Again in contrast to England, there was almost no compounding of rates in Scotland except in the very cheapest houses of under £4 rental. Indeed, it was, apparently, not uncommon for occupiers to pay the owner's share of rates and then to claim them back with the next rent payment. How far this was possible, given the complexity of the rating system, is not clear. But as a city assessor commented 'whoever pays in the first place is not able to transfer the whole burden to the shoulders of another'.[24] In the English city, where compounding was common and owners bore the burden of rates the pressure from the influential was for reductions in the level of rates. In Scotland the better-off had less cause for complaint. Better, therefore, to have low-priced water and gas, with the rate burden spread widely. While there was no enthusiasm for rates, economy parties do seem to have made less headway in Scottish cities in the late nineteenth century than in some English towns.

On the other hand, there were more complaints from working-class rate-payers. The franchise in local elections was a ratepayers' one. In order to get a vote in the November elections in Scotland an occupier had to have paid his rates in full before then. Occupiers of the cheapest property where rates were compounded were automatically excluded.[25] The system effectively meant that the poorest, 'the whole body of men who are ignorant, vicious and irresponsible', as an American observer noted approvingly, were 'practically outside the pale of politics in Glasgow and Edinburgh, Dundee and Aberdeen'.[26] More than a quarter of households in Glasgow were excluded in the 1890s and in 1908–9 35,671 ratepayers failed to pay the municipal assessment on time.[27] The Scottish city electorate was predominantly the better-off skilled working class. In a way this probably made the extension of municipal activities easier since there was less middle-class fear that the 'slum vote' would get control of the political system.[28] On the other hand, the pressure from hard-pressed working-class ratepayers was generally in favour of economy. Not unnaturally, trades councils in their first rather tentative moves in local politics in the 1870s associated with small ratepayers' associations. They were keen for the costs of city improvements to be borne by owners, since they were the ones who were gaining from the increased rents that followed the implementation of the Improvement Act.[29]

Few things so consistently aroused resentment among the working class as the salaries of officials of local authorities—such officials as the city chamberlain or the town clerk or the superintendent of police.[30] There was class resentment at a well-paid group getting privileges not granted to others. There was protest at the financing of superannuation schemes for police and parochial board officials from the rates:[31] 'they should be left to make provision for old age from their own savings the same as other members of the community.'[32] It was this issue, more than anything, which brought the first two trades-council-backed candidates into the Aberdeen Town Council in 1884.[33] It was not, however, easy to find working-men candidates who could attend meetings of the town council held during the day, and throughout the eighties the working class had to depend on sympathetic middle-class candidates to represent their interests. With a new political awareness emerging in the 1880s, however, there were increased demands for the alteration of council meetings to the evening[34] and more determined efforts to overcome the problems of the existing arrangements.

By the 1880s, then, there was little sign that the working class had much enthusiasm for the local improvements that had been carried out. A deep suspicion of the inflated powers of officials made workers resistant to any augmentation of their powers. A rating system that pushed the burden of rates on to occupiers made the working-class ratepayer resentful of rate increases. When an enlightened few active unionists campaigned for popular support for the adoption of the Free Libraries Act they found that they were again and again defeated by the 'antagonism of petty shop-keepers' and 'the indifference of the workers'.[35] Only towards the end of the decade did attitudes begin to change.

II

A second phase of municipal interventionism came in the 1890s with, in Glasgow, the municipalisation of trams, electricity supply and telephones and an extension of earlier activities. The whole period from 1890 through to the war has frequently been seen as the golden age of the 'civic gospel' with Glasgow at its centre. As *The Times* said, it was 'more responsible than any other city or town in the United Kingdom for the spread of the various forms of municipal progress which has been developed by the new munici-palisation'.[36]

The great symbol of the 'new municipalisation' was the municipal trams. As the first major city actually to run its own trams Glasgow attracted the attention of municipal reformers, particularly from the United States, who projected it and much else in the administration of the Scottish city as a model for the United States.[37] From the point of view of this paper its importance lies in bringing organised labour into local politics and it was for long claimed as the first major success of the labour movement in local politics.

In fact, there were a number of issues that turned Glasgow Corporation towards municipal operating. It had always been seen as a possibility under the terms of the Glasgow Tramway Act. Projected plans by the private company to expand into the provision of cabs and carriages in 1887 brought up the issue of the lease in 1887.[38] The Corporation effectively blocked those plans and from this date on there was a possibility of the lease not being renewed. It was decided to make a firm decision five years before the lease was due to run out, and as the date approached there were increasing complaints publicly voiced against the Tramway Company: cars were dirty, irregular and lacked a standardised colour; the drivers and conductors were given no uniforms and were generally unkempt; unsightly advertisements carried by the cars obscured the destination boards and defaced the city.[39] The influential sabbatarian lobby, which included the Trades Council, had been antagonised by proposals to run Sunday cars.[40] There were running skirmishes between the Corporation's Tramway Committee (responsible for the track) and the Company on who should bear the cost of line repairs.

It was as discussions on the future of the lease were getting underway that the Glasgow Trades Council entered the scene. The Trades Council had become involved when it began to assist in the formation of a tramwaymen's union to campaign against the excessive hours, low wages and harsh fining system which were part of the tramworker's lot. Those tramwaymen most active in organising found themselves dismissed.[41] The Trades Council now took up the call for the Corporation to manage and work the service. The iniquities of the private service rather than the positive attraction of municipal ownership were the motivation.

The Company's refusal to discuss conditions of work and other issues with the Corporation merely succeeded in producing a more hostile tramway committee, who laid down stiff conditions for the renewal of the lease, forbidding the Company to move into new areas of enterprise; demanding the replacement of a specific length of track each year, insisting on no more than a 60-hour week for employees, with proper uniforms and adequate lavatories, restricting advertising. The rejection of these terms made municipalisation more or less inevitable. The Trades Council did play its part by keeping the issue at the forefront of the municipal election of 1890, though it had only limited success in bringing forward candidates of its own. But there was widespread popular support for municipalisation. Trams were, after all, middle-class forms of transport and not yet the 'gondolas of the people'. There were plenty business and commercial men who were discontented with the private company. It had offered an appalling service. It had affronted civic pride and dignity and it had few friends. The city's image, control of the streets, efficiency were the main motives for municipalisation. There had always been those around who had seen the possibility of the tramways relieving the overcrowding of the city centre by carrying workers at cheap fares into the suburbs,[42] but this barely surfaced in the debates. The half-penny fare which the municipal trams introduced in 1894 was not part of this policy, nor a demand of the trades council, but a response to the last-ditch tactics of the old tramway company as it tried to defeat the new trams with halfpenny omnibuses.

There were no labour demands for the other two areas of municipalisation undertaken in the 1890s. In 1890 the Corporation obtained a provisional order empowering it to supply electricity, and by 1900 there were nearly 3,000 consumers and the beginning of electric street lighting.[43] The motive for municipal electricity was, at least according to its critics, a desire by the Corporation to block likely competition with municipal gas.[44] But, it was a logical extension of the process of taking over those public utilities that needed to dig up the streets. In 1893, the Corporation, in response to complaints about the high charges of the National Telephone Co. and about the inefficiency of the service, sought to establish its own telephone service, but it was 1899 before the Government granted the requisite licence. By the end of 1900 there were nearly 4,000 subscribers in a telephone area stretching from Clydebank and Busby to Kilsyth.[45]

None of this had anything to do with municipalisation as a first step towards the creation of the socialist state. Indeed for many of the most enthusiastic this extension of municipal power was an alternative to central power.[46] As one of Glasgow's leading progressives, Henry Dyer, wrote in 1894

The development which is at present taking place in every department of local government opens up great possibilities for the future; in fact the chief reason for this development is to make social and industrial reforms possible, for those who really understand the problems have no wish for a highly centralised authority which too often means dull, lifeless, official routine. On the contrary they are of the opinion that it is only possible to carry out their ideas when power is localised, and when those who exercise it can observe all the conditions and problems which they are called upon to solve. Those who do not care for the name socialism may speak of the works of different local bodies.[47]

For others, there was an attraction in the expertise of local officials and councillors as people who could create a new national efficiency free from the partisan political approach of national politics.[48]

By the end of the nineties there was talk of municipal pubs, milk supplies, hospitals, pawnshops and bakeries. Although all of these were to become incorporated in a Fabian programme, presented in a whole series of tracts between 1897 and 1900, they were part of regular ideas of progressive thinking in Glasgow before then. Municipal public houses had a strong appeal to powerful temperance groups who throughout the decade were campaigning for local control over the drink trade. Municipalisation became part of that demand. It could be used to reduce the number of licences and pubs had already been banned from municipal property. The municipal pub manager in a municipalised system could control the drinking of the customers, could eliminate bad liquor and could eradicate the political power of publican and brewer.[49] The demand for municipal milk supplies stemmed from medical concern at the spread of tuberculosis.[50]

Working-class attitudes to municipalisation were in essence different from that of the middle-class progressives, though influenced by some of the same ideas. There was not, for the working class, a faith in the 'expert' who knew best, nor a belief that the local state could somehow be separated from the national state and would act differently. On the municipalisation of public houses they could, to an extent, agree. Temperance and the labour movement was closely linked. Few labour candidates for public office in the years before 1914 failed to preface their election addresses with a statement that they were teetotal. A number of labour candidates were backed by temperance parties.[51] Drink was still clearly seen by the skilled working class as the major social problem, but there was never complete agreement on whether the answer lay in local option or in municipal control. There was always a fear that municipalisation might make the public house 'respectable'.[52]

From 1889 a few labour representatives in Glasgow found their way on to the Corporation. But, it was in 1896, in the special circumstances of an election for the whole corporation of the city, expanded by major boundary changes, that a breakthrough came. Nine Labour candidates, of varied and sometimes divided views were elected. By 1898 there were a dozen of these 'stalwarts', as they called themselves, on the Corporation. The goals of municipal activity for this group were different from the wider progressive demands. They focused on three issues. Firstly, there was a demand for the local authority to become a model employer; secondly, to do something about housing; and thirdly, to provide work for the unemployed.

Not all were enthusiastic about the local authorities directly employing labour. There had been earlier protests by plumbers when the Glasgow water committee employed its own men to undertake repairs.[53] Talk of municipal bakeries was not welcomed by the members of the bakers' union. The large proportion of 'jobbing bakers' in the union feared that it would threaten the casual work on which they depended. Nor were the 30,000 or so co-operators likely to be keen on something that might challenge the extensive Co-operative Baking Society.[54] But the relative ease with which the municipal gas workers achieved an eight-hour day in 1889 and the initial enthusiasm for the improved working conditions for tramwaymen that came with municipalisation encouraged the view that the municipality could set the pace for improved working conditions. There were demands for municipal workshops to produce police and corporation uniforms, as an alternative to the sweater dens of the usual tailoring contractors, with the ILP going further and demanding a direct works department for building and sanitary work.[55] When this made little progress there was a more successful campaign to get fair contracts' resolutions passed by town councils, police commissioners and school boards, pledging to give contracts only to those who paid trade-union levels of wages.[56] By 1898 pressure by the Labour 'stalwarts' on the Glasgow Corporation had achieved a minimum wage of 21s. per week for municipal employees and the demand for a working week of 48 hours was at the forefront of the programme of the Workers' Municipal Election Committee. The intention was that the level of wages and conditions of work among municipal employees would act as a stimulus to raise working standards all round.[57]

The second demand was for action on housing. Although there had been concern about housing conditions in the past rarely had solutions been proposed. Asked by the Royal Commission on the Housing of the Working Classes in 1885 if he thought the Town Council should become responsible for housing, the President of the Edinburgh Trades Council hastened to reject it as something that 'would strike at that industry and enterprise that lies at the very root of our national existence'.[58] However, within the year the same Council was calling for municipalisation of land on the edge of the city where house building could take place.[59]

A heightened awareness of housing conditions was apparent in the 1890s helped by the Medical Officer of Health, J P Russell's exposé of *Life in One Room* and by reports like that of the Glasgow Presbytery on the Housing of the Poor.[60] But there was still a faith that if cheap land were available then the market would provide. Scottish municipalities laboured under the particular disability that, unlike in England, it was not possible under existing legislation to purchase land outside the burgh boundaries for municipal building. Secondly, the maximum period of repayment of local authority loans in Scotland was thirty years, compared with as long as eighty years in England. Both these were a deterrent to the local authority utilising the powers of the existing housing legislation. Changes in the law seemed a first necessity.[61] The Workers' Municipal Programme in Aberdeen and in Glasgow in 1891 said no more than that 'all ground belonging to the City Improvement Trust be utilised, when suitable, for building artisan dwellings'.[62]

In Glasgow the City Improvement Trust had moved into housebuilding belatedly and unwillingly in 1888. A few tenements were built 'for the better class of working people' at rents ranging from £4.10s. for a single apartment to £17 for three apartments. The aim was commercial rather than social, to encourage private developers to move in and to boost the value of the surrounding land in the hope of getting rid of it.[63] However, under the chairmanship of Samuel Chisholm, the City Improvement Committee was stimulated into more action in the 1890s. Two 'family homes' were established where widowed parents with children could obtain accommodation, together with nursery provision.[64] In 1897, a new Act authorised the Corporation to purchase land in the City or up to half a mile beyond it and to erect houses for the poorest class. But, the Corporation successfully petitioned the Secretary of State to be relieved of the duty of making provision for those displaced by slum clearance, on the ground that there was ample accommodation available in the immediate neighbourhood. Strengthened by a strong plea from the chief sanitary engineer that workmen's houses had to be provided by the Corporation if he was to be in any position to enforce the city's by-laws on overcrowding, Chisholm proposed to borrow £750,000 for the provision of workmen's houses. Chisholm had already antagonised 'the Trade', by blocking attempts to have public houses on municipal property. He had antagonised some vested interests by his campaign for municipal telephones. He now took on the Glasgow Landlords' Association and a huge number of rentiers on whose support the Association could draw. The Citizen's Union, formed in 1898 to counter the growing strength of Labour in local politics, immediately moved into action to galvanise support against the measure. Six hundred of the Chamber of Commerce and 800 of the city's largest ratepayers petitioned against the provisional order. The secretary of the Citizen's Union went to London to make contact with groups like the Industrial Freedom League and the Electrical Engineer's Society who were at the forefront of a campaign against municipalisation of public utilities. Perhaps, most significantly he was interviewed by *The Times* and no doubt helped instigate *The Times* articles on municipal socialism that appeared a month later.[65]

The arguments of the opponents was that it was the duty of the Corporation to provide for the 'lowest stratum, the improvident and destructive, but not criminal classes', but that it was not its responsibility to provide for the 'decent poor'. For the municipality to provide housing of that kind would be expensive, and wasteful and uneconomical and tend to push up the price of land. It would deter private enterprise, check wholesome competition and pull the poor back into the cities, when the need was to disperse them. To provide for only part of the working class was iniquitously discriminating. To provide state-aided houses was to reintroduce subsidy in aid of wages and bring a dangerous element into municipal politics of having electors electing their landlord. All these arguments were put forward at the Municipal Commission on the Housing of the Poor set up by Glasgow Corporation in 1902.[66]

On the other side, the labour movement was in favour of the Corporation building houses 'beyond the city boundaries, to be let at such rentals as will meet the cost of erection and maintenance'. As the ILP activist George Carson told the Commission, 'We don't ask them in the meantime to let at less than the cost of construction', but the building of working-class housing was 'an absolute necessity' and the Corporation were 'the proper authorities to build these houses'. The assumption was that the Corporation could supply the houses more efficiently than private enterprise, just as it had with gas, water and trams.[67] There was some concern that houses that were too cheap would perpetuate low wages, and the other ILP witness, Joseph Burgess, wanted the corporation houses to be built for the 'better working class' in the suburbs so that the centre could be left to the poorest.[68] Burgess also floated two ideas that were to be taken up later: that any houses built should be cottages, to get away from the single apartments in tenement blocks in which the Scottish cities abounded and that, as had already been done in Sheffield, money should be borrowed from the tramway surplus to finance such building.[69] Housing gradually came to the forefront of the Glasgow Trades Council's concerns and a number of national conferences were organised by the Council to discuss the issue and press for municipal action.[70] But, the municipal commission stuck firmly to the line that any housing should be only for the poorest and as William Smart, the professor of political economy at Glasgow University, wrote,

The construction of such houses should be based on the well-known destructive habits of this class. They should be houses that the tenants cannot spoil—four bare walls, say of concrete, with an indestructible set in fire place, and an indestructible bed-frame. So far as possible, no wood to hack or burn; no plaster to pull down; no paper to tear away; no fittings to carry off by the light of the moon; well-lit, that there be no concealment of evil-doing; with, of course, a sufficiency of air-space and sanitary appliances.[71]

At the election of November 1902, Chisholm was unseated and this was taken by the loan commissioners as a sign that the citizens of Glasgow were not in favour of the municipality building houses and the loan granted was only £150,000 to finish work in hand.

As yet, most working-class spokesmen were searching for a clear stance on the housing issue. There was a belief that more housing was required to push down rents and help relieve overcrowding. It was accepted that the Corporation should play its part in providing such housing. What was not being proposed was subsidised housing. There was still a view that if more land and more houses were available then prices and rents would fall. It is also doubtful if all the working class was enthusiastic for the Corporation's housebuilding plans. The Citizens' Union was able to make capital out of housing proposals that it could present as doing nothing for the poorest section of society, and the Union was able to bid for working-class votes by suggesting that those Corporation houses that had been built had gone to a privileged few of the Corporation's own workers in trams and gas works.[72]

The third area where the labour movement looked to the local authority to take action was in relief to the unemployed. Since at least the mid-eighties trade unionists had been looking to the town councils to provide work at times of depression. Aberdeen Trades Council had been brushed aside in 1879 when they had asked the Town Council to help.[73] In 1885 they refused to be ignored, and both Aberdeen and Glasgow Trades Council campaigned for relief works. There were a few doubts that to look to the city was to admit the inadequacies of their trade societies,[74] but there was now an acceptance that there should be some concern for the unionised. Chamberlain's Local Government Board circular of 1886 encouraging municipal public works did not cover Scotland and there was no Scottish Board of Supervision equivalent. However, by using common-good funds councils did establish some work schemes. These generally caused resentment because of the low rates paid to those in make-work schemes and at the censoriousness of individuals from the Association for Improving the Conditions of the Poor and the Charity Organisation Society who administered relief funds.[75] Similar criticisms were to be found in the next sharp depression of 1892–3, but, by this time, from socialist groups there was a much clearer sense of the state's (local or national) responsibility to provide work for the unemployed. There was talk of the 'right to work' and a demand that the standard rate be paid for the tasks undertaken. On the other hand, as James Treble has shown, interest in the matter throughout the nineties was 'fitful'.[76] It was easy in the relative prosperity of the last years of the century to succumb to the widely preached middle-class view that the unemployed were the unemployable, or just to push the issue to one side.

There was, then, a difference between the more restricted and pragmatic views of the labour movement towards the municipality and the far-flown schemes that emanated from Fabians and others. Significantly, the most grandiose visions of municipalisation of milk, coal, bakeries, pawnshops came from a new Liberal like Daniel Macaulay Stevenson or from the most professional middle class of the Labour candidates such as Dr James Erskine, a lecturer at Anderson's College.[77] Actual working-class candidates tended to be more restricted in their vision. How far the actual policies put forward by the Worker's Municipal Committee explains the remarkable success in getting some dozen men with labour connections on Glasgow Corporation by 1898 is not possible to assess. The complexity of local politics in the city still waits to be unravelled, and the work of John Ferguson and an elaborate relationship with Irish and temperance groups was probably more important than actual policies. The quality of the alternatives may well have deteriorated. Certainly this is what the Citizens' Union believed and, indeed, was set up to alter. What is significant is that as quickly as it arose the Labour presence on the Glasgow corporation evaporated.

III

By the beginning of the century the whole policy of what was increasingly, if erroneously, referred to as municipal socialism was under sustained attack from a variety of directions. A great deal of the criticism came from vested interests. As H T Muggeridge wrote, 'Scratch a lecturer against municipal trading, in whatever out of the way place you may find him, and beneath the skin you will come across an electrical financier.'[78] But that did not make the criticism any less effective. Perhaps more important, however, was the accusation that it was adding to the level of rates. Rates were undoubtedly rising at the turn of the century from 11.4p in the pound in 1890–1 to 18.7p in the pound in 1913–14, according to Tom Hart's calculations; as expressed in terms of tax per head of population a rise from 71p to 134p.[79] They were rising for a number of reasons. Local authorities were facing increased costs. Steady urbanisation brought greater liabilities: increased expenditure on the poor, on public health provision, on parks and recreation ground, on police stations and on schools. Technological change brought more elaborate and more costly ways of laying sewers and making roads and running hospitals. The coming of motorised transport necessitated improvements in many areas. These expenditures were mainly optional, but central government was imposing greater burdens on local authorities by insisting on increased expenditure on education and on the police. Government grants in aid of rates did not adjust to meet the increased expenditure. After 1906 a very high proportion of the administrative costs of new welfare measures had to be paid for from rates.

It is all too easy for historians to assume that ratepayers are predominantly middle class. As has been argued earlier, the skilled working class bore the rate burden also, indeed perhaps increasingly so as the better off moved further out of the cities. Working-class ratepayers were equally opposed to rising rates. One response was to try to get more of the burden of rates passed to owners. There was also a long campaign, master-minded by John Ferguson, for the taxation of land values, by which the city could gain from the unearned increment on land and property values which municipal improvements like tramway extension brought. It was suggested that 'the taxation of land values, municipal banking, and the municipalisation of the liquor traffic would be sufficient to relieve them of taxes altogether'.[80] Another approach was an end to yearly letting of houses and the bringing in of compounding of rates with rents. In the event the resulting House Letting and Rating Act of 1911 did not bring the expected relief. It left tenants open to gradual rent increases and to a passing on of a share of owners' rates to tenants. It intensified the pressure for municipal housing.[81]

There were signs of disillusionment and disenchantment with existing municipalisation. As an editorial in the *Forward* newspaper admitted once the initial '*eclat* derived from the municipalisation of the tramways' had run its course there was not much left to sustain enthusiasm. After the early success of the new trams those who were preaching municipalisation 'appeared with a strong presumption in their favour'.[82] Now there was no such presumption. Municipal telephones had no great popular appeal and the decision to sell them to the Post Office in 1907 could be presented as a sign of failure. All the talk of municipal milk and municipal coal had not led to action. The blocking of the Corporation's housebuilding scheme in 1902 was an indication of how limited municipal power was. There were doubts about the success of what was already municipalised. There were questions about the much lauded tramways. Wages on them did not compare favourably with other areas. There were too many officials 'all of them better treated in every way than the rank and file' and every bit as authoritarian as private employers.[83] Earnings were not all that high and there was, with increased inspection, a loss of 'opportunities for making a bit on the side that there had been under the old regime'.[84] Attempts to raise the minimum wage of municipal employees to 25s per week had been defeated.[85] The attempts to get the halfpenny fare extended beyond the half mile were constantly thwarted and it seemed that the fares system was more favourable to the middle class of Pollokshields than to working-class areas, while private landowners had made substantial 'unearned increment' from tramway extension. As an anonymous correspondent noted, 'Glasgow is preeminently the paradise not of the municipal or any other worker, but of the shopkeeper and the middle class, who occupy all the comfortable positions and monopolise the advantages of municipal activity, for which the workers have to pay.'[86]

Labour candidates had an abysmal record in elections from 1900 and the Labour 'stalwarts' were ousted from the Corporation. The Glasgow Fabian Society, full of those progressives who had been most enthusiastic for municipalisation in the 1890s, tried to revive commitment to municipalisation with a new municipal programme in 1907. It called for a municipal bank, municipal market gardening in public parks, municipalisation of building land and a direct works department. Tom Johnson pushed the programme in the pages of *Forward* but there is no evidence of much response.[87]

With the emergence of a Labour Party in Parliament and with a government in power that was apparently much more sympathetic to working-class demands than previous governments there was perhaps a tendency to look much more to the central state. As a *Forward* editorial commented, 'Our municipalities do not have the power of German, French and Italian municipalities of promoting many schemes for the public advantage on their own initiative'. Municipal development had outrun national development and it was now necessary to win more power in Parliament.[88] The inadequacies and limitations of the operation of the Unemployed Workmen Act of 1905 quickly became apparent and, especially during the 1907–8 slump, there was a reaction against the variety of treatment by different distress committees. Increasingly, from all sides of the labour movement the demand was for unemployment to be seen as a national problem requiring the use of national resources.[89]

At the end of 1908, the Lord Provost, backed by the *Glasgow Herald,* proposed that the profits of municipal enterprises should go to relieve the rates' burden. This was common practice south of the border and it was claimed that as much as 1s. in the pound could be saved.[90] The threat to the principle of low prices which this seemed to imply stirred a defence of municipal socialism from Tom Drife of the ILP. Its ultimate aim was 'to abolish poverty within the city'.

Municipal enterprise

> steadies the market. It stems the tide of depression instead of quickening it. In times of bad trade it suffers along with other trades. But it does not spread havoc around. Its losses are scarcely felt by anyone. . . . If all the trades of Glasgow were in the hands of the people they would be in the same position as the tramways. When bad times come, they would neither dismiss men nor reduce wages. This would ensure a steady demand for goods of all kinds. And this, again, would almost abolish depression. . . . Municipal socialism will save the city. It will abolish the struggle for a living.[91]

There was now an attempt to separate a Labour municipal programme from the earlier tradition of Glasgow municipalisation. The 'inherent capitalism' of earlier corporation activities had to be recognised, Joseph Burgess declared. The tramways were not municipalised because of labour pressure but because of 'the gradual perception that a municipal tramway could be turned to capitalistic account'. What was needed was a distinct Labour programme for municipal activity. A municipal works department was, he argued, the only means 'pending the collapse of capitalism to remove large bodies of workers from the sphere of competition'. Shades of Alexander Campbell sixty years before, a municipal note issue and a municipal bank were the only ways to free municipal enterprise from the tutelage of being mortgaged to capitalism. There were renewed calls for municipal coal supplies and municipal bakeries.[92]

The formation of a centralised Glasgow Labour Party in the autumn of 1911 to organise for local elections in the city gave a new impetus to delineating a clear municipal programme. It consisted of taxation of land values, equalisation of rates between landlord and tenant, rate relief from the state, a corporation works department, municipal control of pubs (with the intention of reducing licences), of milk distribution ('and should conduct dairy production as far as possible') of coal distribution, municipal bread, municipal laundries and municipal banking. On housing the demand was for a moratorium on slum clearance and instead the provision by the municipality of cheap housing, the renovation of tenements and the building of three or four apartment working men's cottages.[93] John Wheatley's *Eight Pound Cottages for Glasgow Citizens* called for the use of the tramway surplus, by way of the common good fund, to finance house-building. By coming from the common good fund it would not require central government sanction and it would add nothing to the rates. Since no interest need be paid then cheap houses could be provided. In a tone that has a remarkably nineteenth-century ring to it, Wheatley declared, 'Glasgow workers by their own unaided efforts can solve their housing problem.'[94]

The proposals came at a time when there was a growing crisis in housing in parts of the city. There were signs of a militant resistance to rent rises, that was to culminate in the 1915 rent strikes.[95] Not everyone within the labour movement went with Wheatley in his no interest proposals. For some it smacked of subsidised housing. Some suggested that the spread of housing could be greater if low interest were paid to the Fund.[96] But Wheatley pressed his policies hard. In a remarkable lecture early in 1915 on 'The City under Socialism' he conjured up a picture of a new city based on 'better homes for the people' free from smoke so that a new beauty could spring forth in 'Cowcaddens Gardens' or 'Calton Parks'. The rebuilding of the city would transform the local economy:

> To save contractors profits for the workers the city would employ its own labour. . . . The saving thus effected would enable a Labour majority in the Council to pay high wages and supply the public cheaper than profit makers could. This would have the effect of creating a pressing demand for Corporation employment which could only be met by an ever increasing addition of Municipal Departments.[97]

There were hopes in 1915 that the Wheatley scheme might be carried, but the Town Clerk ruled that to borrow from the Common Good Fund was illegal, on the ground that 'it obviously cannot be held to be for the benefit of the community as a whole'.[98] This left only the central state as a possible source of finance and by 1916 Labour was calling for Treasury money.[99] The dramatic rises in the costs of raw materials and of labour by the end of the war made a nonsense of pre-war costings and made central Government aid even more necessary.[100] There was also a new commitment to subsidising the rents of the poorest in the renovated tenements.[101]

In the years after 1918 there were still a few demands for the extension of municipal enterprise. Direct labour for building the corporation houses came and went and came again, with endless debate on its efficacy. There were recurring attempts to float a municipal bank scheme, which had been successfully undertaken in a number of smaller Scottish towns like Kirkintilloch, Irvine, Clydebank and Motherwell, to provide 'the local authority with funds at a low rate of interest, to finance housing and other public enterprises'.[102] But when in 1934 a labour majority was able to give the go-ahead for such a bank it was blocked first by ratepayers' action in the Court of Sessions and then by Parliament.[103] But in the post-war world the demand was for equality between regions. Variation in wages or conditions or services between different regions was increasingly regarded as indefensible and the ironing out of these differences could be achieved by 'nationalisation' of industry and services, not by municipalisation.[104]

ACKNOWLEDGEMENTS

The author is indebted to Dr J H Treble for commenting on a draft of the chapter and to Mrs Irene Scouller for typing the manuscript.

REFERENCES

1. H Pelling 'The Working Class and the Origins of the Welfare State' in *Popular Politics and Society in Late Victorian Britain* (1968), pp 1–18
2. *The Times* 30 September 1902
3. A K Chalmers *Public Health Administration in Glasgow* (Glasgow 1905), p 63
4. J Connell *Glasgow Municipal Enterprise* (1899), p 69
5. J Butt 'Working-Class Housing in Glasgow 1851–1914' in S D Chapman (ed) *The History of Working-Class Housing* (Newton Abbot 1971)
6. Both quoted·in E Gauldie 'The Middle Class and Working-Class Housing in the Nineteenth Century' in A A Maclaren (ed), *Social Class in Scotland* (Edinburgh 1975), p 17
7. C G Brown, 'Religion and the Development of an Urban Society, Glasgow 1780–1914'. Unpublished PhD thesis, University of Glasgow 1981
8. *Ibid.* p 195
9. *Glasgow Examiner* 3 August 1844
10. J D Marwick *Glasgow. The Water Supply of the City* (Glasgow 1901), pp 85–92
11. For the central role played by Ure's report *see* Stephanie M Blackden, 'The Development of Public Health Administration in Glasgow 1842–72'. Unpublished PhD thesis, University of Edinburgh 1976, p 165
12. The most useful accounts of municipal enterprise in Glasgow are in Marwick, *op. cit.* Connell, *op. cit.* and *Municipal Glasgow: Its Evolution and Enterprise* (Glasgow 1914)
13. L C Wright *Scottish Chartism* (Edinburgh 1953), p 78
14. Gauldie 'The Middle Class and Working Class Housing', p 26
15. Blackden, *op. cit.* p 228
16. *Glasgow Sentinel,* 20 November 1858, 8 December 1860
17. *Ibid.* 18 September 1858, 30 August 1862
18. I MacDougall (ed) *Minutes of Edinburgh Trades Council 1859–1873* (Edinburgh 1968), 8 December 1868. The minutes after 1873 are in manuscript. All further references are made as Edinburgh Mins
19. *Ibid.* 12 April 1870
20. *North British Daily Mail,* 8 June 1871; *Glasgow Sentinel,* 10 June 1871
21. A Shaw *Municipal Government in Britain* (1895), p 120; T Hart 'Urban Growth and Municipal Government: Glasgow in a Comparative Context, 1846–1914' in A Slaven and D H Aldcroft (eds) *Business, Banking and Urban History* (Edinburgh 1982), p 206
22. Shaw *op. cit.* p 201
23. *Select Committee on Municipal Trading,* pp 1900 VII, q. 1894
24. Alexander Walker *City Rating* (Glasgow 1911)
25. M Atkinson *Local Government in Scotland* (Edinburgh 1904), p 35
26. Shaw *op. cit.* p 42
27. Walker *op. cit.*
28. Shaw *op. cit.* p. 77
29. *North British Daily Mail,* 18, 25 December 1879
30. See for example, *North British Daily Mail* 15 August 1881, 15 January 1885; Edinburgh Mins 12 February 1884, 6 October 1885
31. *North British Daily Mail,* 24 March 1881; Edinburgh Mins 12 April 1881
32. K D Buckley *Trade Unionism in Aberdeen 1878 to 1900* (Edinburgh 1955), p 122
33. *Ibid.* pp 122–3

34   *Ibid*. pp 127–8; Edinburgh Mins 20 October 1885
35   Glasgow Trades Council, *Annual Report 1884–1885*
36   *The Times* 6 October 1902
37   B Aspinwall 'Glasgow Trams and American Politics 1894–1914', *Scottish Historical Review* 56 1977, p 65
38   Glasgow Corporation *Tramway Committee Minutes,* 10 March 1887
39   Shaw *op. cit.* pp 129–31
40   Glasgow Corporation Minutes 4 July 1889, 6 March 1890; cf. Glasgow Trades Council Mins 18 February 1885
41   *North British Daily Mail* 13, 16 May 1889
42   H R Meyer *Municipal Ownership—Great Britain* (New York 1906), p 98
43   Strathclyde Regional Archives (SRA) PA 3/24 Corporation of Glasgow, *Synopsis of Municipal Undertakings* (Glasgow 1914)
44   Hugo R Meyer *Municipal Ownership in Great Britain* (New York 1906), pp 238–9; *The Times,* 30 September 1902
45   *Report of Proceedings at Conference of Municipal Representatives on Telephone Control and Charges 27 February 1911* (Glasgow 1911); D M Stevenson *Municipal Glasgow: Its Evolution and Enterprise* (Glasgow 1914)
46   H Dyer *The Evolution of Industry* (1895), *passim*
47   *Ibid.,* p 163
48   Aspinwall, 'Glasgow Trams', p 74
49   *Fabian Tract,* no. 86
50   *The Times* 6 October 1902
51   *North British Daily Mail* 6 November 1890; Glasgow Trades Council *Annual Report 1889–1890*; *Scottish Leader* 16 June 1892; *Daily Free Press* 13 October 1887
52   *Ibid*. 13 April 1892; Aberdeen Trades Council Minutes 5 July 1893, 9, 16 May 1894; *Glasgow Echo* 6 October 1894; SDF favoured municipalisation, *see Forward* 9 February 1907, but for Edwin Scrymgeor's view in Dundee, *see Forward* 10 August 1907
53   Glasgow Trades Council Minutes 18 February 1885
54   *Forward* 30 April, 14, 21 May 1910. I am grateful to Dr J H Treble for these references; J Connell *op. cit.* p 78
55   Glasgow Trades Council *Annual Report 1891–1892*; *Glasgow Echo* 22 February, 18 September 1894
56   *North British Daily Mail* 2 August 1888; Glasgow Trades Council *Annual Report 1889–1890*; *Glasgow Echo* 22 February, 5 July 1894
57   *North British Daily Mail,* 2 November 1899; *The Times* 6 October 1902 quoting Glasgow Workers' Municipal Election Committee programmes 1901. Cf. Edinburgh & Leith Workers' Municipal Committee Minutes 31 August 1900
58   Quoted in S Damer 'State, Class and Housing: Glasgow 1885–1914' in Joseph Melling (ed) *Housing, Social Policy and the State* (1980), p 76
59   Edinburgh Trades Council *Annual Report 1886–1887*
60   J B Russell *Life in One Room* (Glasgow 1888). The Presbytery of Glasgow, *Report of the Commission on the Housing of the Poor in Relation to the Social Conditions* (Glasgow 1891)
61   *Forward* 15 June 1907
62   *Trade Unionist* 3 October 1891
63   Shaw *op. cit.* p 105
64   *The Times,* 4 October 1902

65 SRA TD 488/9 Glasgow Citizens' Union Minutes 12 April, June, 10 July 1902; *The Times* 19 August–22 October 1902
66 *Glasgow The Municipal Commission on the Housing of the Poor* 1902, especially the evidence of John Mann & Thomas Binnie
67 *Ibid*. q. 12311 cf. NLS Mf. MSS 135. Edinburgh & Leith Workers' Municipal Committee 14 April 1899; *see also* Carson speech at Housing demonstration, *Glasgow Herald* 22 September 1902
68 *Ibid*. q. 5618
69 *Ibid*. q. 5564
70 *Glasgow Herald* 12 March 1900, 22 September 1902; Damer, 'State, Class & Housing' *op. cit*. p 85
71 W Smart *The Housing Problem and the Municipality* (Glasgow 1902), p 24
72 *Forward* 20 October 1906
73 Buckley *op. cit*. p 75
74 Glasgow Trades Council Minutes 25 November 1885
75 *Ibid*.16, 23 December 1885; Buckley *op. cit*. pp 75–6
76 J H Treble 'Unemployment and Unemployment Policies in Glasgow 1890–1905', in Pat Thane (ed), *The Origins of British Social Policy* (1978), p 162
77 *See* the municipal election campaign report October–November 1898
78 H T Muggeridge *The Anti-Municipal Conspiracy* (City of London Br., ILP n.d. (1902?))
79 Tom Hart 'Urban Growth and Municipal Government', p 200
80 *Glasgow Herald* 2 November 1900. Councillor Forsyth of Townhead
81 Damer, 'State, Class & Housing', p 89; Melling, 'Clydeside Housing and the Evolution of State Rent Control 1900–1939', in Melling (ed), *op. cit*. p 146
82 *Forward* 14 November 1908
83 *See* the references to the Manager of the Tramways as 'Napoleon' in *Forward* 19 August 1911
84 *Ibid*.16 March 1907
85 *Ibid*. 29 June 1907
86 *Forward* 16 March 1907
87 *Forward* 12 October 1907
88 *Ibid*. 14 November 1908
89 Glasgow Trades Council *Annual Report* 1908–09
90 *Glasgow Herald* 21 December 1908; *Forward* 2 January 1909
91 *Forward*, 28 August, 18 September 1909
92 *Ibid*. 9, 23 April, 8, 15, 22 October 1910
93 *Ibid*. 12 July 1913
94 John Wheatley, *Eight Pound Cottages for Glasgow Citizens* (Glasgow 1913)
95 J Melling, *Rent Strikes. Peoples' Struggle for Housing in the West of Scotland 1890–1916* (Edinburgh 1983)
96 *Forward* 4 July 1914
97 *Ibid*. 6 February 1915
98 *Ibid*. 13 February 1915
99 Glasgow Trades Council Minutes 21 June 1916
100 *Ibid*. 28 March 1917
101 NLS 33(5) Glasgow Labour Party *Constitution* 7 April 1915
102 *Forward* 27 October 1928, 29 October 1932
103 SRA D TC 8/1/20/16, *Municipal Savings Bank. Report by City Chamberlain* 30 November 1971
104 W A Robson 'The Central Domination of Local Government', *Political Quarterly* IV (1) 1933

7

POLITICS IN THE SCOTTISH CITY 1832–1982

William Miller

INTRODUCTION

There is a slowly fading notion that normal politics consists of a struggle for power between two class-based parties. By that standard, politics in the Scottish city[1] has seldom, if ever, been normal.

Over the last century and a half politics in Scottish cities has been at times the politics of a one-party regime, at other times there have been three or more significant parties, and at others no significant parties at all. Class divisions have been important and have related to matters like housing, or municipal socialism which could be decided, to some extent, within the city. But other issues have been geographic, and have set the city against areas outside it. Glasgow in particular fought a never-ending series of imperialistic battles to absorb the surrounding burghs. Glasgow and Edinburgh have not only tended to support different parties, they have also repeatedly supported different factions within parties and expressed their rivalry in nakedly geographic as well as ideological terms. A third geographic dimension has been the central versus local axis: local parties have opposed the intervention of national parties in local government, and local governments have (unsuccessfully) fought central governments bent upon the destruction of local political autonomy.

Above all, however, politics in the cities has focused upon issues which could not in any way be decided within the city. Political conflict at all levels, municipal as well as parliamentary, has involved national and even international issues. So political debate and political responses even in municipal elections have been strongly influenced by attitudes towards prohibition, religion, Irish Home Rule, the Coal Strike of 1926, unemployment, Scottish nationalism, the Falklands Affair or generalised evaluations of Central Government's current performance. Politics *in* the city has never been primarily politics *about* the city. Strictly local issues and local political choices have been of secondary importance.

It is convenient to divide the years since 1832 into three periods though it would be wrong to overstress the dividing lines between them. From 1832 until 1885 Scottish city politics was one party, or more realistically, no-party politics. Every MP who sat for Glasgow, Edinburgh, Aberdeen or Dundee in those years described himself as a Liberal—except for a single Conservative elected during the brief period when Glasgow used a system of proportional representation. But this was a time in which the label 'Liberal' meant very little and Scottish politics was between factions in the Liberal Party rather than between parties.

Divisions amongst Liberals in 1885 on religious issues and in 1886 over Irish Home Rule finally led to the defection of the Liberal Unionists who linked up with the Conservatives and introduced competitive party politics to the Scottish cities. But party competition between Liberals and Unionists operated mainly at the parliamentary level: municipal politics did not divide Liberals and Unionists. Instead, a trickle of Labour, trade union, or socialist candidates won election as councillors and their unaccustomed party-political style encouraged the other councillors to think in terms of a defensive, anti-socialist alliance.

From 1920 onwards both parliamentary and municipal politics were dominated by the growth of the Labour Party and reaction against it. In parliamentary elections Labour's main opponent was the Unionist (later called Conservative) Party but until the end of the sixties, resistance to Labour at the municipal level was organised by loose alliances of Conservatives, Liberals and Independents who called themselves either Moderates or Progressives.

During this long period of Labour versus anti-Labour politics there were three short periods when another political dimension assumed some importance. Protestant parties won substantial votes in the 1930s as did the SNP in the late sixties and again in the late seventies. On each occasion the electoral system, with its built-in bias against parties whose support is uniformly distributed prevented the new party from winning large numbers of council seats but the Protestants peaked at seven seats in Glasgow and ten in Edinburgh in the thirties while the SNP reached fifteen in Glasgow and ten in Edinburgh during the sixties.

Liberals enjoyed a minor success at local elections in Edinburgh in the early sixties, leaving the Moderates and Progressives with the appearance of being purely Conservative front organisations, which they were not. Towards the end of the sixties the Conservatives themselves entered local government and speedily brought about the final collapse of the Moderates and Progressives. From then onwards Conservatives provided the main opposition to Labour at all levels. So the modest surge of support for the Liberal/Social Democrat Alliance in the early eighties might be classified as a fourth deviation from Labour/anti-Labour politics, a successor to the Protestant and SNP surges of the thirties, sixties and seventies.

MIDDLE CLASS POLITICS: 1832–1885

The franchise

Prior to the reforms of the eighteen thirties self-perpetuating city corporations ran the cities and elected members to parliament. The five corporations of Dundee, Forfar, Perth, Cupar and St Andrews, for example, formed an electorate of five and elected an MP on the basis of 'one corporation, one vote'.

Parliamentary representation was subjected to democratic election in 1832 and Burgh Corporations democratised in 1833. But the reforms of 1832 were very limited. They introduced the concept of democratic control but the franchise remained very limited and apportionment very unequal: they introduced neither 'one man, one vote' nor 'one vote, one value'. The 1832 Act enfranchised only 4.7 per cent of the Edinburgh population and only 3.5 per cent of the population in Glasgow, Aberdeen and Dundee.

Such a franchise had several consequences. First, the new electors reacted strongly against those who had opposed their new privileges. In consequence the cities of Scotland remained almost exclusively Liberal for half a century after the reform. Second, such a highly restricted franchise increased the electoral significance of those issues which divided the electorate: a middle-class electorate meant that middle-class issue-based politics must receive a great deal of attention. Third, a highly restrictive franchise made the franchise itself an issue and, until such time as the franchise might be extended, it restrained not only the influence but also the political ambitions of the working class. Lastly, very unequal apportionment, which gave too many parliamentary seats to the small burghs and too few to the cities, restricted the political importance of the cities as a whole: the four cities were entitled to nine MPs on the basis of population but received only six.

Limited though the franchise was in the cities, the city electorate was substantially greater than elsewhere and it was not controlled by the landed interest who directly or indirectly dominated the electors both in the counties and the small burghs. Between 1832 and 1868, Dyer[2] calculates that 67 per cent of MPs in the cities were manufacturers, merchants or lawyers compared with only 25 per cent in the small burghs and a mere 16 per cent in the counties. Conversely only 23 per cent of city MPs were landowners, officers or gentlemen compared with 58 per cent in the small burghs and 81 per cent in the counties. Only 13 per cent of city MPs were related to the nobility as against 23 per cent in the small burghs and 51 per cent in the counties. Merchants predominated in Glasgow, lawyers in Edinburgh, though Dundee succumbed to its environment and elected mainly landowners.

Aberdeen was allowed one MP throughout the period 1832–85, Dundee had one MP until 1868 and two thereafter, Edinburgh had two throughout, and Glasgow had two until 1868 and three thereafter. In the two-member cities each elector had two votes and the two candidates with the highest votes were elected. However, when Glasgow briefly had three seats, Glaswegian electors were still allowed only two votes each—an arrangement which produced a primitive version of proportional representation.

In all the years from 1832 until 1885, the only time a non-Liberal was elected from a Scottish city was in 1874 when Glasgow used this proportional representation system. And on that occasion, in addition to the use of proportional representation, the year was particularly favourable to the Conservatives throughout Britain, and five Liberals were competing against each other for the three Glasgow seats.

One-party politics

So up to and including 1885, with one peculiar exception, Scottish cities elected Liberals and only Liberals. Scottish city politics did not have a party dimension. In default of party politics, Scottish cities had the politics of personality, faction and issue. Liberal candidates were frequently elected without opposition from other parties but frequently also they were elected at contests in which they fought fellow Liberals. Out of forty-eight elections in 1832–80 (four cities by twelve General Elections) there were no anti-Liberal candidates at twenty of the forty-eight, but there were more Liberal candidates than seats available at eighteen of the forty-eight.[3]

Liberal challengers defeated sitting Liberals once in Dundee and Glasgow and three times in Edinburgh: incumbency did not guarantee survival.

Different Liberal candidates stood for recognisably different factions within the loose alliance described by the term 'Liberal Party'. Some who used the label 'Liberal' even stood for factions outside it: James Guthrie who stood (unsuccessfully) as a Liberal at the 1868 election in Dundee was known to be an habitual Conservative voter in London where he lived. His father, David Guthrie had contested the seat in 1832 backed by those respectable Liberals and Tories who had tried (unsuccessfully) to prevent the election of the democratic agitator and former outlaw, George Kinloch. Nominally Liberal candidates often disagreed violently on issues such as the franchise, catholic endowment in Ireland, temperance, or disestablishment of the Church of Scotland. Hanham[4] understates the vitality of Scottish city politics at this time when he describes it as 'member-ridden'. No doubt it was a foregone conclusion that a Liberal would be elected but elections involved real policy choices between alternative Liberals backed by rival organisations all claiming to be Liberal. Elections retained their meaning, it was party that did not.

Working-class influence

At first working-class organisations could only hope to influence the electorate from the outside. The reforms of 1832 produced a merchant and shopkeeper electorate, issue politics within the electorate, and interest group politics applied from outside it. There was no possibility of direct working-class representatation either in parliament or on the city councils. But Trades Councils supplied an alternative political platform for the working class. There is a reference to an Edinburgh Trades Council in the 1830s and both Edinburgh and Glasgow Trades Councils showed considerable political activity from the 1850s onwards. When the franchise was tripled in 1868 they gained some influence *within* the electorate. They were partly supported and partly rivalled by Working Men's Associations.

Working-class organisations were split on how to use their increasing influence. They could either throw their weight behind the Radicals in the Liberal Party who were committed to working-class enfranchisement or alternatively support anyone, Radical or not, who would help them in the struggle for legal, social and industrial benefits. Glasgow Trades Council, especially, objected to being caught up in Radical political causes which were not of specific benefit to the working class, and it was more sympathetic to the idea of independent Labour candidates.

In the end, however, the strategy of supporting and influencing the Radicals, rather than opposing them, prevailed. There were no independent Labour candidates in any of the Scottish cities until 1885. In 1868 Edinburgh Trades Council put a long list of questions to the candidates (both of whom were returned unopposed) on a range of topics that went beyond immediate working-class interests to subjects like railway nationalisation and a national library for Scotland.[5] In Dundee that year candidates had to appear before the executive of the Working Men's Association to answer questions on the franchise, factory inspection, master and servant laws, trade unions and Church Establishment.

Party organisation

Modern party organisations seem to have been established later than the Trades Councils.[6] Certainly Kinloch founded a Dundee Citizens Union in 1831 and there was no shortage of political organisations in the early nineteenth century. But Conservative and Liberal party organisations were formed much later.

A Scottish National Constitutional Association was formed in Edinburgh in 1867 and Working Men's Conservative Associations in Dundee and Glasgow two years later, but none showed much sign of life. Conservative organisations really began in 1882 with the National Union of Scottish Conservative Associations. It was reorganised in 1893, theoretically into six districts but in practice it was dominated by the Glasgow and Edinburgh districts. Glasgow would not take orders from Edinburgh, acted as an autonomous central body, and claimed to be the capital of Scottish Conservatism. In 1884 for example the Glasgow Conservatives combined with the Orangemen in a torchlight procession to welcome Lord Randolph Churchill but insisted that any Eastern Conservatives came as individuals and not as an organised contingent. The division between Edinburgh and Glasgow was social as well as geographic: Edinburgh lawyers were neither liked nor trusted outside their own narrow circle.

A similar Glasgow versus Edinburgh rivalry afflicted the Liberal organisation. A West and South of Scotland Liberal Association was founded in 1876 with headquarters in Glasgow followed, a year later, by an East and North of Scotland Liberal Association with headquarters in Edinburgh. Ideological disagreements reinforced the geographic rivalry: Glasgow was Radical while Edinburgh, especially after the retirement of Duncan McLaren was Whiggish. The two Liberal Associations united in 1881 with the Glaswegians demanding proportionality on the Council of the Association (i.e. predominance for the West of Scotland) and the Edinburgh side holding out for parity.

Such unity as was achieved in 1881 did not last long. A National Liberal

Foundation of Scotland was formed in 1886 in Glasgow, with the president of the Glasgow Central Liberal Association as Federation president and a list of Radical ambitions that included Disestablishment of the Church, reform of the House of Lords and, not least, the transfer of party headquarters from Edinburgh to Glasgow.

Annexation

Glasgow had geographic ambitions against less august places than Edinburgh. The Municipal Extension Act of 1846 doubled the area of the municipality, swallowing up the independent burghs of Calton, Gorbals and Anderston. That ended a competition between Glasgow and the independent burghs to annex such places as Woodside. However the struggles between Glasgow and its surroundings continued. Partick, Maryhill, Govan, Hillhead, Kinning Park, Crosshill, West Pollokshields, Govanhill and East Pollokshields all achieved burgh status between 1852 and 1879 and engaged in competition for intermediate areas such as Kelvinside. Glasgow tried to annex the lot, and succeeded in gaining six of them in 1891 though Kinning Park held out till 1905 and Partick, Govan and Pollokshaws till 1912.

Competition for the annexation of adjacent areas was typical of Victorian politics in many parts of Britain. It roused a certain amount of local feeling, and it was important for the proper provision of services such as water and sewage in the nineteenth century, or land for housing in the twentieth century. Perhaps the most significant annexation was the one that did not occur: in 1946 the City Planning Engineer of Glasgow envisaged no necessary extension to the city area. In consequence of that non-annexation the city ran out of housing land and developed its characteristic dish-shaped appearance with the tallest buildings around the perimeter of the city.

THE POLITICS OF SOCIAL GROUPS: 1885–1920

Groups and parties

From about 1885 until shortly after World War I politics centred on bargains between groups and parties—instrumental bargains rather than emotional identification. The franchise had been massively extended in 1868 and was further extended in 1885. The cities of Glasgow, Edinburgh and Aberdeen, though not Dundee, were divided up into single-member constituencies—two in Aberdeen, four in Edinburgh and seven in Glasgow, and these sub-units of the cities exhibited a degree of social variation. The new larger electorate was necessarily less socially homogeneous than that of 1832 and the division of the cities into territorial constituencies exposed that heterogeneity and improved the prospects for working-class candidates.

But the franchise was still limited: the Representation of the People Act of 1918 more than tripled the electorate in the cities without introducing full female suffrage. So in the period before 1918 the working class were still heavily under-represented in the electorate, and the middle class remained a large group, over-represented in the electorate.

At the same time, issues of Church Disestablishment and Irish Home Rule flared up and provided other bases for group politics.

Divisions between the existing political parties did not correspond to divisions between classes nor to divisions between Dissenters and Established Churchmen and neither party was unambiguously linked to Irish aspirations.

So we should picture middle- and working-class electorates of similar size to each other, Church of Scotland and free-church electorates of roughly equal sizes, and small but well organised and very self-conscious Irish electorates particularly in Glasgow and Dundee—all engaged in a bargaining process between groups and parties without entirely obvious natural linkages between a particular group and a particular party.

From the start of this period the Liberal Party was a more natural working-class choice than the Conservative Party but it was external to the working class and its concern for their interests was often suspect. All British parties were inevitably and irredeemably alien to Irish Home Rulers who advised the Irish in Scotland to support whichever party offered the best deal at the time. In 1885 they urged a Conservative vote, thereafter Liberal. The cold calculating detachment of the Home Rulers was shown not only by their opposition to Labour candidates who might split the Home Rule vote but more clearly by their occasional advice to the Irish catholic community to vote for the Unionist candidate so as to demonstrate their electoral muscle to a Liberal who had not given Irish Home Rule sufficient priority. The equivalent in more modern terms would be the TUC advising trade unionists to vote Conservative in 1970 in retaliation for 'In Place of Strife'.

Two issues, Church Disestablishment and Home Rule for Ireland, broke the mould of Scottish politics in 1885–6 and introduced a competitive party system. Apart from the franchise extension which was bound to produce at least temporary instability, one reason why these issues had such a dramatic effect was that the long period of Liberal dominance since 1832 had left the Liberal Party as little more than a name. No interparty competition had stiffened its organisation, discipline or sense of identification in Scotland as they had for example in Birmingham.

Disestablishment 1885

Shortly after the union with England, an Act of the British Parliament in 1712 introduced lay patronage into the Church of Scotland.[7] That produced various secessionist groups of presbyterians who merged in 1847 to form the United Presbyterian Church, committed to Disestablishment of the Church of Scotland. Shortly before the 1847 merger another split in the Church of Scotland, the Disruption of 1843, produced the Free Church of Scotland which wanted the Church of Scotland to remain established but without any interference by the state in its affairs. The Patronage Act of 1874 reversed the act of 1712 and left the Free Church, the United Presbyterians and the Church of Scotland with very little left to divide them. Almost total reunion was achieved by 1929, but in the closing years of the nineteenth century they remained the prisoners of their history, disunited yet with no doctrinal and few other reasons left to justify their disunity. Overall, the official Church of Scotland encompassed about half the Scots Presbyterians.

Because they did not differ in matters of doctrine, the various presbyterian churches were able to agree on a unified system of school education after the Act of 1872, leaving only the Catholics to set up sectarian schools.

Yet without docrinal differences, religious divisions in 1885 still paved the way for the 1886 schism in the Liberal Party over Home Rule.[8] By 1885, the Free Church had swung over to the United Presbyterian's view that the Church of Scotland should be Disestablished. The issue had been raised in parliament and Glasgow Radicals were enthusiastically for it. They wanted a separation of Church and State. They also wanted funds taken from the Church and used to support the new education system. Six of the Glasgow Liberal Association's seven candidates were for Disestablishment and Glasgow Radicals demanded that Disestablishment be treated as a test question. They tried to extend their influence throughout Scotland with attacks on Goshen and Harrison in Edinburgh and Robertson in Dundee.

Naturally enough the Church of Scotland reacted against a possible financial loss and almost all its presbyteries formed Church Defence Associations. Radicals were accused of being pagan, secular, atheistic, or advocating equality between the Church of Scotland and the Roman Catholic Church.

The issue had few overt consequences in 1885. None of the Radicals who challenged a sitting Liberal succeeded, nor did any of the four Churchmen who challenged sitting Radicals. Liberal splits did little to help the Conservatives who won only ten seats in the whole of Scotland—not one of them in the cities. But amongst Liberals the issue produced a sharp religious polarisation and those who were willing to defend the property of the established Church, or indeed defend any property rights against politically motivated confiscation, identified themselves and got used to working and organising together.

So when Gladstone announced his conversion to Irish Home Rule the lines of battle were already drawn.

Home Rule 1886

Glasgow had a special interest in what happened to Ireland. There was the possibility of attacks on the Clyde by hostile fleets based in Ireland. Home Rule might be the beginning of the end for imperial unity and for Glasgow's access to imperial markets. Glasgow businessmen had substantial investments in Ireland. Local industries did a great deal of trade across the Irish sea. And the Irish Presbyterians sent representatives to address all three Scots presbyterian churches on the dangers of a Romish Ascendancy.

Glasgow Chamber of Commerce issued a statement against Home Rule and many of Glasgow's Liberal political activists who had rallied to the defence of the Church the previous year, now came together again to oppose Home Rule. Glasgow's Liberal Unionism was organised by leading businessmen and distinguished professors—Lord Kelvin amongst them.[9] It was not a simple mobilisation of the Orange vote, though the Grand Orange Lodge later sought and obtained representation on the Western Divisional Council of the Conservative Party.

The Liberal Unionists had no candidates in Aberdeen in 1886 and were soundly beaten in Dundee where Robertson patched up his quarrel with his more radical supporters by coming down in favour of Home Rule. Edinburgh's four constituencies elected only one Liberal Unionist in 1886—a sitting member who rejoined the Liberals the following year. Two of his fellow sitting members, who switched to the Liberal Unionists were soundly beaten. But Glasgow's seven constituencies, all of them Liberal and almost all Radical Liberal in 1885, elected one Conservative and two Liberal Unionists in 1886, while the four Glasgow seats retained by the Liberals were all held on narrow majorities.

Glasgow moved still further towards the Conservatives and Unionists later. The year 1900 was admittedly a bad year for the Liberals, but a year in which they held both the Aberdeen, both the Dundee and half the Edinburgh seats, yet lost every one in Glasgow. The stronghold of Radicalism had become a stronghold of Unionism.

Home Rule gave Irish immigrants, their descendants and their coreligionists, a special interest in politics. Kinnear[10] estimates that in 1900 18 per cent of Glaswegians and 14 per cent of Dundonians were Catholics, though only 7 per cent in Edinburgh and 3 per cent in Aberdeen. Many were from Irish families but by the turn of the century few could claim Irish birth. By 1911, the census recorded only 7 per cent of Glaswegians and 2 per cent of Dundonians as born in Ireland (and those figures include Protestants as well as Catholics). Nonetheless Catholic organisations and the Catholic press fostered a sense of ethnic identity and the United Irish League gave guidance on how Irish electors in Scots cities should cast their vote. Generally, Irish organisations threw their weight behind Liberal candidates but it was a tactical and instrumental choice not a matter of deep emotion and identification. At the 1900 General Election in Glasgow Blackfriars the United Irish League attempted to punish the Liberal candidate for lack of enthusiasm over Home Rule by urging Catholics to support the Unionist candidate Bonar Law who then won the seat with the highest pro-Unionist swing in the city. In 1906 the UIL backed the Labour candidate George Barnes who defeated both Bonar Law and his Liberal predecessor.

It would be wrong however to attribute too much influence to the Irish Catholic vote. The total number of Irishmen in Scots cities was not very large even in Glasgow, many did not qualify for a vote, and Protestant Irishmen or Protestant reaction amongst native Scots clearly overwhelmed the Catholic Irish vote. The most notable feature of Glasgow politics was the strength of the Unionist vote.

Labour candidates before the War

At general elections after 1892 there were usually some Labour candidates, of one kind or another, in Glasgow, Aberdeen and Dundee though usually not in Edinburgh. None of them got elected before 1906 when George Barnes won Glasgow Blackfriars and Alexander Wilkie took one of the two Dundee seats. Since the Gladstone/McDonald pact of 1903 did not apply in Scotland, Wilkie like Barnes faced Liberal as well as Unionist opposition. Unlike Barnes he was also opposed by the United Irish League who warned that he was an 'enemy of Ireland'.

Dundee Liberal Association had tried, in 1889, to find a Labour man as one of their candidates for the two-member constituency. The Trades Council secretary declined to stand and the Trades Council recommended Sir John Leng. Leng's newspaper, the *Advertiser*, described Leng and Robertson (the Liberals) as Labour candidates for the 1892 General Election. Keir Hardie's Scottish Labour Party sponsored James Macdonald of the London Trades Council. Dundee Trades Council rejected him by seventeeen votes to six and he received only one percent of the vote in the election.

Leng retired in 1906, and Wilkie set out to be his successor. Wilkie was a trades unionist and founder member of the Labour Representation Committee but he was not a socialist and had been Liberal candidate in Sunderland. He was nominated at the Dundee Liberal Association but failed to find a seconder. Instead the Liberals chose an elderly London stockbroker, Robson, who was currently Mayor of Kensington. Wilkie fought a vigorous campaign, spending as much as both the Liberal candidates put together. Wilkie (Labour) and Robertson (Liberal) won. Very few voters cast a ballot for a single Liberal: 37 per cent of voters voted for Robson and Robertson together. Only 16 per cent cast a straight Labour vote for Wilkie, but he was elected because another 20 per cent voted for Wilkie/Robertson and 6 per cent cross-voted for Wilkie and a Unionist. Wilkie thereby established himself as the successor to Leng and used the electorate to impose a Lib/Lab pact upon an unwilling party organisation.

Robertson was elevated to the peerage shortly afterwards and Winston Churchill, whose services were made available by defeat in Manchester, won the 1908 Dundee by-election with a huge majority over Unionist and Labour opponents. Thereafter Wilkie and Churchill ran in harness.

The class alignment between Liberals and Unionists

Cities and constituencies can be classified by the number of rooms per family and by the percentage of electors qualified by ownership rather than residence.[11] As indicators of social class these measures are far from perfect, not least because they apply to population rather than electorate, but they are the best available from the pre-war Census.

Within cities, the Conservative and Unionist vote tended to be higher in the more middle-class constituencies. The constituencies of Aberdeen and

Edinburgh provide the clearest test because of their social heterogeneity. Dundee was undivided and Glasgow constituencies were too uniformly working-class. At every election from 1885 to 1910 both the Aberdeen seats returned a Liberal but Liberal majorities were consistently higher in middle-class South Aberdeen than working-class North Aberdeen. The difference varied from time to time: 18 per cent in 1885, 25 per cent in 1900, 6 per cent in 1910—but there was no evidence of steadily increasing class polarisation. In Edinburgh the more working-class constituencies, Central and East, elected Liberals at every election. The most middle-class, Edinburgh West, switched to Unionist in 1886 and stayed Unionist thereafter. Edinburgh South, a trifle less middle-class than Edinburgh West went Unionist only in 1895 and 1900 but was only marginally Liberal in 1892.

In Glasgow the presence of Labour candidates distorted the class polarisation between Liberals and Unionists. Glasgow's housing was so poor, and its rate of residence-only qualifications so high, that every Glaswegian constituency should have behaved like Edinburgh Central and Edinburgh East—that is, they should have been uniformly and consistently Liberal if they had obeyed the same rules of class voting as did Edinburgh. Bridgeton fell in with that expectation by electing a Liberal at every election bar 1900. Blackfriars and Camlachie were so working class that they attracted repeated Labour candidacies. In Blackfriars Labour won in 1906 and thereafter. In Camlachie, Labour polled votes as high as 30 per cent in three-cornered fights and 42 per cent in a straight fight but merely handed the seat to the Unionists.

Central, College and Tradeston would have passed for relatively working-class seats in Edinburgh, but they were the most middle-class in Glasgow. Cameron Corbett held Tradeston at every election, changing his label from Liberal to Liberal Unionist, then to Independent Liberal and finally back to Liberal again, fighting off Labour, Liberals, Lib-Labs, Liberal Unionists, Conservatives and Independent Conservatives. We can draw no conclusions about *party* support from Corbett's career. College, however, went Unionist in 1895 and 1900 and Central went Unionist in 1886 and stayed Unionist thereafter.

The special factors of Labour interventions in Blackfriars and Camlachie, added to Corbett's personal achievement in Tradeston, prevent a clear picture of class polarisation emerging from the Glasgow results. Nonetheless the Unionists do seem to have done somewhat better in the more middle-class areas but more significantly, they did much better in Glasgow as a whole than we might expect on class grounds alone. Even the middle-class areas of Glasgow were not middle class enough to elect Unionists by the standards of Edinburgh and Aberdeen.

Municipal politics before the war

The Victorians were perhaps a trifle slow in moving towards universal suffrage but they were notably committed to the concept of elections.[12] Burgh Councils were subjected to election by the 1833 Burgh Reform Act.

Elected Parochial Boards were set up by the 1865 Poor Law Act to take over welfare supervision, and replaced by elected Parish Councils in 1894. Elected School Boards were created by the 1872 Education Act and replaced by elected Education Authorities in 1918. Veto Polls were introduced in 1918 to provide local referenda on the Drink Question. It was not until 1929 that the quantity of electoral opportunities in the cities was reduced by giving the duties of the Education Authorities and Parish Councils to the City Councils. Since then the electoral method has been out of fashion: bureaucracy and patronage have flourished—elected Councils have lost powers to appointed bodies and democratic control has been channelled increasingly through parliament and Whitehall.

In London and Birmingham local government elections were organised on highly disciplined party lines in the latter part of the nineteenth century, though in London[13] the Conservatives fought as 'Moderates' and the Liberals as 'Progressives'.

Such clear party divisions were not apparent in the Scottish cities before World War I. Individual councillors often had known party attachments but these did not add up to party competition for control of local government.[14] Local elections were frequently uncontested. In Glasgow there was no contest in eleven of the sixteen wards in 1846 and no contest in fifteen out of the sixteen in 1878 and 1880. From 1900 to 1911 when there were annual elections for twenty-five (or twenty-six after 1905) wards in Glasgow the average number uncontested was fourteen. City boundaries were extended in 1912 and for the remaining years before the war there were thirty-seven wards. On average, twenty of the thirty-seven went uncontested. The situation was similar in Edinburgh: throughout the 1890s there were, on average, six contests in sixteen wards.

This created something of a political vacuum at lower levels of politics and the Trades Councils set up political committees to get representatives on the lowest levels of the political structure up to and including the city councils themselves.[15] By 1898 there were ten Labour councillors on a Glasgow City Council of seventy. By World War I there were nineteen Labour men on Glasgow's council of 113, ten out of thirty-four in Dundee, seven in Aberdeen and seven also in Edinburgh (including Leith).

But apart from Labour candidates the link between national and local politics was slight. In 1874 a Central Municipal Organization was formed in Edinburgh to 'return candidates irrespective of their political views'. In Glasgow the Glasgow Citizens Union supported by a huge structure of 'Ward Committees' proclaimed a similar objective. However, by the early 1890s its Programme had changed to state explicitly that the Citizens Union opposed in principle all forms of Municipal Socialism and 'Municipal Trading of a competitive character'. In 1906 it was reported to have 3,800 members and it ran candidates against all the socialists, claiming victory in twelve of the fifteen vacant seats. The Citizens Union was especially incensed by a Labour proposal at this time to use the profits from the Municipal Tramways to build houses that might be let at 'uneconomic rents' to 'other than the poorest classes'.

On the Labour side, candidates were assisted and recommended to the electors by the Workers Election Committee which brought together socialists, trades unionists and co-operators. Catholic Irish organisations published their lists of acceptable candidates. So did temperance organisations like the Glasgow Citizens Vigilance Association and the Municipal Temperance Federation while the Traders Defence Association recommended suitable 'wets'.[16] Candidates received multiple endorsements, whether they liked it or not. T R Cosh, elected for Cowlairs in 1908, for example, was backed by the Citizens Union but indignantly rejected their endorsement.

Irish Catholic organisations adopted a flexible and instrumental approach and their endorsements were in no sense automatic. Up to 1906 they co-operated with Labour in Glasgow municipal politics but after that they were increasingly critical of Labour militancy. As in the parliamentary election in Blackfriars, they were willing to punish their friends. In 1909 the Catholic *Star* declared 'Mile-End is a ward where, in all fairness, a Progressive from the Nationalist wing might have been asked to bear the Stalwart colours. The action of the Labour people in ignoring the Irish electorate calls for emphatic resentment'. The Catholic *Observer,* in 1910, recommended a vote against several Labour incumbents (who survived however) and demanded 'a sound reciprocal scheme whereby the Irish electorate in Glasgow would be now and again the climber, and not always the ladder'.[17]

At the turn of the century Glasgow councillors included few small traders or working men. Even one of the Labour candidates was a shipowner who campaigned (sinfully) in a motor-car. But in the period up to the war there was a marked decline in the social position of newly elected councillors. In Edinburgh 80 per cent of councillors were men of property in 1875 but the figure dropped to 72 per cent in 1905 and 57 per cent by 1925—and not because of any substantial influx of Labour councillors.[18]

Some of the old councillors found the more party political atmosphere distasteful. In Dundee several councillors resigned after a particularly abusive council debate between the Prohibitionist leader and his right wing opponents. One Dundee councillor complained that being a member of the council was 'no longer a recreation'.

MODERN CLASS POLITICS: 1920–1982

Labour and parliamentary politics

After World War I, another franchise extension tripled the electorate. At the same time the Liberal party split over the conduct of the war and the personal rift between Asquith and Lloyd George. The public mood ranged from excessive jubilation tinged with jingoism in 1918 to black depression, psychological as well as economic, a year or two later.

In working-class Aberdeen North, a traditionally safe Liberal seat, the sitting member backed Lloyd George's coalition and very narrowly lost to his only opponent, the Labour man. Labour have held the seat ever since, with the single exception of 1931. In middle-class Aberdeen South the Liberal did not receive Lloyd George's coupon and the Coalition Conservative won, as Conservatives have done ever since, with the single exception of 1966.

Middle-class Edinburgh South and West constituencies along with the new Edinburgh North elected Conservatives. Working-class Central went Labour, and East stayed Liberal. In Central Labour offered the only alternative to the Coalition candidate but in East, North and South there were no Labour candidates. Indeed Labour did not contest general elections in Edinburgh with any vigour until 1924 when it put up four candidates for the five seats.

Before the war, the Liberals had been notably more successful in Edinburgh than Glasgow despite the class bias against them. That class bias operated still more sharply against Labour and Labour's failure to contest Edinburgh seats helped the Liberals towards their victory in two out of the five seats in 1922 and three out of the five in 1923. In consequence the Conservatives held a third of Glasgow seats by 1923 but only a fifth of Edinburgh seats.

Labour interventions at the 1924 election in Edinburgh produced one Labour gain from Liberal and helped in two Liberal losses to the Conservatives. The Liberals never won an Edinburgh seat again with the single exception of Edinburgh East in 1931 when the Conservatives gave them a free run against Labour. Labour took a majority of the Edinburgh seats in its good years of 1929 and 1945 and the Conservatives in their good years of 1924, 1931 and 1935. Following the boundary changes of 1950 Edinburgh was allocated seven seats which always split four Conservative versus three Labour until another boundary change in 1983 abolished one of the Labour seats.

Glasgow had fifteen parliamentary seats from 1918 to 1970. They split ten to five in favour of Lloyd George's Coalition in 1918 and the National Coalition in 1931. But they split ten to five in Labour's favour as early as 1922, as late as 1959, and in 1923, 1929, 1935 (nine to six in that year) and 1945. After 1959 the Conservatives were reduced to two seats and by 1983 they had no representation at all in Glasgow. The only times when Glasgow constituencies divided more or less equally between Labour and Conservative were 1924 and the three election years of the early fifties. In sharp contrast to the years before 1920, the class polarisation of the vote that was and is evident *within* cities also operated *between* cities after 1920

The Scottish Prohibitionists in Dundee

In Glasgow, Edinburgh and Aberdeen the tendency towards class polarisation between Labour and Conservative as well as the surges of support for alternatives to the class-based two-party system can best be illustrated by reference to local election results which tell all the story of parliamentary politics and more. Dundee is different. Dundee alone retained a two-member constituency until 1945, with all the complications of split ticket voting. Dundee also had the distinction of dismissing the celebrated Winston Churchill in favour of an obscure Prohibitionist.[19]

Edwin Scrymgeour, the Prohibitionist, had founded the Scottish Prohibition Party and established branches right across the central belt of Scotland but the Headquarters and the man himself were in Dundee. He was elected to the town council in 1905 and launched his (highly profitable) paper, the *Prohibitionist* in 1906.

Scrymgeour combined the most extreme and heartless intolerance for evil and corruption with a very genuine and practical concern for the weak. He had no sense of dignity, decorum or style and, in his early days, no tolerance for even a sympathetic ally who had the misfortune to disagree with him on the smallest detail or who showed the slightest willingness to compromise with the enemy. He called himself a Socialist and received funds from Labour (until 1908) and the trades unions. But an early poster read: 'Vote for Scrymgeour and Death to Drink—have done with Bogus Labour Representation and go in for Socialism.'

On the council he fought successfully for specific and practical benefits for the lower-paid council employees and launched a bitter class war against the high-paid officials and the old councillors. He had 'the gift for uncovering one public scandal after another, revealing in the process incompetence or worse on the part of convenors who had been elected for their putative business acumen or renowned integrity'.[20] Along the way he made many enemies and lost his council seat in 1909.

His first attempt to enter parliament was at the 1908 by-election. Churchill came top of the poll with 44 per cent, Scrymgeour came fourth and bottom with just 4 per cent. Again, at both the general elections of 1910 Churchill came top and Scrymgeour came bottom.

During the war Scrymgeour had ample opportunity to display his fearless and intransigent socialism and pacifism. When Churchill became Minister of Munitions in 1917 he had to seek a renewal of his electoral mandate. Scrymgeour was his only opponent and this time got 22 per cent.

Churchill ran as a Coalition Liberal in 1918 and over half the voters cast a joint vote for Churchill and his sitting Labour colleague, Wilkie. They were opposed by a second Labour candidate and Scrymgeour. Even in the jingoistic atmosphere of 1918 Scrymgeour did better than ever before. Over a quarter of the voters supported him: 10 per cent plumped for Scrymgeour, another 14 per cent cross-voted Scrymgeour and Labour, and 2 per cent cross-voted Scrymgeour and Churchill. Scrymgeour beat the second Labour candidate by a significant margin and confirmed himself as the leading opponent to Churchill.

By 1922 the Coalition had fallen out of favour and collapsed. Wilkie retired and Labour put forward only one candidate, E D Morel who was more famous for his pacifism than his socialism. At the same time Churchill, standing now as a National Liberal, had a fellow National Liberal as a running mate. The only way to make sense of that pattern of choice was to see the two National Liberals in opposition to Scrymgeour and Morel. A Liberal and a Communist merely cluttered the ballot. In the

Table 1

The changing structure of Dundee politics 1895–1945

Per cent of voters casting their votes for

Year	SPP	SPP/ Lab	Lab	Lab/ Lib	Lib	Lib/ LU	LU	LU/ Con	Con
1895	—	—	3	2	54	3	2	32	0
1900	—	—	—	—	58	1	0	38	0
1906	—	—	16	20	37	1	0	18	0
1910J	2	4	3	55	6	0	0	25	0
1910D	3	3	3	50	3	1	1	30	0
1918	10	14	10	(55% Lab/LU)			9	—	—
1922	8	34	2	3	1	5	28	—	—
1923	9	18	3	2	4	(24% Lib/Con)			4
1924	5	32	5	0	0	(37% Lib/Con)			1
1929	2	48	1	1	2	(31% Lib/Con)			3
1931	2	28	2	1	1	(51% Lib/Con)			1
1935	—	—	45	1	1	(50% Lib/Con)			2
1945	—	—	54	2	1	(32% Lib/Con)			2

Notes:

Dundee was an 'undivided burgh', i.e. it elected two MPs from one constituency. Every voter could vote for either one or two candidates. The two candidates with the highest votes were elected

SPP = Scottish Prohibition Party; LU = Liberal Unionist up to 1910, Coalition Liberal in 1918, and National Liberal in 1922

SPP/Lab indicates the percent of voters who cross-voted, i.e. who cast one of their votes for the SPP and the other for Labour

Lab/Lib, Lib/LU, LU/Con, Lib/Con, Lab/LU are defined similarly

The figures do not add up to 100% because a few voters cast their votes for combinations not shown in the table. The only occasions when over 10% voted for such an unlisted combination were in 1923 and 1924 when 16% and 12% respectively voted Lab/Communist. But of course there were usually several unlisted combinations, with a substantial total vote even though no one combination received many.

A single party label heading a column, indicates the percent of voters who cast all their votes for the one party. Depending on the circumstances, such voters may have 'plumped', i.e. used only one of the two votes to which they were entitled, or there may have been two candidates from the one party.

Source Data in this table have been calculated from F W S Craig, *British Parliamentary Election Results 1885–1918,* and *1918–1949*

event 28 per cent of the voters cast a straight vote for both National Liberals and 34 per cent voted for the Scrymgeour/Morel combination which won.

At each of the next four elections, the bulk of the voters cast their votes either for a Scrymgeour/Labour combination or for a Liberal/Conservative combination. Those two combination tickets accounted for 42 per cent of

Table 2

Results in Contested Wards 1920–1938

Glasgow

PPR	Ward	1920	1	2	3	4	5	6	7	8	9	0	1	2	3	4	5	6	7	8
67	Kelvinside	M													M			M	M	
81	Pollokshields	M			M					M			M	M						
93	Park	M									M				M			M		
96	Cathcart	M			M				M	M	M	M			P	M		M	M	M
100	Langside	M				M	M				M			M	M		M			
104	Camphill	M	M			M	M								P	M		M	M	M
136	Dennistoun	M	M			M			M	M		M	P		P	M	M	M		M
137	Whiteinch	M			M	M	M	M			M	M	M	M	M	L	M	M	M	M
137	Pollokshaws	M	M							M			M	L	M	M	M	M	M	M
142	North Kelvin	M	M	M				M	M	M		M	M	M	M	M	M	M	M	M
147	Blythswood	M					M	M			M	M			M	M			M	
148	Partick East	M	M	M	M	M	M	M	M		M		M	M	M	M	M	M	M	M
150	Sandyford	M	M		M	M		L	M	M	M	M		M	M	L	M	M	L	M
152	Partick West	M	M	M	M	M	M	M	M	M	L	M	M	M	L	L	L	L	M	M
164	Govanhill	M	M			M	M	M		M	M	M	M	M	P	M	I	M	M	I
182	Townhead	L	M	M	M	M	M	L	M	L	L	M	M	L	L	L	L	L	L	L
186	Woodside	L	M	L	M	L	L	L	M	L	L	M	L	L	L	L	L	L	L	L
190	Exchange	M	M		M	M	M		M	M	M	M	M		M	L	L	M	M	
193	Kinning Park	M	M	M	M	M	M	L	M	M	M	M	M	P	L	L	L	L	L	L
196	Maryhill	L	M	M	M	M	M	M	M	M	L	M	M	M	L	L	L	L	L	L
197	Fairfield	L	L	L	L	L	L	L	L	L	L	M	L	L	M	L	L		L	L
198	Springburn	L	L	L	L	L	L	L	L	L	L	L	L	L	L	L			L	L
200	Kingston	L	M	L	M	L	L	M	L	L	M	L	L	M	L	L	L	L	L	L
200	Anderston	M	M	L	L	L	L	L	L	L	M	M	L	M	M	L	M	L	I	L
201	Ruchill	L	M	M	M	L	M	L	M	M	L	M	L	L	L	L	L	L	L	L
201	Gorbals	L	L	L	L	L	L	L	L	L	L	L	L	L	L	L				L
204	Whitevale	M	M	M	M	M	L	L	M	M	L	M	M	L	L	M	L	M	M	L
206	Shettleston	L	L	L	L	L	L	L	L	L	L	M	M	I	I	I	I	M	I	I
208	Cowlairs	L	L	L	L	M	M	L	M	L	L	M	M	L	L	L	L	L	L	L
209	Govan	L	L	L	L	L	L	L	M	L	M	L	M	L	L	L			L	L
211	Provan	M	L	L	L	L	M	L	M	M	L	M	L	L	L	L			L	L
214	Calton	M	L	L	M	L	L	L	L	M	L	L	L	I	L	I	I	L	I	I
220	Cowcaddens	M	L	L	M	L	M	L	L	L	L	L	L	L	L	I	L	L	L	L
221	Parkhead	L	L	L	L	L	L	L	M	L	L	L	L	I	I	I	I	I	I	I
241	Hutchesontown	L	L	L	L	L	L	L	L	L		L	L	L	L	L	L	L	L	L
251	Mile-end	L	L	L	L	L	L	L	L	L	L	L	L	L	L	L	L	L	L	L
260	Dalmarnock	L	L	L	L	L	L	L	L	L	L	L	P	I	I	I	I	I	I	L

Edinburgh

PPR	Ward	1920	1	2	3	4	5	6	7	8	9	0	1	2	3	4	5	6	7	8
68	Morningside		M							M	M									
73	Haymarket	M							M	M				M				M		
76	Newington	M							M							M		M	M	M
84	Corstorphine	M				M														M
88	Merchiston		M		M									M						
92	St Bernards	M			M	M		M			M	M						M	M	M
100	St Stephens	M	M		M	M	M		M	M	M	M			M	M	M	M	M	M
106	West Leith	M						M	M				M		M	M	M	M	M	M
107	Colinton	M	M																M	
108	Portobello	M					M	M	M	M	M	M	M	M	M	M	M	M	M	M
110	St Andrews	M												M	M	M	M			M
112	Broughton		M					M	M	M			M	M			M	M	M	M	P

Table 2

Results in Contested Wards 1920–1938

PPR	Year—1920	1	2	3	4	5	6	7	8	9	0	1	2	3	4	5	6	7	8
131 George Square	M	M	M	M	M	M	M	M	M	M	M	M	M	M	M	M	M	M	M
139 Liberton	M	M	M		M		L	M	M	M	M	M	M	M	M	L	L	M	L
140 Calton	M	M			M	M	M	L	M	M	M	L	M	M	M	L	M	M	L
146 South Leith	M	M	M	M		M		M	M	M			M	M	M	P	P	P	P
158 Canongate	M	M	M	M	M	M	L	M	L	L	M	L	L	M	L	L	P	M	L
163 Gorgie	M	M	L	L		M	L	L	L	L			L	L	L	L	P	L	L
163 St Leonards	M	M	M	M	L	L	L	L	L	L	L	L	L	L	L	L	L	L	L
165 St Giles		M	M	M	M	M	L	L	M	L	L	M	M	L	L	M	L	L	M
170 Dalry	M	M			M	M	L	L	M	L	L	L	L	L	L	L	L	L	L
172 Central Leith	M		M	M	M	M	L	M	M	M	M		M	M	M	M	P	L	L
182 North Leith	M	M			L	M	L	L	M	L	L	M	L	L	P	M	L	L	M

Aberdeen

PPR	Year—1920	1	2	3	4	5	6	7	8	9	0	1	2	3	4	5	6	7	8
73 Rubislaw																			
85 Ruthrieston												M	M	M	M			M	M
102 Rosemount								M	M				M					M	M
111 Ferryhill													M					M	M
112 Holburn								M		M		M		M	M				M
125 Woodside								M	M				M		M	M	M	M	
130 Gilcomston								M	M	M		M	M	M	M	M	M	L	L
150 St Nicholas								M	M	M	M	M	L	L	M	L	L	L	
152 St Machar								M	M	M		L	L	L		M	L		
160 Torry									M			M			L	M	L	L	
183 Greyfriars								L		L		L			I		L	I	I
183 St Clements								L				M	L			L	L	L	

Dundee

PPR	Year—1920	1	2	3	4	5	6	7	8	9	0	1	2	3	4	5	6	7	8
83 Tenth				M				M											M
91 Eleventh		M		M	M		M					M		M	M			M	M
123 Second	M			M				M	M	M	M			M	M	M	M	M	M
138 Ninth	M	M		M	M		M	M	M	M		M	M	M	M	L	M	M	L
145 Seventh	M			M			M	M	M	M	M	M	M	L	M	M		M	M
152 Fourth	M	M	L	M		L	M	M	L			M	L	M	L	L	M	M	L
160 Fifth	M			M		L	M		M	M	M	L	L	L	L	M	M		L
163 Third	L	M	M		M		L	M	L		M	M	L	L	L	L	L		
164 First	L	M	L		M		L	M	M	M		M	L	M	L	L	M	M	L
166 Eighth	M	M	L	M	M	L	L	M		L	M	M	M		L	L	L	L	L
167 Sixth	M	M		M	M	M	M	M	M	M	M	M	M	L	L	L		L	L

Notes:

M = Moderate, Progressive or Independent: P = Protestant, or Independent Protestant; L = Labour; I = ILP or Independent Labour

In 1920 three councillors were elected for each ward. In most cases all three represented the same party, but there was split representation in 7 Glasgow wards (Townhead, Maryhill, Kingston, Anderston, Ruchill, Provan and Calton) and in 3 Edinburgh wards (Liberton, Dalry and Central Leith). For these wards the 1920 entry shows the party which won 2 out of the 3 seats in the ward

PPR = number of persons per room (times 100). Figures are the average of those for 1921 and 1931 (except in Aberdeen where the ward boundary changes have forced me to rely on 1931 figures only—which makes little difference for interpretation however)

the voters in 1923, 69 per cent in 1924, 79 per cent in 1929 and 79 per cent again in 1931. The unusually low figure in 1923 resulted from a number of factors—a 16 per cent Labour/Communist vote, a 10 per cent Scrymgeour/Anti-coalition Liberal vote, and a 9 per cent plump for Scrymgeour amongst others.

Scrymgeour was top of the poll in 1922, 1923 and 1929—ahead of the official Labour candidate. But Labour and Prohibition votes became increasingly identical and after a resounding joint victory in 1929 they went down together in 1931. Scrymgeour never stood again and died, forgotten, in 1947.

Labour and municipal politics

There were no local government elections in 1918 because of the war, and in 1919 they attracted little enthusiasm in Edinburgh or Glasgow because a reorganisation of city and ward boundaries was due in 1920 when all councillors (instead of the usual one-third) would be up for re-election.[21]

All Edinburgh and Glasgow council seats were up for election in 1920: 111 in Glasgow, sixty-nine in Edinburgh. In both cities the old medieval guilds contributed another two councillors who always sided with the right wing. The Labour Party had eighty-three official candidates in Glasgow, nineteen in Edinburgh. It won forty-four of the Glasgow seats but only four in Edinburgh. Indeed Glasgow was the only Scottish city where Labour did well in 1920.

For the next five years Labour representation on Scottish city councils remained fairly static. Then in 1926 Labour had another breakthrough in Glasgow and made substantial gains in Edinburgh and Dundee. Though only a third of the council members were up for election, Labour representation jumped from forty to forty-eight in Glasgow and from six to fourteen in Edinburgh. Labour enjoyed no similar breakthrough in Aberdeen until the mid-thirties and its success in Dundee was not to be repeated until the mid-thirties.

Local politics in smaller and more remote communities like Aberdeen remained relatively unpoliticised for a considerable time, but in the big cities local elections were political and were fought increasingly on national political issues. As the Glasgow Herald lamented in 1921: 'The main subjects on which candidates discoursed were national rather than local in their range: for instance, unemployment, housing or the burden of rates and taxes. References to such things as baths and washhouses, open spaces and even so big a subject as the building of bridges over the Clyde to relieve the enormous pressure of vehicular traffic only served to emphasise how relatively small a place these topics occupied in the public mind compared with the great issues—issues which concern the State probably in greater degree than municipal authorities'. Labour's success in 1926 was attributed to class polarisation induced by the Coal Strike.

Moderates and Progressives

Yet though local politics might revolve around national issues it did not present the elector with the same range of party choices. Labour entered local contests sporadically before the war and in an increasingly organised fashion after 1920. But the Conservative Party stayed out of local politics until the late sixties. In all the Scottish cities Labour faced loose coalitions of anti-socialists whose members used labels such as Moderate, Progressive, or Independent. Apart from their single-city parochialisms, the essence of these anti-socialist groupings was instinctive distaste for Labour policies and Labour style plus a desire to avoid splitting the anti-Labour vote. They were a product of the First-Past-the-Post electoral system, without a clearly defined policy and without tight party discipline. Their great success lay in restricting the number of anti-Labour candidates presented to the electorate. Thus although Labour won two-thirds of Glasgow's parliamentary seats in 1922, 1923 and 1929, and even a majority of Edinburgh's parliamentary seats in 1929, Labour never won control of Edinburgh's municipal council and had to wait until 1933 to win municipal control in Glasgow.

Whether anti-socialists were described as Progressives or Moderates was irrelevant in the sense that these were merely alternative labels for the anti-socialist group. In contrast to London, Progressives were not organised to fight Moderates or vice versa.[22] However the Liberals amongst them, particularly influential in Edinburgh, had a distinct preference for describing the (whole) group as Progressive rather than Moderate just to emphasise that it was not a purely Conservative front.

Edinburgh anti-socialists formed themselves into a Progressive Party in 1928. In Glasgow the anti-socialists were organised by the Good Government League and the Glasgow Citizens Union and used the term Moderate through the twenties, formally organising into a Progressive Party only in 1936.

Irish Catholics

The franchise extension of 1918 increased the numerical significance of the Irish Catholics and they had far better propaganda resources than the socialists: the pulpit, the pub and a large circulation Catholic press which was greatly assisted by its football correspondents' close links with Celtic Football Club. Other factors reduced their political influence however. First, few Irish immigrants came to Scottish cities in the twentieth century and the numbers with Irish birth steadily declined. In that sense, the Irish became less Irish. Second, the creation of parliaments in Dublin and Belfast took Home Rule out of British politics. Third, the general collapse of the Liberal Party left them without a credible alternative to Labour. Fourth, the Labour Party which had been for Prohibition in 1920 (by resolutions at both the Scottish Labour Party Conference and the STUC) switched against it in 1921 though the ILP's Scottish conference continued to affirm its commitment to Prohibition annually. Fifth, Catholic schools were at risk after 1918 and whatever the logic of its socialist principles, Labour showed most sympathy for the Catholic education system. The consequence of all these factors was that Irish Catholic organisations could no longer bargain with different parties and deliver a significant vote to whichever offered the best bargain. Increasingly the Irish Catholic vote identified with Labour and Catholic organisations could not credibly threaten to withhold it.

1920 was the end of independent Irish influence. In that year the municipal elections coincided with a Veto Poll under the Temperance Act. All Labour candidates were pledged to support the 'dry' side and they found every pub turned into an anti-Labour committee room.[23] Turnout averaged 79 per cent—never to be repeated in a local election. Despite a general breakthrough in that year Labour failed to win more than two of the nine seats in working-class Provan, Calton and Cowcaddens wards. All three elected Irish wets including several Irish publicans (not *republicans* though they may have been that as well). The Glasgow Citizens Union listed them as Moderate. But after 1920 Labour dropped its commitment to Prohibition and made itself acceptable to the 'wets'.

The 1918 Education Act imposed a further restraint on Irish Catholic political mobility. Catholic schools were in financial trouble. With the consent of the Vatican and the Scottish Hierarchy the 1918 Act transferred Catholic schools to the elected Education Authorities while leaving Catholics in charge of religious education and allowing them a veto on unsuitable teachers. Elections to the Education Authorities were by the Single Transferable Vote method of Proportional Representation. They were contested by Labour, by the Catholic Church, in Edinburgh by the (Protestant) Church Joint Committee and in Glasgow by the Moderates. In 1928, for example, Glasgow's forty-five member Education Authority consisted of thirty Moderates, eleven Catholics and four Labour.[24] Labour and Catholic voters transferred their votes to each other's candidates.

The Good Government League complained that under the 1918 Act 'Glasgow has ceased to be a douce Scottish city. To a large extent it has become an Irish city . . . (with) a very large semi-alien population.'[25] Romanism had been put on the rates by making Protestant ratepayers subsidise Catholic schools. In Scotland, and nowhere else in the United Kingdom, the state took over ownership of Catholic schools, built additional Catholic schools to meet demand, and bore 100 per cent of both capital and running costs. It gave Catholics a special interest in local politics. A combination of Labour sympathy and Moderate antagonism left Catholics with no other choice than Labour if the choice had to be between political parties. In 1929 elected Education Authorities were abolished and the schools were transferred to Municipal Councils. There was no tradition of direct church representation on Municipal Councils—so Catholics had an additional motive to back Labour in municipal elections after 1929.

Protestant reaction

What the *Glasgow Herald* called 'the menace of Romanism' was not just an educational issue however and it prompted Protestant parties in both Glasgow and Edinburgh. The Glasgow party, led by Alexander Ratcliffe, was called the Scottish Protestant League. Oddly enough it was founded in Edinburgh in 1920 but achieved electoral success in Glasgow during the early thirties. It was to be 'evangelical, undenominational and non-political' but would give special attention to the 'Roman Catholic Sinn Fein campaign in this country'.[26] By 1927 Ratcliffe was attacking the Roman Catholic Relief Act (1926) for allowing an 'idolatrous procession of the Host in Glasgow'. The same year he demanded a census of immigrants as a 'precaution to safeguard one of the most notable and certainly one of the most historic races on the face of the earth' and to protect native Scots from 'an alien race that would impose its culture, its traditions, and possibly its faith'.[27] According to the 1931 census he need not have worried about immigration. Even in Glasgow less than 3 per cent had been born in Northern Ireland and only 2 per cent in Southern Ireland. In 1929 the SPL claimed that reducing the Irish in Scotland from 750,000 to 250,000 would end unemployment in Scotland.

Two SPL councillors were elected to Glasgow corporation in 1931, one in 1932 and four in 1933. They took a quarter of the vote in 1933, almost the same as the Progressives. SPL victories in 1931 and 1932 were achieved in wards where it was opposed by both Labour and the Progressives. However in 1933, three of the four SPL victories were in straight fights with the Progressives in wards that were so middle-class they usually returned Progressives without any opposition. Their votes were no doubt inflated by the absence of other candidates. Overall the SPL stood in twenty-two of the thirty-eight wards in 1933 and came first or second in fifteen of them.

The seven SPL councillors did not stick together for long. Two split off in 1933 and another two in 1934, alleging Ratcliffe's methods were 'dictatorial'. He was left with only two followers, electoral support declined, and by 1936 not a single SPL member remained on the council.

Few remember the SPL intervention in Glasgow now. They reached their peak in 1933 when the main political story was the Progressives' loss of control to a coalition of Labour and ILP members. In 1933, the SPL defeated four Moderates, and eleven of the twelve Labour gains were in wards where the SPL intervened. If it succeeded in attracting working-class Protestant votes it clearly did Labour no harm in the process.

Edinburgh's Protestant Action Party, led by John Cormack surged ahead as Glasgow's SPL went into decline. Cormack accused Labour of being permeated by Catholics and the Progressives of being slum landlords. Labour certainly was in alliance with the Catholics, who did influence Labour policy on Catholic and ethical questions, while a majority of the Moderate councillors were property owners. Cormack won North Leith ward in 1934 and was joined by other Protestant Action councillors in 1935 and 1936. At one point they numbered ten in a council of seventy-one.

Cormack lost his seat in 1937 although Protestant Action candidates were first or second in twelve of the twenty-three wards that year. However, he won the neighbouring seat of South Leith in 1938 and retained it after the war, calling himself an Independent and siding with the Progressives for a time, but surviving right through into the sixties as the sole remaining Protestant Action councillor.

Unlike the SPL in Glasgow, Edinburgh's Protestant Action party won its seats in the city's more working-class wards, particularly the three Leith wards but also including places like Gorgie. When the SPL lost all its seats on Glasgow council in 1936 but Protestant Action was at its peak in Edinburgh there were plans to extend its activities to Glasgow. Electorally at least, they came to nothing.

In the long term, both the generous treatment of the Catholic schools in the 1918 Act and the Protestant backlash conspired together to integrate the Irish Catholic community into the Scottish political system. The generosity put the minority in a privileged position and the backlash forced them into a permanent coalition with a British party in order to defend their privilege. They could no longer stand outside the system.

The class alignment between Labour and the Progressives

For the period between the wars the wards in the four cities can be classified by census data on the numbers of persons per room. More direct measures of social class are available for large areas but not for wards. Housing measures are a reasonable substitute however, especially because local politics stressed the housing aspect of class divisions. By 1938 every Glasgow ward (except Exchange) with more than 1.6 persons per room went to Labour or the ILP. All the rest were won by Progressives. No ward on either side of the class divide was entirely safe. A split between rival candidates could deliver a normally safe seat to the class enemy—as happened in working-class Parkhead which Labour lost to the Moderates in 1927, or in middle-class Whiteinch and Pollokshaws in 1933 where SPL interventions handed the seats to Labour. And there could be special local factors like the Irish wets in Provan, Calton and Cowcaddens who beat the Labour candidates in 1920.

Overall however, the pattern is clear (see Table 2) and most exceptions have specific explanations: throughout the interwar years the Moderates or Progressives could almost always count on winning the wards with less than 1.6 persons per room. Labour eventually controlled all the rest except Exchange ward, where the non-resident business voters kept it Progressive until their franchise was abolished in 1970. But between 1920 and 1938 Labour's performance was patchy in its 'natural areas': it took time to establish local organisations and destroy old personal links. Labour took control of the council when and only when it was able to make an almost clean sweep of its own 'natural constituency', that is the areas with more than 1.6 persons per room.

Edinburgh conformed almost as closely to the simple rule. Only five of the twenty-three wards had over 1.6 persons per room and in 1937 Labour won those five wards and no others. The following year, 1938 was an unusually good year for Labour in Edinburgh, however, and it pushed its score up from five to seven.

Labour took longer to establish itself in Dundee and Aberdeen but by 1938 Labour took all Dundee wards with over 1.6 persons per room plus two more. In Aberdeen also, Labour by 1938 was winning all the wards with over 1.6 persons per room plus the three next wards on the class spectrum.

One characteristic of interwar politics recalled pre-war patterns: many wards frequently went uncontested, especially in the earlier interwar years. It reflected the patchy performance of Labour, because most of the uncontested wards were held by Moderates or Progressives. Aberdeen, in 1931, was an extreme example. Only one of its twelve wards was contested and only 20 per cent of the ward electorate turned out to vote.

The simple pattern of class polarisation established by 1938 continued after the war. For the period up to the reorganisation of local government in 1974 I have classified the wards by their proportion of employers, managers and professionals in the 1971 census. This is a very direct measure of occupationally defined social class. Statistics on persons per room were still available right up to 1971 but housing reforms reduced their effectiveness as an indicator of social class and political partisanship. Obviously there were social changes between 1945 and 1971; so my choice of class indicator more accurately reflects social conditions at the end of the period. But it provides a simple yet effective guide to social conditions throughout the period except in a few wards (Cathcart, Knightswood and Provan in Glasgow; Liberton, Sighthill, Colinton and Murrayfield in Edinburgh) where post war peripheral housing estates brought many new electors into the area.

Whatever its deficiences as a perfect social indicator it predicts political partisanship very well throughout the post-war years. In Glasgow, at the 1973 election, Labour won every ward with less than 10 per cent managers and professionals and Conservatives won the rest. Throughout the whole period 1949–73 Labour seldom lost wards with less than 6 per cent managers and professionals while it very seldom if ever won wards with over 9 per cent. Only four of the thirty-seven wards could be described as marginal in the sense that they changed to and fro between Labour and Progressive: Kinning Park (8 per cent Manag & Prof), Parkhead (8 per cent), Yoker (7 per cent) and Govanhill (7 per cent).

In Edinburgh over the same period 1949–73, Labour seldom lost wards with less than 9 per cent managers and professionals and seldom if ever won those with over 16 per cent. The only wards which swung to and fro were Calton (13 per cent) and South Leith (10 per cent).

Boundary changes in Dundee and Aberdeen preclude an analysis of the full 1949–73 period, but over a decade or so they also conformed well to the class model. In Aberdeen, Labour could usually expect to win all wards with less than 13 per cent managers and professionals and could never win those with over 16 per cent.

Dundee ward boundaries were redrawn in 1954 and again in 1964. From

Table 3

Results in contested wards 1949–1973

%PM		Year—1949	1950s 0 1 2 3 4 5 6 7 8 9	1960s 0 1 2 3 4 5 6 7 8 9	1970s 0 1 2 3
Glasgow					
43.6	*Kelvinside	P	P P P P P P P P P	P P P P P P P P C C	C C C C
22.6	*Camphill	P	P P P P P P P P P P	P P P P P P P P P C	C P C C
22.6	*Whiteinch	P	P P P P P P P P P P	P P P P P P P P P P	P P L C
20.1	*Partick West	P	P P L P P P P P P P	P P P P P P P P P P	P P C C
19.1	*Langside		P P P P P P P P	P P P P P P P P P P	C C C C
18.0	*Partick East	P	P P P P P P P P P P	P P P P P P P P P P	P P C C
17.8	*Park		P P P P P P P	P P P P P P P P P P	P C C C
16.7	Craigton	P	P P P P P P P P P P	P P P P P P P S C	C L C C
16.5	Pollokshields	P	P P L P P P P P P P	P P P P P P P P P P	C L L C
15.9	Cathcart		P P P P P P P	P P L P P P P P P C	C L L C
10.9	*Dennistoun	P	P P P P P P P P P P	P P P L P P P P P C	C C C C
9.8	*Woodside	L	L L L L L L L L L L	P L L P L P P P P	P L C L
9.4	*North Kelvin	P	P P L P P P P P P P	P P P P P P P P P P	P L L L
8.0	*Kinning Park	P	P P L L L L L L L P	P L L P P P P P P	P L L L
7.7	Pollokshaws	L	L P L L L L L L L L	L L L L L L L L S L	L L L L
7.7	Parkhead	L	L P L L L L L L L	L L L L L P P P P P	P L L L
7.4	Yoker	P	P P L P P P P L L L	L L L L L L P L S P	L L L L
7.3	*Govanhill	P	P P L L L P L P P L	P P L P L P P C C P	L L L L
6.2	*Anderston	L	L L L L L L L L L L	L L L L L P L L P P	L L L L
5.6	Fairfield	L	L L L L L L L L L L	L L L L L L P L P P	L L L L
5.5	Shettleston	L	L L L L L L L L L L	L L L L L L L L S S	L L L L
5.1	Exchange†	P	P P P P P P P P P P	P P P P P P P P P P	L L L L
5.0	Knightswood	P	P P L L L L L L L L	L L L L L L L L S L	L L L L
4.9	Springburn	L	P L L L L L L L L	L L L L L L L L S L	L L L L
4.7	Maryhill	L	L L L L L L L L L	L L L L L L L S L	L L L L
4.2	Ruchill	L	L L L L L L L L	L L L L L L L L S L	L L L L
4.1	Cowcaddens	L	L L L L L L L L L	L L L L L L L L S L	L L L L
4.0	Townhead	L	L L L L L L L L L L	L L L L L L L L L L	L L L L
4.0	Calton	L	L L L L L L L L L L	L L L L L L L L L L	L L L L
3.6	Cowlairs	L	L L L L L L L L L L	L L L L L L L L S L	L L L L
3.5	Govan	L	L L L L L L L L L L	L L L L L L L L L L	L L L L
3.4	Provan	P	P P L L L L L L L L	L L L L L L L L S L	L L L L
2.7	Mile-end	L	L L L L L L L L L L	L L L L L L L S C	L L L L
2.2	Gorbals	L	L L L L L L L L L L	L L L L L L L L L L	L L L L
2.0	*Kingston	L	L L L L L L L L	L L L L L L P L C	L L L L
1.6	Hutchesontown	L	L L L L L L L L L L	L L L L L L L L L L	L L L L
1.1	Dalmarnock	L	L L L L L L L L L L	L L L L L L L L S L	L L L L
Edinburgh					
44.4	*Murrayfield	P	P P P P	P P P P P P P P P	P P C C
44.2	*Morningside	P	P P P P P P P	P P P P P P P P	P P P R
37.6	*Corstorphine	P	P P P P P P P P P	P R R P P P P P P	P P R R
32.0	*St Andrews	P	P P P P P P P	P P P P C C C	C C C C
31.8	*Newington	P	P P P R P P	R P R R P P P P P P	P P P C
31.4	*St Bernards		P P P P P P P P	P P P P P P P P	P P C C
29.8	*Merchiston		P P P P P P	R P R P P R R	R R R R
29.6	*Colinton	P	P P P P P P P P	P P P P P P P C	P C C C
27.0	*Portobello	P	P P P P P P P P P	P P P P P P P P P P	P P P C
26.8	*West Leith		P P P P P P P	P P P P P P P	P P P P
19.0	*George Square	P	P P P P P P P P P P	P P P P P P P P P P	P C P L

Table 3

Results in contested wards 1949–1973

```
                            1950s          1960s         1970s
%PM              Year—1949  0123456789     0123456789    0123
17.2  Craigentinny     P    PPPLLLLLLL     LLLLLLLLLL    LLLL
16.7  *Broughton       P    P  PP    P       PPPP PPP    PPPC
15.4  Liberton              PPPPLPLLL      LLLLL LCLC    LLLL
12.7  *Calton          P    PPPPLPPPPP     PPLPLLPPSP    LLLL
10.3  *South Leith     P    APPAPPAPLA     PLLLLLLPSP    LLLC
 9.0  *Gorgie          P    PPLLLLLL L     LLLLLLLLSC    LLLL
 8.0  *St Giles        P    PPLLLLLLL      LLLL  LSL     LLLL
 7.0  Sighthill        L    LLLLLLLLL      LL  L SS      LLLL
 6.3  *Holyrood        L    LLLLLLL L      LLLLLLL L     LLLL
 5.3  Craigmillar      L    LL L LL   L    LLLLLLLLSL    LLLL
 4.6  *Central Leith   L    LLLLLLLLLL     LLLLLLLLSL    LLLL
 4.6  Pilton           L     LL  LLL        LLLLLLLL     LLLL

Aberdeen
46.3  *Rubislaw                            PPPPPPP       PCCC
30.6  *Ruthrieston                         PPPPP PPP     PCCC
27.1  *Rosemount                           PPPPPPPPP     PCCC
20.9  *Holborn                             P  PP PPP     POCC
15.5  Ferryhill                            LLLLLLLLL     LLLL
13.9  *St Nicholas                         PLLLLPPPP     LLLL
10.3  Woodside                             LLLLPPLL      LLLL
 9.4  St Clements                          LLLLLLSL      LLLL
 7.0  Mastrick                             LLLLLLLLL     LLLL
 6.9  Northfield                           LLLLLLLLL     LLLL
 6.3  Torry                                LLLLLLLLL     LLLL
 5.5  St Machar                            LLLLLPLLL     LLLR

Dundee
36.5  *Broughty Ferry                      PPPPPP        PPPP
25.2  *Riverside                           PPPPPP        PPPP
21.3  *Balgay                              PPPPPP        PPPP
20.7  Law                                  PPPPPP        PPPP
20.3  Harbour                              PPPPPP        PPPP
14.4  Craigie                              LPPPPP        PLPP
 6.3  Downfield                            LLLLLL        LLLL
 6.0  Douglas                              LLLLLL        LLLL
 5.6  Camperdown                           LLLLSL        LLIL
 5.4  Caird                                LLLLLL        LLLL
 5.0  Lochee                               LLLLLL        LLLL
 4.6  Hilltown                             LLLLLL        LLLL
```

Notes:

P = Progressive, Moderate, Progressive-Conservative, or Independent; A = Protestant Action, or Protestant Independent; C = Conservative; O = Official Conservative (Aberdeen); L = Labour; I = Independent Labour; R = Liberal; S = SNP.

%PM = percent Professional & Managerial (strictly: percent Employers, Managers and Professionals) in 1971 Census.

* = wards where the number of owner-occupied tenures exceeded the number of council tenures in 1971.

† Over a quarter of Glasgow Exchange ward electors were non-resident 'business' electors until their franchise was abolished in 1970.

1964 to 1973 there were thirty-six councillors. After 1966 no party ever had more than nineteen councillors on its side. Yet politics in Dundee was in no way genuinely competitive. Five of the twelve wards had 20 per cent or more managers and professionals: they always elected Progressives or Progressive-Conservatives. Six wards had 6 per cent or less managers and professionals: they never elected Progressives or Conservatives. Apart from one solitary SNP member, elected in 1968, and the occasional internal party quarrel, Dundee had only one ward whose social composition gave both Labour and the Progressives a chance of victory. That was Craigie ward with 14 per cent managers and professionals.

Overall then, class determined party support in all four cities but despite Labour's great strength in Glasgow it did not do quite so well as Glasgow's class composition implied: Dennistoun and North Kelvin should have been marginal while Govanhill and Kinning Park should have been more solidly Labour.

The Conservative entry into city politics: 1967–72

In contrast to the interwar years, the well-established tyranny of class-based political alignments after the war ensured that Labour versus Progressive politics was fairly stable. Spectacular changes involved other political dimensions: the SNP surge in the late sixties, the entry of the Liberals or the rapid replacement of the Progressives by Conservatives.

As long as the Progressives were opposed only by the Labour Party they could maintain their parochial principle of 'keeping politics out of local government'. But if they had to fight Labour, Liberals and Nationalists, they looked very much like stand-ins for the Conservative Party.

A Liberal won Newington ward Edinburgh in 1957 and was joined by others in Merchiston and Corstorphine—all three of them solidly middle-class places. By 1963, there were five Liberals on Edinburgh council—though none on any other Scottish city council.

The SNP put forward a large number of candidates in 1967 and won many votes but no seats in the cities. The next year their vote increased and they won thirteen Glasgow seats, eight in Edinburgh, but only one in each of Dundee and Aberdeen though they ran either first or second in eleven of Dundee's twelve wards. Almost without exception SNP victories were in working-class wards, though they ranged from the most marginal Labour areas to the most solidly working-class. As with the Liberals in the early sixties, SNP support faded as the parliamentary General Election approached and they won only a couple of city wards in 1969.

The Conservative Party entered local government contests from 1967 onwards primarily in order to use them as an aid to success in parliamentary contests. In particular, they wished to capitalise on the unpopularity of the Wilson government and channel the benefits to themselves rather than the SNP. Even hopeless local government wards were to be contested if they lay in marginal parliamentary constituencies so as to reinforce all potential Conservative voters' party identifications, mobilise all the potential activists, and improve the party's parliamentary campaign machine. It was all done in self-conscious imitation of Labour's strategy a generation earlier.

In Glasgow the Progressive Party had by then no real existence outside the council. Ward organisation was sparse. New Progressive candidates were located, approved and allocated to wards by a subcommittee of the existing Progressive councillors, and each Progressive councillor paid his own election expenses. Four-fifths of them had spent all their lives in Glasgow. They were a 'small self-perpetuating clique of long-established Glasgow 'small-businessmen'.[28]

Their lack of any real organisational support left them unable to resist the Conservatives who won over some Progressives, replaced others when they retired, and stood against those who would neither defect nor retire. By 1972 there were twice as many Conservative councillors as Progressives and by 1974 no Progressives at all.

Edinburgh Progressive Association did have ward organisations albeit with few members and some Progressive councillors were Liberals rather than merely parochial Conservatives. Edinburgh Progressives held out quite well until 1972. In that year there were twenty-one Progressives and only nine Conservatives on the council along with thirty-three Labour and five Liberals. No party had a majority but the Progressives hoped the Liberals would side with them to elect yet another Progressive as Provost. Instead the Liberals voted with Labour to elect Jack Kane. After that the Progressives collapsed. Only one Progressive stood for election in 1973 and none thereafter. Some former Progressives threw in their lot with the Conservatives, others left politics and one prominent Progressive councillor even joined the Labour Party. There was no longer any profit in remaining a Progressive.

Progressives in Aberdeen and Dundee had stronger local organisations. In Aberdeen the Progressives hit on the neat solution of relabelling themselves as Conservatives in 1971, forcing the Conservative Party candidates to call themselves 'Official Conservatives'. South Aberdeen Constituency Conservative Association supported the Conservatives (i.e. the Progressives) while North Aberdeen Constituency Association backed the Official Conservatives. The two groups fought each other in four wards. Conservatives beat the Officials in three of the four wards and the dispute ended with the Conservative Party accepting the old Progressives as their representatives.

Dundee had a Progressive Group on the Council but it was supported by the Dundee Ratepayers Association which had a strong ward organisation and little interest in national politics. Dundee Ratepayers raised money locally and was dependent neither on a few business donations nor on candidates to pay election expenses. Progressive councillors had to attend its meetings and often face severe criticism. Many of the councillors were Conservatives though none held office in the Party and others were genuinely non-political Dundonians. The Ratepayers Association was so strong that it was able to negotiate an agreement for joint candidates to be called Progressive-Conservatives. In 1970 there were six Progressive candidates, four Conservatives and three Progressive-Conservatives. Only the Progressives were elected. Gradually the agreement took root however, and in the seventies all candidates came to be Progressive-Conservatives, selected by a Central Liaison Committee containing equal numbers of Conservatives and Ratepayers.

Local government reorganisation 1974

Scottish local government was reorganised in 1974. A two-tier system of Regional and District Councils was introduced, each level having responsibility for different services. Both District and Regional Councils were subject to direct election but the old system of annual election by thirds was abolished and replaced by a system of general elections every four years. Hence there was more possibility of the minority party in a city winning control if the election happened to occur at a favourable time. One purpose of the reform was to put some excitement back into local politics. It failed to do so.

During the introductory phase of this system, District elections (including elections for city councils) were to be held in 1974, 1977 and 1980 before settling down to a four-year cycle. Turnout rose to 51 per cent in the first District elections but declined later. In 1977 turnout rates were 47 per cent in Glasgow and Edinburgh, 43 per cent in Dundee and only 36 per cent in Aberdeen. By 1980 turnout was down to 43 per cent in Glasgow and 45 per cent in Edinburgh though it rose to 49 per cent in Dundee and 38 per cent in Aberdeen.

Reflecting general Scottish (but no longer British) attitudes towards Central Government, Labour did very well in the cities in 1974, very badly in 1977 and very well again in 1980. The SNP took sixteen of Glasgow's seventy-two seats and five of Edinburgh's sixty-four in 1977 but lost almost all their seats in 1980.

In addition to these nation-wide (Scottish) trends Edinburgh and Glasgow diverged especially in the eighties. Labour-controlled Lothian Region, which included Edinburgh District, allowed itself to be manoeuvred into a fight with the 1979–83 Conservative Central Government on the questions of levels of public expenditure. Whatever the rights or wrongs of the issue, Lothian electors lined up behind Central Government: in the 1980 District elections and the 1982 Regional elections Labour won substantially fewer Edinburgh seats than in 1974 but, at the same time, more seats in Glasgow and Dundee and roughly the same as before in Aberdeen. At last the political differences between Glasgow and Edinburgh were as wide as class differences implied.

CONCLUDING REMARKS

Paradoxically the 'Lothian effect' in the eighties demonstrated the power of national forces in local politics because it was central government intervention in Lothian affairs, not competition between rival political elites within Lothian, that produced the electoral response. Its national origins contrast sharply with the local basis for Prohibition and Protestant Party successes in earlier years.

Caught between Labour central governments' desires for equality and uniformity, and Conservative central governments' desires for low levels of public expenditure, local government has lost all scope for initiative or discretion, and the Scottish Secretary of State has led the way in devising legislation to end local discretion. He now determines not only the 'reasonable' level for each local authority's expenditure and adjusts central government grants accordingly, he has also acquired the power to set 'reasonable' levels of rates.

The old unreformed burgh councils prior to 1833 were criticised for being self-perpetuating, unrepresentative and corrupt. But the elected councils of recent decades certainly did not conform to idealistic democratic notions of competition between ideas or between elites for the allegiance of the electorate. Class politics determined a high degree of stability. The Progressive councillors of Edinburgh or the Labour councillors elsewhere were not too far removed from being a self-perpetuating elite. Allegations of corruption were frequently made and not infrequently substantiated. Swings of support between parties owed more to British, or latterly Scottish, factors than to the performance of local councils and could not be interpreted as a judgement on local governments. Local politics was only incidentally and accidentally about political choices within the locality. Instead, political activity within the cities has come to serve other purposes whose significance goes beyond the cities themselves. For the parties local elections provide regular manoeuvres that help to keep the party organisation in trim for a parliamentary election. Collectively, the trends in local politics serve as a barometer of public attitudes towards Central Government. Individually, the political battle most relevant to a particular city is not the battle for control within the city but the battle between Central Government and the city for control of policy within it—and for funds to carry out that policy. Labour leaders in Glasgow have no reason to fear the Conservative opposition on Glasgow Council but they have every reason to fear the consequences for themselves, their policies and their city of an unpopular Labour Government or a determinedly ideological Conservative Government in London.

REFERENCES

1 The *Third Statistical Account of Scotland* gives a good account of politics in Glasgow and Dundee though the chapters on politics in the Edinburgh and Aberdeen volumes are short and uninformative. *See* D G Southgate 'Politics and representation in Dundee 1832–1963' in J M Jackson (ed) *The City of Dundee* (Herald Press, Arbroath 1979), pp 287–328; and R Baird 'The machinery of Local Government and Justice' in J Cunnison and J B S Gilfillan (eds) *Glasgow* (Collins, Glasgow 1958)

2   *See* M Dyer 'Mere detail and machinery: the Great Reform Act and the effects of redistribution on Scottish representation 1832–1868', *Scottish Historical Review* LXII (1983), pp. 17–34

3   For Parliamentary Election Results since 1832 see the series edited by F W S Craig *British Parliamentary Election Results 1832–1885, ditto 1885–1918, ditto 1918–1949, ditto 1950–1970* (all published by Macmillan, London); and the update volumes for 1974, 1979 and 1983 (published by Political Reference Publications, Chichester)

4   H J Hanham *Elections and Party Management: Politics in the Time of Disraeli and Gladstone* (Harvester Press, Sussex 1978), chapter 8

5   *See* W Hamish Fraser, 'Trades unions, reform and the election of 1868 in Scotland', *Scottish Historical Review* L (1971), pp 138–57

6   For the early history of the Conservative and Liberal Party organisations in Scotland *see* D W Urwin 'The development of the Conservative Party organisation in Scotland until 1912', *Scottish Historical Review* XLIV (1965), pp 89–111; and J G Kellas 'The Liberal Party in Scotland 1876–1895', *Scottish Historical Review* XLIV (1965), pp 1–15

7   *See* H Pelling, *Social Geography of British Elections 1885–1910* (Macmillan, London 1967), chapter 16, for a description of the religious controversy plus statistics on the distribution of Established Churchmen and free presbyterians in different parts of Scotland

8   *See* D Savage, 'Scottish politics 1885–1886', *Scottish Historical Review* XL (1961), pp 118–35, for the link between Disestablishment and Home Rule

9   J F McCaffrey 'The origins of Liberal Unionism in the west of Scotland', *Scottish Historical Review* L (1971), pp 47–71

10 M Kinnear *The British Voter* (Batsford, London 1968), p 130

11 *See* Pelling *op. cit.* for tables of figures on social class

12 For an account of the creation of democratic institutions in the nineteenth-century city *see* J E Shaw *Local Government in Scotland* (Oliver and Boyd, Edinburgh 1942); or J J Clarke *History of Local Government in the United Kingdom* (Greenwood Press, Connecticut 1978), chapter 25

13 *See* K Young *Local Politics and the Rise of Party: The London Municipal Society and the Conservative Intervention in Local Elections 1894–1963* (Leicester University Press 1975)

14 *See* B Elliot, D McCrone and V Skelton 'Property and political power: Edinburgh 1875–1975)', in J Garrard, D Jary, M Goldsmith and A Oldfield (eds) *The Middle Class in Politics* (Saxon House, Farnborough 1978)

15 *See* W Hamish Fraser 'Trades Councils in the Labour Movement in nineteenth century Scotland' in I MacDougall (ed) *Essays in Scottish Labour History* (John Donald, Edinburgh 1975). On the general point that there was a sub-municipal level of democratic political competition in Victorian times (though not now) *see* D Fraser *Urban Politics in Victorian England* (Leicester University Press 1976), chapter 13. Although this book is about England, the same sub-municipal layers of politics existed in Scots cities, sometimes with slightly different titles and responsibilities

16 The *Glasgow Herald* frequently included these endorsements in its account of the local election candidatures and results.

17 Quoted by I McLean *The Legend of Red Clydeside* (John Donald, Edinburgh 1983), p 187. McLean gives a detailed account of local politics in Glasgow during the twenties

18 Elliot, McCrone and Skelton, *op. cit.*

19 *See* Craig, *op. cit.* for the full record of cross-voting in the two-member constituency of Dundee. For an account of the battle between Scrymgeour and Churchill see Southgate *op. cit.*; or W M Walker *Juteopolis: Dundee and its Textile Workers 1885–1923* (Scottish Academic Press, Edinburgh 1979); or W M Walker 'Dundee's disenchantment with Churchill', *Scottish Historical Review* XLIX (1970), pp 85–108

20 Walker (1979), p 358

21 I have relied mainly on the *Glasgow Herald* and the annual election booklet of the Glasgow Citizens Union for reports of municipal elections up to 1973. Results from 1974 onwards have been collected in a series of reports by J M Bochel and D T Denver which are obtainable from the Election Studies Unit in the Department of Political Science, University of Dundee

22 *See* Young, *op. cit.*

23 McLean, *op. cit.* p 183

24 E Lakeman *How Democracies Vote* (Faber, London 1974), p 220

25 *See Glasgow Herald,* 22 October 1921

26 For a report of its inaugural meeting at the Free Gardeners Institute, Edinburgh, see *Glasgow Herald,* 30 September 1920

27 *See Glasgow Herald,* 1 March 1927

28 C J Wyke *The Conservative Party: History, Organization and Entry into Local Government* (Masters Thesis, Edinburgh University Politics Department 1978)

8

THE CHANGING CHARACTER OF URBAN EMPLOYMENT 1901-1981

John Butt

What went wrong with the Scottish economy in the twentieth century has become a burning issue for many social scientists in recent years and since the 1930s has been a fundamental question to which public policy has been directed. Effort by government has not been continuous nor has it been consistent; rarely has the examination of the structure of employment gone beyond the shallows; solutions have been sought in special agencies, some of them national, in regional economic measures, and—by some—in political independence.[1] This chapter is first concerned with examining what happened to the employment structures of the major growth points which arose out of the Victorian economy, the urban centres and, in particular, the cities of Aberdeen, Dundee, Edinburgh and Glasgow. Thereafter, analysis of the nature and causes of change will no doubt provoke further controversies as well as, one hopes, illuminate present ones.

EMPLOYMENT IN THE CITIES BEFORE THE GREAT DEPRESSION

Although it is certainly a mistake to imagine that the development of the Scottish economy in Victorian times was an unalloyed story of success, the additions to employment were substantial and highly significant. Clive Lee, in two stimulating articles, has painted the broad picture and also indicated important regional differences within the British Isles and particularly within Scotland.[2] Within Great Britain the labour force increased from 6.9 million people in 1841 to 18.3 million in 1911; new jobs had clearly been created and filled, and contraction had occurred elsewhere, notably in agriculture, indicating that the net growth in employment of about 11.4 million jobs, which these figures reveal, was by no means the full story.[3] In the same period Lee demonstrates that in Scotland total employment more than doubled, the labour force increasing from 1.01 millions in 1841 to 2.06 millions in 1911. Mining accounted for 13.1 per cent of new jobs, the metal and engineering industries for 21 per cent and the service industries for 41.7 per cent.[4] Thus, the macroeconomic guidelines are clearly drawn within which the experience of the cities can be judged.

Table 1 delineates the dimensions of the total 'occupied' and 'unoccupied'—in terms of the Census Report of 1901— population of the four cities by sex. Dundee and Glasgow were strikingly comparable in terms of percentage of males employed and, to an even greater extent, so were Aberdeen and Edinburgh. The major differences, however, existed in female employment. Aberdeen had the least percentage of its women, Edinburgh

Table 1

Occupied and Unoccupied Population 1901

City	Total Male	Total Female	Male Occupied	% Total	Female Occupied	% Total
Aberdeen	52,822	64,634	43,381	82.13	21,836	33.78
Dundee	53,677	72,723	46,504	86.64	37,567	51.66
Edinburgh	113,982	142,231	93,595	82.11	53,658	37.73
Glasgow	288,039	303,143	250,441	86.95	111,472	36.77

Source: Census of Scotland 1901

slightly more than Glasgow, but Dundee had more than half its women at work. Miss M L Walker of the Dundee Social Union noted in 1912 that this percentage had risen to 53 at the Census of 1911 and pointed out that the proportion of married women in employment in the city was 23.4 per cent compared with 5.1 per cent of this group in Edinburgh and 5.5 per cent in Glasgow.[5] These facts reflect underlying economic necessity: Dundee in 1901 had more women heads of household than any other Scottish town—not far short of a third of all householders. Working to pay the rent and to provide subsistence was clearly an imperative.

Table 2

Major Categories of Male Employment 1901

Category	Glasgow	%	Edinburgh	%	Aberdeen	%	Dundee	%
Commercial	20,708	8.26	8,173	8.73	2,671	6.16	2,618	5.63
Transport etc.	38,988	15.57	13,120	14.02	7,630	17.59	6,026	12.96
Metals etc.	53,382	21.32	7,911	8.45	4,948	11.41	6,662	14.33
Construction	25,538	10.20	13,614	14.55	5,291	12.20	4,409	9.48
Textiles etc.	19,909	7.95	5,707	6.10	3,248	7.49	13,771	29.61
Food, Tobacco etc.	21,901	8.74	10,580	11.30	3,818	8.80	3,876	8.33
Other Trades	20,874	8.33	4,254	4.55	3,137	7.23	NA	NA
Without spec. occupation	37,598	15.01	20,387	21.78	9,441	21.76	7,173	15.42
Totals	238,898	95.38	83,746	89.48	40,184	92.64	44,530	95.76

Source: Census 1901

Table 2 sets out seven major categories of male employment and a catch-all category for the relatively high proportion in all four cities who could not specify a precise and regular occupation. As might be expected, the Census Report categories are not as helpful as the enumerators' returns in defining exact occupation in any category. Transport, for instance, includes 'the conveyance of men, goods and messages'; textiles cover the production of clothing as well as mill employment; metal manufacture takes account also of general engineering. Not surprisingly Glasgow and Edinburgh had higher percentages of employed males in commerce than Aberdeen and, more particularly, Dundee. Apart from those without a specific occupation, transport employed more males in Aberdeen than any other economic activity, although the proportions elsewhere were also relatively high. The emphasis on industrial employment was greatest in Glasgow and Dundee, metal manufacture dominating in the former and textiles in the latter. The construction industries were major employers everywhere but were of particular importance in Edinburgh and Aberdeen.

If the service sector within Table 2—commerce, transport, construction and food, drink, tobacco and innkeeping—is measured, the differences between the cities become more significant: 42.77 per cent of male employment was derived from this source in Glasgow, 48.6 per cent in Edinburgh, 44.75 per cent in Aberdeen and 36.4 per cent in Dundee. The two cities with the greatest reliance on industrial employment for males had the weakest service sector. If we consider further that Edinburgh, the leader in this employment, had much the most significant proportions of males employed in government, defence, professional and domestic service—elsewhere providing relatively little employment for men in 1901—then a picture of three out of every five males finding jobs in services seems substantially different from the pattern elsewhere: 41.2 per cent in Dundee, 51.8 in Aberdeen, and 48.07 in Glasgow compared with 61.57 in Edinburgh.

Consideration should also be given to the large group without specific occupations. The Census enumerators in Glasgow treated those 'unoccupied' as belonging to this group, the third in order of magnitude, ranking after those males employed in metals and transport. In both Edinburgh and Aberdeen this category was the largest, and in Dundee the second in importance. Apart from the problems of unemployment and old age which this category encompasses, the size and significance of it reflects the importance of the unskilled casual and seasonal force in an often chronically glutted labour market, the singular but complex problem of urban poverty which poorly paid and insecure male employment often produced.[6]

Table 3 sets out six major categories of employment for women in 1901, covering in all four cities between 85 and 96 per cent of all females in jobs. Variations are quite marked. The dominance of the jute industry in the pattern of female employment in Dundee is no surprise, but the relatively few alternative occupations are most striking. Even domestic service, a traditional urban employer of women, was unimportant, although in second place. In Aberdeen, a city with the smallest percentage of occupied females, there was a much more diverse pattern. Textiles—wool, linen and jute—flourished,[7] and nearly a third of all occupied women worked in these mills or in associated outwork. The expansion of the white fish industry provided a substantial stimulus to employment in the food industries, the third sector following domestic service which employed slightly more than a quarter of all jobs.

Table 3

Major Categories of Female Employment 1901

Category	Glasgow	%	Edinburgh	%	Aberdeen	%	Dundee	%
Domestics	24,094	21.61	22,823	42.53	5,597	25.63	3,007	8.00
Paper etc.	6,579	5.90	4,484	8.36	1,742	7.98	295	0.79
Textiles etc.	42,178	37.84	9,017	16.83	6,898	31.59	29,719	79.11
Food, Tobacco etc.	13,397	12.02	4,731	8.83	3,359	15.38	1,952	5.20
Professional services	5,745	5.15	4,170	7.77	1,507	6.90	1,048	2.79
Transport	3,275	2.94	732	1.36	394	1.79	207	0.55
Totals	95,268	85.46	45,957	85.68	19,497	89.27	36,228	96.44

Source: Census 1901

Edinburgh's female labour market was dominated by domestic service which provided more than two of every five jobs. The food industries, paper and publishing, and particularly textiles also made significant contributions to women's employment. As compared with Dundee and to a lesser extent, Glasgow, the great majority of Edinburgh women working in textiles was concerned with the production of clothing rather than with millwork. Openings for women in professional services were greatest in Edinburgh and Aberdeen, insignificant in Dundee, with Glasgow ranking a moderate third.

Female employment in Glasgow was dominated by three sectors—textiles, domestic service, and the food, tobacco and drink trades. Although textiles was first in importance, employing over three in every eight occupied women, it was nowhere near so dominant as in Dundee. More positively, domestic service and the food group were much more significant in Glasgow; moreover, in textiles Glasgow employed more women in garment production rather than in millwork. Sewing sacks in Dundee provided some employment for men and women, but the clothing sector of textiles was unimportant.

Within these six categories of female employment, four could be counted as part of the service sector—domestics, food, professional and transport—and the other two as manufacturing. When female employment is considered in terms of these two simple divisions, the differences between the four cities become even more apparent. In Dundee the service sector absorbed 16.65 per cent of female labour, in Glasgow 41.72, in Aberdeen 49.7, and in Edinburgh 60.49 per cent. The manufacturing sector in Dundee, in turn, employed 79.9 per cent of occupied women covered in Table 3, in Glasgow 43.74 per cent, in Aberdeen 39.57 per cent, and in Edinburgh 25.19 per cent.

It is tempting to suggest that both male and female economic activity given in Tables 2 and 3 reflected differences not only in economic structure but also in regional incomes. Edinburgh probably enjoyed a greater *per capita* income and more widely spread affluence; Dundee a narrower economic base and smaller wealthy middle-class with a mass of poorly paid male and female employees heavily dependent on one industry. It is also reasonable to argue that Aberdeen and Glasgow, despite their differences in population, approximated closely to one another in terms of *per capita* income. Certainly, the occupational patterns in both these cities show a number of similarities, but undoubtedly, the Granite City was less dependent on manufacturing and more on services than Glasgow. However, these speculations simply point to the need for more research.

Why Dundee eventually ran into economic difficulties should not occasion surprise for one-industry towns are notoriously vulnerable. But, in a sense, this is tautology for the decay of the jute industry might have happened more quickly, and consequently, the need to diversify the city's economic structure been apparent much earlier than the 1920s and 1930s. But the social composition of this city seemed most appropriate for a dependence on textile manufacturing. The jute industry required a substantial supply of female and young male labour. The latter—and at least one third of the males in jute in this period were under the age of twenty—mostly worked in dead-end jobs, usually as labourers. Dundee had a surplus of females: at the Census of 1901 there were three women aged between twenty and forty for every two men, and in 1921 females outnumbered males by 37 per cent.[8]

This sex composition of the working population reflected both the relative decline of local employment opportunities for men which had begun in the late nineteenth century and the long-term imbalance between the sexes. The drill sergeant and the Empire may have gained, but the ossification of the economic structure was the prime regional consequence. The simple fact is that Dundee's ability to generate jobs for men was long suspect, and permanent positions with prospects were locally at a premium. Hence Dundee men—after training in engineering—made their way to the shipyards of Clydeside and the Tyne and the Wear or joined the colours usually through the local Volunteers or serviced Dundee's investments in Calcutta jute as mechanics, mill foremen and overseers.[9] Opportunities for men decreased as Dundee's whaling declined, as the shipping tonnage based in Juteopolis fell and as the number of shipbuilding firms contracted. Confectionery, preserves and journalism were never adequate substitutes, and alternative engineering jobs were slow to emerge.[10]

If Dundee businessmen became more concerned with foreign than local investment, this probably reflected both the optimal use of capital and the inadequacy of local opportunities. Dundonians through their investment trusts had foreign assests of £4.1 million in 1900, £10.8 million by 1914, £11.2 million by 1920 and £23.8 million by 1930. Their interests ranged wider than the jute mills of Calcutta which competed very effectively with Dundee's factories already by 1900.[11] No doubt diversification into finer hessian and linoleum backings was induced as an indirect consequence of this locally sponsored Indian competition, but direct investment would have been preferable. Stagnation was the price which the local economy paid.[12]

Alternative local investment depended initially on regional purchasing power, and levels of demand reflected income. Jute was a poor payer! Spinning and weaving were dominated by women, many of them young. The reversal of economic roles—so that often women were the main bread-winners—and the shortage of jobs for men were reflected in low wage rates. In 1906 the average wage for females working in the jute industry was about 67p per week, but more than a quarter of women over eighteen years old earned between 75p and £1 per week. The average wage for males was £1.07, and nearly one-eighth of men aged over twenty-one earned 75p or less, and about one half less than £1. Considering that Dundee had a high cost of living in 1906 compared with Glasgow or Edinburgh, disposable income—beyond that required for rent and food—was never sufficient to form the basis upon which a range of locally made consumer goods could be sold.[13] Low regional purchasing power reinforced the existing industrial and occupational structure.

Despite the fact that jute was obviously a strategic material in great demand during World War I and unionisation proceeded apace after 1914, as the historian of the textile workers' experience has shown,[14] by 1917 the import of raw jute was one of many pressures on precious shipping space which caused the Government to restrict production in the city temporarily, causing short-time working. After the immediate boom in the two years after the war, deflation led first to further short-time working and then to unemployment. A Trade Board established in 1919 to regulate wages in the industry, a clear indication of a low wage problem, engineered the lowest rates by 1923 sanctioned by any such Board.[15] Unemployment rose to 11 per cent in 1923, and attempts to raise productivity in order to maintain competitiveness from 1927 led to the displacement of many spinners, and therefore, a fall in the demand for female labour. The international depression adversely affected exports as did rising tariff barriers from 1929 onwards. By 1931, despite the preceding displacement of labour, nearly 50 per cent of jute workers were unemployed.[16]

As we have seen, in 1900 Aberdeen's occupational structure showed great diversity, although manufacturing—engineering, textiles, paper—accounted for over a third of total employment. Extractive industries—fishing and quarrying—provided about an eighth, and service occupations not quite a half of all jobs. Up to 1914, save for a sharp but short depression in 1908, Aberdeen was remarkably prosperous.[17] One of the leaders was the white fish industry which employed about 3,000 men at sea in 1907 and another 6,000 people on shore. Fish landed at Aberdeen increased from 911,260 cwts. in 1900 to 2,268,860 cwts. in 1914, and thus on the eve of World War I, the city was the first fishing port in the United Kingdom. Markets for cured and filleted fish grew rapidly, and the export market for salted fish in Spain and Latin America also was buoyant. However, landings by foreign trawlers were already significant before 1914.[18]

Although fishing was less intensive during the war, the trawler fleet increased as a consequence of Admiralty action. However, the twenties witnessed stagnation in the industry, and Hull and Grimsby with their key advantage of greater proximity to centres of population in the north and south of England took over the leadership. The industry in Aberdeen was over-capitalised, and firms were highly individualistic and slow to integrate. Hull and Grimsby re-equipped so as to exploit distant and more lucrative fishing grounds, and thereby successfully intensified competition as home and middle distance waters were gradually over-fished.[19]

Granite, Aberdeen's other extractive industry, had its fortunes closely linked to the construction industries and also to the highly specialised market for monuments.[20] Although the industry was also represented in south-west Scotland and also in Devon and Cornwall, between 70 and 80 per cent of granite manufacturing, measured by sales, was concentrated in Aberdeenshire and controlled from the Granite City.[21] After World War I foreign granites flooded into Britain, particularly from Germany, Finland and Czechoslovakia, and the United States imposed even more substantial tariffs on British granites. Most Aberdeen firms were small compared with their continental competitors, and the typical unit employed less than fifty employees. By 1930 the number of firms had fallen to 53 from the 91 of 1914, but the numbers employed stabilised at about 2,000.[22]

However, it would clearly be mistaken to ascribe too much significance to the employment effects produced by the difficulties of the granite and fishing industries. Other economic activities were more important. Compared with 1901 there was an increase in the occupied population by 1921—to 49,379 males and 24,550 females—representing 14 per cent for men and 12 per cent for women. Securing employment in the 1920s was inevitably a more competitive exercise. Five groups of industrial workers were numerically more important than the number employed in granite working: workers in metal, 6,103; workers in wood and furniture, 4,089; textile workers, 3,697; process workers in food, drink and tobacco, 3,477; makers of textile goods and clothing, 3,331. The whole picture for 1931 is given in Table 4. Over the decade the increase in occupied males and females was respectively 5 per cent and just under 9 per cent. Compared with 1901 the most striking feature is the increase in employment in commerce, the professions and government service. A significant component in the rise in commercial employment was the continued growth of the transport sector, which in 1931 provided jobs for 10,515 compared with 8,024 in 1901. The infancy of the welfare state increased the demand for teachers, doctors, nurses and other professional people. The natural development of limited liability companies stimulated the growth of employment opportunities for lawyers, accountants and bankers, not to mention the expansion of the number of clerical jobs, especially for women. There were in 1931 5,696 clerks—2,209 men and 3667 women.[23]

Table 4

Categories of Employment in Aberdeen 1931

Type of Occupation	Male	Female	Total	Percentage
Government Service and Defence	4321	1871	6192	7.9
Professions	2640	2381	5021	6.4
Domestic and Personal Service	1716	5646	7362	9.4
Commercial	19,605	7144	26,749	34.0
Agriculture and Fisheries	4370	180	4550	5.8
Manufactures	18,350	8828	27,178	34.6
Miscellaneous	879	644	1523	1.9
Total occupied	51,881	26,694	78,575	100.0

Source: Census 1931

The manufacturing sector had marginally declined by 1931, but changes in the composition of employment within industry were significant. Textiles continued a decline which had begun in the middle of the nineteenth century, and increasingly, the emphasis was on employment in the clothing and hosiery trades. In 1931 there were only 5,016 employees in textiles compared with 10,146 in 1901, the major decline falling into two periods 1901–09 and immediately following the boom years of World War I, the Indian summer of Aberdeen's woollen, jute and linen industries.[24] The engineering and metal industries, including shipbuilding and marine engineering, took up some of the slack. These variegated trades benefited in the 1920s from the diverse needs of the local economic structure and, in specialised lines, remained efficient exporters. The over-capitalisation of the fishing industry already mentioned produced a boom for the three shipyards before 1920 but problems of adaptation later. Alexander Hill and Company developed from 1923 a new market for steam dredgers and tugs, turning out by 1935 thirty-three of the former and thirty of the latter.[25] This enterprising firm was imitated by the other two, Hall, Russell and Company and John Lewis and Sons. The general engineering firm of John M Henderson and Company specialised in mechanical handling equipment, aerial cableways and cable drag scrapers. Alexander Wilson Ltd specialised in quarrying equipment and granite cutting, shaping and polishing machinery. Other firms added to the product range with agricultural machinery, crushing machinery, plantation equipment and paper-making machinery.[26] The city also provided workers for nearby paper mills often outside its boundaries, but specifically the opportunities in box-making, furniture, and general wood-working increased. Aberdeen had the advantages of a broader base for industrial employment than Dundee and at the same time less dependence on it.

Comment on the contrasts between the employment structures of the two northern cities before 1931 could equally be made about Edinburgh and Glasgow. The seat of government in Scotland, a great banking centre and the birthplace of the Scottish insurance industry, Edinburgh was and is also an important distributive centre for its region and, through the port of Leith (absorbed within its boundaries in 1920), is advantageously placed for trade with Europe and coastwise. A renowned tourist centre, the city also has a substantial industrial base, although even by 1901, as we have seen, the service sector was much the most important for the generation of employment. Not far from the city boundaries and certainly within Edinburgh's hinterland there are a number of settlements whose resources have fed the industry and trade of the capital: the coal-mining district around Dalkeith and Tranent, the oil-shale settlements of West Lothian and Midlothian, the paper mills of Lasswade, Penicuik and Polton, the rich agricultural areas of East Lothian and Berwickshire.[27] Although not so sparsely populated as the hinterlands of Aberdeen and Dundee, the population density did not really compare with Glasgow's satellite areas—for example, the iron and steel and coal-producing areas of North Lanarkshire, the shipbuilding towns of Greenock, Port Glasgow and Clydebank, and the great and ancient textile town of Paisley.

The major difference between the two cities resided in the export-orientated and capital goods emphases within Glasgow's industrial base, dependent as it was on a narrow range of industries—heavy engineering, shipbuilding and associated trades with the regional substructure of coal and iron and steel.[28] Edinburgh's industries were for the most part concerned with supplying the domestic market, more weighted towards consumer goods production and relatively diverse. Even Leith with its greater commitment to industry than the rest of the city had its quota of food warehouses, flour mills and bonded stores. The shipyard of Henry Robb Ltd was an important employer but not outstandingly so. For most of this period the largest firm in the city was the North British Rubber Company, second only in this sector to Dunlop. Its principal products were rubber boots and shoes, rubber sheeting used for floor covering, tyres and hard rubber combs. Printing was the principal industry of the city and between 1921 and 1931 increased its labour force by 19 per cent. Here there were a relatively large number of firms, more than fifty employing over twenty workers each in the 1920s and 1930s. This industry had clear connections with the paper industry and the publishing of books, periodicals and newspapers. Stationery-making was also a specialist Edinburgh activity related to paper-making and with a buoyant local market provided by the city's professional services sector—education, the law, insurance and banking.[29]

Among Edinburgh's engineering firms of the period 1900 to 1931 there was much commitment to serving growing markets, some of them international but many of them domestic. An example of the latter was the specialisation in the production of gas meters and heavy electrical engineering goods such as rectifiers and transformers for the production of which Bruce Peebles established a large new factory in 1925. Brown Brothers, operating in the difficult marine engineering market, managed by technical expertise and the application of science to develop the telemotor and other hydraulic steering and handling gear which made the firm a favoured supplier to the Admiralty and other fleets. Type founding, printing machinery, paper machinery, baking and brewing plant and structural engineering were other employers of skilled and unskilled labour throughout the period.[30]

The food and drink industries were well represented in Edinburgh. A noted centre of the brewing, distilling and blending industries, the city had a well-developed export trade in whisky to Canada and before Prohibition to the United States. The brewery firms increasingly attacked the English market, and two, William McEwan's and William Younger's, exported beer to a number of countries, including Australia, Canada, India and South Africa. In 1930 these two large firms combined under the title Scottish Brewers Limited.[31] Food products were well established as Edinburgh specialities before 1900 but became increasingly important—bread, biscuits, oatmeal products, sweets including chocolates, tea-blending, ham-curing and dairy production (including bakery margarine) forming the main output. In this sector the Scottish Co-operative Wholesale Society and the largest Edinburgh retail society, St Cuthberts, were exceedingly important.[32]

Table 5

Categories of Employment in Glasgow and Edinburgh 1931

(a) The Service Sector in 1931

Occupation	Percentage of total labour force	
	Edinburgh	Glasgow
Personal services	15.0	9.7
Commerce	13.7	13.6
Clerks	11.1	9.2
Transport	10.9	11.2
Professional	6.3	3.8
Food and drink	2.3	2.2
Public administration	1.7	0.8
Totals	61.0	50.5

Nonetheless, the service sector remained the principal employer of labour throughout the period: over 60 per cent of total employment was generated by this group of economic activities with manufacturing in all its forms declining to about 27 per cent by 1931. Significantly, engineering decreased from 25.8 per cent of all manufacturing jobs in 1921 to 18.8 per cent in 1931. The five largest groups in Edinburgh's occupational structure provided personal, commercial, clerical, transport and professional services in that order of ranking.[33] However, by 1931 there had been an intercensal decline of 1736 in the number of professionals working within the city whereas Glasgow had witnessed an increase of 1949. In both cities relative to London the proportion of professional service jobs was small, and the differences between Glasgow and Edinburgh were becoming less significant.[34]

Comparisons between Edinburgh's occupational structure and that of Glasgow in 1931 are possible by reference to Table 5 which covers separately the service and manufacturing sectors. Personal services, principally domestic jobs for women were much more significant in Edinburgh than in Glasgow; clerical posts including local authority and civil service as well as commercial firms were slightly more important also in the capital. Professional services—especially solicitors, nurses and doctors, teachers and ministers—although beginning to converge in the decade 1921–31 were still a greater proportion in Edinburgh than in Glasgow. Otherwise the major difference between the service sectors in their patterns of employment remained that relating to proportion.

Turning to the manufacturing sector, what is most striking is the similarity of certain components. Only in the metals and textile categories are there significant differences. These were critically important for

Table 5

(b) The Manufacturing Sector in 1931

Occupation	Percentage of total labour force	
	Edinburgh	Glasgow
Metals	5.3	12.9
Wood and furniture	3.0	3.3
Textile goods	2.8	4.5
Construction	2.4	2.4
Printers	2.3	1.2
Paper etc.	1.3	0.9
Electrical	1.1	1.0
Unskilled	8.7	11.4
Totals	26.9	37.6

Source: Census 1931

Glasgow since metals, in particular, represented the tip of the iceberg of reinforced integration within the regional economy which began to melt away as world trade contracted after 1920. But the opportunities for men were declining also in Edinburgh after 1924, but probably more women sought and obtained work in the capital because of this. Nonetheless unemployment doubled in Edinburgh between 1923 and 1932.[35]

After 1920 shipbuilding faltered on the Clyde, and Glasgow's economy caught cold. Regionally, there were never less than 14 per cent unemployed, and throughout the 1920s desperate measures were taken to cut costs and often to cut capacity. Contracts taken by many of the shipbuilding and marine engineering firms proved to be loss-makers; a reduction of costs leading to greater competitive efficiency appeared an obvious solution. So too did the national policy of returning to the pre-1914 gold standard days when British exports of coal and heavy engineering goods were buoyant. Deflation with high interest rates reduced employment and investment and made it less likely that new product ranges would emerge from established firms in Glasgow's engineering sector. Beardmores, the great experimentalists with motor vehicles and aircraft, for instance, went into progressive decline which only rearmament after 1936 was to halt.[36]

The convergence of wage rates in Glasgow and Edinburgh with national rates, markedly occurring from the 1890s might not have been significant had Scotland's share of the net output of Britain not fallen after 1924 for labour productivity diverged adversely also. Thus in many economic activities there were more cost efficient firms elsewhere in Britain, although shipbuilding on the Clyde was exceptional in that this competitive disadvantage was not apparent.[37]

There problems were more deep-seated. World demand for ships was relatively stagnant in the 1920s, and in any case economic nationalism, widely prevalent as it was, ensured that the Clyde was unlikely to maintain the share of world tonnage which it had enjoyed before 1914. In the British market it did relatively well, but capacity had to be reduced from wartime levels; this was undertaken by National Shipbuilders Security Limited, established in 1930.[38] Affecting the Glasgow economy and the region was the downward spiral in demand for steel and coal. The objective of returning to world trade based on the gold standard proved incapable of achievement, as the world's economic crisis deepened after 1929. National solutions were initially inadequate; the Industrial Transference Board of 1928 encouraged migration of labour rather than the creation of new jobs within the city; derating of industrial premises (1929) represented the classic institutional attempt to reduce costs which failed. The dominance of heavy industries in the West of Scotland region constituted a major problem for the economy more widely, and more radical solutions were needed as unemployment mounted. Although Glasgow had marginally changed its structure of employment by 1931, that movement proved to be too slight.

COLLAPSE, RECOVERY AND THE QUESTION OF
DIVERSIFICATION

The concept of achieving relatively full employment through policies leading to the revival of international trade so commonplace in the 1920s disappeared gradually as the weight of the depression made itself felt. In terms of scale Glasgow and its region was worst affected with unemployment rates in the heavy industries varying from over 75 per cent in shipbuilding in 1932, averaging at about 30 per cent and never less than 25 per cent. Even three years later in the summer of 1935 Dundee had 37.7 per cent while recovery in engineering had reduced Glasgow's unemployment rate to just under 25 per cent. Edinburgh and Aberdeen fared better with rates of 14.2 per cent and 15.5 per cent respectively.[39] Restructuring of civic economies was less difficult for these two cities and more urgent for Dundee and Glasgow.

Dundee was particularly vulnerable for its dependence on jute, if not total, was highly significant. Technical change in the 1930s reduced the demand for labour, especially for women. Thus, even with recovery in demand there was bound to be a surplus of labour: in 1930 approximately 35,000 Dundee jute workers registered under the Unemployment Acts and even in 1938 there were over 24,000. Just before the outbreak of war in 1939 unemployment was running at about 20 per cent. No wonder Eastham described the industry as 'precariously balanced on the edge of a precipice, and, if it falls over, the city of Dundee will be largely dependent on Unemployment relief'.[40]

Self-help was practised by all the cities, often as in the case of Dundee and Glasgow taking the form of industrial exhibitions. Attempts were made in Dundee to find additional finer uses for jute notably in art fabrics and in linoleum, to extend the market for heavy linens and particularly, to diversify into engineering. This latter sector gradually and unevenly increased its labour force from 1934 onwards as shipbuilding recovered but other engineering trades were slower to recover. Printing and publishing, textile furnishing, and the food and drink industries showed significant gains as did the distributive trades.[41]

By 1951 changes were underway, but the percentage of occupied labour employed in manufacturing still remained higher than in any of the other cities, 49 per cent as against Aberdeen's 28 per cent, Edinburgh's 30 per cent and Glasgow's 42 per cent. Textiles, employing 19,698, remained the largest occupational category, and jute provided jobs for 15,684 people of which 8,787 were women. Distributive trades employed 12,188, engineering 9,409, professional services 6,627 and transport and communication 6,447. The growth of the welfare state under the Labour government accounts very largely for the increase in employment provided by professional services, and alternative jobs for women in medicine and education were particularly welcome.[42]

The survival of jute reflected a number of favourable circumstances. Demand had risen with rearmament and World War II, and in the immediate post-war period the expansion of international trade stimulated fresh investment in the industry. Modernisation and greater technical efficiency made the search for alternative uses for jute more rewarding as productivity gains were achieved. By the end of the 1950s about £11 million had been invested in new spinning and weaving machinery. The major new product arose from the development of tufted carpeting which required a coarse wide backing which the jute industry could provide. In the United States and Britain this new market grew rapidly especially in the 1960s and 1970s. Other high quality products, notably wall hangings, diversified the range still further.[43]

Engineering, especially light engineering, was the panacea for many regional economists in the post-war period. Industrial estates and new towns were alike constructed in the expectation that the growth industries of the inter-war Midlands and South East would make their way further north. It was a slow process.

In Dundee shipbuilding, after a wartime boom, declined relatively and was replaced by the textile machinery sector in 1951. In turn electrical engineering superseded both as an employer by 1961. Office machinery, watches and clocks, domestic electrical appliances of various kinds, machinery for use in food-processing greatly widened the product range. Some new industries were attracted to Dundee by abundant supplies of cheap female labour such as National Cash Register, makers of office machinery, in 1946 and Timex, also established in 1946. Industrial estates were planned as early as 1939 but developed significantly only after 1945. By 1966 employment on them accounted for over 11,000 jobs.[44]

Table 6 indicates that for male employment the 1970s presented some problems even for these new industries, but Dundee was midway between Edinburgh and Glasgow in terms of unemployment. Female economic characteristics are indicated in Table 7 with Dundee having a much greater percentage of unemployment than either Aberdeen or Edinburgh but only marginally more than Glasgow. Manufacturing was strongest as a sector in Dundee as Tables 8, 9 and 10 indicate, but the range of products has greatly

Table 6

Male Economic Characteristics 1981 (percentages)

Category	Aberdeen	Dundee	Edinburgh	Glasgow
Full-time employment	83.5	73.6	78.6	67.0
Part-time employment	0.7	0.6	0.8	0.5
Unemployed	7.2	15.6	9.7	21.6
Economically inactive	8.7	10.2	10.8	10.9
Students	5.5	5.7	7.0	4.9

Source: Census of 1981

strengthened the civic economy since 1939. Yet Dundee remains vulnerable because of the weakening of international trade since 1974, and if it is to maintain its manufacturing base, it must continue to expand its electrical and electronic engineering sector. Services have greatly increased their significance in the city's economy since 1901 and by 1981 provided approximately 70 per cent of total employment.

Aberdeen's relatively low unemployment rate in the 1930s was fundamentally a consequence of the variety of its economic activities which Table 4 already has demonstrated. Textiles were in the doldrums, but high-quality hosiery production and woollens maintained their place in domestic and export markets. Food, drink and tobacco processing, shipbuilding and engineering were the largest employers of labour by 1938 but what impresses is the stability provided by reasonably efficient small industries such as paper-making, wood-working, printing and publishing which assisted in widening the base.[45] Working granite into facings for shops and

Table 7

Female Economic Characteristics 1981 (*percentages*)

Category	Aberdeen	Dundee	Edinburgh	Glasgow
Full-time employment	39.9	39.6	42.1	38.9
Part-time employment	25.6	19.9	22.4	16.3
Unemployed	3.3	8.8	4.2	8.4
Economically inactive	31.2	31.7	31.4	36.4
Students	5.1	5.6	6.4	4.8

Source: Census of 1981

Table 8

Male Occupational Characteristics 1981 (*percentages*)

Category	Aberdeen	Dundee	Edinburgh	Glasgow
Agriculture	1.6	1.3	0.8	0.1
Energy	9.0	2.7	2.8	1.8
Manufacturing	21.2	36.3	22.0	30.5
Construction	12.3	12.4	10.6	15.6
Distribution & Catering	19.0	13.2	16.3	15.3
Transport & Communication	10.3	8.3	10.8	11.9
Other services	25.2	25.0	36.1	23.9

Source: Census of 1981, 10 per cent sample.

public buildings and into monuments became more closely linked with imports of foreign stone which totalled just under 20,000 tons in 1938.[46]

Aberdeen, as a regional market centre, provided distributive and commercial services to a wide area. Wholesale and retail activities grew in significance after 1931; so did the amount of employment by hotels, professional services and local government. By 1938 23,310 jobs were in this sector, representing about 33 per cent of total employment. Essentially, the major contribution was distribution, with 18.75 per cent of this total. Retailing had expanded greatly in the 1920s and 1930s, and outlets for other services such as laundries, leisure activities and general wholesaling showed an expansion.[47]

War brought a boom to many sectors except granite. Intensive cultivation of the land increased the demand for agricultural machinery; armaments production also became a significant component of heavy engineering

Table 9

Female Occupational Characteristics 1981 (percentages)

Category	Aberdeen	Dundee	Edinburgh	Glasgow
Agriculture	0.2	0.4	0.3	0.04
Energy	3.6	0.5	1.5	0.8
Manufacturing	11.5	22.7	10.4	18.0
Construction	1.2	1.1	1.5	1.5
Distribution & Catering	30.5	24.2	22.0	24.6
Transport & Communication	3.6	2.4	3.3	3.7
Other services	48.3	48.1	60.4	50.5

Source: Census of 1981, 10 per cent sample.

Table 10

Total Occupational Characteristics 1981 (percentages)

Category	Aberdeen	Dundee	Edinburgh	Glasgow
Agriculture	1.0	1.0	0.5	0.1
Energy	6.7	1.8	2.2	1.3
Manufacturing	17.0	31.9	16.8	25.0
Construction	7.5	7.8	6.5	9.4
Distribution & Catering	24.0	18.9	18.8	19.4
Transport & Communication	7.4	6.0	7.4	8.3
Other services	35.3	36.9	47.0	35.7

Source: Census of 1981, 10 per cent sample.

activity; the shipyards produced a variety of mainly small vessels for the Admiralty and tank-landing craft for the invasion of Europe. Repair facilities were very busy during the war, and frigates, corvettes, mine-sweepers and destroyers found Aberdeen a safe haven during refitting. By 1944, 4,357 people were employed in shipbuilding and marine engineering compared with 1,942 in 1938.[48]

After the war medium-sized trawlers became the main product of Aberdeen's shipyards and these were supplied to many other fishing ports in Britain. Engineering took an even more diverse pattern with motor repairs, brass-fitting, welding and light castings becoming more important. Over-head electrical cranes, aerial cableways, wire ropes for suspension bridges, mechanical excavators and handling equipment all feature in the product range.[49]

By 1951 2,194,665 people were employed in Scotland, and 40 per cent of this employment was provided by the cities. Aberdeen had 79,708 people gainfully occupied or 3.6 per cent of Scotland's total, Glasgow 514,104 or 23.4 per cent, Edinburgh 220,042 or 10 per cent and Dundee 87,026 or 4 per cent. The five largest categories of employment in Aberdeen in 1951 were distribution, 19.39 per cent, professional services, 10.65 per cent, transport and communication, 11.1 per cent, miscellaneous services, 8.6 per cent, and building and contracting, 8.1 per cent. These five, therefore, accounted for almost three jobs in every five.[50]

Whereas each of the other cities encountered serious difficulties with employment in the 1970s, Aberdeen maintained its record of stability and indeed as its commitment grew to the exploitation of the energy resources of the North Sea, the city widened the base of its economy. For in November 1970 oil was first tapped at a point on the sea-bed 176 km. north-east of Aberdeen. Many discoveries have been made since, and in 1975 the giant Forties field came on stream. By 1981 about 250,000 barrels a day were being supplied to the petro-chemical plant at Grangemouth by pipeline.[51] Apart from direct employment on the oil rigs, there was an increase in onshore service jobs, and Aberdeen gained a helicopter base in addition. By 1974 16,000 jobs were provided to the Scottish economy in consequence of these discoveries in the North Sea, and roughly 40 per cent of them accrued to Aberdeen. In 1981 at least 25,000 jobs were so derived, and as Table 8 most clearly indicated, Aberdeen was the principal beneficiary.[52]

Edinburgh's low point in terms of unemployment was 1932, when 26,000 were idle or about 17 per cent of the labour force. As opposed to the experience of many in Glasgow and Dundee, Edinburgh's unemployed were rarely out of work for long periods, because the city's service sector provided many opportunities for temporary, casual and seasonal employ-ment. Juvenile unemployment in the mid 1930s was, however, a particularly intractable problem, and Leith had an unemployment record of over 23 per cent in 1935, revealing its vulnerability as a port and shipbuilding centre.[53]

Gradually, the situation improved as growth points emerged: vehicle construction and repair, the production of wire ropes, and the extension of electrical engineering, the growing importance of the building industry and the under-pinning provided by the service sector. Many small and medium-sized firms catered for the regional economy only and did not seek the pleasures and perils of expansion. Leith's experience reflected the dangers arising from a commitment to trade in the wider world. Edinburgh's printing trade remained wedded to the home market and by 1936 had no unemployment problem. Specialist printers such as Bartholomews, the cartographers, found new markets such as providing maps for motorists. Printing demanded paper, inks and a range of skills in other trades, notably the lithographers. Experience was not uniform but diverse. Brewing, the food industries and the rubber industry, nonetheless, were not held back by the depression.[54]

The war brought new firms to Edinburgh, notably Ferranti, the electrical engineering firm (1943) which specialised in high value to volume products assembled from a range of components. This firm required a high proportion of skilled labour for its products were highly sophisticated—all types of electronic equipment and electro-mechanical devices. But by 1951 engineering accounted for only 5.2 per cent of employment, compared with 14.2 per cent in distribution, 12.8 per cent in professional services, 10.3 per cent in miscellaneous services, 9.8 per cent in transport and communications, 9 per cent in public administration and defence, 8.7 per cent in construction, and 8.4 per cent in the food, drink and tobacco sector.[55]

In some categories of occupation women predominated notably in professional services such as medicine, dental care and education. But the most significant feature of Edinburgh's employment pattern remained the strength of its service sector. Although this included many low-paid jobs, especially for women in distribution and catering, the balancing feature was the range of well-paid professional positions provided by the financial, legal and administrative groups.

The growth of tourism, the creation of the Edinburgh Festival and the expansion of the leisure industries of the city in the 1950s, 1960s and 1970s continued a well-established pattern.[56] By 1981 Edinburgh compared with Aberdeen in its lack of dependence on manufacturing as a source of employment, as Table 10 indicates. Aberdeen's greater connection with North Sea oil was bound to reduce its percentages in other categories but it approached closest to Edinburgh. The latter in 1981 had nearly 80 per cent of its occupied population engaged in services whereas Aberdeen had 74.2 per cent.

The real problem because of its scale occurred in West Central Scotland where the regional capital was Glasgow. As in Dundee, recovery from the depression arose from the revival of the traditional industries. Influential exponents of business wisdom like the writers for the *Glasgow Herald Trade Review* or the *Clydesdale Bank Annual Survey* indicate how retarded recovery was before rearmament became a significant influence.[57] The need for structural adjustment in the civic economy was widely recognised by contemporaries but was much more difficult to achieve. A wage-cutting policy in the 1920s made the possibility of generating new growth in consumer goods and light engineering industries more incapable of realisation in the dark days of the 1930s when purchasing power was reduced even further as a consequence of widespread unemployment.

However, leading businessmen such as Sir James Lithgow and Sir Steven Bilsland recognised the implications of a disarmament policy for the city and its region. Shipbuilding was bound to be in grave difficulty when alternative world markets were depressed. Bilsland became committed to the policy of industrial diversification and a regional policy based upon the creation of industrial estates.[58] For Glasgow government policy was not helpful since it was not included within the terms of the special areas legislation. Yet the gradual revival of shipbuilding on the Clyde beginning in 1934 with the completion of the *Queen Mary*, the orders for the sister ship, *Queen Elizabeth* (1936), and for a growing number of naval vessels was accompanied by government 'scrap and build' incentives which further assisted the shipyards and associated marine engineering works.[59]

The Scottish Economic Committee was given a mandate to prepare a plan for the restructuring of the economy and pinned its faith in 1939 to light engineering and the development of industrial estates.[60] By then Glasgow had already acquired the Hillington Estate (1937) and nearly seventy tenants had been found to take up industrial premises built there. At Shieldhall another estate followed, both being financed partly from the Special Areas Fund.

Yet jobs for men depended fundamentally upon rearmament and the re-emergence of heavy industry in its more stream-lined, 'rationalised' form. World War II appeared to have cured Glasgow's social disease of unemployment but really it remained dormant. The deficiencies within the industrial structure were masked as shipbuilding and the armaments industries boomed. Rolls Royce aero-engines production came to Hillington, and light engineering for civilian demand was placed in abeyance.[61]

After 1945 greater government control over industrial location favoured a further movement towards the diversification of the civic economy, but the expansion of world trade assisted the heavy industries to maintain their hold particularly over male employment. By 1951 the number of metal workers in the city was about 6,000 greater than in 1931. Shipbuilding and engineering provided jobs for 54,593 men and 6,610 women. The prosperity, despite post-war controls, of the city was reflected in the increase in jobs in distribution which by 1951 employed 42,219 men and 41,799 women. Transport and communication, including railways, civic transport and working in shipping and road haulage, had 46,416 male and 9,224 female employees. The growth of professional and other service employment was also marked: 16,931 men and 25,785 women in professional occupations and 13,199 males and 22,379 females in miscellaneous service jobs.[62] The five main categories of employment for men and women are given in Tables 11 and 12.

The impending problems for the Glasgow economy were effectively masked in the 1950s by the great growth in world trade. In particular, the Clyde shipyards did not take advantage of all the opportunities offered because order books appeared satisfactory. But world competition was growing, backed by more effective subsidy policies elsewhere. By 1960, despite attempts made to maintain and to improve competitiveness, shipbuilding was in difficulties.

In that decade the infrastructure had been greatly improved: electrification of suburban railways had begun, plans for new urban motorways were drawn up and the airport developed. Yet new industries were slow to come to the city and, apart from American investment on the periphery, reluctant to expand in the 1950s. In the 1960s performance was better as output in electronics increased by about six per cent per annum. By 1971 there were 170,700 jobs in this sector in Scotland, but Glasgow's share was relatively meagre. Firms like International Business Machines and Burroughs Engineering either made their way to new towns like East Kilbride or Cumbernauld or to Greenock where modern premises and lower rates

Table 11

Male Employment in Glasgow 1951

Occupation	Percentage of all occupied men
Metal manufacture etc.	22.28
Building and contracting	6.06
Transport etc.	12.59
Commercial	8.76
Unskilled	12.23
Total	61.92

Source: Census 1951

Table 12

Female Employment in Glasgow 1951

Occupation	Percentage of all occupied women
Textiles	10.35
Commerce	14.81
Personal service	17.78
Clerks, typists	22.37
Professional and technical	7.66
Total	72.97

Source: Census 1951

awaited. However, commercial headquarters were commonly located in the city.

In shipbuilding nemesis beckoned. In the 1960s about 70 per cent of British orders for ships went to foreign yards and Scottish output, especially on the Clyde, fell. Restructuring of the industry around Upper Clyde Shipbuilders at Govan and Scott-Lithgow at Port Glasgow and Greenock followed the Geddes Report into the industry in 1965–6. Employment fell by 25,000 in that decade. Nationalisation, save for Yarrow's naval yard, followed in 1977 but could not halt the slide, as world depression began.[63]

By 1981, as Table 6 indicates, Glasgow once more had a very substantial male unemployment problem. Apart from Dundee its commitment to manufacturing was greatest, and this was most obvious in terms of male employment (Table 8) but true also of female employment (Table 9). Jobs for both men and women were clearly becoming more difficult to obtain in the 1970s and 1980s. A reputation for poor industrial relations, no matter how ill-deserved, and for social deprivation, no matter how true, did little to attract either new firms or the necessary professional and skilled labour.

CONCLUSION

The rise of the service industries in the twentieth century is the story of all the Scottish cities. By 1981 Glasgow derived, as we have shown, 72.8 per cent of its employment from this sector, Dundee 69.6 per cent, Aberdeen 74.2 per cent and Edinburgh 79.7 per cent. However, we must be careful not to assume that it was only the slow transference of labour to these activities which retarded the economies of Dundee and Glasgow. Undoubtedly the development of urban infrastructure, especially facilities for road transport, has made the urban population increasingly the servants of a wider region.

The attractions of new towns clearly affected Glasgow's capacity to lure new industrial firms to the city, and the development of Livingston may yet have an effect upon Edinburgh's slighter industrial base. If there is a lesson arising from this twentieth-century experience, it is perhaps best found in Aberdeen; it is best to have little in the way of an integrated industrial base as the negative experience of Dundee and Glasgow had demonstrated. Edinburgh had the advantage of its industries being essentially concerned with high value to volume products which tended to offset other disadvantages. A combination of diversity in economic activity linked with constant industrial innovation is perhaps the safest policy.

ACKNOWLEDGEMENTS

The author would like to thank Mrs Irene Scouller for help in typing this chapter.

REFERENCES

1   For example, cf. S Mukherjee *Scotland and Unemployment: A Fresh Look* (1973); G C Cameron and G L Reid *Scottish Economic Planning and the Attraction of Industry* (1966); Scottish Council (Development and Industry), *Inquiry into the Scottish Economy 1960–1961* (The Toothill Report) (Edinburgh 1961); A MacGregor Hutcheson and A Hogg (eds) *Scotland and Oil* (Edinburgh 1975); H J Hanham, *Scottish Nationalism* (1969)

2   C H Lee 'Regional Growth and Structural Change in Victorian Britain', *Economic History Review* 1981, pp 438–52; *idem* 'Modern Economic Growth and Structural Change in Scotland: the Service Sector Reconsidered', *Scottish Economic and Social History* 1983, pp 5–35

3   Lee *Economic History Review,* pp 443–4

4   Lee *Scottish Economic and Social History*, pp 6–7

5   *British Association Handbook, Dundee Meeting, 1912*, p 69

6   Cf. J H Treble 'The Market for Unskilled Male Labour in Glasgow, 1891–1914', in *Essays in Scottish Labour History* Ian MacDougall (ed) (Edinburgh 1978), pp 115–42; cf. also his *Urban Poverty* (revised edition 1983) where attendant social deprivation is analysed. Dr Treble is presently preparing a book on casual labour in Glasgow, the first four chapters of which he has kindly allowed me to read.

7   A Keith *The North of Scotland Bank Limited 1836–1936* (Aberdeen 1936), pp 143–4

8   Census of Scotland 1901 and 1921

9   *British Association Handbook, Dundee Meeting 1912*, pp 118–20

10 *Ibid*. pp 263 ff; B Lenman, C Lythe and E Gauldie *Dundee and its Textile Industry* (Dundee 1969), *passim*; D R Wallace *The Romance of Jute: A Short History of the Calcutta Jute Mill Industry 1855–1927* (1928), *passim*; S G E Lythe 'Shipbuilding at Dundee down to 1914', *Scottish Journal of Political Economy* IX 1962, pp 219–32; *British Association Handbook, Dundee* (1939), p 86

11 W H Marwick *Economic Developments in Victorian Scotland* (1936), pp 81 ff; *British Association Handbook, Dundee* (1912), pp 118–20, 349–56; J C Gilbert *A History of Investment Trusts in Dundee* (1939), *passim*; *British Association Handbook, Dundee* (1939), pp 89 ff; W T Jackson *The Enterprising Scot* (1968), *passim*.

12 H A Silverman *Studies in Industrial Organisation* (1946), pp 235 ff

13 W M Walker *Juteopolis: Dundee and its Textile Workers 1885–1923* (Edinburgh 1979), pp 90–100

14 *Ibid*. pp 394 ff, Silverman *op. cit.* p 235

15 D Sells *The British Trade Boards System* (1923), pp 99 ff

16 J K Eastham 'An Economic Survey of Present-Day Dundee', *British Association Handbook, Dundee* (1939), pp 94–9

17 A Keith *op. cit.* p 244; *idem, A Thousand Years of Aberdeen* (Aberdeen 1972) pp 459 ff

18 *Third Statistical Account: The City of Aberdeen*, p 164

19 *Ibid*. pp 165 ff

20 The best treatment of the granite industry is by T Donnelly *The Granite Industry 1750–1939* (unpublished PhD thesis, University of Aberdeen 1976)

21 *Third Statistical Account: Aberdeen,* pp 231 ff

22 *Ibid,* pp 234 ff; Census of Scotland 1931

23   Census 1931
24   A Keith *Northern Bank,* pp 55, 122, 138, 144; *idem, A Thousand Years,* p 459
25   *Ibid.* p 462
26   C A Oakley, *Scottish Industry Today* (1937), pp 11–14
27   *Ibid.* pp 130 ff
28   Cf. S G Checkland *The Upas Tree* (Glasgow, 1976), pp 34 ff; A Slaven *The Development of the West of Scotland* (1975), pp 183 ff
29   *Third Statistical Account: Edinburgh* (Glasgow 1966), *passim*; C A Oakley *op. cit.* pp 131–2, 135–41
30   C A Oakley *op. cit.* pp 142–6
31   *Ibid.* pp 148 ff; I Donnachie *A History of the Brewing Industry in Scotland* (Edinburgh 1979), pp 234 ff
32   C A Oakley *op. cit.* pp 149 ff; J A Kinloch and J Butt *History of SCWS Ltd* (Glasgow 1981), p 382
33   Census 1931
34   N Milnes *A Study of Industrial Edinburgh and the Surrounding Area 1923–1934* (1936) I, pp 35–9
35   *Ibid.* p 9
36   A Slaven *op. cit.* pp 183 ff; S G E Lythe and J Butt, *An Economic History of Scotland 1100–1939* (1975), pp 214 ff; R H Campbell *The Rise and Fall of Scottish Industry 1707–1939* (Edinburgh 1980), pp 56 ff; J R Hume and M S Moss *Beardmore* (1979), *passim*
37   R H Campbell *op. cit.* pp 76 ff; Lythe and Butt, p 215 Table 31
38   N K Buxton 'The Scottish Shipbuilding Industry between the Wars: A Comparative Study', *Business History* X, 2 1968, pp 101–20; Lord Aberconway *The Basic Industries of Great Britain* (1927), pp 226 ff
39   Cf. A Slaven *op. cit.* pp 198 ff; *Third Statistical Account of Aberdeen* (1953), p 146; N Milnes, *op. cit.* pp 80 ff
40   *British Association Handbook, Dundee* (1939), pp 96–101; *Third Statistical Account of Dundee* (Arbroath 1979), p 85; C A Oakley *op. cit.* pp 116–17
41   A M Carstairs 'The Nature and Diversification of Employment in Dundee' in *British Association Handbook, Dundee* (1968), pp 322 ff; C A Oakley *op. cit.* p 126
42   Census 1951
43   A M Carstairs *op. cit.* pp 329 ff
44   *Ibid.* pp 333–6; *Third Statistical Account, Dundee,* pp 97 ff
45   *Third Statistical Account, Aberdeen,* pp 143 ff
46   *Ibid.* p 239
47   *Ibid.* pp 294 ff
48   *Ibid.* p 265
49   *Glasgow Herald Trade Review* 1945–51
50   Census 1951
51   Information kindly supplied by British Petroleum Industries Ltd
52   Census 1981; *Glasgow Herald Trade Review 1975*
53   N Milnes *op. cit. passim*
54   I Donnachie *op. cit.* pp 234–5; C A Oakley, *op. cit.* pp 131–58
55   *Third Statistical Account, Edinburgh,* p 615; Census 1951
56   *Ibid.* pp. 833–44
57   R H Campbell *op. cit.* pp 164–6
58   *Ibid.* p 167
59   A Slaven *op. cit.* pp 187–90

60 Scottish Economic Committee *Scotland's Industrial Future: The Case for Planned Development* (Edinburgh, 1939), *passim*
61 *Third Statistical Account, Glasgow,* pp 222–31
62 Census 1951
63 *Glasgow Herald Trade Review* 1960–70; The Geddes Report, *passim*

9

MANAGEMENT AND CONSERVATION OF THE HISTORIC CITY

George Gordon

Conservation has been variously described as a proper balance between preservation and change and the control of the rate of change.[1] Many writers emphasise the theme of heritage. 'A city without old buildings is like a man without a memory.'[2] An associated but significantly distinctive view stresses the beauty of many historic buildings, streets, skylines and portions of towns and cities.[3] To some extent the two points are fused by the argument that preservation satisfies a psychological need for historical roots.[4] Equally, the question of economic viability is of central concern to owners and developers. The success of substantial schemes of urban conservation depends to a large degree upon persuasive evidence of economic benefits although there will undoubtedly be additional, even crucial, aesthetic and social advantages which accrue from the projects.

THE DEVELOPMENT OF THE LEGISLATIVE FRAMEWORK

The concept of managing the historic townscapes in cities as distinct from preserving particular buildings (Listed Buildings) is a comparatively recent component of British planning, though it has a longer history in some European countries.[5] For example, in 1815 Friedrich Wilhelm III of Prussia passed an act allowing intervention where public buildings of historical value were threatened with destruction or alteration.[6] Early in the twentieth century legislation in Germany was enacted against the disfigurement of settlements and landscapes. The 1967 Civic Amenities Act introduced an areal viewpoint into British conservation planning by stating that every local planning authority should determine 'Areas of Special Architectural or Historic Interest, being areas which contain a building or group of buildings or land of Special Architectural or Historic Interest and other buildings or land adjacent thereto, the character and appearance of the whole of which it is desirable to preserve or enhance'. Since Victorian times there had been some interest in Britain in conservation of particular buildings and monuments. The Society for the Protection of Ancient Buildings campaigned for preservation and Sir John Lubbock unsuccessfully, in the 1870s, attempted to introduce a National Monuments Preservation Bill.[7] The Ancient Monuments Protection Act 1882 heralded a series of legislative measures related to preservation. For example, the Ancient Monuments Act 1900 protected unoccupied medieval buildings whilst the 1931 Act allowed local authorities to establish preservation schemes for areas around scheduled monuments. An important procedural development was the inclusion of preservation within the terms of the Town and Country Planning Act 1932. Authorities were given extended powers relating to unoccupied buildings of historic interest, the establishment of schemes to protect buildings or groups of buildings, to control advertising hoardings and preserve trees and woodland. The Town and Country Planning (Scotland) Act 1947 required the Secretary of State to compile lists of buildings of architectural or historic interest. Principles of selection were established relating to period, style, quality and architectural or historical importance and buildings were classed under three categories (A, B, C). Category A buildings were of national or more than local importance as architectural, historic or little altered examples of a particular style or period. Buildings listed in Category B were primarily of local importance whilst those in Category C included buildings which had been considerably altered or were only fair examples of a style or period. Category C also referred to buildings of limited individual merit which constituted part of a spatial grouping of Category A or B buildings. Financial provisions for preservation grants featured in the Historic Buildings and Ancient Monuments Act 1953 and the amount and terms were increased and extended respectively in the Local Authorities (Historic Buildings) Act 1962. As mentioned earlier it was the Civic Amenities Act 1967 which introduced the statutory mechanism to enable planners to develop management policies for conservation areas in addition to the established function in relation to the preservation of Listed Buildings. Successive legislation defined the statutory position but that did not constitute a comprehensive, or even a representative, summary of contemporary interest in conservation. For example, over a century ago, the founder of the Cockburn Association in Edinburgh said that the 'dilemma of conservation at the expense of impoverished living rarely, if ever, occurs'.[8] Whilst Lord Cockburn's views apparently had limited influence upon the development process in the Victorian city in Scotland, if judged by the respective roles of demolition and preservation, the recent shift in emphasis in favour of rehabilitation of residential property echoes that plea for improvement of living conditions within existing structures. The broad founding objectives of the Cockburn Association were 'preserving and increasing the attractions of the city and its neighbourhood'.[9] The statement implied a concern with diverse environmental and functional matters within the spatial span of the local area of the city to the urban region of Edinburgh. Thus the society was not solely concerned with the preservation of particular buildings or monuments but with wider developmental and management issues. Equally, one can cite the late Victorian endeavours of Patrick Geddes and his friends to revive the residential quality and character of the Old Town of Edinburgh as another atypical example of a wider vision of the concept of management and conservation than that embodied in contemporaneous legislation.

THE NEED FOR CONSERVATION AREAS

The Town and Planning Act 1947 extended and enhanced the powers of town planners, particularly in relation to development control. Reviewing the efficiency of the Act, Wilson observed that 'development has been achieved more or less in the right places with adequate services, safe access, necessary amounts of open space, etc.'.[10] He criticised the prevailing planning attitudes in the post-1947 era which equated progress with modernisation, the replacement of the old by the new, 'a lack of respect and concern for our traditional built environment'.[11] Wilson recalled 'contesting an appeal where an authority wished to demolish an old but attractive housing area in 1965—one year before the General Improvement Area became established, and the inspectors' report did not even consider conservation and improvement as a possible alternative'. Apart from the ravages of comprehensive redevelopment concern was mounting in the 1960s about the threat to the historic city from powerful, physical and economic forces. Physical decay had prompted the phase of comprehensive redevelopment. Increasing levels of traffic stimulated a plethora of traffic studies and planning proposals, many involving substantial demolition of old properties and threatening townscapes, built environments and distinctive communities. Economic, technological and organisational change promoted demands for additional space and new or different buildings. In some cases conversion of existing buildings was either impracticable or too expensive, thereby creating a persuasive argument for demolition and radical change. Equally, there was a substantial amount of conversion notably in properties occupied by shops and offices. Here the impact of conversion varied considerably from minor internal modifications to major facade and structural alterations. Many of these changes were localised within the central business districts of cities and Sim studied the patterns and processes of renewal in central Glasgow.[12] Nonetheless the demolition of residential areas involved tracts of the inner city, road proposals and developments spread tentacles towards the urban periphery which was, in any case, the location of a substantial proportion of new development whilst industrial change had a more dispersed geographical impact dependent upon the distribution of older industrial areas in a particular city. The actual and potential scale of change in the 1960s produced a renewed interest in conservation with an emphasis upon townscapes and areas rather than single buildings and upon function and community in addition to architectural and historical characteristics. The Civic Trust, founded in 1957, provided a practical force in areal conservation through some 400 street improvement schemes. The Council for British Archaeology published a list of over 300 town centres deemed worthy of preservation and, in 1966, Government commissioned preservation studies of four towns; Bath, Chester, Chichester and York. In 1967, the President of the Civic Trust, Duncan Sandys, MP, successfully introduced, as a Private Member's Bill, the Civic Amenities Act. Local authorities were urged: to ensure that the traffic and land use objectives of plans considered the character of conservation areas; to prepare preservation and enhancement programmes for conservation areas; to protect historic buildings; to finance the repair and maintenance of historic buildings; to set an example in the conservation of their own properties; and to publicise proposals and seek public participation in the planning and conservation processes. The Town and Country Planning (Scotland) Act 1972 superceded the earlier legislation. Different levels of the local authority system in Scotland were required to prepare structure and local plans respectively. The designation of conservation areas became the responsibility of District Councils and the Secretary of State. Additionally, authorities could seek approval from the Historic Buildings Council for the special status of outstanding conservation areas, thereby gaining access to special financial aid for conservation work. At the risk of condensation and over-simplification of lengthy and complex legislation, the various Acts cumulatively produced a framework in which alterations to Listed Buildings required Listed Building Consent and changes within conservation areas were subject to development control policies. Regulations defined permissible advertising in conservation areas and powers were given to ensure the protection of trees in conservation areas. A statutory requirement was placed upon local authorities to give public notice of proposals related to subjects covered by the various regulations.

The General Development (Scotland) Order 1975 defined over a score of classes of development which did not require planning permission. However authorities could seek a direction from the Secretary of State under Article 4 which restricted the application of the concept of permitted development. These restrictions on development and the exercising of tighter controls could be applied to part or the whole of a conservation area. Under Article 4 directions planning permission was necessary for an extensive range of alterations including such diverse phenomena as stands for milk churns and extensions of industrial premises. Most commonly local authorities sought control over developments related to the enlargement, improvement or alteration of dwelling houses, or parts thereof, to minor works involving walls, gates, fences and external paintwork, to streets and footpaths, the location and erection of domestic oil tanks and the character of lamp standards and other street furniture. Frequently development and alteration of buildings may be dependent upon the use of traditional materials and the preservation of the architectural or historic features of the property.

'What is a prerequisite of any enhancement is a thorough understanding of a Conservation Area. This entails the appreciation of its history, development, style of building, landscape and social factors. . . . Enhancement can be very minor treatment such as planting a few trees, replacing an area of rough ground with stone setts and cobbles, or it can involve reorganisation of a town centre closing streets to traffic, and demolishing eyesores.'[13] Successful conservation demands skill and sensitivity but it also needs careful planning and co-ordinated action.

THE FINANCING OF CONSERVATION

Only limited amounts of additional public funds were made available to finance conservation schemes. The precise ratios depended upon the technical status of the conservation area and of the particular building involved but generally the additional monies required proportionate contributions from national government, the local authority and the owner of the property. Generally the latter could expect to contribute between 25 and 50 per cent of the costs, thus the owner must be prepared to accept a significant financial commitment although that should largely be offset by the enhancement to the value of the property. However, in a financial sense the enhancement is a potential gain which matures on sale whereas the expenditure is a current cost requiring immediate funding. Similarily the local authority must make budgeting provision for a share of annual expenditure on approved conservation projects. For example, since 1972 Edinburgh District Council (or its predecessor) has allocated nearly £1 million towards conservation work in the New Town of Edinburgh.[14] That scale of expenditure is exceptional in Scotland and most authorities operate more modest conservation budgets. There is also scope for conservation work to be funded in other ways. Residential property may qualify for improvement grants, again with costs shared in a ratio between the owner and the local authority. Although the respective proportionate contributions to costs have varied through time, improvement grants have proved an important vehicle of assistance in many conservation areas. Grants may also be made by private bodies, voluntary trusts and amenity groups. In aggregate they constitute a small portion of the total sum but these contributions often represented pioneering projects which established possibilities and provided substantive proof of the economic practicalities of conservation. Housing Associations and developers have participated in conservation schemes in Edinburgh, Glasgow and Aberdeen. Additionally, the private sector has gradually become involved in conservation work. Shops, offices and banks have implemented enhancement work, often at their own expense, after consultation with, and guidance from, conservation experts of the local authority.

In particular conservation areas of each Scottish city the respective University constitutes a major institutional use. Their record has been neither equal nor unblemished but, in general, they have contributed to local conservation.

It has been argued that the local authorities could achieve enhancement goals 'through the implementation of other local authority programmes'.[15] For example pedestrianisation and street closures might be handled and funded from monies allocated to transport policies. In Scotland, the division of functions between the different tiers of local government complicates the situation, because transport is a regional function whereas conservation is the responsibility of district councils. The postulated alignment of programmes is, therefore, dependent upon inter-authority consultation, collaboration and agreement.

The Scottish Development Agency has operated in a dual capacity in relation to conservation. Firstly, it has been actively involved in the field of environmental improvement in the Scottish cities and one scheme, in Leith, is sited within a conservation area. Secondly, the SDA operates a Conservation Bureau which is based in Edinburgh. The Bureau collects and disseminates information about the availability of conservation skills, sources of materials for conservation work and of grants for training in practical conservation.

Finally amenity bodies have performed a variety of functions, sometimes simultaneously, ranging from channelling comment and protest to, in the case of Edinburgh New Town Conservation Committee, administering the funds from local and national government allocated towards conservation work in the New Town and operating a salvage scheme, 're-cycling building materials, railings, doors, fireplaces etc. recovered from historic buildings, and available for re-sale within the Edinburgh District'.[16]

CRITICISMS AND RESERVATIONS

Although there has been a shift in opinion in favour of conservation, particularly recently, various criticisms and reservations have been expressed by both opponents and supporters of the policy of conservation areas. It has been argued that conservation is opposed to development.[17] A number of points are often subsumed within the claim. There is a widely-held fear that potential economic developments may not be attracted to a city, or an area of a city, because of conservation regulations. The essence of the argument is that the possibility of additional costs and/or procedural obstacles and delays, could tip the balance unfavourably in a situation in which there are numerous suitors pursuing a comparatively limited supply of new enterprises. The substantial increase in Aberdeen, Edinburgh and Glasgow in conservation projects involving the enhancement of existing offices or conversion to use by offices appears to provide counter-evidence to that view. It may be that developers have made a virtue of necessity but the pre-release advertising of prestigious conserved office buildings suggests that there is a buoyant demand for these properties. Another strand of the argument is that conservation, presumably like planning in general, is interfering with the natural processes of change. However unless functional or economic efficiency was seriously impaired, or working and living conditions adversely affected, it is difficult to see an automatic need for the replacement of buildings which are structurally sound and patently usable. Prevention of change of use can pose more serious problems. An absolute ban would create fossilisation but even lesser areal limitations can have the practical consequences of deflecting pressures on to other areas and as will be discussed later, this has happened in the Scottish cities. A further thread in the argument is that artificial constraints and restraints distort the property market. In that context conservation is not significantly distinct from a whole myriad of planning measures which, it is widely recognised, will have complex and varied economic and social consequences in both space and time.

Conservationists are also criticised by the advocates of social justice in the city.[18] There are three principal components in the argument. Firstly, it is argued that conservation does little for the quality of life of the poor. Secondly, it is claimed that money spent on conservation should be devoted to improving the lot of the poor. Thirdly, it is suggested that conservation involves 'the displacement of those unable to conserve, by those with the will and the wealth'.[19] In residential areas the outcome would be the process of gentrification as the areal enhancement displaced working-class households and attracted middle-class residents. In shopping areas traditional retailers might be replaced by specialised sectional users such as antique shops and boutiques. Clearly such processes cannot occur in the absence of demand but the social injustice debate hinges around the question of which sections of society gain and lose respectively as a result of acts of policy.

It should be recognised that staunch supporters of conservation question the efficacy of certain aspects of existing policies. To generalise the reservations relate to the absence of precise guidelines determining which townscapes should be conserved, to the limited financial provision for conservation and to the absence of statutory retrospective powers to enable the enforced restoration of buildings or the restitution of properties or aspects thereof.

Discussion and debate of a technical and conceptual nature has occurred. Slater[20] noted that 'Though techniques of conserving historic areas are now better understood . . . there are few theoretical constructs upon which basic techniques can be built'. He added that 'conservation areas within historic towns are still very much at the mercy of local government planning departments and the often conflicting political pressure groups of town-centre developers and conservationists'.[21] Slater advocated that the 'development of ideas based on a thorough understanding of the development of the fine detail of *town plans* might offer a useful way forward in the management of historic towns'.[22] Fine detail referred to the pattern of streets, lanes, plots and townscapes and also to the architectural minutiae of individual buildings. Worskett[23] suggested a five-stage procedural model for conservation policy commencing with survey and culminating in the issuing of detailed policy statements. A vital intermediate stage after the setting of goals involved testing for feasibility and also evaluating the compatibility with other planning strategies. Bygrave noted that local plans had become the primary policy documents for conservation but argued for a separate and detailed conservation area document and for the publication of design guidelines.[24] In several instances, such as Edinburgh New Town conservation area, guidelines have been published but there are considerable differences in practice and no generally accepted normal procedure.

The remainder of the chapter presents a detailed account of conservation areas in each of the Scottish cities.

EDINBURGH

For most people Edinburgh conjures up images of the famous shopping thoroughfare of Princes Street, one of the jewels of the Georgian New

Town, set against the dramatic backcloth of the Castle and the Royal Mile, rather than pictures of extensive suburbs, peripheral local authority estates, industrial districts or the harbour complex at Leith. The city is steeped in history, a fact which colours the views of visitors and residents. The latter may bemoan the inconveniences which result from an historic infrastructure, notably parking and transport problems, but the trenchant opposition to inner ring-road proposals bears witness to the ingrained respect for the distinctive inheritance of the city and the desire to protect various and varied residential environments.

'Edinburgh, Scotland's history in her every grey stone, with her grave and kindly people, and her heritage of lore and learning, looking out for ever northwards across the Firth of Forth, and southward to the Pentland Hills. . . . '[25] Thus Sillar endeavoured to capture the complex interplay of the various elements which have affected the character of the city; site, situation, function as capital and seat of learning, historical development and population.

Victorian Edinburgh was a gathering place and educational centre for national elites and a national intelligentsia.[26] In part these functions dated from medieval times but the building of the Georgian New Town reinforced the social and cultural pre-eminence of the capital for Scottish society. The city remained the effective national administrative focus, the seat of the legal profession, of many national institutions and a major educational, medical and financial centre. These functions generated substantial development pressures on the historic built environment. If unrestrained the powerful centripetal forces would cause horizontal and/or vertical growth of the central business district which in Edinburgh coincides with the historic Old and, more particularly, the New Town. Desmond Hodges, Director of the Edinburgh New Town Conservation Committee, has described the threat.

In 1966 it seemed as though central Edinburgh was about to be changed by the same combination of road transport, property investment and chain stores, which tore the hearts out of other cites at that time. George Square on the south side of the Royal Mile was being partly demolished for new university buildings, great chunks of the south side were demolished, inner ring roads, urban motorways and tunnels were being proposed for the central area; James Craig's shabby St. James Square was to be replaced by the concrete fortress of St. James Centre. Offices spreading into the residential streets of the Moray Estate brought the inevitable pressures for alterations, extension and even demolition which follows change of use, and they added to the car parking problems, then totally uncontrolled.[27]

In essence there were three principal sources of pressure for change namely, development, decay and congestion, although the relative importance of each varied within the central area. Traffic congestion was greatest in the principal shopping thoroughfares, the Royal Mile and the main service arteries whereas acute physical decay was primarily located in the Old Town and adjoining South Side. In contrast, whilst Matthew[28] found extensive decay of stonework in many properties within the New Town conservation area only one street, Jamaica Street, had reached such a state of physical unfitness that demolition was considered necessary by the local authority. In 1966 there were no conservation areas in Edinburgh. By the beginning of 1983 twenty-six conservation areas had been declared (Figure 1). Subsequently, a further area, Grange, has been designated. Indeed the historical and architectural importance of Edinburgh and the history of development of the city presents the District Council with a sizeable challenge in terms of conservation policy. Edinburgh is second only to London in Britain in the number of listed buildings. 'The majority of these buildings are in the New Town area but significant concentrations also exist in the Old Town, South Side, Leith, and other former village settlements such as Duddingston and Swanston.'[29] The scale and diversity of the heritage places significant financial demands on the District Council in connection with sharing the costs of maintenance and restoration, in addition to the work involved in the management of development within the designated areas.

It could be argued that Edinburgh District Council should declare further conservation areas. The city has many fine Victorian villa and high quality tenement districts, such as Morningside and Marchmont, that are certainly comparable in aesthetic, social and historical merit to areas in other cities which have been deemed worthy of preservation and conservation. Concerted local action could encourage the local authority to designate areas, as the campaign in Grange illustrated,[30] but there may be a reasoned reluctance to add to the list if areas are not believed to be at risk and when there is little probability of substantial increases in the level of public funding of conservation work. The pressures upon policy-makers in Edinburgh are substantial for they must respond to the opinions of influential and distinguished persons who have charged the city with the guardianship of a national treasure. 'Indeed, in Edinburgh, what was built between 1760 and 1860 provides still the most extensive example of a romantic classical city in the world.'[31] 'It is for those who inherit the achievement of Edinburgh's classical age to understand it, to use it, and to enjoy it.'[32] Betjeman urged the maintenance not only of buildings but of a sense of place and a style of living: 'So Edinburgh is what a city ought to be (or could be), somewhere to live and walk about in.'[33] Equally, policymakers are subject to pressure from developers, particularly those engaged in the burgeoning office and tourist sectors, searching for new sites preferably with speedy planning approval and minimal restrictions. The planners have also recognised that the pre-1760 townscapes, notably in the Old Town, deserve a high priority in conservation policies. The spatial distribution of the medieval and classical districts has resulted in an extensive series of conservation areas between Inverleith and Grange, including almost all of the city centre. It would be impracticable and unwise to attempt to prohibit change and development within a zone of such dimensions. A rigid policy could precipitate fossilisation and displace development into other areas generating problems and conflict in these areas in turn. Moreover, the planners must grapple with the sustenance and furtherance of the functional and economic efficiency of the city. Whilst Edinburgh has retained a

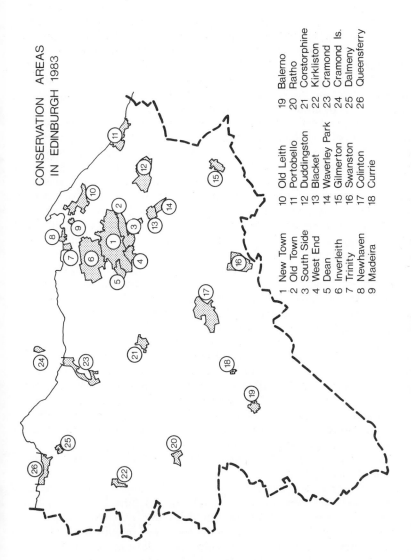

Figure 1 Conservation areas in Edinburgh, April 1983.

considerable degree of centrally-located residences, substantial decentralisation of population and place of residence has occurred. The city draws shoppers and workers from an extensive catchment. Collectively these components generate public and private transport demands in terms of parking and access which still focalise upon the central area. Somehow policies must serve these suburban dwellers without prejudicing the environment of the conservation areas. Planners are, of course, acutely aware of these conflicting priorities and forces but, when evaluating policies, critics should recognise that invariably some balance must be struck in order to attain a viable equilibrium.

There are noteworthy examples of successful restoration and conservation work outwith designated areas. For example, the Lister Housing Co-operative with a grant of £135,509 has completed an award-winning project involving Georgian residential tenements in Lauriston Place (Figure 2). Strangely, some of the fiercest controversy has surrounded road and building proposals not directly related to conservation areas. For example, a sustained, political and cultural debate has focused upon the 'hole in the ground' in Castle Terrace. The site of the demolished Synod Hall, which had accommodated a cinema, the offices of societies and meeting rooms, was originally planned as the location of the proposed opera house because of the juxtaposition of the Usher Hall and the Lyceum Theatre. Ultimately the project was abandoned due to escalating costs and the site became the subject of various proposals for hotels. In truth, subject to proper safeguards about skyline and façade the negotiations should have been comparatively simple. Edinburgh needed additional central hotel accommodation and the frontal view of the Castle and restricted angular vista of Princes Street were valuable site attributes for the proposed use. The ensuing heated controversy paid little attention to the general character of the area or to the various office and road developments happening in the vicinity. It is difficult to escape the conclusion that politicians, vested interests and the media exaggerated the significance of the use of the site during a prolonged debate which was primarily concerned with opposing the abandonment of the plan to build an opera house. On 1 March 1984 Edinburgh District Council unveiled a plan for a multi-purpose theatre on the Castle Terrace site.

Paralysing, or greatly delaying, decision-making has sometimes resulted in some adventitious benefits. For example, the extended debate over transport proposals meant that Edinburgh delayed action over major road developments. Subsequent changes in the climate of opinion and reductions in the estimates for level of car ownership now make it unlikely that some of the Buchanan[34] proposals will be implemented in the foreseeable future. To date the only major new road developments have been the western approach road terminating in Lothian Road and a section of the outer ring road. Nonetheless delaying tactics are not entirely beneficial. Traffic problems continue to affect the central area and the major approach routes, notably that leading from the M8 to the city centre, and new proposals have been formulated for a major western relief road from Corstorphine to Lothian

Figure 2 Restoration of properties in Lauriston Place, Edinburgh. *Source*: Edinburgh District Council.

Road. The scheme has aroused considerable opposition, especially from amenity groups. The Cockburn Association,[35] for example, whilst accepting that there is a need for transport improvements, favour increased use of park and ride schemes, extensions to the suburban rail network and completion of the outer ring road as primary priorities and oppose a major new traffic artery which they believe will increase the levels of vehicular traffic in the city centre, thereby endangering the environmental quality of central districts. Doubtless other parties would question plans for the completion of the outer ring road. Uncertainty about the outcome of road proposals in the 1960s and 1970s led to a degree of planning blight in central and inner districts such as Tollcross which added to the existing requirements for planning controls, commercial and residential regeneration, redevelopment and rehabilitation.

Space does not permit a detailed survey of each of the twenty-seven conservation areas in Edinburgh. Instead four very different examples (New Town, Old Town, South Side, Grange) are used to illustrate some facets of conservation and management of the historic areas of the city. The selection encompasses an interesting range of historical, architectural, spatial, developmental and technical situations.

The New Town

The New Town conservation area (Figure 3) embraces the original New Town based on Craig's plan and the subsequent western, eastern and northern Georgian extensions along with the development on the Moray estate.[36]

As a result of commercial pressures in the nineteenth century, many of the Georgian houses in the original New Town were replaced or adapted for other purposes. The replacements were designed as individual units and reflected architectural fashions of the period. These, and later, changes caused Abercrombie[37] in the 1940s to comment that conflict existed between the continued original uniformity of Charlotte Square and the anarchy of the architecture of Princes Street. In the 1950s and 60s the planning department exercised a measure of control over new developments particularly in terms of skyline infringements and through the mechanism of plot ratios. Nonetheless considerable change occurred, most noticeably in Princes Street and at Leith Street (St James Centre). Indeed the recommendations of the Princes Street Panel Report (1967) implicitly assumed the accumulative redevelopment of properties in that street and sought control by height regulations and plot ratios.[38] The Panel, which consisted of a small group of local authority officials, considered that a unified design could be achieved by controlling the materials to be used, floor levels, the width of frontages and the modelling of elevations. A standard section was devised which made allowances for a walkway with shops at first floor level and an example of the design exists west of the junction with Hanover Street. Contemporaneously, the planning department tried to encourage new office developments[39] to locate at various suburban and peripheral

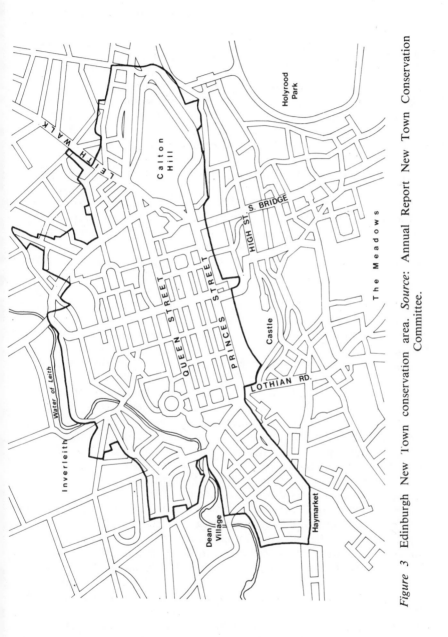

Figure 3 Edinburgh New Town conservation area. *Source*: Annual Report New Town Conservation Committee.

central sites in order to restrict further invasion of the western and northern extensions of the New Town.

A central component in the objectives of the Recommended Transport Plan (1972)[40] revolved around the need to secure the highest degree of accessibility to the principal shopping and office districts whilst safeguarding the unique architectural and landscape heritage of the city. The Plan recommended stabilisation of total employment in the Central Area at the early 1970s level and accepted that there would be some increase in retail activity in Princes Street and in office employment within the Central Area. In fact in the 60s and 70s Princes Street experienced a significant invasion by chain stores with a consequent displacement of cinemas, clubs and family businesses. Until the early 1980s these changes resulted in major structural alterations to frontages, internal layout, complete buildings and plots. The traffic strategy of the Buchanan Plan involved diversion of inter-suburban and regional traffic from the Central Area, short-stay parking in the city centre, improvements to the bus system and to access routes and the provision of a limited amount of additional central car-parking facilities. To date strict control of parking has been a central tenet of policy aligned with the commitment of Lothian Regional Council to the maintenance of a substantial public transport system. Pedestrianisation has been implemented in part of Rose Street. Originally a residential area for tradesmen and servants Rose Street had degenerated functionally and socially but pedestrianisation has provided a stimulus for regeneration in a potentially attractive commercial location proximate to Princes Street. Various traffic management strategies have been adopted to smooth flows and reduce congestion, especially in Princes Street, but there is still a considerable daytime traffic problem. In autumn 1982 the Regional Council produced a new set of proposals for traffic management in the original New Town (Figure 4) which were intended to lead to a substantial improvement in conditions in Princes Street. However, one almost unavoidable consequence appeared to be correspondingly heavier traffic loadings in certain other streets in the New Town conservation area.

A conference organised in 1970 on the theme of the conservation of Georgian Edinburgh resulted in the creation of the influential and successful Edinburgh New Town Conservation Committee although the current extensive outstanding conservation area was designated in parts over a lengthy period. The conservation area now covers 318 hectares in which some three quarters of the buildings are listed and houses approximately 24,000 people. Between 1971 and 1981 over £2.5 millions of grant aid have been devoted to external restoration in the area, mainly stone repair which was highlighted as a priority requirement in the voluntary survey conducted in 1970 by Edinburgh Architectural Association. The District Council, central government, residents associations, Scottish Civic Trust, Scottish Georgian Society and the Cockburn Association are represented on the New Town Conservation Committee. In 1982 the Committee reported[41] that careful planning and vigilant building control combined with the active support of residents and amenity societies meant that the historic develop-

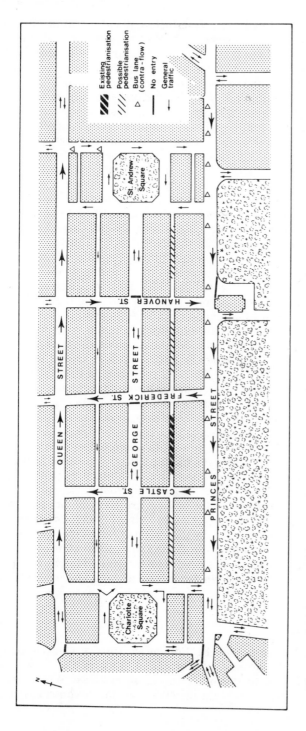

Figure 4 Traffic management proposals for the original New Town of Edinburgh. *Source:* Lothian Regional Council 1982.

ment remained largely intact. Nevertheless attention was drawn to the cost
of repairs using stone, slate and lead. 'Without public subsidy the buildings
will not be repaired to the required standard and in some cases will not be
repaired at all. Since 1970 three buildings have had to be demolished for
structural reasons and it is significant that none of them has been
replaced.'[42] Reviewing ten years operations the Report noted that 53
comprehensive conservation schemes had been completed or were in
progress, that technical advice was provided by the Conservation Centre
and by means of various publications,[43] that public interest in conservation
had been awakened and conservation encouraged and that administrative
and legal techniques had been developed to help proprietors undertake
common repairs in the major building type, flatted properties. In addition
to support for co-operative policies for conservation in the extensions of the
original New Town which have been organised by the Edinburgh New Town
Conservation Committee, early in 1982 the District Council issued a statement of planning policies for the first New Town.[44] The document set fairly
exacting guidelines for the design of new buildings and revealed an
increasing morphological awareness in the requirement that the design of
new buildings should reflect traditional feu divisions. In effect the intention
was to prevent the continuation of a trend involving the invasion of rear
lanes and of the rear of adjoining plots by extensions of shops and offices.
Specific instructions were given about heights, roofs, materials, shopfronts,
exterior painting and advertising. Maximum plot ratios were set at 1:4.5 for
Princes Street, 1:3.5 for George Street and 1:2.5 for Queen Street. Detailed
recommendations were made for most properties in Princes Street and for
many properties in other streets such as listing of buildings, the removal of
additions and extensions, and the retention of particular frontages. The
policies paid particular attention to developments in minor streets and lanes
which had suffered invasion and conversion in a phase of extension by
several major Princes Street stores. In essence the policies attempt to
prevent further anarchy of style, impose stricter control of future development and encourage desirable restorative work. An illustration of the latter
was the voluntary removal of a modern shopfront in George Street and the
replacement with a replica of the original neo-classical facade. It should be
appreciated that, with the exception of Princes Street, Georgian buildings
predominate in most streets in the original New Town. In the case of
Princes Street the policy basically aimed at the preservation of interesting or
meritorious designs of various periods and styles and the encouragement of
the highest standards of design and the use of particular materials in future
developments.

The Old Town

In the financial year 1981–82 Edinburgh District Council contributed
£112,000 towards the cost of restoration work in the New Town and
£213,000 grant aid to the other conservation areas. Whilst that was a
comparatively substantial sum in relation to many conservation budgets

there were a large number of competing claimants. The District Council appreciated the severe physical and financial problems confronting certain conservation areas and in the Old Town and South Side increased levels of grant were made available to cover the exceptional cost of rehabilitating housing. Both areas are classed by the Historic Buildings Council as outstanding conservation areas.

In January 1980 the District Council adopted a series of conservation policies[45] for the Old Town area relating to conservation, new buildings, advertisements, traffic and street improvements. With reference to new buildings guidance was offered about elevations, roofs, windows and materials. It was suggested that arcades could feature in new buildings and developers were encouraged to incorporate closes and wynds in any new developments. The policy included detailed instruction that the closes and wynds included in new building projects should be surfaced with flagstones and small stones laid on edge.[46] The traffic policies urged the identification of sites for short-stay car parks and a review of traffic management and pedestrianisation schemes both of which required liaison with, and implementation by, the Regional Council. The conservation section of the policies stated the development controls, the financial policy and the intention to pursue strict enforcement of the policy for replacement windows. The Old Town was designated an area of archaeological interest and the City Archaeologist must be notified of all new developments. Encouragement was given to coordinated improvement schemes and it was stated that unoccupied listed buildings owned by the District Council should be disposed of to agencies who could guarantee restoration. One policy specifically sought to resolve a problem of the area, namely gap sites, by stating that planning . permission would not be granted for the demolition of buildings until contracts for replacement buildings had been accepted. Unfortunately in the high-risk building industry, particularly in times of economic recession, that policy cannot prevent the possibility of the abandonment of a project after demolition but before rebuilding because of the closure of the firm of builders, developers or contractors.

Until the second half of the eighteenth century Edinburgh had been confined to the crest and flanks of the sloping ridge linking the Castle with Holyrood. Within that relatively small compass were variously distributed the military, administrative, craft, merchant, market, religious and residential functions of the city. After the development of the Georgian areas the Old Town experienced progressively rapid social and commercial decline. Thus when Littlejohn surveyed mid-Victorian Edinburgh[47] the Old Town emerged as an unhealthy, squalid, overcrowded and insanitary area in desperate need of remedial action. An important strand in the subsequent response by the authorities was the demolition of unfit housing and the implementation of Improvement Schemes. Several new streets were constructed with the specific purpose of locally truncating the dense network of closes and wynds. In some cases modern tenements were erected but the Improvement Schemes were also associated with the construction of a number of institutional buildings. The net effect was some gains in terms of access and environmental conditions but considerable losses in the total, albeit defective, housing stock. The latter trend initiated a progressive depopulation of the historic heart of the city which accelerated in the post 1950 period.

Various measures have effected a substantial improvement since the mid 1960s to the visual appearance of the Old Town although there are still sizeable areas of decayed or under-utilised property. For example, there are relatively low usage rates of upper floors in many properties in the High Street. Restoration and rebuilding by various agencies have preserved properties and skillfully recreated a sense of the traditional morphology (Figure 5). Effective conservation must combine the preservation and restoration of buildings with the retention and recapturing of the sense and spirit of community. The local authority has sought a reversal of the process roundly criticised eighty years ago by Patrick Geddes, the process he called dehousing. The local authority, Edinburgh University, developers and other agencies and trusts have all contributed in some measure by renovating existing buildings for residential use or constructing new buildings to acceptable standards of design for the area. However, it is difficult to control all facets of the process. In particular it can be difficult to recreate a balanced social and demographic structure when many agencies are involved. There may be practical and financial problems in converting units into flats suitable for families, and particularly low income families, but without some resolution the area would develop a biased demography with a preponderance of single people and childless couples. Whilst the spirit of the policies intended restoration and rehabilitation to produce permanent residences it is difficult to preclude any speculative venture involving short-stay executive flats for visiting businessmen which may make a useful contribution to the goals of physical conservation within the area. This issue furnishes another example of the practice of conservation policy which touches upon the sensitive topic of social justice and can provoke vigorous political debate.

Many parts of the Old Town have acquired an important role in the tourist trade of the city. Preservation of particular buildings and of their setting is a fundamental matter if that function is to be maintained. Equally, the tourists pose serious problems for conservation policy. They require access to conveniences, eating places, gift shops and transport as well as historical buildings and sites. The development of a small restaurant in the crypt of St Giles is an excellent example of the intelligent use of surplus space to satisfy an important demand

Several large institutions are situated in the Old Town and many of them have generated demands for additional space and new buildings. Such expansion affects the balance of the land use pattern and invariably creates increased demands for parking facilities. Conversely the institutions point to the administrative convenience of centralising around the existing site. When there was a low level of competition for space in the Old Town institutional growth went largely unchallenged but that situation should alter if the overall conservation strategy is successful.

Figure 5 Restoration and conversion of properties at James Court, Lawnmarket, Edinburgh. *Source*: Edinburgh District Council.

Figure 6 Restoration of residential property, Pleasance, Edinburgh. *Source*: Edinburgh District Council.

The South Side

Conservation policies for the area were a constituent part of the Local Plan.[48] The area contains eighteenth- and nineteenth-century stone built terraced and tenement properties, some major institutions of which the University of Edinburgh is the largest, and various retail, office and industrial premises. The immediate policy objectives of the Local Plan were twofold. Firstly, the maintenance of investment in the area, particularly in the rehabilitation and redevelopment of housing, in order to restore confidence, reverse the decline of population and protect existing employment. Secondly, the conservation and enhancement of the architectural and historic character of the area.[49]

In the 1960s proposals were formulated for the redevelopment of a substantial portion of the South Side with the clearance and replacement of extensive tracts of decayed and substandard housing. Although there was a substantial reduction in the resident population comprehensive redevelopment did not occur. By the mid 1970s rehabilitation and conservation had become fashionable and the South Side was recognised as an outstanding conservation area, despite the advanced state of structural decay of many properties. The problems of dilapidated housing and cleared land necessitated rehabilitation and in-fill housing being allotted prime importance in the first phase (1–5 years) of the Local Plan. Prominent amongst the other pressures and problems experienced in the area were the construction of new buildings for Edinburgh University in the George Square area (with the loss of some Georgian terraced houses), increased volumes of traffic along the three major north–south thoroughfares and the closure of a number of industrial premises.

Restoration (Figure 6) and rehabilitation have been carried out by several agencies including Edinvar Housing Association (Figure 7), Edinburgh University and the Royal College of Surgeons. Additionally new private housing has been built by the Crown Estate Commissioners and Barratt Developments.

Without doubt a promising start has been made to the regeneration of an inner city area but much remains to be done. The future progress of the project will be watched with interest because most major cities possess comparable problems in inner areas.

Grange

Like the Blacket and Waverley Park conservation areas Grange, an area of Victorian and Edwardian villas, was designated after representations from local residents. In this instance the residents not only organised meetings and exhibitions, but conducted a substantial piece of research which was published in support of their case.[50] The work had four objectives. The primary goal was the presentation of conclusive evidence of the special historic, architectural and landscape qualities of the area in order to petition for designation as a conservation area. The other objectives were the

Figure 7 Restoration to residential accommodation, Hope Park Square, Edinburgh. *Source:* Edinburgh District Council.

establishment of the identity of the area, the promotion and enhancement of community feeling by active co-operation and the achievement of participation of residents in planning and conservation.[51] The study presented an account of historical development, an analysis of a household survey, a parking survey, a study of images of the area based upon small samples of children and parents and chapters on architecture and townscape, trees, threats to the character of the area, means of protecting the area, public participation and recommendations and conclusions. A reviewer described the study as a 'thorough, readable and useful document'.[52] The section[53] which dealt with pressures upon the area discussed six problems: demolition and redevelopment, infill of gardens, sub-division of villas, change of use, over-parking and through traffic. There had been a small number of instances of demolition of villas and replacement by modern flats but infill of gardens and sub-division of villas were more widespread threats. There had been some invasion by non-residential uses. The heaviest traffic flows occurred in Grange Road but other streets were affected by through traffic particularly at peak times.

The Grange Association won its case with the designation in 1983 of the Grange conservation area. Their tactics may interest other residents associations and the results of their research provided a possible framework for the analysis of risk in other residential areas in Scottish cities.

GLASGOW

The phase of sustained urbanisation and industrialisation which earned the title of Second City of the Empire[54] for late Victorian Glasgow destroyed or transformed much of the medieval, post-medieval and early Georgian districts. The burgeoning city which spawned numerous new industrial and densely-packed tenemental areas also witnessed the construction of many elegant middle-class terraced houses and suburban villas. Contemporaneously, within the city centre many Georgian houses were progressively replaced by massive ornamented blocks of offices and newly fashionable department stores. After 1945 the industrial decline and urban decay which had affected many areas of the city were attacked through an extensive programme of redevelopment and urban regeneration. Several local authority housing estates were built in the interwar period but that phase was eclipsed by the scale of postwar activity in that sector of the housing market. The massive growth in road transport led to problems of congestion, access and parking in and around the city centre, to which the local authority responded by implementing a succession of road building and traffic management schemes including the construction of the Clyde Tunnel, Kingston Bridge, the northern portion of the Inner Ring Road, the Clydeside Expressway, and the urban sections of the M8.[55] Many areas were affected, often radically altered, by these developments but the older middle-class suburbs and, to a lesser extent, the city centre, were unharmed. Thus Lord Esher could observe in 1971 that 'Glasgow is now the finest surviving example of a great Victorian city'.[56] His report to the local authority proposed the designation of nine suburban conservation areas, namely: Kelvinside, Partickhill, Dowanhill, Hillhead, Dumbreck, Pollokshields, Strathbungo, Crosshill and Dennistoun.[57] The report further recommended a ten-year programme of repair and restoration in the Park Circus conservation area and the provisional declaration of a Central conservation area.[58] Coincidentally, planning policy switched from comprehensive clearance and redevelopment of old residential districts to selective clearance of hopelessly decayed or structurally unfit properties, with an emphasis upon the rehabilitation of the majority of substandard buildings.

By 1982 sixteen conservation areas had been designated and the spatial distribution is shown in Figure 8. In 1983 the West End conservation area was extended and the small Farme Cross conservation area in Rutherglen was designated. Seven conservation areas have been approved as outstanding areas. The local authority hopes to obtain Article 4 directions for all conservation areas in order to effect the maximum degree of development control. Preservation and enhancement statements have been made in policy reports or Local Plans. In connection with the latter, public consultation has resulted in representations by groups of residents, particularly in Jordanhill and Newlands, for the designation of a number of Victorian and Edwardian residential areas.

The seventeen conservation areas vary markedly in scale ranging from one or two streets (Queen's Crescent, St Vincent Crescent, Walmer Crescent) to extensive zones (Central, West End). A broad interpretation of the statutory definition has been adopted. For example, Victoria Park conservation area consists of several rows of late nineteenth-century sandstone cottages. The initial development of three rows was for workers on the Scotstoun Estate but over a period of ten years a somewhat larger townscape unit emerged by westward extension. Nowadays most of the buildings have been painted and the abundance of colour is one of the striking features of the conservation area. Although there are no listed buildings in the area, designation could be justified on the dual criteria of continued unity and distinctiveness of the townscape. Similarly, the Farme Cross area is of historical interest as an early example of co-operative housing and Hyndland is a superb example of a red sandstone middle-class tenement area.

Queen's Crescent, Walmer Crescent, St Vincent Crescent

The small, outstanding, conservation areas tend to share common problems related to change of use, physical alterations or physical decay and the proximity of major thoroughfares. Queen's Crescent consists of a semi-circular pattern of two- and three-story early Victorian terraces with a central garden. There has been some invasion by non-residential uses and a new elevated section of road skirts the north-eastern boundary of the area. The District Council would wish to extend the conservation area to include adjacent streets. At present limited restoration has occurred in the conservation area although there is greater activity in some adjoining streets.

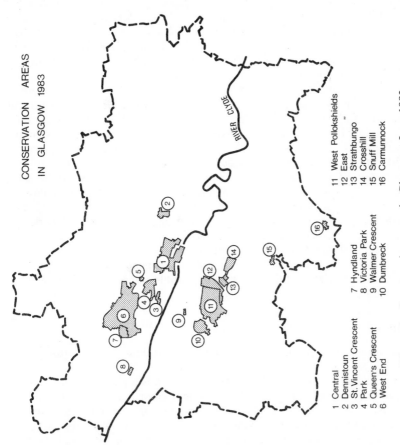

CONSERVATION AREAS
IN GLASGOW 1983

RIVER CLYDE

1 Central
2 Dennistoun
3 St. Vincent Crescent
4 Park
5 Queen's Crescent
6 West End

7 Hyndland
8 Victoria Park
9 Walmer Crescent
10 Dumbreck

11 West Pollokshields
12 East   "
13 Strathbungo
14 Crosshill
15 Snuff Mill
16 Carmunnock

Figure 8 Conservation areas in Glasgow, June 1983.

Walmer Crescent was built in the late 1850s to a design by Alexander 'Greek' Thomson. A single-storey commercial frontage on the busy thoroughfare of Paisley Road West occupies part of the original front gardens. Although the surrounding area is dominated by later Victorian tenements, designation was recommended because of the importance of Walmer Crescent as an early example of Thomson's work in which he achieved the impression of a continuous curve by subtle angling of individual frontages.

The three- and four-storey tenements of the St Vincent Crescent conservation area were built at the middle of the nineteenth century. Most of the properties in Minerva Street, Corunna Street and St Vincent Crescent have been declared listed buildings. The area remains predominantly residential although there is a modern office development at the south-western part of St Vincent Crescent. As a one-sided residential development the southern view from the houses in St Vincent Crescent is of some significance. Additionally access to the offices can only be effected from the east along St Vincent Crescent, thus inevitably increasing the loading of non-residential traffic in the area. Restoration work is in progress on several properties in St Vincent Crescent with housing associations as leading agents of rehabilitation. Equally several properties await restoration. In a functional sense the success of this conservation area will depend upon the control over sub-division of flats and the fostering of a stable owner-occupied residential community.

Suburban areas

Snuff Mill and the village of Carmunnock are unique, almost rural conservation areas.

In detail, each inner and intermediate suburb is a particular and distinct spatial outcome of build, development and environment but, to varying degrees, they share the problems of maintenance and repair, physical alteration, change of use, parking and through traffic. With the exception of the Park conservation area where the mid-Victorian terraces have been converted to offices and institutional uses, most suburbs remain in residential occupation.

In West Pollokshields and Dumbreck the policy is to maintain the residential character by controlling sub-division of, and extensions to, existing villas, the number, design and materials of new buildings and change of use.[59] For example, change of use will be refused unless the application refers to a recognised local public, social or education need within the area. The policy on extensions restricts the increase in floorspace to fifty percent, limits total site coverage to forty percent and prohibits protrusion beyond the front elevation of the existing building. Similarly, the principal objective of the strategy for the tenements in East Pollokshields and Hyndland is the preservation of the residential character of these areas through the control of physical alterations to the exterior of the buildings and the implementation of environmental measures relating to the maintenance of stonework and roofs, to greenery, to parking and the management of traffic.

The Victorian terraces and squares of the Strathbungo outstanding conservation area constitute a unique architectural townscape which retains detailed original features of properties and street furniture, e.g. iron work and lamp standards. Because construction spanned a period of seventy years there is a variation in style and detail but the potential heterogeneity is subsumed by the unifying force of the areal design of terraces and squares.

The Victorian and Edwardian district of Crosshill contains a mixture of villas, cottages, terraces and tenements. Victoria Road is an important district shopping centre and non-residential uses have invaded properties fronting onto Queen's Park. The villas and monumental terraces in the eastern and south eastern portions would seem to face the greatest dangers of alteration, demolition or invasion by other uses. The monumental terraces in Queen's Drive are listed buildings but preservation of the other properties at risk would be aided by the acquisition of an Article 4 direction.

Between 1860 and 1910 the Dennistoun area was developed by the architect James Salmon for Alexander Dennistoun. Originally intended as an area of large villas for wealthy merchants, the project was subsequently adjusted to incorporate several terraces. Part of the criteria for defining the conservation area was the contrast between the informal layout of the villas and the strict grid iron plan of the adjoining tenement district. Paradoxically, there is considerable rehabilitation in progress in the tenement area but little restorative activity in the conservation area. The latter has suffered from traffic using local streets as a route betwen two major thoroughfares and in order to discourage this practice narrowed and constricted sections have been constructed on the connecting thoroughfares.

The extensive Glasgow West outstanding conservation area encompasses several separate districts in terms of history and character. In Hillhead yellow sandstone tenements are dominant whereas Kelvinside and Dowanhill contain a mixture of terraces and villas. In many cases there is an urgent need for restorative work and rehabilitation and enhancement schemes have been completed on tenements in Hillhead and several Victorian terraces in Kelvinside, e.g. Great Western Terrace, Kirklee Terrace, Kew Terrace, Westbourne Gardens.

Specific conservation briefs have been prepared for Partickhill Road area, Westbourne Gardens and Kingsborough Gardens. The basic features of the policies are the encouragement of high standards of maintenance and the control of new developments including the sub-division of existing properties. However, there is a general policy towards the limitation of further sub-division and the promotion of regular maintenance within the conservation area as a whole.

In the 1970s contentious proposals were advanced for the widening of Great Western Road which involved the removal of lines of mature trees and which threatened the environmental quality of terraces and villas in the section westward of the Botanic Gardens. Fortunately, the plans were vigorously and effectively opposed by amenity groups such as the New Glasgow Society.

Institutional uses, such as the University of Glasgow, have generated pressures on space with demands for new or additional buildings and parking facilities and on property with the need for student accommodation. Associated services added further pressures, especially in the vicinity of the institutions. Collectively, these stresses caused considerable change in some parts of Glasgow West, both in terms of adaptation and construction.

Development in the Park area started around 1830 and finished almost fifty years later with the completion of the upper terraces on the crown of the hill. Parts of the area became the site of a cluster of medical consulting rooms and by the 1930s office and commercial uses occupied many of the terraced properties. In 1970 Park was designated a conservation area. The conservation policy recognised the attractions of the location for office uses and proposed the development of prestigious office accommodation within preserved Victorian terraced buildings. Strict controls were formulated with respect to car parking, the retention of gardens and open spaces and the preservation of the architectural and townscape character of the area. The policy has achieved a considerable measure of success, although some new office buildings were built and parking remains a thorny problem.

Central area

In 1965 about half of the total floorspace in the Central area was classed as obsolete[60] but it was estimated 'that of this obsolescence about two-thirds could be matched with replacement demand'.[61] The excess of supply over demand 'ensured the survival of so many old buildings, good and bad (except in the case of public housing where market factors do not operate)'.[62]

The Central area conservation area was designated in 1975 and in 1976 it was redesignated as the Central conservation area which included the Blythswood Square and Royal Exchange Square conservation areas. In 1979 an extension incorporated the area around St Andrew's Square. The present area embraces a wide range of architectural and historical heritage spanning the medieval to Edwardian eras. The limited remnants of medieval Glasgow are situated on the eastern periphery of the area in the vicinity of High Street and Glasgow Cross. During the eighteenth century the Merchant City emerged and several new streets were developed to the west of the High Street. Contemporaneously, a small development occurred at St Andrew's Square. From 1780 until 1830 there was a phase of rapid urban growth which progressively created the Georgian terraced streets between George Square and Blythswood Square. The business centre migrated westwards as commercial uses followed the dominant direction of urban expansion. Substantial numbers of plots in the city centre were redeveloped during the Victorian period, particularly in the zone bounded by Buchanan Street and Hope Street. Changes in building technology meant that new buildings were larger, higher, more massive and more flamboyant than the

Georgian terraced dwellings. Thus the city has inherited a striking contrast in architectural styles in different parts of the Central area.[63] A simple tripartite division on the basis of architectural form delineates an area of early nineteenth-century classical buildings in the vicinity of Blythswood Square, of mainly late eighteenth-century classical buildings around the axis of Ingram Street and an extensive intervening, largely commercial, Victorian zone.

Whitehand[64] examined the piecemeal redevelopment in central Glasgow, 1840–1969, and found that the rate which was consistently high throughout the Victorian and Edwardian periods plummeted in the inter-war era and only returned to about two-thirds of the peak by the late 1960s. In an exhaustive study of change in Central Glasgow, 1950–70, Sim[65] concluded that the highest rate of redevelopment had occurred in Victorian properties with very low rates in the high plot ratio Edwardian buildings. Plot ratios were an important instrument of post-war planning control. In most Georgian, Victorian and Edwardian buildings the ratios exceeded those permitted in new developments but Edwardian properties had the greatest concentration of very high ratios.[66] The continued imposition of controls over plot ratios and skyline has encouraged a commercial reappraisal of the merits of existing properties. At present there is a shift in the office sector in favour of retention and restoration rather than redevelopment. There are numerous examples of restored and refurbished properties in Georgian (e.g. Blythswood) and Victorian (e.g. St Vincent Street) areas. For example, the office refurbishment at Nos 6 and 7 Blythswood Square by the Mountleigh Group was forward funded by British Rail Pension Fund.[67]

The westward migration of the centre of business activity resulted in the Merchant City becoming a zone of discard with a haphazard mixture of institutional, commercial, industrial, and residential uses. Abandonment of the area in the 1970s by industrial, wholesale and warehouse uses left a number of empty buildings. Demolition created gap sites which have mainly been used for car parking. A major change involved the relocation of the fruit market from Candleriggs to Blochairn. After some indecision the old market building was refurbished and re-opened as a market for small traders. Conservation policy in this section of the Central area is aimed at the regeneration of the Merchant City and the retention of economic activity is a vital component of the strategy. Another strand relates to residential re-occupation of restored commercial buildings. A small pioneering venture at Albion Chambers involved the conversion of a redundant warehouse to residential use and every unit was sold before the completion of the project. Further schemes are in progress or under consideration involving empty warehouses in the Merchant City. Indeed, if there is sufficient demand the policy could be adopted in other parts of the central area, such as Broomielaw, where an excess of warehouse space exists.

There has been a considerable amount of redevelopment in the penumbra of the Central area. Hotels, offices, the Anderston Centre and the Ring Road dominate the new construction on the western flank. The northern periphery has also attracted redevelopment with a marked eastern concentration of education uses. The boundary of the conservation area excluded the site of former St Enoch Station and the adjoining eastern approaches and commercial redevelopment is finally in progress in that area.

Within the Central area parts of Buchanan Street, Gordon Street and Argyle Street are pedestrianised and there are widespread controls over street parking and extensive schemes of traffic management. The recent revival in the popularity of Sauchiehall Street as a shopping area, may, in part at least, be related to the fact that it is outside the Conservation area and possibly subject to slightly less stringent controls over redevelopment and alteration.

Finally, conservation should benefit from the determined attempts by the local authority to project a positive image of the city through the 'Glasgow's Miles Better' campaign. The attraction of tourists offers economic opportunities and the promotion of heritage and visual qualities of the city places a firm emphasis on preservation, restoration and regeneration.

DUNDEE

Dundee District Council control seven urban conservation areas (Figure 9). Designation of a further area, The Crescents, is pending. The local authority also has responsibility for four rural conservation areas (Murroes, Longforgan, The Knapp, Fowlis) but they are not of relevance for the present study.

At the dawn of the Georgian era Dundee was a small settlement focused upon the broad High Street (Marketgait) which was served by Nethergait and Overgait to the west and Murraygait and Seagait to the east.[68] Narrow wynds led from High Street to the harbour. The rapid development in the nineteenth century of the jute industry provided a major catalyst to industrial and residential growth. Industrial zones and tenement districts flanked the Scouring and Dens Burns. A western higher status suburban area developed around Perth Road and the opening of the Dundee-Arbroath railway led to the construction of an eastern outlier at West Ferry. Later northward spread encroached upon the slopes of the Law. In the present century substantial estates of local authority and Scottish Special Housing Association houses were built on the western periphery of the city and to the north of Kingsway. In the 1960s the emphasis switched to the clearance and development of areas of obsolescent housing in the inner city and industrial districts. One consequence was the construction of a number of blocks of multi-storey flats.

The central area experienced three major phases of development and redevelopment: Georgian, mid-Victorian and modern. Several new streets were constructed in the Georgian period including Reform Street which provided a northern point of access to Murraygait. Development connected with the 1871 Improvement Act included the widening of lower Commercial

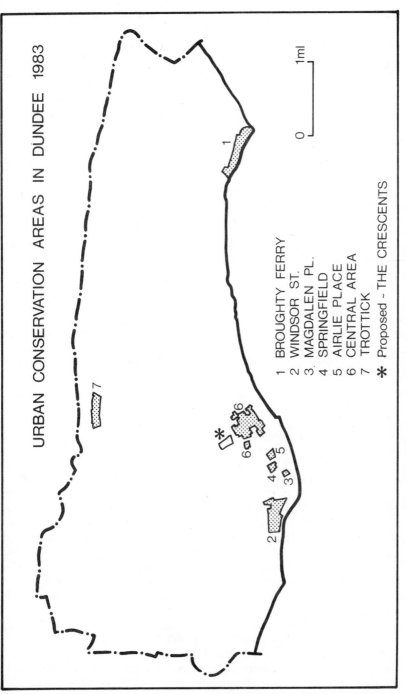

Figure 9 Urban conservation areas in Dundee, October 1983.

Street and the demolition of old properties to facilitate the construction of upper Commercial Street, Whitehall Street and Whitehall Crescent.[69] Prominent amongst the modern changes have been the development of the Overgate, Nethergate and Wellgate shopping centres, the building of the multi-storey office block for the Regional Council and road improvement schemes on the western, northern and southern margins of the central area.

The massive contraction of the jute industry resulted in a glut of empty factory premises. Some were converted to other commercial and industrial uses although the heavy floors and cast-iron pillars of the old mills presented technical problems. Most recently interest has been shown by housing associations and a private builder in the conversion of the buildings or sites to residential use.

It is surprising that efforts have not been made to preserve at least one mill as part of the industrial heritage of the city. The designation of Trottick conservation area was associated with the history of the textile industry for the area includes an old mill, millpond and a number of weavers' cottages. However, in the absence of the allocation of financial resources, little action has been taken to restore properties or even arrest decay. Indeed there is a general problem in terms of enhancement work in Dundee given the comparatively modest level of budgetary provision for that purpose. Nonetheless there have been significant successes such as the stone-cleaning in South Tay Street. Additionally the authority has sought maximum possible statutory powers by obtaining Article 4 directions for all conservation areas. The officials have pursued a policy of encouragement and persuasion in relation to development, alteration and restoration which has paid such dividends as the enhancement of Reform Street and the commencement of restoration at Springfield.

> Only five Georgian terraces exist in Dundee. . . . There was no enlightened and strong-minded landowners like the Heriot Trust in Edinburgh, or the Blythswood Campbells in Glasgow.[70]

These terraces constitute the cores of the Airlie Place and Springfield conservation areas and the eastern section of the Windsor Street conservation area. The modern design of the Students' Union detracts from the visual character of Airlie Place and many of the properties in Springfield require external restoration work. Both areas have been subject to invasion by the nearby educational institutions of the University of Dundee and Duncan of Jordanstone College. The veracity of Windsor Street has been impaired by the construction on the western side of the street of post-1950 housing. Part of the section of Perth Road within this conservation area contains a varied mixture of properties in terms of age and style and there have been some conversions to commercial uses such as hotels, clubs and bed-and-breakfast establishments.

The small enclave of villas at Magdalen Place retain a peaceful secluded setting although most properties are in need of maintenance to stonework and boundary features. By comparison the villas at the serpent-shaped The

Figure 10 Restoration and rehabilitation of residential property, Fisher Street, Broughty Ferry. *Source*: Dundee District Council.

Figure 11   Restoration, Reform Street, Dundee. *Source*: Dundee District Council.

Crescents proposed conservation area are in a comparatively good state of repair. However, the area does suffer from the demands of street parking generated by the neighbouring college and hospital. The problem is exacerbated by the proximity to the tightly controlled central/parking zone.

There has been some restoration of buildings in Broughty Ferry (Figure 10) but the prime objectives of the conservation policy are the control of development and alterations and the preservation of the character of the area. The varied townscapes of the former fisher village, the classical terrace at James Place[71] and the Victorian villas married to the social history of the area constitute the ingredients of that character.

The outstanding Central conservation area contains many listed buildings in substantial tracts of Georgian and Victorian townscapes. The pedestrianised Murraygate and adjacent Wellgate Centre represent the core of the shopping area although the Overgate Centre and Reform Street are also very popular. By contrast, the Nethergate Centre appears to be an example of supply outpacing demand.

Mention was made earlier of the enhancement of properties in Reform Street. (Figure 11) It might be possible to foster similar attitudes in upper Commercial Street, Whitehall Street, Whitehall Crescent and Union Street where listed buildings predominate.

Not surprisingly consideration is being given to the designation of further conservation areas around the high-status axis of Perth Road. Traffic volumes along that thoroughfare have reduced significantly with the diversion of the primary flow onto the riverside approach road.

ABERDEEN

With the development of North Sea oil Aberdeen has enjoyed substantial economic growth and experienced powerful developmental pressures in relation to commerce, industry and particular sectors of the private housing market. However, in 1968, the local authority had designated six conservation areas. Subsequently there have been extensions and additions and the District Council now has ten conservation areas (Figure 12), although one, Cove Bay, involves a separate village to the south of the city. The early initiation and sustained development of a conservation policy allowed the authority to control the impact of redevelopment on the historic areas of the city. The stated aims of the policy are: to ensure the preservation of listed buildings and control minor developments; to ensure the retention or replacement of trees; to preserve and enhance the conservation areas by creative planning; to achieve a high standard of environment; to require proposals for new developments to conform with the character of the area in regard to scale, height, materials used and general appearance of buildings; to encourage and assist the formation of associations or bodies willing to undertake co-ordinated improvements of streets or areas; and to awaken and sustain the interest of citizens in their heritage.[72]

Aberdeen grew around the twin foci of the harbour at the mouth of the Dee and the medieval burgh of Old Aberdeen. The latter contained the

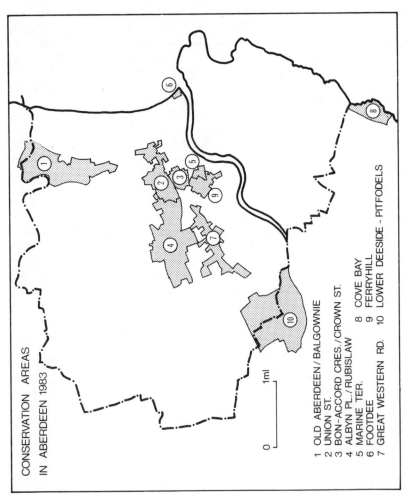

Figure 12   Conservation areas in Aberdeen, October 1983.

cathedral, market and university. However, after the development of Union Street and the ensuing phases of Georgian and Victorian urban expansion, Old Aberdeen became the more static of the early nuclei.[73] The terraces and squares on and behind Union Street stimulated a migration of wealthy citizens from the old town and initiated a prolonged phase of westward sectoral growth.[74] Ultimately the residential areas encompassed Rubislaw Quarry, the prime source of the distinctive local building stone.

This western sector accounts for six of the conservation areas. The Bon Accord Crescent, Marine Terrace and Ferryhill areas are located to the south of Union Street. Bon Accord Crescent, Square and Terrace and Marine Terrace are examples of the prodigious output of the architect Archibald Simpson (1790–1847).[75] Marine Terrace is still a residential area but the properties in Bon Accord Crescent and Square have been converted to office and other commercial uses. Pressure upon parking space has led to the adaptation of former rear gardens into car parks for office staff. In spite of the demand for extra parking space it is essential that the garden in the centre of Bon Accord Square is retained since it is an integral component of the areal design.

Most buildings in the Bon Accord Crescent–Crown Street conservation area are two-storey granite terraces. Attics are a ubiquitous feature but, with the exception of one section of Springbank Terrace, front gardens are absent. Several properties are used as hotels or guest houses and there has been sub-division of dwellings. Proximity to the city centre is a causal factor promoting change of use and generating substantial traffic flows along several streets.

The adjoining small Marine Terrace conservation area remains over-whelmingly residential in character. There has been a substantial amount of alteration to the rear gardens of properties on the north side of Ferryhill Place, primarily associated with the creation of parking space. Obviously it has been decided to permit such alterations in order to preserve the frontal views of the properties because conservation controls include the vetting of sundry works such as the removal of boundary walls and the altered use of garden space.

Ferryhill conservation area encompasses a variety of styles and types of building ranging from a pinkish three-story tenement at the corner of Caledonian Place to some large detached houses in Fonthill Road. In the case of Ferryhill designation may have been primarily intended as a defensive tactic. One noticeable sign of change in the area is the fact that several semi-detached villas are used as guest houses.

The Union Street conservation area encompasses most of the central area, a fact which has profoundly influenced the development of the functional structure of the area. The overwhelming majority of ground floor frontages are devoted to commercial uses and many plots have been redeveloped. Nonetheless, a large proportion of the upper floors remain unaltered. Indeed several sections have been enhanced by recent stone-cleaning enterprises, and some upper floor properties have been developed as speculations in the refurbished office market. Upgrading of buildings has also occurred in Golden Square although the replacement of the central garden by a large parking lot is most regrettable. Plans were prepared for the reclamation of Golden Square[76] which involved a recommended reduction in parking provision to a maximum of forty spaces but the plans were not implemented.

It is noteworthy that every sign advertising new or redeveloped office space in and around the central area lists as a major feature the number of parking spaces incorporated in the development. Whilst this policy should restrict any increase in demand for street parking by the office sector it will have little effect on the present volume of demand. Moreover, a proportion of that demand is, in any case, associated with shopping trips.

The heart of the shopping area is situated in the portion of Union Street between the viaduct over the railway and St Nicholas Street. The latter is the site of Marks and Spencer and the St Nicholas Centre but the other leading variety and chain stores are located in Union Street. Most stores occupy modern buildings although the adaptation of the distinctive nineteenth-century Trinity Hall by a leading retail company is an interesting example of the marriage of development with conservation. Just beyond the boundaries of the conservation area office development is occurring at Guild Street and Union Row and conversion of residences to offices at Waverley Place and Victoria Street. Another interesting development within the conservation area is a small residential speculation involving a block of refurbished flats on the west side of Bon Accord Terrace.

Shopping redevelopment in St Nicholas Street was confronted with the presence of an important historic building, Wallace Tower, a Z plan tower house. The dilemma was resolved by demolishing the Tower and rebuilding it in Seaton Park in the Old Aberdeen conservation area. Whilst purists might criticise the decision, and the Scottish Civic Trust opposed the shopping development, it did at least ensure the preservation of the building.[77]

Office development has spread into the eastern parts of the Albyn Place–Rubislaw conservation area. The substantial terraced properties in Albyn Place, Rubislaw Terrace and Queen's Terrace were readily adapted into offices and the situation combined the qualities of a prestigious address with a considerable measure of centrality. However, the majority of the conservation area has remained an important high status residential district with terraces giving way to some of the largest villas in Aberdeen in the Rubislaw Den neighbourhood.[78]

Great Western Road conservation area includes some 1930s granite bungalows. There are heavy flows of traffic along Anderson Drive and Great Western Road and there has been some change of use in Great Western Road from residences to hotels and guest houses. One test of success for conservation policy in this sort of area will be control of extensions to, and alterations of, dwelling houses.

Pitfodels and Footdee are completely contrasting residential conservation areas. The wooded Pitfodels is a large area but contains few residential units being mainly given over to institutions, allotments and farms.[79] Royle assumed that designation was defensive, aimed at preventing residential growth.[80] However, some executive houses have been built near Inchgarth.

At the beginning of the nineteenth century a small development of single-storey cottages was erected at Footdee. Subsequently a second storey was added to many houses. Improvements were made to the houses in the 1960s and the area was one of the six original conservation areas in the city. Footdee continues to flourish as a vigorous community despite the juxta-position to the busy harbour. There have been transgressions of the official policy on window replacements, much to the annoyance of architectural purists, but provided it does not spell the collapse of controls the departures from approved policy need not seriously detract from the character of the area.

The longitudinal Old Aberdeen outstanding conservation area extends from Brig o' Balgownie in the north to Spittal at the southern extremity. St Machars' Cathedral dominates the Chanonry district and commands northern vistas across Seaton Park and the Don valley.

Nowadays the University is the largest landowner in Old Aberdeen and it has played a crucial role in terms of the erection of new teaching accom-modation and halls of residences and the conservation of old buildings. A notable example of the latter was the restoration of small vernacular eighteenth-century houses in Wrights' and Coopers' Place. The University has endeavoured to harmonise and integrate new developments into the historic townscape and morphology of the old burgh and to minimise the amount of alteration involving properties flanking the central axis of The Chanonry, High Street and College Bounds.

Royle[81] concluded that the local authority had pursued successful and positive conservation in spite of the contemporaneous industrial and commercial expansion of the city. Nonetheless signs of stresses and strains are increasingly evident in the central historic areas. At present the tensions are not excessive but further industrial growth would inexorably add to the pressures for change in the shopping and administrative districts, thereby threatening particular buildings and townscapes. Unlike the situation in Glasgow or Dundee, in Aberdeen there is a paucity of centrally-situated empty sites which could be used to act as a safety valve by deflecting demand away from the conservation areas.

CONCLUSION

The foregoing discussion has highlighted the conservation policies of the Scottish cities and examined the problems in specific areas of each city. Common strands are identifiable such as the problems of the management of change and of parking and the organisation and funding of enhancement and restoration. Nonetheless differences resulting from the distinct contextual framework of each city complicate comparative analysis. The localised resolution of the set of influencing factors means that transference of successful policies to other situations requires cautious evaluation.

Additional divergence originates in inter-city differences in the perception of areas worthy of designation and in policy and budgetary priorities.

Conservation policy must strike a delicate balance between the control of development and excessive restriction, between preservation and fossilisation. Inevitably there will be specific issues which cannot be resolved by compromise and which generate heated debate. The various inner ring road proposals for Edinburgh are an example of the generation of heated debate. Similarly the route of the proposed eastern flank of the inner ring road in Glasgow was opposed by amenity groups because of the threat which it posed for the remaining elements of the medieval burgh.

A matter of major importance concerns the approval of intrusive or massive developments. Occasionally reprieve has come at the eleventh hour as in the case of the planned, high rise office development near Haymarket in Edinburgh which would have caused a serious visual intrusion into the prevailing skyline of the Georgian West End. Cancellation of planning approval involved payment of compensation. Controversial massive or intrusive buildings have been constructed during the past twenty years such as St James Centre[82] in Edinburgh and St Nicholas House in Aberdeen.[83] In neither case could the new uses have been accommodated by restoration of the existing buildings but on many occasions that is a feasible solution. The provision of grants would probably encourage that course of action but there is scope for proselytising work of conservation bodies to persuade developers of the case for restoration. The increasing recognition that restoration can produce economic, aesthetic and perceptual benefits for the individual and the community is a testimony to the successful dissemination of advice and information by planners, architects, and amenity groups. There has been a measurable shift in philosophy in the past twenty years in relation to the value, potential and usefulness of old buildings. In central areas controls over plot ratios for new developments contributed to the shift in opinion but that factor does not explain the revival of interest in maintaining older residential properties. In part the latter stemmed from a change in planning policy in favour of rehabilitation rather than redevelopment but in certain areas of the cities it also reflected the existence of consumer demand for the style, structure, character and location of older houses and areas.

Whilst a high level of faithfulness is essential in the restoration of unique properties or in areas with negligible alteration of even the minutest detail lesser standards of accuracy, without loss of quality of workmanship or materials, could be applied in more heterogeneous areas. At the areal scale it may be necessary to consider operating a tiered system of controls on similar lines to those outlined above with stringent measures applying to particular sections or buildings and a slightly relaxed set of criteria for a secondary category of properties. However, such a policy would require careful articulation and implementation and it raises the spectres of neglect, stigmatisation and abuse.

There is a need to develop systems for monitoring and evaluating the effectiveness of conservation policies with the measurement of gains and the computation of costs and negative side effects. For example, in every Scottish city there is a significant concentration of new development at sites adjacent to the central conservation area. However, traffic-related pressures may continue to affect the central area and, additionally, the spatial concentration of new developments can cause subsidiary traffic and parking problems in adjoining areas previously free from such difficulties.

Ideally, conservation should be an integral part of an integrated planning policy dealing with buildings, uses, communities, environmental quality and the quality of life and applicable at various temporal and spatial scales. Much has been achieved in the field of conservation planning within a comparatively short period of time and there could be further significant conceptual, technical and practical advances in the future in the management and conservation of historic areas of the Scottish cities.

ACKNOWLEDGEMENTS

The author is indebted to officials of the Cockburn Association, the Edinburgh New Town Conservation Committee, the Scottish Civic Trust and the District Councils of Aberdeen, Dundee, Edinburgh and Glasgow for information about conservation areas and restoration projects. Particular thanks are due to Mr O Barratt, Mr J Gerard, Mr J Gillon, Mr N Grieve, Mr R Henderson, Mr D MacDougall, Mrs S McGowan, Mr D Martin and Mr J Souter.

REFERENCES

1   P Ward (ed) *Conservation and Development* (Newcastle 1968), p 15
2   K Smigielski quoted in introduction to P Ward (ed), *op. cit.*
3   A J Youngson 'Britain's Historic Towns' in P Ward (ed), *op. cit.* p 3
4   A J Youngson *op. cit.* p 4
5   T R Slater Conservation and planning in historic towns: theory and practice in Stratford-upon-Avon. *Historical Geography Research Group, Anglo-German Conference* (1982a)
6   B Von Der Dollen 'City Planning: Conservation and Urban Historical Geography in Germany', *Planning History Bulletin* 5, 3 (1983), p 39
7   A Bygrave *Conservation in Practice.* Unpublished thesis Urban and Regional Planning, University of Strathclyde, 1982, pp 10–14
8   G Bruce *Some Practical Good* (Edinburgh 1975), p 8
9   Bruce *op. cit.* p 8
10 C Wilson 'Planning in a historic city', *The Planner* (February 1983), p 60
11 Wilson *op. cit.* p 60
12 D Sim *Change in the City Centre* (Aldershot 1982)
13 Wilson *op. cit.* p 61
14 Edinburgh New Town Conservation Committee *Annual Report* (Edinburgh 1983)
15 Wilson *op. cit.* p 61
16 Edinburgh New Town Conservation Committee *op. cit.*

17   J Stewart 'Conservation—A Plea for a Rational Approach', *Planning Outlook* 15 (1974), pp 35–47
18   D Eversley 'Conservation for the Minority', *Built Environment* (January 1974), pp 14–15
19   R Pahl 'Social Aspects of Conservation', *Architects Review* (December 1970), p 369
20   T R Slater 'Preservation, Conservation and Planning in Historic Towns. *Department of Geography, University of Birmingham, Working Paper Series* no 17 (1982b), p 1
21   Slater *op. cit.* (1982b), p 1
22   Slater *op. cit.* (1982b), p 14
23   R Worskett *The Character of Towns* (London 1969)
24   Bygrave *op. cit.* p 110
25   E Sillar *Edinburgh's Child* (Edinburgh 1979), pp 1–2
26   R Q Gray *The Labour Aristocracy in Victorian Edinburgh* (Oxford 1976), p 17
27   D Hodges 'The Conservation of Edinburgh's Georgian New Town', *Building Technology and Management* (February 1982), p 9
28   R Matthew 'The State of the Fabric' in Scottish Civic Trust, *The Conservation of Georgian Edinburgh* (Edinburgh 1972), pp 40–61
29   Edinburgh District Council *Planning Report* (Edinburgh 1977), p 60
30   The Grange Association *The Grange: A Case for Conservation* (Edinburgh 1982)
31   H R Hitchcock quoted in p 3 of D Hodges (*et al*) *The Care and Conservation of Georgian Houses* (Edinburgh 1978)
32   A J Youngson *The Making of Classical Edinburgh* (Edinburgh 1966)
33   J Betjeman 'The Stones of Edinburgh' in Scottish Civic Trust *op. cit.* p 32
34   C Buchanan (*et al*), *Edinburgh: The Recommended Plan* (Edinburgh 1972)
35   The Cockburn Association *Newsletter* no 26 (1983), pp 30–1; personal discussion with Secretary of Cockburn Association
36   G Gordon 'The status areas of early to mid-Victorian Edinburgh', *Trans. Inst. Brit. Geog.* (new series) (1979) 4, 2, pp 168–91
37   P Abercrombie and D Plumstead *A Civic Survey and Plan for Edinburgh* (Edinburgh 1949) p 65
38   Edinburgh District Council *Planning Policies for the First New Town* (Edinburgh 1982), p 3
39   J Fernie 'Office activity in Edinburgh', *Ekistics* (January 1979), pp 25–32
40   Buchanan *op. cit.*
41   Edinburgh New Town Conservation Committee *Annual Report 1982–83*
42   *Ibid.*
43   Hodges (*et al*) *op. cit. The Care and Conservation of Georgian Houses*
44   Edinburgh District Council *Planning Policies for the First New Town op. cit.*
45   Edinburgh District Council *Conserving Edinburgh's Old Town* (Edinburgh 1982)
46   *Ibid.* p 2
47   H D Littlejohn *Report on the Sanitary Conditions of Edinburgh* (Edinburgh 1865)
48   Edinburgh District Council *South Side Local Plan* (Edinburgh 1982)
49   *Ibid.* p 3
50   Grange Association *op. cit.*
51   *Ibid.* p 8
52   Cockburn Association, *op. cit.* p 42

53 Grange Association *op. cit.* pp 62–5
54 C A Oakley *Second City* (Glasgow 1947)
55 A Gibb *Glasgow—The Making of a City* (London 1983) pp 147–85
56 Lord Esher *Conservation in Glasgow* (Glasgow 1971) Introd.
57 *Ibid.* p 25
58 *Ibid.* p 26
59 Glasgow District Council Planning Committee 21 February 1977
60 G Eve *Central Area Report* (Glasgow 1965)
61 Esher *op. cit.* p 13
62 *Ibid.* pp 13–14
63 A Gomme and D Walker *Architecture of Glasgow* (London 1968)
64 J W R Whitehand 'Long-Term Changes in the Form of the City Centre: The Case of Redevelopment', *Geog Annaler* 60B, 2 (1978), p 86
65 Sim *op. cit.* p 105–7
66 *Ibid.* p 105
67 *Glasgow Herald* 16 November 1983
68 S Jones Historical Geography of Dundee in S Jones (ed) *Dundee and District* (Dundee 1968), p 268
69 *Ibid.* p 276
70 D M Walker 'The Architecture of Dundee' in S Jones (ed) *op. cit.* p 286
71 *Ibid.* p 288
72 Aberdeen District Council, *Conservation Areas—Aberdeen* (Aberdeen 1982) quotes policies approved by District Council in 1977
73 R Jones 'The Growth and Development of Aberdeen' in C M Clapperton (ed) *North East Scotland Geographical Essays* (Aberdeen 1972), pp 34–8; I H Adams *The Making of Urban Scotland* (London 1978), p 79; G Gordon 'Urban Scotland' in K J Lea (ed) *A Geography of Scotland* (Newton Abbot 1977), p 214
74 R Jones *op. cit.* pp 36–7
75 C Graham *Portrait of Aberdeen and Deeside* (London 1972), p 33
76 Corporation of City of Aberdeen, *A study in the reclamation of a civic square* (Aberdeen 1972)
77 S A Royle, 'Conservation in Aberdeen', *The Planner* (April 1982), p 48
78 J Souter 'Conservation Area Contrasts', *Aberdeen's Own* (1983), p 30
79 Royle *op. cit.* p 48
80 *Ibid.* p 48
81 *Ibid.* p 49
82 Bruce *op. cit.* p 51
83 Royle *op. cit.* p 49

10

RENEWAL, REDEVELOPMENT AND
REHABILITATION IN SCOTTISH CITIES 1945–1981

M Pacione

All major cities of the United Kingdom have experienced a number of common development trends during the post-war era. In terms of population and housing this has generally meant a centrifugal movement from the inner cities to peripheral estates, leaving behind a residue of older and less mobile residents and a decaying housing stock often intermixed with declining industrial and commercial land uses. The area of vacant land and levels of unemployment have also grown. A key development of the post-war era was the increasing municipal involvement in housing provision. This has been accompanied by a sharp decline in the private-rented sector. In the immediate post-war period the planning response to the overcrowding and housing shortages centred upon wholesale slum clearance and comprehensive redevelopment, followed in many cities during the 1950s and 1960s by high-rise building. Concern over the effectiveness of the physical planning machine to achieve socially-sensitive solutions, and the alienation of people from the planning process culminated in a review of planning policy and practice in the mid 1960s, and by the early 1970s, greater attention was given to the rehabilitation of urban neighbourhoods. As a direct result of earlier post-war policies however British cities have, since the 1970s, faced the major problems of excessive loss of population and enterprise from the inner areas, the decaying physical, social and economic condition of these residual areas, and the social and economic problems which have emerged in the peripheral housing areas built to receive the surplus population created by renewal.

These national trends are clearly represented in the four main Scottish cities of Glasgow, Edinburgh, Aberdeen and Dundee (Table 1) but, to differing degrees, each also exhibits a unique problem or particular emphasis which demands attention. This chapter provides a detailed discussion of the general developments in post-war Scottish housing strategy taking Glasgow as a frame of reference, and then considers the local variations on these general themes represented in the other cities.

GLASGOW

Housing in post-war Glasgow continued to reflect the legacy of the past when rapid city growth in the nineteenth century and a shortage of suitable building land created an intense form of urbanism (Pacione 1979). In the mid 1960s 85 per cent of dwellings were soot-stained tenements. Those classic nineteenth-century four-storey structures, with a doorless entry from

RENEWAL, REDEVELOPMENT AND REHABILITATION

Table 1

Population and Housing Characteristics in the Four Scottish Cities, 1961–81

	1961	Population 1971	Population 1981	% Change 1961–71	% Change 1971–81	% Population of pensionable age
GLASGOW	1,140,078	982,315	765,915	− 13.8	− 22.0	18.7
EDINBURGH	483,854	476,531	436,936	− 1.5	− 8.3	19.6
ABERDEEN	206,319	211,848	203,927	+ 2.7	− 3.7	18.0
DUNDEE	195,258	197,371	179,674	+ 1.1	− 9.0	18.3
SCOTLAND	5,179,344	5,228,963	5,130,735	+ 1.0	− 1.9	16.8

Housing 1981

	Households	% Owner occupied	% Council owned	% Private rented	% With over 1 ppr	% Lacking or sharing bath
GLASGOW	273,582	24.9	62.9	12.1	19.9	4.6
EDINBURGH	164,692	52.7	33.0	14.3	10.6	4.0
ABERDEEN	75,076	36.4	52.7	10.9	12.9	4.0
DUNDEE	67,352	26.6	61.7	11.8	13.8	4.3
SCOTLAND	1,785,936	34.7	54.6	10.7	14.1	2.6

the street and common stone staircase, dominated the housing stock. The tenure pattern had changed since 1914, reflecting the growth of public intervention in housing provision; in 1965 private landlords owned 38 per cent of houses, owner occupiers 19 per cent, and the Corporation 43 per cent (Cullingworth 1968). The amount of private house building since 1945 has been negligible; Miller (1970) estimated that only 75 houses per year had been built for sale. Until recently the Corporation's insistence that it retains building sites for subsidised housing had driven private contractors outside the city boundaries. Since 1977 vacant inner city sites and land within the peripheral council estates have been offered to private builders but the scale of development remains low. In 1980, for example, a total of 887 new private houses were completed in the city. The amount of land currently available indicates a potential for only another 6,500 at an average development density of 25 dwellings/hectare unless land is released by other agencies such as the Scottish Special Housing Association (SSHA).

In the post-war period policy disputes between central and local government began over the recommendations in the Clyde Valley Plan of 1946 (Abercrombie and Matthew 1949). Its essence was that in the interests of the city and the region as a whole there should be a planned decentralisation of both population and industry from Glasgow. The report also expressed concern about the tendency towards urban sprawl and recommended that a green belt policy should be adopted to limit urban growth and to preserve agricultural land and recreational space. The Scottish Office accepted the report's recommendation that a substantial proportion of Glasgow's population should be transferred to New Towns and that overspill agreements should be concluded with existing towns. The Corporation of Glasgow disagreed strongly, and argued against any loss of land within the city's boundaries for the proposed green belt. In 1947 the Secretary of State designated East Kilbride a New Town site, and prevented the Corporation from building on a large section of land at Castlemilk, less than five miles from the New Town. East Kilbride was in easy commuting distance of Glasgow and clearly represented a new and rival source of jobs and houses.

Faced with a desperate post-war need for housing, estimated in the early 1950s between 80,000 and 90,000 families, the Corporation responded by planning and by building large housing estates on green field sites around the perimeter of the city with higher densities than previously considered acceptable for such projects. Some of the schemes still contained a significant proportion of cottages, as in the inter-war estates (such as Knightswood), but the trend was to rows of three- and four-storey walk-up flats. Peripheral largely working-class dormitory suburbs such as Drumchapel (8,660 houses), Easterhouse (8,720), Castlemilk (8,902), Pollok and Priesthill (8,600) were founded and absorbed approximately 10 per cent of Glasgow's population (Figure 1). In spite of the experience in Blackhill, where 980 low cost houses were built in the 1930s, there was minimal provision of amenities and community facilities. Preoccupied with the construction of houses, the Corporation was ill-organised to provide shops and entertainment; private enterprise was generally dubious about

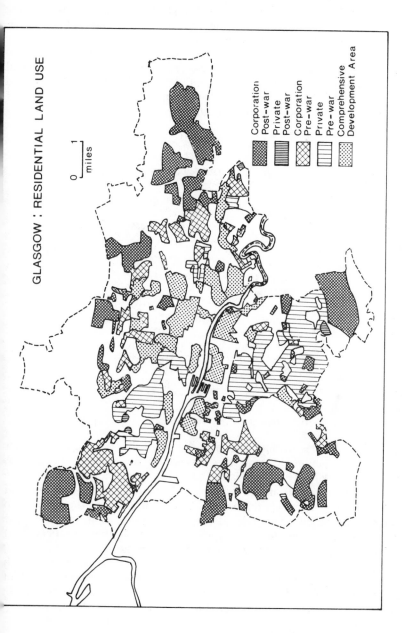

Figure 1 Housing areas in Glasgow by tenure and age.

participating in the schemes on economic grounds; and there was a long standing Corporation resolution dating from 1890 that public houses should not be provided on Corporation property. Not until 1971 with the development of Easterhouse Township Centre were these difficulties overcome. Today in many post-war estates, distant from the traditional centre of Glasgow life, the resurgence of social problems and the demand for housing transfers (Table 2) are strong reminders that the provision of houses is not sufficient to create a humane environment.

Table 2

Requests for Transfers out of
Council Housing Areas in Glasgow, 1977

Area	Total no. of houses	No. of transfer requests to other areas	Transfer requests as % of total households
Anniesland	16,171	784	4.84
Bardowie Street	15,093	2245	14.87
Castlemilk	9735	2754	28.28
City centre	11,804	1241	10.51
Drumchapel	10,339	3361	32.50
Easterhouse	15,040	4731	31.45
Gallowgate	12,700	1602	12.61
Mid-east	11,075	1421	12.83
North-east	16,685	3183	19.07
Pollok	11,595	3542	30.54
South	12,633	877	6.94
South-west	14,279	662	4.63

Source: Glasgow District Council (1978)

In the 1950s the dispute between the Scottish Office and Glasgow Corporation ameliorated, and the concept of an overspill policy was accepted by the city. The Corporation agreed to operate a voluntary scheme that would allow people and firms to leave Glasgow. The out-movement of industry was not positively advocated by the Corporation, the decision to relocate being based on individual firms' judgement of their needs. The Corporation did undertake to buy the land and buildings of firms that wanted to relocate under the scheme. The Corporation estimated in 1960 that approximately 200,000 people would move from Glasgow by 1980 with the probability of more later. The figure was challenged with the argument that between 400,000 and 500,000 people would have to be rehoused outside Glasgow in new or expanded towns (Forbes and MacBain 1967).

The overspill policy

The redistribution of economic activity within metropolitan areas and in particular the increase in manufacturing activity on the periphery at the expense of the inner city has been noted in several cities, especially ones that grew rapidly in the nineteenth century and early twentieth century. This tendency for firms to move out from the inner city areas has frequently been used as an argument for planning objectives to decrease urban congestion. In Glasgow, with its surfeit of old dilapidated industrial and commercial properties, industrial overspill has been considered an essential policy because it is not enough to provide houses in the reception areas. Jobs must be made available for the people who move to them (Farmer and Smith 1975). In 1959 the Corporation considered that many of these jobs could be provided by Glasgow firms, either by complete relocation or by the establishment of offices and factory extensions in the reception areas. A basic assumption behind the overspill policy was that there would be a sufficient volume of industry both able and willing to move out of Glasgow to the designated reception areas, although neither the Clyde Valley Regional Plan (1946) nor Glasgow Corporation (1959) had actual figures. Henderson (1974), based on a study of manufacturing establishments which moved from Glasgow over the period 1958–68, found that at the time of moving the firms employed a total of 5,486 people (3,744 males). Subsequent closures and rationalisation reduced the employment loss to the city to 4,978 jobs (3,142 males). It is doubtful whether the relocation of 107 manufacturing plants in eleven years reflects the anticipated scale of movement. Furthermore the majority of establishments deciding to relocate preferred to remain in Glasgow. Between 1958 and 1968, 79.5 per cent of all transfers that originated in the city remained within the urban area, defined to include places adjacent to the city that are an integral part of its labour market. Even if places such as Barrhead, Johnstone and Linwood are excluded, only 12.8 per cent of all transfers originating in the city actually moved from the city's travel to work area. Over the period, closures accounted for almost four times (79.6 per cent) as many firms lost to the city as did outmigration (20.4 per cent). The volume of industry that would be prepared to leave the city seems, in retrospect, to have been overestimated. A second assumption also proved by subsequent events to have been overstated was that redevelopment would act as a major stimulus to outmigration. Although redevelopment caused 27.8 per cent of the moves it was not the principal push factor, being overshadowed by the firms' need to expand. In addition only 18.1 per cent (27 firms) of all moves originating in the city as a direct result of redevelopment had destinations outside Glasgow, which suggests that the greatest demand was for alternative premises within the city. Furthermore, although the comprehensive development areas were expected to be major contributors to overspill, establishments located in these areas showed no greater desire to move out of the city than firms from other parts of Glasgow. Finally there was no evidence to support assertions that redevelopment, by forcing some firms to move, disrupted them so severely that they were subsequently forced to close. None of the 26 concerns which moved from eight comprehensive development areas had closed by the end of 1968, whereas 12.1 per cent of all transfers from the city had closed by this date. A third assumption was that Glasgow would benefit from the industrial overspill policy because the creation of employment opportunities in the reception areas would entice Glaswegians from the city and thereby would increase the rate of urban renewal. In practice firms seem to have transferred their skilled rather than semi-skilled or unskilled workers, and the skilled: unskilled ratios of 2.9:1 in Glasgow and 14.6:1 in East Kilbride indicate a gross imbalance in favour of the New Town. The overspill policy contributed to the depletion of Glasgow's skilled labour force, and as Cameron and Johnson (1969) have stated 'the objective of any policy which causes the dilution òf the skilled content of the Glasgow labour force without compensatory programmes of skill creation must be seriously questioned'. The empirical evidence suggests that many of the assumptions underlying the industrial overspill policy are open to question, because despite a number of theoretical attractions the policy has not worked effectively in practice. The policy incorporated a potential conflict between the physical and economic planning needs of the city. As Henderson (1974) observed a policy of encouraging industrial over-spill to pursue physical planning objectives may conflict with the need to create new employment opportunities in order to reduce the continually high levels of unemployment in the city itself. It was assumed that popula-tion overspill would decrease the supply of labour in the city and enable Glasgow to export industry, but despite the loss of 160,000 people between 1961 and 1971, unemployment rates remained above the Scottish average (Table 3).

Table 3

Comparative Rates of Unemployment, 1973

| | Unemployment rates (Jan. 1973) | | |
	Male	Female	Total
Glasgow	11.4	3.0	8.0
Scotland	7.8	3.4	6.1
GB	4.6	1.6	3.5

The population encouraged to leave Glasgow was directed to New Towns developed on the few remaining buildable sites in the area, and to existing towns with which agreements had been concluded under the Town Develop-ment Act 1952. The authors of the Clyde Valley Plan thought that the New Towns should be near Glasgow if decentralisation of population and industry was to be popular. In this they were probably affected by the criticism levelled at the first garden city, Letchworth, which at 35 miles from London was said to be too distant to attract industry from the capital. In the event, the planners could find only three sites that were large enough to accommodate a self-contained town of 50,000, and where physical separation from the existing conurbation could be maintained. These were at East Kilbride, Cumbernauld and Bishopton. Only the first two were selected, and East Kilbride was designated to serve as an outlet for the surplus population of the Clyde Valley. In one sense this objective has been fulfilled. In March 1963, 57 per cent of all tenants had been drawn from the city of Glasgow and 34 per cent from other centres in the county of Lanark. The estimated population was then 36,500 or 73 per cent of the original projection of 50,000. In another sense, however, East Kilbride has not fulfilled its intended function. Its construction has had little effect on the population pressures of Greater Glasgow, and the New Town has not provided an escape for the families most urgently in need of new housing. At first the housing allocation policy in East Kilbride gave preference to the employees of its industries, but they were not necessarily the Glaswegians who were homeless or living in overcrowded or sub-standard dwellings. This policy was relaxed in 1959. In order to speed the movement of population from the redevelopment areas in the city, the East Kilbride Development Corporation agreed to allocate houses to people from Glasgow irrespective of employment in the New Town. The proximity of Glasgow, however, makes commuting to work in the New Town easy and as early as 1959 it was estimated that 50 per cent of the labour force lived outside East Kilbride. The comparatively high rents and rates meant that some people found it cheaper to travel to work from south and east Glasgow rather than move to East Kilbride. There has also been very little relocation of industry from Glasgow to East Kilbride. The major industries have been drawn from further afield, a major attraction being the town's location in a development area. East Kilbride has become more of an industrial growth point in an economically depressed area than an instrument for the redevelopment of Glasgow (Smith 1967).

A second New Town, Cumbernauld, was designated in 1956 as a result of the continuing urgency of Glasgow's housing problems. The city's needs in 1955 were no less than they were ten years earlier despite the construction of 40,000 new dwellings. The immediate need for houses for homeless families, for new families and for occupants of condemned properties was estimated at 100,000 units. That figure included no allowance for the population that would be displaced by the plans to redevelop the congested inner quarters of the city. In an attempt to avoid repetition of the indecisive outcome of East Kilbride's housing allocation mechanism it was decided from the outset that at least 80 per cent of Cumbernauld's houses would go to Glasgow residents approved by the city corporation as persons in need of accommodation. In most other respects, however, the progress of Cumbernauld has been similar to its predecessor; the initial target population of 50,000 was later raised to 70,000. Commuting meant that the ideal of a self-contained town physically and economically distinct from the conurbation has only partly been realised and there has been almost no industrial relocation from Glasgow. Another New Town not formally envisaged as part of the overspill policy became linked with Glasgow's housing problem. Under the terms of the Housing and Town Development (Scotland) Act 1957 new financial incentives were offered to towns willing to accept migrants from Glasgow. The Glenrothes Development Corporation, stimulated by the slow growth rate of the town, entered into an overspill agreement with the city of Glasgow, and by 1960 Glenrothes had virtually become a third New Town for Glasgow. The need for a fourth New Town was created by the final acceptance of plans to redevelop Glasgow's worst housing areas. The reasoning behind this was contained in the draft designation order for Livingston New Town.

> Over the next twenty years a massive redevelopment programme will be under-taken by Glasgow Corporation in twenty-nine separate areas. Some 100,000 families at present living in bad housing conditions will be displaced by the entire operation, and although the redeveloped sites will include residential accommoda-tion to the greatest densities acceptable by modern standards, it will not be possible to rehouse more than about 40,000 of the original 100,000 families (Department of Health for Scotland 1962).

Further overspill pressure from Greater Glasgow led to the designation of Irvine in 1967 and of Stonehouse in 1972 as New Towns, although the latter was abandoned in 1976 due to a government decision to devote more direct attention to the problem of multiple deprivation in the east end of Glasgow.

Comprehensive redevelopment

When the large housing schemes began to exhaust the available open sites near the periphery of the city, the Corporation, faced with a housing shortage, a waiting list which stood at 100,000 by the mid-1950s and a lack of developable land, turned its attention to the redevelopment of decayed areas nearer the centre. Not only was most of the housing there intolerable but the industrial premises, built mostly for heavy industry, were unsuitable for modern industries and, being in a poor state of repair, were unattractive to new ventures. A report to the Housing and Planning Committees of the Corporation proposed the comprehensive redevelopment of three inner-city areas as early as 1953. By 1957 the magnitude of the redevelopment problem was apparent and the City Architect and Planning Officer submitted a report suggesting that 29 comprehensive development areas (CDAs) should be established in order to achieve a realistic clearance and redevelopment programme. These covered a total area of 5 square miles (8 per cent of the city). The sizes varied from 25 acres to 270 acres, and populations ranged from 4,000 to 40,000. Approximately 2,500 industrial concerns were within the CDA limits. The comprehensive redevelopment programme set out in the report depended on the city pursuing an overspill policy:

> It cannot be too strongly emphasised that the provision outwith the city of accommodation for the reception of Glasgow's overspill is the governing factor in all proposals made in this report. Without this provision little or no redevelopment can be undertaken.

From its inception the comprehensive development area programme had far reaching implications for city planning beyond the clearance of slum housing and the creation of modern residential areas (Hart 1967). Each

CDA was planned to be reasonably self sufficient in terms of support facilities for the new population. Areas were thus zoned for commercial development, education, open space and industry. The planners hoped that these new developments would assist in city-wide rationalisation and modernisation of commercial activities, especially shopping, in the release of land for new industrial development and in the development of an improved highway network. Although 29 CDAs were identified in the 1957 report, initiation has not been uniform. The time scale for the physical redevelopment can be spread in phases over a period of up to twenty years, but plan preparation and implementation for a single CDA, together with the legal difficulties associated with compulsory purchase and compensation, stretched to the limits the resources of the Corporation. Thus there have been long intervals between the approval of one CDA and of another. Of the nine CDAs that have been approved, the first was accepted in 1957 and the most recent in 1973. The original goal to complete a considerable portion of the redevelopment programme by 1980 could not be realised. There is no doubt, however, that the comprehensive redevelopment programme has brought about massive changes in the physical and social environment in the city. A detailed discussion of the Gorbals CDA is provided elsewhere (Pacione 1983). Of the remaining comprehensive development areas on which work is proceeding the majority are located within the innner city (Townhead, Cowcaddens, Woodside and Anderston) and work in these areas will continue well into the 1980s.

The high-rise solution

In spite of the comprehensive development areas and the overspill policy, Glasgow's housing problem in the mid-1960s was still severe. Earlier housing construction was hopelessly inadequate to keep ahead of the rate of decay in the old tenements. The problem was exacerbated by the scarcity of building land in the city. With increasing scarcity of sites, and possibly because of contemporary architectural fashions, Glasgow Corporation began to erect multi-storey housing. This move was a revolutionary step for the city since it meant altering the whole meaning of urban living for many people. Although some planners expressed misgivings the policy was implemented on the argument that high-rise buildings would increase the number of housing units more rapidly than other programmes. From the late 1950s the Corporation was committed to the new high-rise formula. A major change in the city's skyline occurred during the 1960s. By 1968 there were six multi-storey housing units being built to every low-rise, and by the following year 163 tower blocks were occupied. By 1969 the Housing Management Department had 15,000 high-rise units and 121,500 low-rise homes on its books. The new form of building reached its extreme at Red Road, a 22-acre complex of 31-storey blocks designed to house 4,000 people at a density of 180 ppa. Many tenants appreciated the modern facilities that were so different from their previous living conditions but with use several major disadvantages soon appeared in the form of lift breakdowns; maintenance of stairs, communal areas and landscaped surrounding; isolation of the elderly; and lack of space for families with young children. Although high-rise buildings put a large population in a small area in a short period of time, the land economies have been less than anticipated. Moreover, the cost of constructing high-rise flats has often proved expensive (Miller 1970). It has also become clear that the high-rise of today may be the slums of tomorrow (Pacione 1984). Partly in response to the doubts about the programme, Glasgow has retreated from its policy of multi-storey building and has returned to the familiar four-storey structures.

A change of philosophy
The beginning of the 1970s was an opportune time to assess the city's progress. There had been a major improvement in the quality of Glasgow life in the thirty years since the war. The high residential densities had all but disappeared and the crowded core of the city, inherited from the nineteenth century, had been remade. More than 100,000 municipal houses had been built since 1945 and during the same period 200,000 of the city's population dispersed. The percentage of households with exclusive use of hot and cold water, a fixed bath and an inside toilet, though lower than the steadily rising British average, improved between 1961 and 1971 from 58.9 per cent to 75.2 per cent. The percentage of the urban population living at more than 1.5 ppr fell from 46.9 per cent in 1951 to 26.0 per cent in 1971. Partly because of judicious amendments to the boundaries of the inner city CDAs, a new urban motorway had been inserted in the highway system to ease traffic congestion in the centre and speed cross-city movement (Pacione 1977). Despite these achievements planning in Glasgow continued to be dominated by the two major issues of housing and unemployment. Development plans in the early 1970s rested on the dual strategies of overspill and redevelopment. The comprehensive development programme continued, and in 1972 a sixth New Town was designated at Stonehouse, 17 miles from Glasgow, to provide 30,000 new jobs and accommodate 70,000 people. The CDA programme had not been completely effective, and of the 29 CDAs proposed in 1957 only 9 had been approved by 1973. Doubts were expressed on the efficiency of large scale redevelopments that create prolonged disruptions of community life. The land use zonings of the 1947 Town and Country Planning Act were used rigidly as prime controls in the redevelopment programme so that the boundaries of the CDAs were tightly drawn and virtually unalterable once approved. The results were inflexible and slow responses to changing ideas on the restructuring of urban areas. Such criticisms may be levelled at the redevelopment of the Gorbals. The original report on the area proposed that development should take place in three sections but to date only the central unit (Hutchesontown-Gorbals) has been completed. The plans for the western unit (Laurieston-Gorbals) were only finally approved in 1966, almost a decade after the development of the whole area had begun, and this section will not be completed until the mid-1980s. The third sector (Hutchesontown-Polmadie CDA) has been dropped from the comprehensive redevelopment programme.

Changes occurring in the planning profession affected urban redevelopment schemes. In the immediate post-war period architects, engineers and surveyors who dominated the planning process saw planning problems mainly in terms of the physical environment. By the 1960s the profession included geographers, economists and sociologists. The change to an interdisciplinary approach shifted the focus from physical land uses to the consideration of socio-economic problems. Two government reports were commissioned in the mid-1960s and became instruments of the change toward a more flexible planning (Planning Advisory Group 1965; Skeffington Committee 1969). The first report recommended that the range of planning activity should be widened in economic and social terms to provide an integrated planning framework from regional to local levels, and that the CDA procedure should be discontinued and replaced with a less rigid and less time-consuming system. The second report dealt with public participation and outlined in detail a mechanism for public consultation at each stage of the planning process. The government incorporated the principal recommendations of both reports in major planning and housing legislation of 1968 and 1969, especially the Town and Country Planning Act 1968, in which the planning process was divided into a two-tier system of structure planning and local planning. Under this new system the CDA approach to urban renewal has been replaced by a process that identifies 'action areas'. These areas may be defined in a local plan for either improvement or redevelopment. They are generally expected to be much smaller than the CDAs and all development is required to be completed within a ten-year period. For the older areas of Glasgow the decision to include improvement of existing stock or rehabilitation along with redevelopment is most important, because one of the major disadvantages of the CDA programme was that it often removed fit houses along with the unfit and efficient businesses along with the inefficient in order to comply with the overall master plan. In practice, progress with rehabilitation of existing dwelling houses was slow, despite the fact that improvement grants have been available since 1949. Between 1960 and 1972 the grants approved by the Corporation were insignificant for the scale of the problems of obsolescence and insanitary conditions (Glasgow Corporation 1974). By 1975 rehabilitation had been accepted as a major policy. The social motives behind this change were supported by figures from the Corporation on the relative costs of rehabilitation and redevelopment. From the limited information available on costs, long term rehabilitation proves to be cheaper than new construction in comprehensive development areas, 'but the difference is not sufficiently great to recommend one method at the expense of the other' (Glasgow Corporation 1974). The strongest argument in favour of rehabilitation is the effect that demolition can have on long established residential areas, such as Partickhill, Hillhead, East Pollokshields and Dennistoun. A total commitment to rehabilitation would be impractical because a large proportion of the city's 31,000 sub-tolerable houses is beyond repair. The city has thus embraced a dual programme involving both rehabilitation and redevelopment. In view of the sensitive structure of local economies and communities, wherever and whenever possible the emphasis is placed on improvement rather than redevelopment.

There are approximately 16,000 pre-1919 tenement dwellings in Housing Action Areas for Improvement. By 1981 Housing Associations had rehabilitated more than 4,500 of these, the District Council 2100 and the SSHA about 100. Clearly, the rate of progress in tackling the remaining homes will depend on the flow of capital funds to the agencies involved. The longer the delay in treating these older properties the greater the cost and the likelihood of irrepairable decay. There are also 27,000 inter-war council houses (on estates like Blackhill) in need of modernisation or improvement. Much of the post-war council housing is also in need of attention. In approximately 30,000 homes rewiring is necessary and dampness is a major problem; while the 25,511 dwellings in 263 multi-storey blocks present special maintenance and improvement problems (Glasgow District Council 1981).

A novel approach to housing rehabilitation is the Homesteading Scheme initiated in Easterhouse in 1980–1. This seeks an alternative to the demolition of council housing stock which, due to resource constraints or the existence of more urgent priorities, the council would be unable to improve, repair or rehabilitate within a reasonable time. Under this scheme the council undertakes basic repairs to the house which is then offered for sale, with the assistance of a local authority loan. The advantages of the Homesteading Scheme include the contribution to urban revitalisation and the provision of more properties to supply a demand for owner-occupied housing from people in the lower-income brackets who might otherwise be unable to enter the private sector.

Glasgow eastern area renewal

The new planning philosophy has been applied in the east-end of Glasgow, where the various symptoms of urban deprivation are seen at their most virulent. Glasgow's east-end is one of the bleakest urban areas in Britain—3,500 acres of wasteland from which population and industry have consistently retreated since 1961. Partly as a result of the city's overspill policy of the 1950s and 1960s and partly by choice, 85,000 people have left the area in the last twenty years. More than half of the remaining population of 55,000 live in single rooms or room and kitchen dwellings. Unemployment rates are well above the city average, reaching 36 per cent in places, and vast areas of derelict land blight the landscape.

In order to cure what had almost become a terminal case of urban decay, drastic measures were called for. To this end the most ambitious urban renewal programme in Britain is being undertaken jointly by Glasgow District Council, Strathclyde Regional Council, and SSHA under the general direction of the Scottish Development Agency. The aim of the Glasgow Eastern Area Renewal Project (GEAR), for which an initial sum of £120 million over eight years has been assigned, is to revitalise the area by halting the drift of population, re-establishing industries, and improving the quality of the general environment. The GEAR project, announced on 21 May 1976, was primarily a response to the 1971 Census statistics. Supported by this evidence the local authorities argued that the development of Stonehouse New Town as a rival source of housing and employment would only serve to increase Glasgow's problems. Amid growing pressure the government decided to abandon the New Town project and concentrate resources on regenerating the inner areas of Glasgow. First thoughts were to place the problem in the hands of an experienced New Town development corporation (such as that no longer required at Stonehouse), but in the interests of maintaining harmony with existing authorities this idea was dropped and the work was entrusted to a multi-agency group which included the district and regional authorities.

The GEAR project area comprises the five local plan areas which have been designated in the east-end, together with the existing Bridgeton-Dalmarnock comprehensive development area and the Cambuslang recovery area. Public perception of the problems and priorities for the area varied. In Camlachie the main concern was with atmospheric pollution from a local chemical works, while in Dalmarnock attention focused on the lack of local shopping. Generally however, the major issues were seen as crime and vandalism, the physical environment, shopping needs, employment, leisure and recreation, public transport, and uncertainty about the future of the area.

Insight into the problems and prospects for the east-end can be obtained by examining the situation in the Camlachie local plan area. Here the main problems include the poor quality of the environment including housing, the lack of social and community facilities, industrial pollution, and the presence of obsolescent and physically run-down property which is unattractive to both industrialists and workers. In this area the closure and demolition of houses in poor sanitary and structural condition has proceeded steadily since the early 1960s and the population has fallen considerably, as has the number of shops and range of community facilities. Many of the industrial firms have closed down as a result of clearance, poor structural condition, or simply because of the inadequacy of the premises for modern industry. The considerable time-lag between demolition and redevelopment has resulted in a marked deterioration of the physical and social environment in which derelict buildings, unkempt vacant sites, closed-up tenements and shops, and scrap yards dominate the scene (Pacione 1983).

An ambitious housing programme is underway in each of the five local plan areas within the east-end (Table 4) with the emphasis now on renovation and rehabilitation where possible rather than clearance. This should help to prevent the break-up of existing communities, and reduce the acreage of derelict wastelands which discourages developers and despoils the townscape. Although the physical problems of the east-end can be resolved to a large extent by redevelopment, the social problems engendered by such an impoverished environment and manifested in high tenancy turn-over, abscondences, eviction and vandalism are less tractable to physical

Table 4

Population and Housing Changes in East End Local Plan Areas, 1971–81

	Camlachie	Calton	Dalmarnock	Shettleston–Tollcross	Parkhead	Total
Population 1971	9374	6437	9000	21,839	20,030	66,680
Population 1981	3611	3100	4558	16,702	9545	37,516
% change	−62	−52	−49	−24	−52	−44
Housing stock 1971	1437	2656	1983	7831	7805	21,712
Loss due to clearance and rehabilitation	206	1902	300	381	846	3635
New built additions	315	470	69	160	250	1264
Housing stock 1981	1542	1224	1742	7610	7209	19,327
% change	+7.3	−53.9	−12.2	−2.8	−7.6	−11.0

planning in the short term. The modernisation of the Barrowfield housing area in Camlachie, for example, has eliminated some of the environmental factors which underlie anti-social behaviour, but a major problem remains in the high level of unemployment throughout the east-end. Job opportunities are divided between traditional small-scale manufacturing in which more than half of the firms employ less than ten persons and service industries with low growth prospects. The attraction of new employment opportunities suited to the characteristics of the local labour force is of paramount importance for the success of the GEAR project (Pacione 1980).

The partnership of agencies involved in the GEAR project is committed to the difficult task of bringing about the economic revival of the area at a time when throughout Britain the forecast is for increased levels of unemployment as a result of economic and technical change. The GEAR management has been criticised for not paying sufficient attention to the wishes of the local people, and friction among the constituent agencies has been suggested to explain the slow rate of progress. Whether the present management structure is retained or replaced by an urban development corporation similar to that proposed for the London docklands and the Merseyside dock area, the problem remains immense.

EDINBURGH

The general trends and problems identified in post-war Glasgow were also experienced in Edinburgh. Whereas in the years up to 1950 a major problem of the inner city was overpopulation, the major planning issue for Edinburgh District now is the need to stem the further outward movement of population. The dominant trend of outmigration by the younger age groups has resulted in an ageing population structure, a decrease in the average household size, and a fall in the number of children being born (Table 1). The main sources of outmigration are the inner tenement areas, e.g. the four central wards of St Giles, St Andrews, Holyrood and George Square, with similar losses recorded in Gorgie/Dalry, Leith, Broughton, and Calton. While the inner areas lost population the peripheral areas of the city District and other receiving settlements in Lothian, Central and Fife Regions have expanded. Continued decline and ageing of the population is both socially and physically undesirable. Socially, an increasingly unbalanced demographic structure would have repercussions for the provision of facilities with, for example, inner city paediatric services underutilised and geriatric services oversubscribed. Physically the loss of population is made manifest in the continuing dereliction of parts of the urban fabric and loss of community identity, while on the periphery pressure on the green belt intensifies. In recent years, for example, private sector housing has encroached on good quality agricultural land at Currie, Queensferry and Baberton; and other potentially attractive sites exist at Kirkliston, Ratho, Balerno and Brunstane. Apart from the loss of agricultural land development of green field sites requires the local authority to provide service infrastructure. Such developments could also exacerbate the commuting problems into the city. Understandably therefore the main aims of local authority population and housing policy are to guide development to potential housing sites within the city and away from peripheral greenfield locations wherever possible; and secondly, as a general principle, to undertake rehabilitation rather than demolition of sub-standard housing. The latter is closely related to the city's conservation strategy.

The major population dispersal of the post-war years has been energised by slum clearance in the inner urban area and the development of new public and private sector housing in the peripheral areas and surrounding settlements (Figure 2). While the growth in suburban housing has altered the city's character from one with a preponderance of high-density Georgian and Victorian housing to one more representative of the majority of British cities, Edinburgh does retain a large element of inner area housing, particularly in the New Town and south of the city centre. Detailed insight into the situation in Edinburgh can best be gained by considering the examples of (1) the rehabilitation of Georgian and Victorian property in the South Side, and (2) the problems of multiply-deprived peripheral council housing estates in Craigmillar ward.

The South Side

The South Side originally developed in the eighteenth century as a relief from the problems of overcrowding in the Old Town and thereafter continued to expand on an *ad hoc* basis. The area now contains a mixture of land uses and architectural styles including many buildings of historic and architectural merit. While there is the diversity of function typical of an inner city the residential element remains dominant despite the presence of major institutions, including the University of Edinburgh.

There has been considerable planning activity in the South Side since World War II; unfortunately the area has not benefited to the extent that might have been expected from almost thirty years of activity (City of Edinburgh 1975). The first major plan relating to the South Side was the Civic Survey and Plan 1949. Many of the proposals were radical including, for example, a major road development through the area, and redevelop-ment of the zone around George Square to facilitate expansion of the University. The Survey also concluded that the majority of the housing suffered from multiple deficiencies and should be redeveloped. As the Civic Survey and Plan 1949 was advisory not all of the recommendations were included in the 1957 Development Plan for the city. In particular no comprehensive treatment was proposed for the sub-standard housing in the South Side. Comprehensive development areas were proposed, however, in several subsequent amendments to the 1957 Development Plan. For example in 1962 the Corporation agreed to process the University/Nicolson Street CDA initially put forward by the University to secure coordinated development in the South Side and deal with problems of decay, piecemeal redevelopment and traffic congestion. The proposed CDA was not

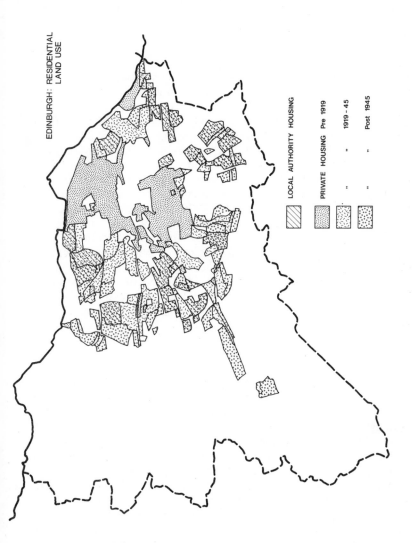

EDINBURGH: RESIDENTIAL LAND USE

LOCAL AUTHORITY HOUSING

PRIVATE HOUSING Pre 1919

"   "   1919 – 45

"   "   Post 1945

Figure 2 Housing areas in Edinburgh by tenure and age.

approved finally by the Town Council until May 1968, with the codicil that it was not to be submitted formally to the Secretary of State for Scotland until cost and feasibility studies had been prepared. These studies were never prepared, however, being overtaken by a wider study of planning and transportation strategy for the whole city centre.

The first Quinquennial Review of the 1957 Development Plan submitted in 1966 recommended the South Side as an Action Area for comprehensive development. Early in 1968 the Secretary of State instructed that the proposed Action Area be deleted from the statutory map and that the 1957 zonings be restored. Despite such clear instruction the Review was not approved formally until October 1974. This considerable delay added to the uncertainty over the future of the South Side and effectively placed a pall of planning blight over the area. In keeping with the national changes in planning philosophy following the reports of the Planning Advisory Group (1965) and the Skeffington Committee (1969) it was decided in November 1973 that renewal work in the South Side should proceed on the basis of a Local Plan rather than a CDA plan. In 1975 the South Side was declared an Outstanding Conservation Area and conservation and rehabilitation are key factors in the local plan. The South Side is now in the anomalous position of being subject to special protection and restriction by reason of its conservation interests while at the same time containing many buildings in an advanced state of structural decay due to prolonged uncertainty as to their future.

Craigmillar

The Craigmillar ward is located at the eastern extremity of Edinburgh separated from the centre by Arthur's Seat and Holyrood Park. This relatively isolated position is exacerbated by the city road network which is essentially radial rather than orbital. The housing legislation of the 1920s and its subsequent developments provided the basis for most of the residential expansion in Craigmillar. The first public housing scheme to be built was Niddrie Mains, a rehousing area for slum clearance families from St Leonards and Leith. Although conceived as a single entity the scheme was built as a series of piecemeal developments between 1930 and 1936. The second scheme at Craigmillar was built in 1938–9 and again drew tenants from slum clearance areas in central Edinburgh and Leith. The national housing shortage which followed World War II prompted further large estate developments at Bingham and Magdalene. Emergency accommodation was also erected at Southfield and Greendykes. In the late 1950s and through the 1960s additional public housing was built at Niddrie Mill and Niddrie Marischal, and the Greendykes and Southfield areas were redeveloped. By 1970 the present housing stock was complete although sporadic infilling continues. In general the area's housing typifies the majority of British public housing schemes of this generation although as shown elsewhere (Pacione 1982) significant spatial variations in residential environmental quality can exist within these areas.

Some of the problems of inter-war housing schemes such as those in Craigmillar have been attributed to the original selection of tenants. In the 1920s tenants for new Corporation estates were drawn usually from the higher income groups on the housing waiting lists, but under the Housing Acts of 1930 and 1935 it was necessary to rehouse all the people who had been moved out of substandard housing. Rather than mixing groups of different social backgrounds and incomes certain estates, including Niddrie Mains and Craigmillar Castle, were set aside to take only the lower income groups and those from problem slum areas. Both schemes have progressively deteriorated since completion for a number of reasons including the high concentration of problem families, the unattractive tenements, the stigma of the area, and neglect by officialdom. By the 1970s the areas exhibited all the characteristics of the worst of local authority housing. The reality of multiple deprivation in Craigmillar is seen in the following suite of problems; (a) externally generated traffic which creates high accident rates, (b) poor public transport, (c) unsatisfactory townscape and environmental management, especially excessive litter, unpleasant house exteriors and poor maintenance of open space, (d) lack of social facilities for all groups but especially teenagers, (e) a high rate of tenancy turnover, (f) a concentration of crime, (g) unfavourable publicity by the mass media, (h) official or unofficial neglect by the Council, (i) low involvement of schools in extra mural activities and low parental participation in children's education, (j) lack of particular types of shops, (k) high male and female unemployment, (l) poor accessibility to actual and potential sources of employment, (m) existing industry creates environmental problems, and (n) pockets of housing have deteriorated to a state where they are unfit for human habitation. Not surprisingly, the local authority has great difficulty in finding families willing to accept a tenancy in the older schemes and many houses lie empty and prey to vandals. As in Glasgow, the number of tenants wishing to be re-allocated from these areas is well above the city average.

The need to rehabilitate the worst estates was recognised officially in the mid 1970s and work commenced in the Craigmillar Castle scheme. Physical renewal involved internal improvements such as the installation of central heating and the modernisation of electrical installations and sanitary fittings; as well as painting of house exteriors and general environmental improvement of the surrounding area. Acknowledging the social dimension to the problem the city Housing Department has also adopted a screening procedure before allocating rehabilitated dwellings to new tenants in an attempt to create a more balanced population structure and reduce the proportion of likely problem tenants. Although conditions in the inter-war 'general needs' housing have been most pressing, increasing attention is being focused on the deficiencies of some of the post-war council stock for modern living. This development underlines the fact that housing rehabilitation is an on-going process. Higher minimum tolerable standards and rising public aspirations inevitably mean a need to continuously improve the quality of the residential environment throughout the council stock.

ABERDEEN

The morphogenesis of housing areas in Aberdeen mirrors that of Glasgow though at a smaller scale (Figure 3). The factors which dominate the housing debate in Aberdeen are the shortage of private and public stock to satisfy a demand fuelled by the development of North Sea oil, and the scarcity of land in the city to meet an estimated need for an additional 7,100 houses between 1980–5. In addition to the physical constraints on the city's ability to satisfy its housing requirements the financial cuts imposed by Central Government have meant that only 84 new local authority houses were started in 1981–2. This will obviously have an adverse affect on the council house waiting list which currently stands at over 3,500 applicants. Lack of finance for new public sector housing may also bring undue pressure to approve large areas of land for private housing or to release existing Council owned land to the private sector. Administrative constraints arise as a result of policy decisions made by adjacent authorities. Gordon District Council, for example, in its local plan has not classified land at Cairnie as intended for housing even though the site is owned by Aberdeen District Council who wish to proceed with development.

Of the existing housing stock in the city 5,800 houses, the majority of which are in the private sector, failed to satisfy the tolerable standard in 1980. Of particular concern is the standard of housing in the private rented sector where in 1981 one-third of households lacked at least one basic amenity (that is exclusive use of WC and/or bath). A major policy instrument for the improvement of sub-standard housing in the city is the declaration of Housing Action Areas following the provisions of the 1974 Housing Act, and there are now more than thirty HAAs in Aberdeen. Housing Associations also play an important role in meeting housing need, particularly for special groups such as the elderly or disabled. A Housing Association is the body in charge of a government defined Housing Action Area within which general environmental, structural and amenity improvements are planned. In order to operationalise these plans the Association can apply for improvement grants from the Housing Corporation. In the past the local authority has assisted by providing sites for development and properties for rehabilitation, but the land shortage makes it increasingly difficult to set aside sites which are large enough to sustain a viable Housing Association development. It may be argued that the attention which Housing Associations have attracted is out of proportion to the scale of their activities, which provide less than 700 houses in Aberdeen. The significance of the Housing Association movement, however, lies in the direct contribution it has made to taking over part of the role of the declining private rented sector and widening the choice of housing available, especially to those who fail to pass the eligibility tests of the managers of council houses and building societies. Overall, as far as existing housing is concerned, although Aberdeen has a proportion of decaying stock, difficult-to-let houses, and problem areas, the city's housing difficulties are far less pressing than those confronting Glasgow or Edinburgh.

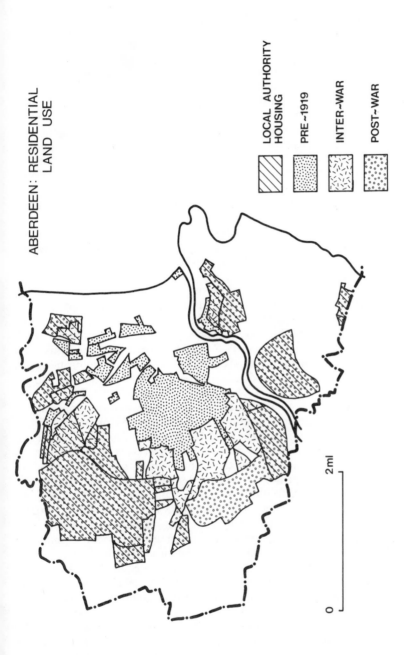

ABERDEEN: RESIDENTIAL LAND USE

LOCAL AUTHORITY HOUSING

PRE~1919

INTER~WAR

POST~WAR

0   2ml

Figure 3   Housing areas in Aberdeen by tenure and age.

DUNDEE

Like many large industrial cities in the United Kingdom housing opportunities in Dundee have, for the majority of the population, traditionally relied on renting. A combination of low incomes and high unemployment rates have tended to make council housing a major form of tenancy (Table 1). The evolution of Dundee's housing followed the pattern described in the other Scottish cities, largely in response to national legislation (Figure 4). Thus the Victorian tenement building era was followed by the expansion of municipal housing in the inter-war period. Major developments of the post-war period were the continued expansion of council estates on the urban periphery, the rise of multi-storey blocks which account for one in five of the city's house-building since 1945, and the rapid decline of the private rented sector largely as a result of property demolition in CDAs designated in the 1950s and 1960s.

Most of the remaining private-rented stock consists of tenement flats, many of which are in poor condition. Approximately 6,400 are below the tolerable standard, 97.0 per cent of which are located in the inner city. Housing Action Area activity is of importance in improving these units. By December 1980 there were 28 HAAs encompassing 2,674 houses, which will be reduced to 2,059 modern homes through demolition and integration. There are also 14 Housing Associations active in Dundee, all but two of which concentrate on special needs housing. The Housing Association stock falls into three categories, recent new build, rehabilitated tenements, and tenements awaiting rehabilitation. Acquisition of the tenement property has been on a voluntary basis and has often involved stock in the poorest condition.

In addition to the rehabilitation of older sub-standard property a comprehensive maintenance programme is essential to ensure the continued utility of the existing satisfactory stock. Modernisation is also necessary to keep pace with rising standards and expectations. This process normally involves decanting residents from their home for several months but the majority of tenants appear to accept the temporary inconvenience as the price to be paid for their improved living conditions. As in the other Scottish cities, the need to improve council stock is not confined to pre-1945 housing. In Dundee some of the immediate post-war schemes suffer from a host of social and physical problems, ranging from poor community amenities to inadequate thermal and sound insulation in houses. These areas are currently among the least popular in the council stock and it is clear that any lengthy postponement of remedial action may create extreme letting difficulties. Progress is dependent, however, on resource availability, and under the existing programme this stock will be forty-five years old before it is considered for modernisation. Looking further ahead, the prolific council house building rates in the 1950s and 1960s, when over half of the public stock was constructed, were such that modernisation programmes to deal with this age of stock are likely to be of significantly greater magnitude.

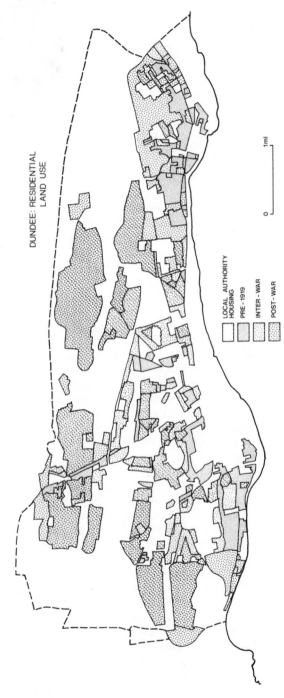

DUNDEE: RESIDENTIAL LAND USE

LOCAL AUTHORITY HOUSING

PRE - 1919

INTER - WAR

POST - WAR

0   1ml

Figure 4   Housing areas in Dundee by tenure and age.

Four estates comprising 13.0 per cent of the council housing stock have been identified as being of low-letting demand. These are at Beechwood, Magdalene's Kirkton/West March, Mid-Craigie and Whitfield Skarne. All exhibit a higher than average incidence of vacant houses, relets/transfers, evictions, moonlight flittings, rent arrears, DHSS direct payment of rent and fuel bills, and maintenance work orders. Other evidence of multiply-deprived environments include the high levels of unemployment, low school-leaving ages, high receipts of DHSS benefits, and numbers of children in care. There is little immediate prospect of the poverty and social stress in these estates being alleviated, since an increasing proportion of the houses relet are allocated to vulnerable families in the homeless and badly-housed categories. In addition, between July 1979 and June 1980 63.0 per cent of households moving from a home in these four areas were rehoused in the same or another low demand estate. Of the four low demand estates two (Beechwood and Mid Craigie) were built in the 1930s, one (Kirkton) in the 1950s, and the fourth (Whitfield) in the 1970s. These areas cannot simply be 'written off'.

It is important to underline that these low demand estates represent a significant part of Dundee's housing stock. If past investment is to be secured and optimum use made of present resources the problems of these areas must be tackled effectively. Given the complex of social and physical problems in the estates it is unreasonable to expect a single approach to be sufficient to resolve the problem. Clearly, any physical remedial actions could be rendered ineffective unless they are supported by programmes from other relevant agencies to deal with the social and economic aspects of the situation. In 1979 the local authority commenced a five-year phased programme of environmental improvement in the four estates but even with a degree of self-help response from community groups this is a palliative rather than a cure. The experience of the successful homesteading schemes pioneered in Glasgow may have direct relevance here.

The regeneration of Dundee's inner city areas is also of particular importance. A principal objective of the Inner City local plan is to encourage investment in the housing market by indicating the local authority's commitment to the area through new building and rehabilitation, by environmental improvement programmes, and by rationalising development proposals so as to remove the effect of planning blight from large areas and thus form the basis for improved confidence by building societies and other investors. The West End is typical of the inner city environment. Problems relate to an ageing fabric, ageing infrastructure and outdated layout which manifest themselves in a low environmental quality with a large number of tenement flats below tolerable standard, lack of local social facilities, problems of servicing shops and pedestrian-vehicular conflict. Earlier attempts to remedy conditions in the form of CDA proposals and ambitious road plans have only served to exacerbate the situation by their piecemeal implementation. This has resulted in a lack of confidence in the future of the area, demonstrated by a low level of investment in routine maintenance and new building. To date most progress towards rehabilitating the inner city has been made in the Hilltown area where the first of the city's HAAs were designated. There are also several Housing Association sites, a site for private housing, a SSHA scheme, and a local authority sheltered housing development. The longer term aim is to extend this initiative to the other parts of the inner city.

REFERENCES

P Abercrombie and R Matthew *The Clyde Valley Regional Plan* (HMSO 1949)
G Cameron and K Johnson 'Comprehensive urban renewal and industrial location' in J B Cullingworth and S C Orr *Regional and Urban Studies* (Allen and Unwin 1969), pp 242–80
City of Aberdeen District Council *Housing Plan 1983–1988* (Aberdeen 1982)
City of Dundee District Council *Inner City Local Plan* (Dundee 1979)
City of Edinburgh *South Side Local Plan* (Edinburgh 1975)
J B Cullingworth *A Profile of Glasgow Housing 1965* University of Glasgow Social and Economic Studies Occasional Papers No. 8 (Oliver and Boyd, Edinburgh 1968)
Department of Health for Scotland *Draft New Town (Livingston) Designation Order* (HMSO, Edinburgh 1962)
E Farmer and R Smith 'Overspill Theory', *Urban Studies* 12 1975, pp 151–68
J Forbes and J MacBain *The Springburn Study,* (Glasgow 1967)
Glasgow Corporation *Planning Policy Report: Housing* (Glasgow 1974)
Glasgow District Council *Housing Plan 4,* (Glasgow 1981)
T Hart *The Comprehensive Development Area* University of Glasgow Social and Economic Studies Occasional Paper No. 9 (Oliver and Boyd, Edinburgh 1967)
R Henderson 'Industrial overspill from Glasgow: 1958–1968'. *Urban Studies* 11, 1974, pp 61–79
R Miller 'The New Face of Glasgow' *Scottish Geographical Magazine* 86(1) 1970, pp 5–15
M Pacione 'The revivification of the transition zone in Glasgow' *Norsk Geografisk Tidsskrift* 31 1977, pp 137–41
M Pacione 'Housing Policies in Glasgow Since 1880' *Geographical Review* 69(4) 1979, pp 395–412
M Pacione 'New Patterns for deprived Clydeside' *Geographical Magazine,* August 1980, pp 756–62
M Pacione 'Evaluating the quality of the residential environment in a deprived council estate'. *Geoforum* 13(1) 1982, pp 45–55
M Pacione 'Glasgow' in M Pacione (ed) *Urban Problems and Planning in the Developed World* (Croom Helm, London 1983), pp 189–222
M Pacione 'Evaluating the quality of the residential environment in a high-rise public housing development' *Applied Geography* 4(1) 1984, pp 59–70
Planning Advisory Group *The Future of Development Plans* (HMSO, London 1965)
Skeffington Committee *People and Planning* (HMSO, London 1969)
P J Smith 'Changing objectives in Scottish New Town policy' *Ekistics* 23 1967, pp 26–33

LIST OF PERSONAL NAMES

INDEX OF SUBJECTS